Diplomacy and Murder in Tehran

Alexander Griboyedov
and Imperial Russia's
Mission to the
Shah of Persia

Laurence Kelly

I.B.Tauris *Publishers*
LONDON • NEW YORK

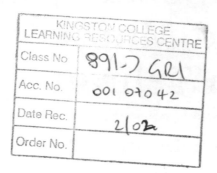

Published in 2002 by I.B.Tauris & Co Ltd
6 Salem Road, London W2 4BU
175 Fifth Avenue, New York NY 10010
www.ibtauris.com

In the United States and Canada distributed by St. Martin's Press
175 Fifth Avenue, New York NY 10010

ISBN 1 86064 666 2

A full CIP record for this book is available from the British Library
A full CIP record for this book is available from the Library of Congress

Library of Congress catalog card: available

Typeset in Bookman by Dexter Haven Associates, London
Printed and bound in Great Britain by MPG Books Ltd, Bodmin Cornwall

Contents

Acknowledgements

There is no full-length biography of Griboyedov in English; considering his importance as a literary figure in Russia, there has also been comparatively little written about him in the West. In part this may be due to the shortage of the necessary literature about him in university or academic libraries. I should exemplify this by explaining how much biographical material relating to Griboyedov and his contemporaries is to be found in those two repositories of 19th century Russian history, *Russky Arkiv* and *Russkaya Starina*: even the London Library, with its first-class Russian collection, does not possess these series in full. Of necessity, this book has been something of a pioneering work, involving a decade of research, and including journeys to Russia, Georgia and the Crimea. I am enormously grateful for the help and generosity I have received on the way.

Among Western academics, my greatest debt is to Professor Evelyn Harden, late of Fraser University, Vancouver. I have been able to draw extensively from her PhD thesis from Harvard University in 1966, analysing Yuri Tynianov's historical work *The Death of the Vazir Mukhtar* (i.e. Griboyedov). This exhaustive piece of scholarship has provided me with many illuminating insights into Griboyedov's diplomatic role, and the history of Georgia, Persia and Armenia in the 1820s. I am also grateful for her patience in reading a number of draft chapters, and pointing out errors and omissions.

The search for rare books and studies of Griboyedov's activities in Georgia has led me to have recourse to the kindness of many inhabitants of that most ancient corner of the world, notably Tamila Mgaloblishvili and Irakli and Gela Charkviani; I am also very grateful to Liya Kiknadze and Tamara Dragadze for checking the archives at their disposal for details of Griboyedov's role in repatriating Russian deserters to Tiflis. Regrettably their researches have proved fruitless, perhaps because files have been removed; the thorny problem of the deserters' fate, and the numbers involved, is still unsolved. My friend Gyorgy Ploutnikov, in Moscow, has been equally unsuccessful in finding the answer.

On Persian questions, which involved a language I regret I cannot speak or read, I owe a special mention to Sir Claus Moser for introducing me to Dr John Gurney of the Oriental Institute in Oxford; thanks to Dr Gurney I was able to enlist the help of the distinguished Persian historian

Dr Negin Nabavi in researching and interpreting Persian sources. Thanks also to Dr Homa Katouzïan of Oxford for his professionalism in defining the pound/toman exchange rates. I am deeply grateful to Shusha Guppy and Shirin Mahdavi for their help and introductions. It is also pleasant to record the high quality of the Persian section of the Library of the Royal Geographical Society.

To the extent that this book makes a fresh contribution to our understanding of the tangled story of Russian and Anglo–Persian relations in the late 1820s, I have to express my gratitude to the helpful staff of the India Office Library, and to Michael Blake and Dr Anthony Farringdon. I must also offer my thanks to Sir Denis Wright, who with his encyclopaedic knowledge of Anglo–Persian history, gave me many generous leads, and unstinting encouragement at the right moment. I must thank Lord Jellicoe for introducing me to Dr C.M. Woolgar at Southampton University (Hartley Library), thus enabling me to use their database of the Duke of Wellington's papers in relation to British policy decisions on Persia, Russia and the defence of India. The kindness of Professor Malcolm Yapp in emerging, as it were, from retirement to consider again the roles of Lord Ellenborough and the Duke of Wellington in this area, was also very marked. I should also like to thank Martin Tyson and the Duchess of Buccleuch for giving me access to the McNeill papers in the Scottish Record Office; also Robin Smith at the Scottish National Library; and Linda Shaw of Nottingham University. I owe warmest and very special thanks to Professor Michael Rogers of SOAS both for his meticulous and helpful reading of my final text, and for investigating the records of the Turkish Foreign Office to see whether, as suggested by the French Consul Charles de Gamba in Tiflis, the Turkish Government had a hand in instigating Griboyedov's murder. To the best of my knowledge this work has never been attempted before; his negative conclusions effectively dispose of the suggestion.

In Moscow, I have to thank Gyorgy Ploutnikov and Evgenii Tsymbal for procuring out-of-date articles, and for their scholar's instincts in rooting them out. In St Petersburg I owe thanks to Irina Chistova of Irli, Pushkin House, for including me in the Griboyedov bicentenary celebrations in January 1995, and to Anna V. Kornilova for her unbounded help and expertise over picture research. Thanks also to Galina Andreyera at the Tretyakov Museum in Moscow for help over the Teleshova portrait. Among Russian friends in the West, Nathalie Brooke, Nina and Nikita Lobanov Rostovsky, Sophie Lund, the late Victor Volkov-Muromtsov (whose father owned Khmelita), George Vassilchikov and Kyril Zinoviev have given me generous help and advice. Lastly Professor Alexander Bonduriansky at the Moscow State Conservatoire for his help identifying *opera seria* played in the first half of the nineteenth century.

Acknowledgements

During the long gestation of this book I have been greatly indebted to those who culled sense from my first drafts, and helped later with the laborious task of straightening out the manuscript and notes: Linda Deschampneufs, Elizabeth Hord, Carolyn Madden, Mary Young and Mary Scott, whose skills at her word processor solved many problems. My daughter Rosanna has made a most valuable contribution, especially in helping with translations. I owe a further debt to my editor, Dr Lester Crook, and to Robert Hastings and Linda Robinson. Finally, my heartfelt gratitude goes to my wife Linda, for her work in editing the manuscript, and for her support in the aftermath of a debilitating stroke. Without her help, this book would never have progressed to a manageable state.

List of Illustrations

Plates

List of Illustrations

List of Illustrations

59. Griboyedov casually watches the weighing of the idemnity bullion at Turkmanchai. Original, V.I. Moshkov; engraving, K. Beggrov.

60. Sir John McNeill (1795–1883).

61. Abbas Mirza and Paskievich signing the Treaty of Turkmanchai. Original, V.I. Moshkov; engraving, K. Beggrov.

62. I. Mal'tzev (1807–80).

63. The enforced repatriation of up to 40,000 Armenians from Azherbaijan in 1828 under the Treaty of Turkmanchai. Original, V.I. Moshkov; engraving, K. Beggrov.

64. A.S. Griboyedov. Drawing, A.S. Pushkin.

65. Cover of catalogue of State Literary Museum exhibition celebrating the two-hundredth anniversary of Griboyedov's birth, 1995. Silhouette of Griboyedov, N.Ya. Simanovitch, 1929.

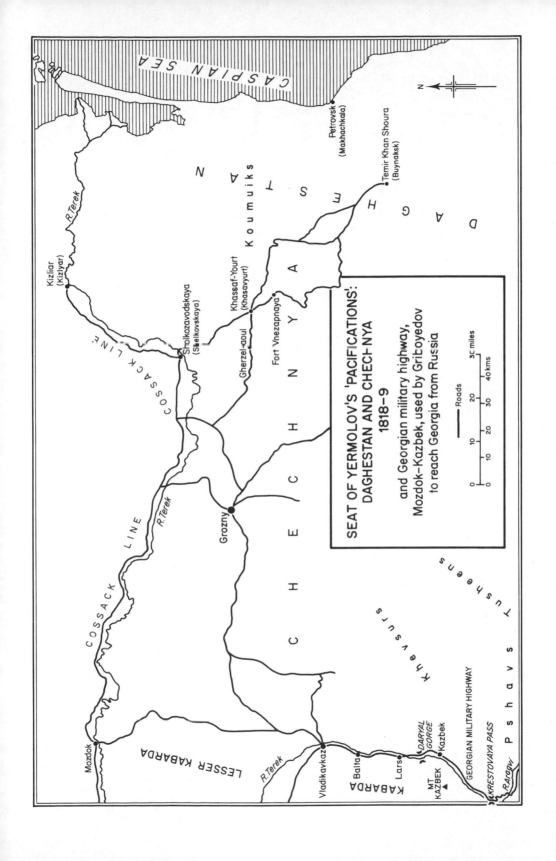

SEAT OF YERMOLOV'S 'PACIFICATIONS':
DAGHESTAN AND CHECHNYA
1818–9

and Georgian military highway,
Mozdok–Kazbek, used by Gritoyedov
to reach Georgia from Russia

CASPIAN SEA

Petrovsk
(Makhachkala)

Temir Khan Shoura
(Buynaksk)

D A G H E S T A N

K o u m u i k s

Kizliar
(Kizlyar)

R. Terek

COSSACK LINE

Sholkozavodskaya
(Shelkovskaya)

Khassaf-Yourt
(Khasavyurt)

Gherzel-aoul

Fort Vnezapnaya

C H E C H N Y A

R. Terek

Grozny

COSSACK LINE

Khevsurs

Tusheens

Pshavs

Mozdok

LESSER KABARDA

KABARDA

R. Terek

Vladikavkaz

Balta

Lars

MT KAZBEK

DARYAL GORGE

Kazbek

GEORGIAN MILITARY HIGHWAY

KRESTOVAYA PASS

R. Aragw.

Roads

0   10   20   30   40kms
0   10   20   30 miles

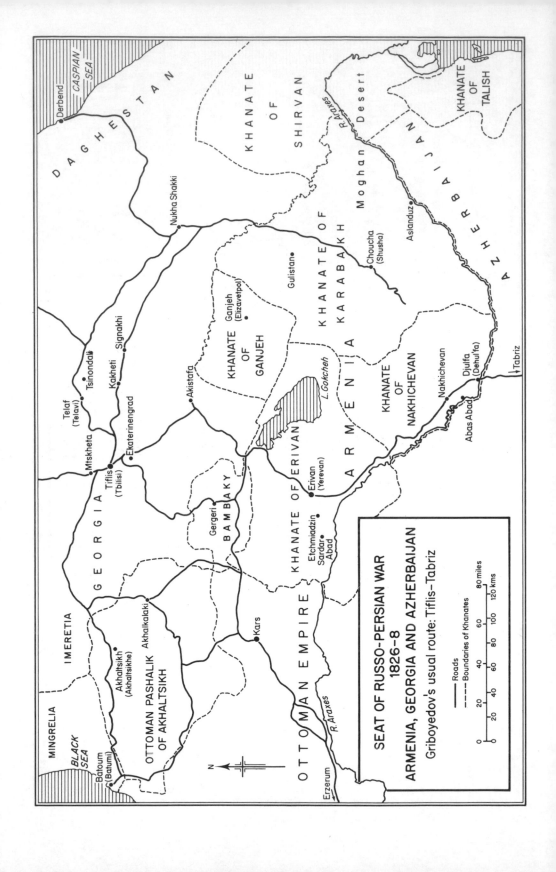

CASPIAN SEA

Derbend

DAGHESTAN

KHANATE OF SHIRVAN

R. Araxes

Moghan Desert

AZHERBAIJAN

KHANATE OF TALISH

Nukha Shakki

Gulistan

KHANATE OF KARABAKH

Choucha (Shusha)

Aslanduz

Signakhi

Kakheti

Ganjeh (Elizavetpol)

KHANATE OF GANJEH

L. Gokcheh

KHANATE OF NAKHICHEVAN

Nakhichevan

Djulfa (Dehul'fa)

→Tabriz

Tsinondali

Telaf (Telavi)

Ekaterinengrad

Akistafa

ARMENIA

Abas Abad

Mtskheta

Tiflis (Tbilisi)

GEORGIA

Gergeri

BAMBAKY

KHANATE OF ERIVAN

Erivan (Yerevan)

Etchmiadzin

Sardar Abad

IMERETIA

Akhaltsikh (Akhaltsikhe)

Akhalkalaki

OTTOMAN PASHALIK OF AKHALTSIKH

Kars

OTTOMAN EMPIRE

MINGRELIA

BLACK SEA

Batoum (Batumi)

R. Araxes

Erzerum

N

SEAT OF RUSSO-PERSIAN WAR
1826–8
ARMENIA, GEORGIA AND AZHERBAIJAN
Griboyedov's usual route: Tiflis–Tabriz

Roads
Boundaries of Khanates

80 miles
120 kms
60
100
40
80
20
60
40
0
20
0

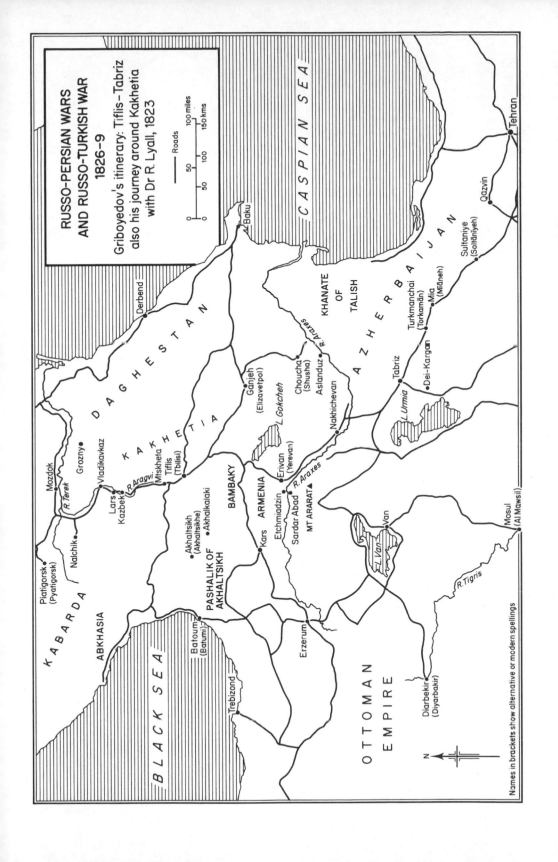

RUSSO-PERSIAN WARS
AND RUSSO-TURKISH WAR
1826–9

Griboyedov's itinerary: Tiflis–Tabriz
also his journey around Kakhetia
with Dr R. Lyall, 1823

Roads

100 miles
150 kms

50   100
50
0   0

CASPIAN SEA

Tehran

Qazvin

Sultaniye
(Soltāniyeh)

Mia
(Miāneh)

Derbend

Baku

KHANATE
OF
TALISH

DAGHESTAN

Turkmanchai
(Torkamān)

Dei-Kargan

Ganjeh
(Elizavetpol)

Choucha
(Shusha)

R. Araxes

Aslanduz

A Z H E R B A I J A N

Mozdok

Grozny

Vladikavkaz

L. Gokcheh

Nakhichevan

Tabriz

L. Urmia

K A K H E T I A

Lars
Kazbek

R. Aragvi

Mtskheta

Tiflis
(Tbilisi)

Erivan
(Yerevan)

R. Araxes

Piatigorsk
(Pyatigorsk)

Nalchik

R. Terek

BAMBAKY

Akhalkalaki

Etchmiadzin

Sardar Abad

MT ARARAT ▲

Van

Akhaltsikh
(Akhaltsikhe)

ARMENIA

Kars

K A B A R D A

ABKHASIA

PASHALIK OF
AKHALTSIKH

L. Van

Mosul
(Al Mawsil)

Batoum
(Batumi)

R. Tigris

B L A C K   S E A

Erzerum

O T T O M A N

E M P I R E

Trebizond

Diarbekir
(Diyarbakir)

N

Names in brackets show alternative or modern spellings

Introduction

In the spring of 1829, Alexander Pushkin was travelling to the Caucasus, on his way to see his brother, who was serving on the Russo–Turkish front. On his journey through the mountains, he met with an extraordinary sight:

> Two oxen harnessed to a cart were descending the steep road. Some Georgians were accompanying the cart. 'Where do you come from?' I asked them. 'From Teheran.' 'What do you have on your cart?' 'Griboyed.' This was the body of the slain Griboyedov, which they were taking to Tiflis.

Two months earlier, Alexander Sergeyevich Griboyedov, the Russian Minister Plenipotentiary to Tehran, had been murdered with most of his embassy by an infuriated Persian mob. It was the culmination of the second Russo–Persian War, and its ensuing peace treaty, the Treaty of Turkmanchai, whose humiliating terms Griboyedov had been sent to Persia to impose. Although he had been largely responsible for drafting the treaty, he had been full of foreboding about his mission.

> I did not believe I would ever meet our Griboyedov again!' wrote Pushkin. 'I parted with him last year, in Petersburg, before his departure for Persia. He was sad, and had strange forebodings. I thought of reassuring him; he said to me: 'Vous ne connaissez pas ces gens-là: vous verrez qu'il faudra jouer des couteaux.' He assumed that bloodshed would result at the death of the Shah and the ensuing feuds among his seventy sons. But the aged Shah is still alive, and yet Griboyedov's prophecy came true.

Pushkin had first become acquainted with Griboyedov in 1817, when he and Griboyedov, aged eighteen and twenty-two, had been among the rising stars of literary and theatrical St Petersburg. Everything about him, wrote Pushkin,

> his melancholy character, his caustic wit, his good nature, his very weaknesses and vices, those inevitable companions of mankind – everything in him was unusually appealing. Although born with ambition equal to his talents, he was long trapped by petty needs and obscurity. The abilities of the statesman remained unapplied; the talent of the poet

was not recognised; even his cold and brilliant courage were for a time under suspicion. Some friends recognised his value and encountered that distrustful smile, that inane, unbearable smile – every time they would speak of him as an unusual person.

Griboyedov was forced to leave the capital two years later, following a duel, to serve in semi-exile as a diplomat in Persia and Georgia. Pushkin, writing of his life, described it as being 'darkened by certain clouds: a consequence of fiery passions and powerful circumstances': the duel in question was certainly one of these. From then on he would lead a double existence, on the one hand as an increasingly important player in the game of Russo–Persian relations, on the other as a writer of genius whose verse comedy *Gore ot Uma*, variously translated as *Woe from Wit* or *The Misfortune of Being Clever*, is one of the greatest masterpieces of Russian theatre.

On leaving St Petersburg Griboyedov spent five years in Persia and Georgia, first as Chargé in the Persian diplomatic capital of Tabriz, then in Tiflis as diplomatic adviser to General Yermolov, a legendary figure in the history of the area, dominating its unruly tribes with his policy of terror and scorched earth. They were years of honing his diplomatic skills, of perfecting his knowledge of the Persian language, of travelling in gruelling conditions in the wild and awesome mountains of the Caucasus. His letters describing his experiences place him among Russia's great letter writers; a collected edition in English is long overdue. Above all, it was during this period that *Woe from Wit* took shape.

On leave in Moscow in the spring of 1823, Griboyedov was able to refresh his memory of the intrigues and hypocrisies of upper-class society which he was to satirise so brilliantly in *Woe from Wit*; he completed the play that summer. Almost immediately, it began to circulate in manuscript, and at readings at which Griboyedov would 'scatter its sparks' to chosen audiences. But its denunciations of society were too near the bone, too subversive, to pass the censors in St Petersburg; only after eight months of effort were a few scenes allowed to be printed in Bulgarin's magazine *The Russian Thalia*. Meanwhile his friends had taken matters into their own hands, as teams of young officers and students set about making copies of the play. In an early form of *samizdat*, the copies were copied and re-copied, so that by 1830 it was reckoned that more than 40,000 manuscript versions were in circulation, and that there was scarcely a town in Russia where the play had not been read.

The play, wrote Pushkin, had an 'indescribable effect', immediately placing Griboyedov on a level with Russia's foremost poets. Written in rhyming couplets of irregular length, its verses rapidly acquired the status of popular sayings; Pushkin, at first reading, predicted that more than half of them would become proverbs. The subtlety, wit and precision of the language are almost impossible to convey in translation – one reason perhaps why the play is comparatively little known outside Russia, though a recent stage version by Anthony Burgess at the Almeida Theatre in Islington did something to improve the situation.

In Russia, scores of phrases and aphorisms from the play have passed into everyday speech; according to a recent estimate, it is the most quoted single work in the language. References to *Woe from Wit* permeate Russian literature. Pushkin, quoting from it in *Eugene Onegin*, was the first of a long line of writers for whom it has been a touchstone. Here is Goncharov:

> The salt, the epigrams, the satire, the colloquial verse one feels will never die, any more than the sharp, biting, lively Russian intelligence which is sprinkled throughout them and which Griboyedov locked up, as a wizard might some spirit in his castle, where it bursts into peals of malicious laughter. It is impossible that speech should ever be more natural, more simple, more completely derived from life.

Appearing a year before the failed Decembrist uprising of 1825, *Woe from Wit* has been taken as the manifesto of the doomed generation of liberal aristocrats to which Griboyedov belonged, notably by Herzen. Arguments as to how far the play was political, how far the protest of any young idealist against the corruption of his elders, have raged ever since, culminating in the claims of Soviet historians that Griboyedov was an honorary Marxist. The failure of the conspiracy, ending in death or long years of exile for many of Griboyedov's greatest friends, was undoubtedly another of the dark clouds which overshadowed his life. Arrested himself, he escaped unscathed after three months of questioning, but the fate of his friends would always haunt him, driving him on to his own very different martyrdom.

In the post-Decembrist blight which marked the opening years of Nicholas I's reign, literary protest was stifled, political conformity rigidly imposed. For Griboyedov, escape lay in the Caucasus and the civilised warmth of Georgia. Always intensely nationalistic, his patriotism could find an outlet in his diplomatic career, and expanding Russia's territory at the expense of her Persian and Turkish neighbours. In the context of Russian imperialism, he was a maker of history; the Treaty of Turkmanchai was as important to the area as the Congress of Vienna was to Europe, and (unlike the Congress of Vienna's) the borders then established still hold good today.

Griboyedov's life, with its immensely varied backdrops, ranging from the literary salons of St Petersburg to the snowy peaks of the Caucasus, has never been the subject of a full-length biography in English. The only literary biography in France, Professor Jean Bonamour's *A.S. Griboyedov et la vie littéraire de son temps*, concentrates almost entirely on his place in Russian literature, and deals only briefly with his life as a diplomat. In Russia, studies of his diplomatic career have long been dominated by the conspiracy theory, the nub of which was the allegedly treacherous role played by the British in bringing about his death in Tehran. This was in line with Soviet Cold-War attitudes, but also because British sources, in particular the records of the Foreign Office and India Office Library papers about Persia, were not available to Soviet scholars during the communist period. It is one of the aims of this book to right this picture, and to re-assess the whole question of British and Russian relations in Persia in this period. It is also a chance to examine Griboyedov's own role in the 'Great Game', then starting. There was scarcely a major player on the eastern chess board with whom he was not familiar, from the Shah, the Crown Prince Abbas Mirza and their ministers, to Sir John Macdonald and Dr McNeill, the key figures in the English mission, and Yermolov and Paskievich on the Russian side.

For Russians, Griboyedov will always be loved as the poetic author of an immortal comedy, whose alienated hero, Chatsky, expressed the hopes and disillusions of the Decembrist generation and who, like Pushkin and Lermontov, died young, cut off by violence in his prime. His role as a diplomat is less well known, but his life – and death – are impossible to understand unless the Georgian and Persian dimensions are taken into account. His years of unwilling exile in the east had helped to form his character; the warmth and exoticism of Tiflis, the majestic beauty of the landscape, the brief but intense happiness of his marriage to the Georgian princess, Nina Chavchavadze, had reconciled him to the idea of living permanently in Georgia. Had he lived, he would have resigned from the imperial service for a life of writing and study on his father-in-law's estates. In the end it was only his body that returned to Georgia. He was buried as he had wished, in the monastery of St David, on a steep hillside above Tiflis, looking out towards the distant mountains of the Caucasus.

I

A Moscow Education

Alexander Griboyedov's family left no papers, and at best we only have a sketchy picture of his parents' position in the ranks of the minor nobility in the province of Vladimir. Tradition had it that the family originally came from Poland, settling in Russia and changing their name from Gribovsky to Griboyedov some time before the sixteenth century. The first official reference to the family was in 1614, when Tsar Mikhail Fyodorovich rewarded Mikhail Yefimovich Griboyedov 'for his many services' against the Poles and Lithuanians with some villages in the district of Vyazma. In 1650, Ivan Griboyedov escorted Tsar Aleksei Mikhailovich to Kashin, and in 1669 Fyodor Akimovich Griboyedov wrote *A History of the Tsars and Grand Dukes of the Russian Land* for the benefit of the imperial children. Another Griboyedov served Peter the Great. Griboyedov's mother, a distant cousin of his father, was also a Griboyedov, with a lineage traceable back to the 1630s and certain high-ranking civil servants round Kazan.

By the early eighteenth century, the Griboyedovs had been accepted as part of the Vladimir nobility, with records going back to 1685.[1] The writer's grandfather, Ivan Nikoforovich (1721–1800) served in the Life Guards Preobrazhensky Regiment in the Russo–Swedish wars. In 1755, he was commissioned as a captain in the Siberian Grenadiers, and finally retired in 1782 with the rank of Court Counsellor (Nadvorny Sovietnik; see Appendix II). He is recorded as owning five villages, together with 88 male serfs or 'souls', in the 1780s.

The few facts available about his son, Griboyedov's father, point to what seems to have been a rather unsatisfactory career. Born in 1760,

5

Sergei Ivanovich Griboyedov joined the Smolensk Dragoons as a cadet in 1775. Promotion came when Prince Yuri Trubetskoy, a Lieutenant General in the Crimea, took him onto his regular staff as a captain in the Kinburnsky Dragoon Regiment. But he served in no campaigns, and in 1785 was allowed to retire on the grounds of illness, with the rank of 'Sekund-Major'.[2]

Already before his retirement, on temporary leave in 1782, he had joined the ranks of the heavy-gambling landowners in the Province of Vladimir. Here he was caught up in a disagreeable local scandal, when he fleeced an inexperienced sixteen-year-old, Nikita Artamonovich Volkov, an orphan and the ward of the public prosecutor, of 14,000 roubles at cards. The ensuing outcry reached the ears of the provincial governor, who insisted that the money be repaid.

Once retired, the Major spent most of his time in the country, neglecting his estates and refusing to take part in the local assembly of Vladimir gentry on the grounds of ill health. His wife did not encourage him to join her in Moscow, and he may well have sought consolation among the serf girls on his estate. It seems likely that Alexander's so-called foster-brother, Alexander Gribov, later his devoted servant and companion, was actually the Major's son; according to the convention of the time, children born out of wedlock were often given a shortened version of the father's surname.

The Major was certainly not a father to help his son get on in worldly terms, and Alexander's ambition, touchiness and extreme sensitivity in matters of honour may well have owed something to his negative example. His mother, Anastasiya Fyodorovna, on the other hand, was tight-fisted and authoritarian, determined to keep up her position in society despite her unfortunate marriage. Good-looking and intelligent, she was known

The Griboyedov family crest,
courtesy of N. Volkov-Muromtsov

for her blunt judgements and sharp tongue; Alexander would find her overbearing attitudes increasingly irritating as he grew up.

Alexander Sergeyevich Griboyedov was born on 4 January 1795; his sister, Mariya, was born four years later.[3] The two children spent most of their childhood in Moscow. The family house (destroyed in the great fire of 1812) was 17 Novinsky Boulevard, on the corner of today's Tchaikovsky and Devyatinsky Streets.[4] The freehold belonged to Alexander's mother's brother, Aleksei Fyodorovich, who had rented it to his sister and her husband, presumably on favourable terms.[5] It was a spacious two-storey building to which, in 1806, Alexander's mother added a servants' wing, selling part of a family estate in the Kropkovka region to do so.

Even though she was badly off herself, Alexander's mother had grand connections.[6] One of her sisters was married to the Minister of Education, Count Razumovsky, while her brother, Aleksei Fyodorovich, was a landowner on a splendid scale. He had been married twice, first to a Princess Odoyevsky – one of their daughters, Lisa, married Alexander's future patron and Commander-in-Chief Prince Paskievich – and then to Princess Naryshkina, a country neighbour. Alexander's mother had been lent a house on her brother's estate at Khmelita, and she spent her summer holidays there each year, leaving her husband behind to drink and gamble with his cronies.

Khmelita, near Vyazma, about 150 miles from the provincial capital of Smolensk, was one of Russia's great estates.[7] It extended for over 21,000 acres, and gave employment to 3000 serfs. The main house stood on an eminence on the lower slopes of the Valdai Hills, with two of the estate's three churches visible from its windows. Originally built in the Russian baroque style, probably by the architect of the Stroganov Palace in St Petersburg, it had been enlarged and remodelled on classical lines by Griboyedov's uncle. The house was destroyed in the Second World War, but we have a description of it, much as Griboyedov would have known it, from the son of its last pre-revolutionary owner, Nicholas Volkov-Muromtsov, who was brought up there.

Writing in 1991, two years before his death at the age of ninety-two, he described it as consisting of a central building, with two 120-foot two-storeyed wings and a parade square in front, with low walls linking two side annexes and a triumphal entrance arch. At the back of the house a *pente douce*, or ramp, led to the ballroom in the centre, and there was a formal park of 25 acres, whose main avenue of limes formed a second approach. Beyond the park, a road ran through a wilderness across an artificial river with a pseudo-marble bridge. There was a *manège* and a stud farm nearby – 'In my time,' wrote Volkov, 'this did not exist'[8] – a series of stables, barns and cattlesheds, and an enormous building that housed the serf actors and a gypsy choir.

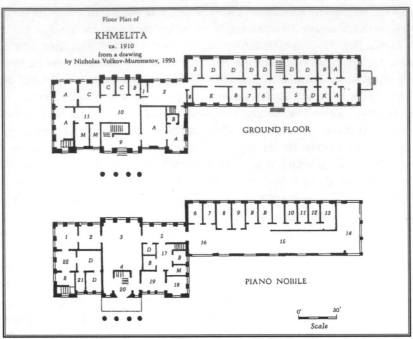

Floor Plan of

KHMELITA

ca. 1910
from a drawing
by Nicholas Volkov-Muromstov, 1993

GROUND FLOOR

PIANO NOBILE

0'   30'

Scale

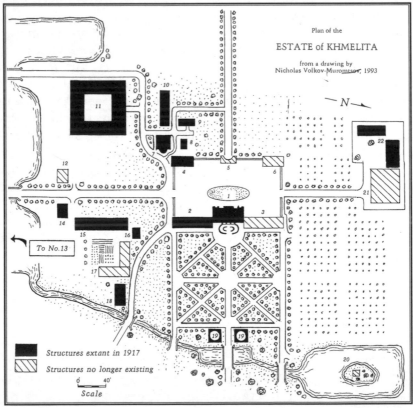

Plan of the

ESTATE of KHMELITA

from a drawing by
Nicholas Volkov-Muromtsov, 1993

N

To No.13

Structures extant in 1917

Structures no longer existing

0'   40'
Scale

Other serfs lived further away. One of them, a certain 'waterman' called Prokop, was still alive when Volkov was born. He had been born in 1799, a date Volkov's father verified from the church records, and died at the age of 112, having insisted on working until the day before he died. 'This was nothing extraordinary in strong Russian country people,' wrote Volkov. 'In our district around Khmelita there were three other people over 110, two women and one man.'[9] Prokop remembered Alexander's visits as a boy. 'He was much older than me,' he said – four years is a big gap to the very young. 'They say he wrote something.'

Khmelita was reduced to only a few walls in the Second World War. It is now a museum directed by the dynamic Viktor Kulakov dedicated to the memory of Alexander Griboyedov. 'The restorers had no idea of what the house was like,' wrote Volkov.

> On knocking off the stucco they found that the house originally was built in the Russian baroque style. When my book with photos (of the house before the Revolution) reached the restorers it was too late. The house had been restored in baroque. The restorers now pretend that the house was converted [to the classical style] in the 1830s. Poor A.S.G. would never recognise Khmelita as now restored.[10]

In the days of Alexander's uncle, Khmelita was a hive of activity. It had every sort of workshop. There were cabinet-makers, mirror-makers, gilders, architects, gun-makers; as Prokop said proudly, 'There was no need to buy anything, everything was made at Khmelita'. The immediate household included the usual French tutor, in this case an Abbé Baudet, a German drawing master, Herr Mayer, and an English harpist and musical director, Mr Adams. There was a house theatre, built in the south wing, with its own troupe of serf actors and actresses and a gypsy band; in the summer there would be as many as three performances a week, attended by the local gentry. Every summer too there would be several grand balls. The house would be illuminated, and neighbours came from far and wide: Volkonskys, Lobanov-Rostovskys, Sheremet'yevs, Naryshkins and so on. From an early age, Alexander was mixing with some of Russia's leading families.

Aleksei Fyodorovich was a genial and expansive host, gallant to the ladies, and, in the eyes of Alexander's childhood friend and neighbour Vladimir Lykoshin, a 'heedless merry sort of fellow'.[11] But his geniality was only skin-deep. In an undated sketch, entitled *The Character of My Uncle*,[12] Alexander gave a cold appraisal of his mother's brother:

> It will fall to the lot of historians to explain why such a mixture of vices and amiability was so prevalent and widespread in that [his uncle's] generation. On the surface they were chivalrous and gallant, but in their hearts there was not an ounce of feeling... In plain words, everyone had the spirit of dishonesty in their souls, and deceit on their tongues. It

seems that at present this is no longer the case – but my uncle belonged to that epoch. He fought like a lion against the Turks under Suvorov, then fawned his way into the drawing rooms of those in favour in St Petersburg and in his retirement lived off gossip. His favourite moral admonition was, 'As I see it, my dear fellow...'[13]

The character of Famusov, the fussy, self-serving bureaucrat of *Woe from Wit* was perhaps already there in outline.

The long holidays at Khmelita, giving Alexander his first taste of life in the grand manner, must have also underlined his sense of being a poor relation. For his mother, disillusioned by her marriage, the worldly establishment of her two children would become an overriding passion. Extremely cultivated herself, she devoted herself to their education. Both children were intensely musical. There is a strong possibility that they studied with the Irish pianist and composer John Field (the inventor of the nocturne), who was living in Russia at the time.[14] Alexander would derive solace all his life from music, the piano and composing, while his sister Mariya was one of the finest amateur harpists of the day.

At the age of eight, Alexander entered the Pension for the Sons of the Nobility, or Noble Pension, in Moscow;[15] his friend, Vladimir Lykoshin, a country neighbour from Khmelita, joined the school at the same time. Founded in 1779, the Noble Pension adjoined the buildings of the Imperial University, which for most of its pupils would be the next stage in their education, leading to an eventual career in the civil service or the army. The links between the university and Pension were close. The university literary society, where distinguished poets, such as Zhukovsky, recited their poems, held its meetings in the hall of the Pension; there were many shared lectures and teachers, and the university bookstore and printing press were housed on the pension's premises.

Alexander attended the Pension as a half-boarder. A German tutor, Johann Petrosilius, later librarian of Moscow University, was engaged to coach him at home. There was a French tutor for Lykoshin, and it is probable that the two boys shared lessons. Alexander was surely recalling their tutors when Chatsky, the hero of *Woe from Wit*, reminisces about his schooldays:

> Our mentor, you remember his cap and gown,
> His index finger and all the signs of education,
> How our tender minds would quiver like a leaf
> How from our early days we were brought up on the belief
> That without Germans there is no salvation.
> And Guillaumet, the Frenchman, always on the town –
> Is he married yet?[16]

In 1806, at the precocious age of eleven, Alexander was admitted to the University. Lykoshin, two years older, was admitted at the same time.

With the agreement of their parents, the boys were allowed to install themselves under the supervision of their tutors in a rented flat on Gazetny Pereulok; other friends and cousins from the Khmelita circle soon moved in as well.

Situated next to the Mokhovaya, the great street leading from the Kremlin, the Imperial University had been founded in 1754 by the Empress Elizabeth; its statutes had been renewed by Alexander I in 1804. Degrees from the university – bachelor ('candidate'), master and doctor – approximated to ranks in the civil and military hierarchies and determined the level of entry to them. They were obtainable in four faculties: political and moral sciences; physical sciences and mathematics; medical sciences; and literature, or *belles lettres*. Both Alexander and Lykoshin entered this last faculty. The courses included Greek Literature and Grammar, Rhetoric and Russian Poetry, World History, History and Statistics and Geography of the Russian empire, Oriental languages, German, French and English. It was an ambitious curriculum, comparable with that provided for Pushkin and his galaxy of friends at the Lycée at Tsarskoye Selo. But whereas the Lycée was always an elitist institution, with students personally approved by the Tsar, Moscow University was open not only to the aristocracy, but to commoners (*raznotchintsy*) and the children of the lower clergy (*popovichi*). There was little mixing between groups, however, and the *popovichi* especially, with their ugly yellow-collared uniforms, were generally looked down on by their better-off contemporaries.

In June 1808, Alexander and Lykoshin took the examination which entitled them to the rank of candidates for degrees. Both presented a thesis, their special subject being 'The Migration of the Slavs'. Maubert, Lykoshin's French tutor, and the German Petrosilius were present at their formal examination by Professor Aviat de Vattoy,[17] a good-natured figure who had supervised their studies and given them the run of his French library.

Having gained their rank as candidates (which brought with it the privilege of wearing an embroidered collar), both Alexander and Lykoshin moved from the faculty of literature to that of law. Alexander obtained his degree when he was only fifteen. He then planned to take his doctorate in natural sciences and mathematics; he was only prevented from doing so by the war of 1812.

Looking back on his friend's university career, Lykoshin commented that Alexander had been no more than an average student, lively and amusing, but with no sign of a literary vocation, beyond a 'certain indeterminate power of concentration'.[18] All the same, the range of his studies, covering literature, law and the sciences in a few short years, was remarkable. So too were his interests. He had a natural gift for languages, reading both Latin and Greek, and speaking French, German, Italian and English fluently. He was widely read in foreign literature, a lover of Shakespeare, Schiller and Goethe, a passionate admirer of Voltaire, 'that bronze bust come alive,' as he described him, 'the picture of decrepitude and withered genius'.[19] Like most of his university contemporaries, he was steeped in the ideas of the Enlightenment and, despite the horrors of the French Revolution, had begun to question his own country's institutions. But, like them, he remained an ardent Russian patriot, fiercely interested in the progress of Russian arms in the Napoleonic campaigns. He was devoted too to the rituals of the Russian Orthodox Church, and had studied the Bible closely; years later, his friend Küchelbecker recalled how, in a period of doubt, Griboyedov had brought him back to a belief in the immortality of the soul.

According to his friend Beguichov, whom he would first meet in 1813, Griboyedov's tastes and literary judgements were already formed by the time he left Moscow University.[20] It is hard to trace specific influences, but one of the most important, according to Griboyedov himself, was that of Professor Johann Gottlieb Bühle, with whom he studied aesthetics and philosophy. Bühle, already a well-known European figure when he joined the university in 1804, was one of the most remarkable philosophers and political scientists of the day, and, as editor of *Revue des Beaux Arts*, a pioneer in the study of Russian art and antiquities. Deeply read in Russian history, he was firmly anti-Napoleon, even at a time when the Tsar was swearing friendship to the Emperor at Tilsit. From him Griboyedov imbibed a hatred of the then fashionable Gallomania, which would later be echoed in *Woe from Wit*. In a long tirade against 'a little Frenchman from Bordeaux',[21] who is greeted like a king at Moscow parties, Chatsky denounces society's 'sickening love for foreign ways':

> Let them call me a believer in the faith of old,
> But our northern land is worse a hundred fold
> Since we gave up our customs, language and the good old days.

Another important influence during his university years was the German Johann Gottlieb John, who in 1810 replaced Petrosilius as his tutor. Eleven years older than his pupil, he would become a close friend. His particular speciality was the classics, but he was also passionately interested in the theatre, both at the university and thereafter – he was later to run the German theatre in St Petersburg.

It was a passion Alexander shared. His apprenticeship as a playwright began in Moscow, where there was a thriving theatrical tradition dating back to the days of Peter the Great. The Petrovsky Theatre, founded by the Empress Elizabeth, offered a varied diet of German, French and Russian plays to the Moscow public, while many of the nobility, Alexander's uncle among them, had their own troupes of serf actors and actresses, and gave lavish entertainments in their homes. The Pension and the university also had their own theatres, where stagecraft was taught by two professors, and students played the female roles. Alexander's first attempt at play writing, a parody of Ozerov's patriotic tragedy *Dmitri Donskoy*, was performed at the university theatre when he was only fifteen. The play, entitled *Dmitri Dyranskoy* (or 'nonsense')[22] has been lost, but, according to his friend Stepan Beguichov, who read it in manuscript, it was a spoof on the quarrel between the Russian and German teaching bodies at the university. The dénouement was a witty one, not unknown in the groves of academe today: Professor Dryanskoy comes forward to read the first number of his new academic journal; all the Germans fall asleep.

Alexander's years at the Imperial University, immensely formative in many ways, laid the foundation of some lasting friendships. They included some of the leading liberal figures of his generation, future Decembrists or sympathisers, among them Peter Chaadayev, his very close friend at university, later to fall foul of the authorities for his Western ideas, Artamon Muravyov, Ivan Turgeniev and Sergei Trubetskoy, all to be exiled to Siberia for their part in the Decembrist rising of 1825. At the same time, through his mother's assiduously cultivated contacts, he was able to plunge into the pleasure-loving world of Moscow society, that upper-class ant-heap which the French invasion of 1812 was soon to overturn.

In contrast to the official world of St Petersburg, centring around the court and government, pre-invasion Moscow had a reputation for informality and jollity. Its essence, in Byelinsky's phrase, was a kind of 'patriarchal domesticity'. Its leaders of society tended to be landowners, gossipy and sociable, their easy-going way of life supported by a substantial income from the country estates to which they would return from May to October each year. Its masculine headquarters was the English Club,[23] a kind of Moscow Athenaeum or Brooks's, which Griboyedov would have visited with his uncle. Tolstoy describes the typical club members as being 'elderly and respected persons, with broad self-confident faces, fat fingers and resolute gestures and voices'. Count Rostov, fussing about Bagration's dinner party at the club in *War and Peace*, epitomises his kind.[24]

For the young and old of both sexes there was a constant flow of visits and receptions. Every day of the week had its pre-determined host, 'at home' for any friend who came to call, the Razumovskys on Thursdays, the Arkharoviches on Fridays and so on, often several on one day. Amongst the most welcoming salons, supposedly a source for many of the characters from *Woe from Wit*, was that of Griboyedov's kinswoman, Marya Ivanovna Rimskaya-Korsakova.[25] Warm-hearted and

hospitable, she was the mother of eight children, for whom she entertained and intrigued endlessly: there were daughters to be married,
sons to be placed in smart regiments. Her house on the Gazetny
Pereulok was large and spacious, on two floors, with two dozen rooms
and a ballroom large enough for theatricals and masquerades and
concerts; service wings behind housed the multitude of servants who
kept the household going. For the young, there was a round of balls and
dinners, impromptu breakfast parties, sleigh rides in the winter and
trips to the country in summer, while for Maria Ivanovna, who had her
serious side, there were church visits and charitable duties to be fitted
in as well. Her diary, perhaps, was not dissimilar from Famusov's in
Woe from Wit:

> Get me the diary...
> Wait just a moment – in the space
> Where it says 'next week', write out
> 'To Praskovya's place
> Next Thursday to eat trout'...
> Note down that on that day – no wait!
> On Thursday I'm invited to a lying in state...
> On Friday or even Saturday, there's nothing in it
> I'm due at the doctor's widow to give her child a name
> She's not yet given birth, but she should do any minute.[26]

In common with most of her contemporaries, Marya Ivanovna habitually
lived beyond her means. The income from her husband's estates was
never quite enough; her sons had expensive tastes; she was always
behind with tradesmen's bills. It was rumoured that she owed money to
the whole of Moscow. But this did not affect her position in society, above
all as a directress of the Assembly of the Nobility, to which Griboyedov,
like any young man of his background, would naturally belong.

Founded by Catherine II, the Assembly's main feature was an
enormous ballroom, with columns in mock marble and a bronze statue
of the Empress. The hall (much frequented by the Soviet establishment:
Stalin lay in state there in 1953) held 3000 people, and there was an
upper gallery to allow great numbers of spectators; in lateral halls there
could also be gaming tables, or dancing if the main hall was full.
Membership was strictly confined to the aristocracy, subscription rates
were 50 roubles for men, 25 for ladies, and 10 for unmarried girls. Every
Tuesday in winter was an assembly day, when there would also be a
ball, except in Lent, when there were evening concerts instead. For
matchmaking parents and aunts, the Assembly was a kind of marriage
market. Readers will remember how in Pushkin's *Eugene Onegin*
Tatiana, still dreaming of Onegin and the Russian countryside, is taken
there to find a husband.

They take her too to the Assembly
The crush, the heat as music blares
the blaze of candles, and the
trembly flicker of swiftly twirling pairs
the beauties in their flimsy dresses,
the swarm, the glittering mob that presses
the ring of marriageable girls –
bludgeon the sense; it faints and whirls.
Here insolent prize dandies wither
all others with a waistcoat's set
and an insouciant lorgnette
Hussars on leave are racing hither
to boom, to flash across the sky
to captivate them to fly...[27]

As a directress of the Assembly, Maria Ivanovna was one of the leaders of Moscow society. It was her daughter who opened the ball with the ADC General Trubetskoy when the Tsar came to Moscow, and with the other autocrats of the assembly she received the imperial family. On this occasion the King of Prussia was present, an episode recalled by Famusov in *Woe from Wit*.

His Highness the Prussian King came to visit us one day.
On seeing the Muscovite young ladies he was mightily astounded,
Not at the beauty of their faces but at their arrogance unbounded...[28]

In the winter of 1811–12, the mazurka, which allows the dancer to kiss his partner's hand while on bended knee, made its first appearance in the Moscow ballrooms. There were dancing classes to practice the new steps, presided over by the famous dancing master I.A. Yogel (Natasha in *War and Peace* was said to be his favourite pupil). Amongst the various private houses where Yogel taught the mazurka was that of Griboyedov's mother, and the seventeen-year-old Alexander, his sister and cousins must have twirled and galloped to its intoxicating strains.

The new craze was still at its height when in the spring of 1812 the cheerful rituals of Moscow life, with its balls, its gossip and its visits, were thrown into confusion by the threat of war. The uneasy peace between Russia and France, established at the Treaty of Tilsit five years before, was coming to an end. Napoleon was gathering his forces on the Russian border. On 24 June 1812, with no official declaration of war, the Grande Armée crossed the Niemen onto Russian soil.

II

The War
of 1812

The recently discovered diaries of Erik Gustav Erström, a Swedish student at Moscow University, published in Stockholm in 1981 under the title *Moscow is Burning*, give a vivid picture of the crisis of 1812 as seen through a student's eyes.[1] They come as close as we are likely to get to what Griboyedov's own experiences during the months of uncertainty leading up to the burning of Moscow must have been.

Erström's father was a modest clergyman in Finland, part of the kingdom of Sweden till 1809, when by the terms of the Treaty of Friedrichmans, Alexander I annexed the country and proclaimed himself Grand Duke of Finland. Erström, having become a Russian citizen, was able to enrol at Moscow University, where he arrived in January 1812.

By the spring of that year, the calm of student life was already disturbed by fears of the coming invasion. Erström's diary for 11 April 1812 notes prosaically that there were no university orderlies, as they had all been dragged off to the army; instead the soldiers' wives kept house for the students, receiving a meagre salary of 10 roubles a month.

On the evening of 12 July, the Tsar arrived in Moscow to appeal for troops, officers and funds from his loyal merchants there. His proclamation to the Russian people, declaring that he would defend the empire come what may, had reached the city 10 days earlier, plunging its citizens into great emotion. Erström was among the crowds awaiting him.

> Every road near the Kremlin was packed with people. I stood by the famous stairs leading up to the Imperial Palace; by 5p.m. excitement

16

was at fever pitch. All the senior aristocracy and members of the court in formal dress and wearing orders and stars were there, together with a group of long bearded merchants in their kaftans...At 8 p.m. there was a sudden rumour in the crowd. 'He is coming, he is coming,' cried a thousand voices. In effect a small carriage appeared and from it emerged the chief of police! The Emperor only arrived at 1 a.m. He immediately entered the Uspensky Cathedral for a service under the Metropolitan Augustin. The people greeted him with great enthusiasm and threw themselves onto the ground, and tried to kiss his feet. All foreigners on this day were told to evacuate Moscow by barge.

Amongst the Tsar's entourage on this occasion was the former Prussian Minister, Baron Shtein, a vociferous anti-Napoleonic intellectual in the mould of Madame de Staël, and an old friend of Griboyedov's tutor Professor Bühle. It was a sign of Bühle's regard for his young pupil that he introduced him to Shtein during his brief visit. Griboyedov, who recalled the meeting with pleasure, would certainly have agreed with Shtein's views on the importance of preserving Russia's national characteristics. 'Russia,' wrote Shtein, 'should keep her original customs, way of life, and sartorial appearances...She has no need of French clothes nor cuisine, nor of any foreign social model.'[2]

The Tsar stayed in Moscow for eight days, before setting out for St Petersburg, leaving the eccentric Governor Rostopchin to prepare for the coming invasion. Urged on by an almost hysterical patriotism, he plastered the streets with posters calling on Moscow to defend itself; the Muscovites would cross themselves as they read them. Searches and arrests followed the posters. To be taken for a Frenchman was to risk summary execution. Any German in Moscow was told to wear a distinguishing sign in his hat to show that he was not French. At the theatre, plays were put on commemorating former Russian victories. Newspaper articles sought to stimulate the mood of national resistance. Glinka, the journalist, led the outcry against French as an aristocratic language and denounced the Russian gentry for employing French tutors. He was rewarded by the Tsar with the Order of St Vladimir, and joined the militia as a major.

On 2 August, the miracle-working ikon of the Smolensk Mother of God was brought in great state to the Kremlin to be placed in the Uspensky Cathedral. On 11 August, however, came the announcement that Smolensk had fallen to the enemy, and the Kremlin's treasures were evacuated by barge. The news sent shivers through Moscow society. The churches were full; every mother was pulling strings with any general she knew to find places for her sons in a good regiment. By early September, most of those who could afford to had left for Nizhny Novgorod or Saratov, the grand hostesses of yesterday now scurrying round to look for flats and houses, followed helter skelter by their French or German governors and tutors.

In the university everything took on a martial aspect. Students fashioned wooden rifles for themselves. A regiment was created, and they all drilled from dawn to dusk, and took turns at sentry duty. Already there was talk of evacuating the university to the east. The Rector told Erström to be prepared to leave with him, first to Vladimir or Nizhny Novgorod, or eventually to Kazan.

> The chests of the university's treasures had already gone. We had no horses…The Rector announced he could not commandeer them any-where. The Governor-General has forgotten us…By 4 September [four days after Borodino] there was panic and terror in the capital. For a whole week after the battle we saw the wounded, though the French had ordered no prisoners should be taken. At ten o'clock on 14 September we saw our first French troops…Finally the university was allocated fifteen horses. Once they arrived the cry resounded, 'Faster, faster!' On 18 September our student group reached Nizhny Novgorod.

Griboyedov did not leave Moscow with the university. Instead, like most of the young aristocrats of his vintage, he had responded to the Tsar's appeal for volunteers for the army. A number of Griboyedov's closest friends, among them the Chaadayev brothers, Yakushkin and Rayevsky, were accepted in the elite Guards regiments and saw action almost imme-diately in the bloody slaughterhouses of Borodino and Shevardino. Griboyedov himself, through no fault of his own, remained in the comparative safety of the Moscow Reserve, obtaining a commission as a Cornet in the newly formed Moscow Hussars. He proudly ordered his newly designed uniform:

> The shako to be yellow with yellow tufted rosettes and bronze trims and froggings, bronze trimmed pelisses, dolmans and sabretaches in black with yellow laces and braid, with bronze buttons; cherry boots with yellow facings and yellow embroidery; black saddlecloths with cherry toothed edgings and yellow laces.

The Moscow Hussars had been created by the immensely wealthy Count P.I. Saltykov, a retired cavalry officer who had served in the Guards, and who from motives of pure patriotism had demanded the Tsar's permission to raise a regiment at his own expense. He had originally intended to raise ten squadrons, but recruitment was slow, and most of the men, many of them serfs donated to the regiment by their owners, had no military experience. The Tsar had intended to strengthen the regiment by allocating 40 NCOs from the Nizhegorodsky, Narva and Borisoglebsky Dragoons, but as the regiments in question were hundreds of miles away, the order was changed, and only 12 NCOs could be spared from another cavalry squadron.

Saltykov, as Colonel, tried valiantly to equip and train his men, with the help of Rostopchin, who issued them with firearms and sabres from the Moscow Arsenal, and gave them the Khamovnitchesky Barracks for their use. But despite anxious enquiries from the Commander-in-Chief, Kutuzov, as to whether the regiment was fit to fight, the Governor General was forced to admit that the regiment was 'lost' for the time being. The junior ranks were quite untrained, and would be useless in the defence of Moscow; moreover, they were unruly and had been causing disturbances in the city. On 21 August, Saltykov recommended to Rostopchin that the regiment should finish its training near Kazan, several hundred miles away. Not only would this give him a chance to instill some order into his troops, now numbering nearly a thousand, but he would be better able to find them horses. Rostopchin agreed, and forwarded his recommendation to the Tsar, but permission in those chaotic times was slow in coming, and the choice of Kazan was neither approved nor disapproved.

On 13 September, with the terrified population already streaming from the city, Kutuzov made his momentous decision not to defend Moscow. The costly battle of Borodino had failed to stem Napoleon's advance; Kutuzov dared not risk his weakened troops in a second confrontation. In the confusion of the evacuation, Saltykov found himself in dispute with Rostopchin, who first ordered him to escort a party of French prisoners-of-war to Orenburg, then told him to use his own judgement as to when and where to withdraw. The regiment eventually left for Kazan a few hours before the first French troops entered Moscow. The following evening, clearly in view to the withdrawing Russians, the first flames from the burning city lit the sky.

Griboyedov was delayed on the journey to Kazan. En route through the province of Vladimir he fell ill, and was granted sick leave on 21 September. His mother and sister hurried to nurse him, renting a house from a local priest, where he spent a month in bed, coughing blood and with a high fever and rheumatic pains. Later, because of the great number of sick and wounded evacuated to the provincial hospitals, he was allowed to convalesce on his parents' estate, complaining of 'nervous sleeplessness' and 'continuous colds', hardly the most martial of complaints.

Meanwhile, the Moscow Hussars had reached Kazan, where serious efforts were made to instil some order into the regiment, and to remedy their worst deficiencies, especially their lack of horses.[3] In December 1812, their Colonel and founder, Saltykov, died, but despite his death the regiment was not disbanded. The Irkutsk Dragoons had suffered severe losses in the ferocious fighting of the early months of the war and then at Borodino, while the Moscow Hussars were still untrained and incomplete. It was decided that the two regiments should be amalgamated and renamed the Irkutsk Hussars. They were to fall under the orders of the experienced cavalry General Andrey Semyonovich Kologrivov, who had been recalled from retirement by the Tsar and made GOC (General Officer Commanding) of the cavalry reserves. In May 1813, Griboyedov, finally recovered, joined the Irkutsk Dragoons at Kobrin with the rest of his regiment, and was inscribed onto its roll the following month.

Having failed to see active service, Griboyedov was now able to hear at first hand of the exploits of those who had fought at Smolensk and Borodino. In the last battle especially, the Irkutsk Dragoons had been in the thick of the fighting in the defence of the Rayevsky Heights, and, as well as many individual awards for gallantry, had collectively been awarded the Medal of 1812. In such company any mettlesome young man, with the war still thundering about his ears, might easily develop an inferiority complex, or at least a burning desire to distinguish himself in one way or another. We may imagine Griboyedov felt the same.

Griboyedov served for only a few months in the routine duties of a regimental officer, and seems to have missed any action during this time. He was then offered the more interesting post of Adjutant or private secretary to General Kologrivov, stationed in Brest-Litovsk in western Russia. Perhaps strings had been pulled for him in Moscow, but he had probably also been recognised as a clever young man with a pen. By November 1813 his secondment had gone through.

His new chief, Kologrivov, belonged to a large and influential family, with links to the court, and friends and relations amongst the leading figures of the time. He himself had been a protégé of Tsar Paul I. He was a humane and civilised man, popular with his officers and men. The following year, when the Tsar awarded him the Order of St Vladimir, with star and ribbon, they arranged a banquet, attended with trumpets, fireworks and triumphant salvos of artillery, to celebrate the honour. Griboyedov's account of the occasion, 'Letter from Brest-Litovsk',[4] was published in the *Herald of Europe*, a well-known Moscow magazine, in June 1814. Written in the name of all his brother officers, it was a panegyric to the General, half in rhyme, half in somewhat sycophantic prose, and was noteworthy above all as being his first published work.

The cavalry reserves constituted a kind of phantom army, spread out over a wide territory stretching from Grodno to Minsk and Ostrolenkov.[5] Their task was to recruit and train fresh squadrons for the depleted regiments of the serving army on active service. The whole exercise was on an enormous scale, with 12,000 troopers and 90,000 horses to be foraged and provided for. Kologrivov's Adjutants would have accompanied their commander in the course of his inspections of units, remounts and scattered squadrons. They would also have acted as couriers, bearing secret orders to destinations as varied as Minsk and Grodno and Warsaw, and perhaps as recruiting officers too; Griboyedov's own parents, inspired by patriotic feeling, were among those who contributed serfs to the reserves.

In a second article for the *Herald of Europe*, published in October 1814, Griboyedov described the role of these reserves, praising the far-sighted attitude of the Government in setting up the operation, and Kologrivov's efficiency in carrying out his orders; out of a target of 130 new squadrons, 56 had already been provided for active service. We may assume that Kologrivov, who would have checked the article in draft, was well pleased with his hyperactive private secretary.

Taking Griboyedov's two articles together, it is easy to see them as naive, if not obsequious, in their enthusiasm for the authorities, and Kologrivov in particular. It is true that as a young officer, under the very eyes of his commander, he could do little else than stand to attention, as it were, in print. The curiosity is that, psychologically, he felt impelled to do so. Perhaps he was preparing the ground for the kind of brilliant conformist career his mother desired for him, in strong contrast to his father's failures. Perhaps he was simply inspired by wartime patriotism, and pride in his country's achievements. The Tsar's entry into Paris, as the 'Liberator of Europe' in the spring of 1814, had seemed to herald a new age. 'Strange destiny of the Slavonic race!'[6] wrote one of his Generals, A. Mikhailovsky Danilevsky, as the Russian army approached Paris. 'The united forces of Europe, led by a Slavonic Tsar, were now approaching to attack that capital, the conquest of which re-established universal peace.'

The active and dedicated role which the Tsar had played in the French campaign of 1814, his magnanimity of spirit in setting the liberal tone for the Russian occupation of Paris, the generosity of his announcement to the French Senate that all French prisoners-of-war in Russia were to be released, were tributes to Alexander's lofty principles and enlightened outlook. Such indeed seemed the noble and heroic figure to whom Griboyedov and his generation – the generation of 1812 – looked for the salvation of Russia.

It soon became clear that the Emperor's liberal attitudes were not for home consumption. The first military change which affected Griboyedov's generation was the death of the heroic architect of Russia's victory, Marshal Kutuzov, in 1813, and his replacement by the sinister martinet General Arakcheyev, who while the Tsar was enjoying the plaudits of his allies in Paris was ruthlessly tightening discipline at home. Under Arakcheyev, service in the army gradually lost all glamour;

the thrill of fighting a great patriotic war to liberate the motherland, and of riding through the kingdoms of Europe, whose social structures seemed to work reasonably well without serfdom or an absolute autocracy, would become an emotion of the past. There was nothing left for idealistic young officers in the army but soulless drill work and parades, and the senseless brutality of public knoutings and floggings. The wide-scale creation of so-called military colonies, a disastrous piece of social engineering in which farming was carried out under army discipline, added a new dimension of horror to military service: 'the blood was never dry on the floors of the rural offices,' wrote Herzen in *My Past and Thoughts.*[7]

For Griboyedov, on the periphery of events, disillusion would come slowly. He seems to have enjoyed the camaraderie of his army years, and taken pleasure in the routines of cavalry life. There are echoes of his feelings in *Woe from Wit*, as Chatsky reminisces with his old army friend Platon Mikhailovich.

> Do you remember how it used to be…
> When I knew you in the regiment at the end of last year,
> Your foot was in the stirrup as soon as it was dawn
> And off you went on your sprightly steed,
> Paying the autumn wind not the slightest heed,
> Whether it blew from the front or from the rear.
> Yes, friend, that was the life to lead.[8]

He also made a number of new acquaintances, most importantly his fellow adjutant, Kologrivov's nephew Stepan Beguichov.[9] Beguichov, who would become his closest friend, was eight years older than Griboyedov, well-read, warm-hearted and open-handed, all appealing qualities for an aspiring intellectual stranded in the backwater of Brest-Litovsk. 'Beguichov,' said Griboyedov later, 'was the first person who respected me'. The young officers found what amusements they could in local society. On one occasion, according to his friend A.A. Zhandr, Griboyedov arrived on horseback in a first-floor ballroom.[10] On another, having offered to play the organ at a service in the local Jesuit church, he broke into a spirited version of the 'Kamarinskaya', a popular Russian folk dance.[11]

By the end of 1815, the war was won and over; it was time for Cornet Griboyedov to plan his return to civilian life. He had already spent some time on sick leave, following a recurrence of his rheumatic fevers, visiting St Petersburg for an extended 'cure' at the beginning of the year. He had also suffered from a riding accident, which had left him with chest injuries, and now sought permission from the Tsar to retire from the Irkutsk Hussars on grounds of ill health.[12] He invoked the help of Kologrivov to support his application, and his commanding officer, in his covering letter, stressed how zealously and well Griboyedov had carried out his duties. He also requested that Griboyedov should be allowed to enter the civil service with a higher rank than that to which he would have been entitled had he left university with a doctorate three years before.

The point was important. For a young man of Griboyedov's background, without a sufficient income to survive independently, the civil service was the only alternative to a career in the army, and both salaries and prospects were determined by the level at which he entered it. Under the so-called Table of Ranks (see Appendix II), comprising fourteen grades which governed the military and civil hierarchy, Griboyedov's doctorate would have entitled him to enter the service at the level of 'guberniya secretary', tenth class. Kologrivov argued that his patriotism in volunteering for the army in his country's hour of peril had put him at a disadvantage with his civilian contemporaries, and that he should therefore be allowed to jump two ranks to the eighth class.

In the event, the promotion was refused and Griboyedov was credited with only tenth-class rank; however, since he had not actually taken his doctorate, he had at least been given some credit for his military service. On 25 March 1816, he received his official release from the army. His four years there had helped to form his character in many ways. As secretary to Kologrivov, he had polished his administrative skills and learned the rudiments of working within an autocratic system, under a chief he could respect and admire. He had made a number of new friends, one of whom, Stepan Beguichov, would be a lifelong confidant and ally. Above all, he had been thrown out of his studies and his mother's social values into a world of real activity and responsibilities, and had enormously widened his experience of life.

III

Literary Beginnings: St Petersburg

Griboyedov's first call after leaving the army must have been to see his mother and sister in Moscow. At the end of 1815 his father had died. Quite apart from any natural sorrow Griboyedov may have felt, there were family matters to be discussed. The Major had left large debts, most of them to his wife, and his three small estates were heavily encumbered. The widow's first consideration was to safeguard the modest dowry of her daughter, Mariya, and with the consent of Alexander, who agreed to stand down in his sister's interest, the whole inheritance was ceded to her, on condition that she assumed her father's liabilities. Mariya, in due course, married a local landowner, M.S. Durnovo, like her a talented amateur musician.

Alexander, in the long run, could expect to inherit property from his mother, who still owned several estates, but meanwhile had no means of his own beyond what allowance she could give him. Anastasiya Fyodorovna, though willing to scheme and pull strings for her family, was chronically short of ready money; Alexander would always be worse off than most of his contemporaries of a similar background.

Having dealt with his affairs in Moscow, where the old patriarchal way of life was beginning to re-assert itself after the trauma of the war, Griboyedov must have been eager to set out for St Petersburg. Moscow might be rising from the ashes, with broad new streets and fine classical buildings, but little else had changed. 'In my view,' says Skalozoop in *Woe from Wit*, 'the fire did much to improve it'.[1]

> Famusov: Don't remind me, everyone's gone raving
> Ever since about new roads and paving,
> Houses and everything in the modern mould.
> Chatsky: New houses, but the prejudices are old;
> Neither years will destroy them, nor fashions
> nor fires! What confidence that inspires!

After four years of independence, the old cocoon of Moscow friendships and relationships must have seemed unbearably restrictive. St Petersburg, the capital of the empire, offered far wider social and intellectual horizons. He hoped eventually to join the Foreign Ministry, but in the meantime, despite the disapproval of his mother, he was determined to try his chances at a literary career.

It was one of the paradoxes of Russian literary life in the early nineteenth century that almost all its practitioners were aristocrats. Some, like Griboyedov, belonged by birth rather than wealth to the ranks of the nobility. But the results were the same; few of them expected to make a living by their writing, though the theatre, and to some extent journalism, offered the best chance of doing so. Censorship, particularly in the theatre, was a further problem. Griboyedov's *Woe from Wit* never passed the censors in his lifetime, but was copied and handed round in manuscript – an early form of *samizdat*.

'One shouldn't judge Russian writers by the same criteria as foreign ones,' wrote Pushkin.

> There they write for money, and here (except for me) they write from vanity. There they earn their living by writing poetry and here Count Khvostov [who published all his works at his own expense] ruined himself by doing so. There if you have nothing to eat, you write a book; here if you have nothing to eat, you enter the government service and don't write.[2]

It was a dilemma which Griboyedov would soon have to face. For the moment, however, he was bent on enjoying his new surroundings. In a letter to Beguichov, dated 9 November 1816,[3] he urges him to hurry up and join him in St Petersburg, where he has taken a splendid flat on the Catherine Canal. He sings the praises of the Shuster Club, an offshoot of the St Petersburg English Club to which, by special dispensation, ladies are admitted. He is to go there in a party with Vassily Sheremet'yev, a golden youth from the Chevalier Guards regiment, and his delectable mistress, Avdotiya Istomina, the leading ballerina of the day. He himself, he admits, has had to forswear the fair sex for a time, and is in the hands of a pharmacist who prescribes grey sarsaparilla (a homeopathic treatment for venereal infections). He ends his letter with the naive declaration, 'How much porter there is to drink here and how cheap!'

Griboyedov was twenty-one when he arrived in St Petersburg, a slight, bespectacled young man lacking the heroic aura of his contemporaries who had fought in the 1812 campaigns, but already armed with something of a literary reputation. His two articles from Brest-Litovsk, though published in a Moscow paper, had attracted notice in St Petersburg. More importantly, his adaptation of a fashionable French comedy, *Le Secret du Ménage* by Creuzé de Lesser, had been performed there at the Maly Theatre the previous year. Written as a curtain-raiser for a benefit performance for the young dancer and actress Nimfodora Semyonova, it had starred her elder sister, Yekaterina Semyonova, St Petersburg's leading actress, and had been repeated successfully both in Moscow and the capital.

The play tells the story of a newly married wife who pretends to have an intrigue in order to influence a lawsuit in her husband's favour. Her husband, who has been planning a real affair, is first jealous, then won over by his wife's ingenuity. It was an amusing but not altogether successful attempt to graft a light-hearted French view of morality onto the sterner, more oriental values of a Russian household. An almost harem-like seclusion was still to be found in certain Muscovite homes. Even in St Petersburg, too much of the spirit of *The Marriage of Figaro* could lead to trouble, as Pushkin's fatal duel, fought later over his wife, would demonstrate.

The Newly Weds, as the Russian play was called, had been written and produced with the encouragement of Prince Shakhovskoy, a playwright himself and a leading figure in the theatrical world of St Petersburg.[4] Griboyedov had first met Shakhovskoy in 1813, when he was bringing recruits from his home region of Ostseisky to Warsaw. Since then, Shakhovskoy had returned to his peacetime occupations. Now in his thirties, a cherubic figure with twinkling eyes and a high domed forehead fringed with scanty curls, he was Director of all the repertoire in the imperial theatres, and had just written a highly successful comedy, *The Lipetsk Spa*, himself. His so-called garret, not far from Theatre Square, was a meeting place for actors and actresses, rakish officers, learned academics (the Prince was a member of the St Petersburg Academy) and writers of all descriptions. The star of the salon was the poet I.A. Krylov, whose fables, drawn from Russian folklore, had earned him the title of the Russian La Fontaine. Other leading figures included the playwrights Katenin, Zhandr and Khmel'nitsky, and later the young Pushkin; Pushkin would recall a reading by Katenin at the garret as one of the happiest evenings of his life.

Refreshments at the garret gatherings were modest, 'at very best a cup of tea', but the Prince's geniality and enthusiasm for all things theatrical made up for it. A first-class actor himself – 'had he not been a prince,' wrote a friend, 'we would have had our own Talma or Garrick' – he loved to bring on and encourage new talent. He also took great trouble in finding suitably rich and honourable protectors for young actresses emerging into the corrupt world of St Petersburg. Rumour had it that he sometimes took a commission for such placings, but this was never proved.

Years later, at a dinner following the jubilee performance of *Woe from Wit*, an elderly actress, who had been taken there as a girl by Semyonova, entertained the company with her reminiscences of Griboyedov at these garret evenings. Griboyedov, she said, 'would gather us young actresses together and would begin to tell us some extraordinary long fantasy; we would shriek and scream and giggle'. He was especially inventive, apparently, in making up party games. In one of them, called 'The Monk and the Nine Virgins',[5] the girls had to line up, and singly enter a darkened room where the Monk, played by Griboyedov, wrapped in a capacious shawl, would wait to hear their confessions. Once Shakhovskoy, disguising himself in a scarf, joined the queue:

> We all awaited his return from the dark room with excitement. 'What a monk! What a spiritual confessor!' Shakhovskoy exclaimed on emerging. When the holy father came out from his confessional, we all quizzed him as to whose kisses had been the most enchanting. 'The fifth,' said Griboyedov, 'though the little hussy regrettably did not make a proper confession of her sins…' The joke was that the fifth was Shakhovskoy.

For all the pranks that took place there, the garret was a serious literary centre and Griboyedov learnt much of his craft as a playwright from its genial host.[6] The American critic Simon Karlinsky, in his book on nineteenth-century Russian drama, goes so far as to suggest that *Woe from Wit* would not have been possible without the example of Shakhovskoy's *The Lipetsk Spa*.[7] St Petersburg at the time was riven by the debate between the so-called archaists and romanticists.[8] Shakhovskoy was an archaist or conservative by temperament, disliking the excesses of romantic sentiment, which he mocked in many of his plays. Paradoxically, however, he was an innovator in his attitude to language. *The Lipetsk Spa* is regarded as a turning-point in the transition from the artificial literary usages of eighteenth-century Russian comedy to a more natural and colloquial style and as such was enormously influential on Griboyedov and his successors.

Woe from Wit, Griboyedov's masterpiece, was still six years ahead, but his next theatrical enterprise, *The Married Fiancée*, first performed in 1817, was written in collaboration with Shakhovskoy. In his introduction to the play, Shakhovskoy explained the circumstances in which it was written:

Wishing to compose a new comedy for the benefit performance of Miss Valberg (who adorned *The Lipetsk Spa* with her enchanting talent), I selected a subject in which she could show her varied talents and I strove to connect the episodic scenes with a simple plot as best I could. There was a short time left before the day set for the benefit performance, and for fear of not keeping my promise, I asked Alexander Griboyedov and Nikolai Khmel'nitsky to help me out. Out of the friendship which they bore me, they agreed; the first wrote the entire beginning of the second act...and the second wrote the third act scene in which Biriulkin gives Natasha an examination. Both gratitude and justice require that I make this known, so as not to usurp other people's property.[9]

The Married Fiancée was Shakhovskoy's most successful play, a sparkling comedy centred on the wiles of the penniless young ward of an aristocratic family who has secretly married an orphan, and who must win the approval of his relations if he is to inherit under his parents' will. Griboyedov's contribution shows how much he had advanced from the more mannered style of *The Newly Weds*, and displayed a verve and fluency that, according to Karlinsky, he could only have learned from his collaborators.

As well as his contribution to *The Married Fiancée*, Griboyedov had collaborated with his new friend Pavel Katenin[10] on a comedy called *The Student*. Katenin was a confirmed archaist, and the play poked fun at the romantics and sentimentalists, as typified by the court poet Zhukovsky. Perhaps for this reason, it did not pass the censors, though it was widely read in the drawing-rooms of St Petersburg. Its theme was the defeat of a newcomer from the country, full of romance and idealistic daydreams, by the implacable realities of money and power. Zvezdov (Mr Star), its cynical anti-hero, is the original wheeler and dealer, an influential senior civil servant whose surface geniality conceals a scheming heart. Benevol'sky, the hopeless young Candide, was said to be a portrait of the critic and playwright Mikhail Zagoskin. He thinks and speaks in clichés: girls are 'celestial creatures', the sky is 'the blue firmament'. As foils to his artificial commonplaces, the servants use a naturally vigorous Russian which must have sounded a radical note to the ears of its fashionable audience. The satire is further sharpened by the contrast between the hero's naivety and the cheerful hypocrisy of the Zvezdovs.

In caricaturing Zagoskin as the country bumpkin of the title, Griboyedov had a personal axe to grind: Zagoskin had written a mildly critical review of *The Newly Weds* in the *Northern Observer*. Not content with lampooning him in *The Student,* he also attacked Zagoskin, together with the editor Nikolai Grech, who had reviewed his play unfavourably, in a skit called *The Puppet Theatre*. The title referred to a popular Punch and Judy show much frequented by the common people in their morning strolls:

> See here your Zagoskin the Observer and the Son of the Fatherland, his
> competitor,
> One of them writes rubbish,
> The other analyses it,
> And between the two it is not easy,
> To decide which is the greatest fool.[11]

He was accused of indulging in personal abuse; undeterred, he hired copyists to produce copies of the pamphlet, which his friends distributed all round St Petersburg. Zagoskin, a gentle, inoffensive figure, was deeply wounded by this unprovoked vendetta; Grech, who was made of tougher fibre, simply laughed at the whole affair.[12]

Katenin had had his own troubles with reviewers the previous autumn, when his translation of Bürger's famous ballad 'Leonore' had been attacked for its excessive earthiness and realism. An earlier but more insipid version by Zhukovsky had softened and romanticised the harshness of the German original. In a review for *Son of the Fatherland*,[13] which in many ways expressed his own artistic credo, Griboyedov had ridiculed Zhukovsky's prudery and flowery paraphrases, praising Katenin's version for the directness and simplicity of its language, which derived from the everyday rhythms of popular speech rather than the poetic conventions of the past.

Such literary battles were commonplace in the capital, which in the years immediately following the war was effervescent with creativity and new ideas. Shakhovskoy's garret,[14] where Griboyedov was soon accepted as a star, was only one of a number of salons which a young man of letters would have known. Grech, as editor of *Son of the Fatherland*, was an influential figure whose drawing-room welcomed all shades of literary opinion. So too did that of O.I. Senkovsky,[15] the editor of *The Reader's Library*, a well-known orientalist who received his guests wearing eastern costume, and puffing scented tobacco from a Persian *kalyan*. The group surrounding Admiral Shishkov,[16] the Conversation Club of the Friends of the Russian Language, were arch-conservatives in literature, determined to defend the traditional forms of literary Russian against foreign encroachments and linguistic innovations.[17] Their opponents, in the lighter-hearted Arzamas Club, stood up against the ancients for modern idioms and a simpler, more colloquial style; their meetings, where the members (including the young Pushkin) wore red caps and consumed a jellied goose for supper, were little more than excuses for carousing.[18]

On a more serious level, but still allowing for a plentiful consumption of champagne, was the Green Lamp Society. Founded in 1818 by the millionaire Alexander Vsevolozhsky, an old friend of Griboyedov's from

Moscow University, its members were mostly army officers, brilliant young roués who had earned their spurs in 1812, and, 'lost among the braid and frogging', a few select civilians. They met once a fortnight in a large room lit by a green lamp, symbol of hope; all the members wore a special ring, with a lamp engraved on the stone. Here Pushkin read his latest poems, there were talks on Russian history, discussions of the theatre, and rowdy late-night suppers with ladies of the town. Here too, since members were bound to secrecy about the society's proceedings, the social and political questions of the day were freely discussed. For those who had campaigned across Europe, the evidence that civilised societies could exist without the twin evils of serfdom and autocracy was clear. Aristocratic liberalism was the fashion. The Green Lamp, though too frivolous to be a centre of conspiracy, was at least a place where revolutionary ideas were aired.

Griboyedov would leave St Petersburg soon after the Green Lamp was founded, but some of his theatrical sketches would have their first readings there, and many of its members were close friends. Its real significance in his life was as a forerunner of those secret societies in which the Decembrist movement took shape, and in which, through his friendships and acquaintances, he was indirectly involved.

Of similar significance was Griboyedov's enrolment in the Freemasons[19] soon after his arrival in St Petersburg. Probably nowhere else in Europe did Freemasonry play so important a part in the development of the cultural life of three or four generations as it did in Russia. It first reached the country in the early years of Catherine the Great, and was rapidly taken up by the aristocracy. Orthodox theology provided no strong alternative in a written form of sufficient emotional depth or intellectual rigour to satisfy an increasingly literate and demanding public. One need look no further than *War and Peace*, and the tortured doubts of Pierre Bezukhov, to learn of the spiritual solace which Freemasonry could provide.[20] By 1816, when Griboyedov joined, some of the earlier intensity had disappeared; the gossipy writer F.F. Vigel' described the Masonic lodges as nothing more than clubs or inns, to which a certain secretiveness and a few minor difficulties in joining gave curiosity value. Later historians, however, see the Masonic lodges, with their exclusiveness and secrecy, as natural precursors to the secret societies in which the Decembrist manifestos were prepared.[21]

Amongst the members of Les Amis Réunis, the lodge which Griboyedov joined in 1816, were P.I. Pestel', M.I. Muravyov-Apostol and I.A. Dolgorukov, all leading future Decembrists, though the Masons themselves had no direct concern with politics. In the same year, however, Pestel' became a founder-member of the small and dedicated Union of Salvation, with an active programme of reform, including the elimination of serfdom and the end of the autocracy. It was followed in 1817 by the founding of the Union of Welfare in Moscow, and its linking body the Military Society, one branch of which was directed by Griboyedov's theatrical collaborator Katenin. Stepan Beguichov was another member. Griboyedov could not have failed to have known their views, but he made no attempt to join them. He may have found the Masons' secret rituals and search for spiritual enlightenment an acceptable substitute for his friends' political idealism, which in any case was alien to his sceptical nature and personal situation at the time.

IV

The Duel

During his stay in St Petersburg, Griboyedov had become a significant figure on the literary scene, attracting attention not only by his writing, but by the sparkle of his personality and conversation. He was witty, high-spirited, almost always jolly and good-humoured; friends would recall his gentle manners and the modest, tentative smile with which he would begin a conversation. He could also be proud and touchy on occasion, quick to take offence and with a bitingly sarcastic tongue. But the roll-call of his friendships, with some of the most brilliant members of his generation, point to a likeable and attractive character, and those who knew him best, like Beguichov, always insisted on his sincerity and underlying seriousness.

Behind the dazzle of his literary life, however, lay a darker reality. Although he was too fastidious for the drinking and debauchery of his wilder friends, he had expensive tastes: new books, a piano, visits to the opera and theatre, were necessities of life to him. He was already living well beyond his means and was in debt to several of his friends. His mother did what she could to help, but her own affairs, according to Beguichov, had become 'confused and dissipated'. While Griboyedov's contemporaries preached liberal values and the emancipation of the serfs, she had recently embarked on an unsavoury property speculation in which she had behaved so tyrannically towards the peasants involved that they had been driven to mutiny against her.

The story began in 1816, when she had purchased an estate near Kostroma, with 780 'souls'. She had borrowed heavily to make the purchase, and was eager to make a quick return. She accordingly raised the peasants' quit-rent (*obrok*, or payment in cash rather than services) to four times its previous level, and hugely increased payments in kind. She backed up her demands with threats. Those who refused would be sent to a distillery or cotton mill, or compulsory labour at the plough; unmarried girls faced forced marriages and removal to Moscow. The peasants, stunned at the exorbitance of her demands, appealed for justice to the Tsar; their luckless spokesman (or *khodok)* was later sentenced to be flogged and exiled to Siberia. Meanwhile, a committee of provincial landowners was called in to arbitrate, but although they suggested a somewhat lower figure, it was far above the local average and the peasants still refused to pay. They continued to sue for justice from the Tsar, but their messengers were intercepted and arrested as runaways by the widow's agents before they reached St Petersburg. In the end, at Griboyedova's insistence, the military was called in: the ringleaders were placed in irons and taken off to jail, the rest were forced into submission. The widow was victorious, but the affair had seriously besmirched her reputation; she sold the estate soon after.

These events, outrageous even in the context of the time, were taking place while Griboyedov was living in St Petersburg, dependent on his mother for an allowance. They were well known to his Moscow contemporaries. The Decembrist Yakushkin, a childhood friend from Khmelita, writes in his memoirs of the 'wickedness' of Griboyedov's mother in laying unbearable burdens on her serfs and in calling in the military.[1] In his few surviving letters of this period, Griboyedov makes no reference to the affair. His mother was self-willed and despotic, and would probably have paid no attention to his protests.

But it may well have been to lessen his financial dependence on her that in the summer of 1817 he applied to join the Collegium (Ministry) of Foreign Affairs. At least as a civil servant he would have an income, regardless of her speculations; he had probably seen enough of journalism and the theatre to realise the problems of making a living by his pen.

Griboyedov's application was accepted on 9 June 1817, on the same day as two other young men whose names are familiar from Russian history, and whose paths in various ways were to cross his over the next few years: they were the Decembrist Wilhelm Küchelbecker (later nicknamed 'Kukliya') and Alexander Pushkin, then barely eighteen.[2] Thanks to Griboyedov's outstanding academic record, he was not made to serve an apprenticeship period in the archives, but reported to the Ministry straight away. It was an imposing building on the English Embankment, once a baroque gem by Quarenghi, but now transformed into a stern, office-like, classical building, well suited to ambassadors and the state bureaucracy. Founded by Peter the Great, the Collegium of Foreign

Affairs became a Ministry only in 1802, though the term 'Collegium' continued. It was only a nominal reform. Like other Tsars before him, Alexander I was very much the master of his own foreign policy, and his insistence on playing a personal role added greatly to the difficulties of conducting routine business. At the time Griboyedov joined the Ministry, there were two official Foreign Ministers, Count Nesselrode and Count Capodistrias. Both were foreigners. Capodistrias, a Greek, was an expansionist whose dream was to free Greece from Turkish rule. (He would later become first President of the Greek Republic.) Nesselrode, a German with little sympathy for Orthodoxy or Russian culture, was more cautious, unwilling to risk war with Turkey or disturb the balance of power in the Balkans. Despite their differences in outlook, the two men worked together in apparent harmony. 'Sometimes when a foreign diplomat addressed a matter to one the other would answer,' writes Patricia Grimsted, in her study of Russia's foreign policy. 'There was no rhyme or reason to the division of work between them,[3] a situation which added immeasurably to the inefficiency of the Chancellery and made it difficult for the members of the diplomatic corps to know to which of these chiefs of Foreign Affairs it was best to present oneself.'

The Ministry was grossly overmanned; according to Vorontsov, the Russian Ambassador in London, it contained more people than the offices of all the Secretaries of State in Europe combined, and was shockingly ill-organised. It is noteworthy that Griboyedov left this subject for satire alone – no doubt it was too close to the hand that fed him. But he later complained that all he did was to attend the Ministry once a month, and sleep in its padded armchairs or talk about the Trojan War. Fortunately, however, he had superiors who recognised his outstanding abilities and his brilliance as a linguist. They included the heads of the Department for Asiatic Affairs, K.K. Rodofinikin, a corpulent Greek bureaucrat, directly responsible to Capodistrias, and the actual Under Secretary, A.S. Sturdza, a Moldavian by birth. It was probably at their suggestion that Griboyedov decided to become an Asiatic specialist, enrolling himself at St Petersburg University to study Arabic and Persian. His aim was to become a professional translator for the Ministry, a prestigious post which would ensure his continued presence in the capital.

He had scarcely begun his new studies when, in November 1817, he was struck by one of those arbitrary blows of fate which destroy the sense of control which rational people,[4] especially when they are very clever, imagine they have over their destinies. In his *Journey to Erzerum*, Pushkin had referred to the dark clouds in Griboyedov's life: 'the consequence of ardent passions and imperious circumstances'. Without doubt the darkest of these clouds was his involvement in a four-sided duel, or *partie carrée*, whose tragic dénouement would change the course of his career.[5]

Central to the duel in question was the eighteen-year-old Avdotiya Istomina, the leading ballerina of St Petersburg immortalised in *Eugene Onegin*:

> The house is packed out; scintillating,
> the boxes; boiling, pit and stalls,
> the gallery claps – it's bored with waiting
> and up the rustling curtain crawls.
> Then with a half ethereal splendour
> bound where the magic bow will send her,
> Istomina, thronged all around
> by Naiads, one foot on the ground,
> twirls the other slowly as she pleases,
> then suddenly she's off and there
> she's up and flying through the air
> like fluff before Aeolian breezes…

Much admired by the young men of St Petersburg and the butt of some bawdy verses by Pushkin,[6] Istomina had been the mistress of the young Count Vassily Sheremet'yev for the previous two years. Sheremet'yev was twenty-four, and a captain in the ultra-fashionable Chevalier Guards regiment. Beguichov, who served in the same regiment, described him later as a 'very amiable, frivolous and empty headed prankster'; his only surviving portrait shows a handsome, tousle-haired young man, with full lips, deep-set eyes and a rather self-indulgent face. He had been Istomina's first lover, but she had recently left him after a blazing row and gone to stay with a friend, a certain Azarova. Sheremet'yev, furiously jealous and still in love with her, kept her under constant surveillance.

Griboyedov was living at this time with a friend, Count Alexander Zavadovsky, a junior member of the court. He was twenty-three years old, rich and dissolute, just returned from travelling in England, where he had acquired such a passion for the country's customs that he was nicknamed 'the Englishman'. We catch a glimpse of him perhaps in *Woe from Wit*:

> What a character – we all die laughing when he tells a story.
> He's spent his life with Englishmen – he's English through and through.
> He talks through his teeth, just like they all do.[7]

Also in the Anglophile tradition, Zavadovsky had brought back a reputation as a duellist or *bretteur*; his *beau idéal* was a certain Captain Ross, famed for being able to shoot swallows on the wing. He was clearly something of a social lightweight, but Griboyedov, although very poor himself, tended to gravitate to the company of his richer contemporaries. Zavadovsky's grandfather had been the lover of Catherine the Great, and his large hospitable family seemed the living incarnation of the values of her splendid reign; they were also potentially useful for his own career.

Griboyedov was on good terms with both Sheremet'yev and Istomina; his first letter to Beguichov after arriving in St Petersburg had described visiting the Shuster Club in their company. A few days after Istomina's break with Sheremet'yev, he met her after a performance and invited her back to drink tea at the flat he shared with Zavadovsky. Istomina agreed, although in order to throw Sheremet'yev off the scent she arranged to leave the theatre alone, and meet Griboyedov at a separate rendezvous, when she could exchange carriages.

Griboyedov's role seems to have been that of a confidant. Zavadovsky, however, had long had amorous designs on Istomina. He arrived at the flat while Istomina was pouring out her troubles, and seized the occasion to make her 'proposals of love'[8] – in other words he offered to become her financial protector instead of Sheremet'yev. The interview appears to have been inconclusive, and after some delay Griboyedov took her back to Azarova.

Sheremet'yev, meanwhile, had not been deceived by Istomina's ruse, and had followed her to Zavadovsky's flat. Immediately suspecting that Istomina was planning to deceive him with Zavadovsky, he flew to Griboyedov, threatening to shoot Zavadovsky and asking Griboyedov to be his second. Griboyedov did his utmost to smooth the quarrel over, but Zavadovsky had lost no time in following up his proposition to Istomina. A few days later, Sheremet'yev sought out Istomina for a reconciliation, threatening to kill himself out of despair. He then pulled a pistol from his pocket and put it to her head, swearing he would kill her if she did not tell the truth. The terrified girl admitted that she had slept with Zavadovsky.

Sheremet'yev was now determined on a duel. He turned for backing to another friend, Alexander Ivanovich Yakubovich, the fourth member of the future *partie carrée*.[9] Yakubovich was a Cornet in the Life Guards – Uhlan Cavalry Regiment, a raffish, daredevil figure, later famous for his roles in the Decembrist rising and the Caucasus. A watercolour portrait, painted in 1831 by his fellow Decembrist N.A. Bestuzhev, gives a vivid impression of his formidable character: prominent, slightly mad eyes bulge out under curling lashes, a huge twirly moustache droops over the firm mouth, an enormous sloping forehead suggests indomitable obstinacy and willpower. All in all, it is the head of an athlete, set on a strong torso and shoulders, the open-necked shirt disclosing a hairy chest.[10]

If Griboyedov had done his best to make peace, Yakubovich did exactly the opposite. According to Griboyedov's cousin D.A. Smirnov, who interviewed Griboyedov's friend A. Zhandr and his former tutor Dr John some years after his death, Yakubovich was all for a fight. It was obvious, he said, that a duel should be fought to the death, but with whom? 'Your Istomina,' he reasoned, 'was with Zavadovsky. Griboyedov brought her there. There are two people here calling for bullets.' With glee, the duel-hungry fanatic concluded, 'This calls for a fighting foursome, a *partie carrée*, you fire at Griboyedov and I will take on Zavadovsky'.

Interrupting Dr John, who was recounting this exchange, Smirnov said, 'Yakubovich had nothing to do with Zavadovsky, how could he get involved?' Zhandr replied simply, 'He was that sort of man'. John added that both Sheremet'yev and Yakubovich were drunk when they went to issue their challenges to Griboyedov and Zavadovsky.

Griboyedov refused to fight Sheremet'yev, but declared that he would take on Yakubovich. The benevolent Dr John, who had recently arrived in the capital as director of the German theatre there, agreed to be his second; another of his friends, Pyotr Kaverin, a young Hussar and duelling enthusiast, would also be present as a witness.

The conventions governing duelling in the the early nineteenth century seem so remote today that it may be worth restating them. Established in Clonmel in Kilkenny, Ireland some 50 years before, they applied over most of Europe and were followed by the hot-headed *jeunesse dorée* of Moscow and St Petersburg. According to this Clonmel code, firing could be regulated by a signal, a word of command, or at the duellists' pleasure; in the last case, either party might advance till their pistols' muzzles touched. In the favourite continental version, however, a stretch of ground at mid-distance could not be trespassed on. This was called *la barrière* (a term stemming from the oldest form of pistol duel, the French one, which was fought on horseback, with the combatants divided by posts placed some ten yards apart). It was the role of the seconds to mark the ground at a certain number of paces. The combatants, after a given signal, were allowed to reduce the distance by walking towards each other, generally leaving a space of twelve paces in the middle; usually the outer and inner limits of this space were marked by the coats or capes doffed by the combatants.

After the pistols had been loaded by the seconds, the principals would take their position at the extreme ends of the ground, facing each other and keeping the muzzles of their pistols pointing down. At a given signal, 'Marchez!' they would advance towards the *barrière*, and could fire whenever they thought fit. If, after the exchange, they still felt aggrieved, they could have the pistols re-loaded and begin again.

The duel was planned for the morning of 12 November, but was delayed by snow, which impeded visibility; the four protagonists finally met at two in the afternoon in the Volkovy (or 'wolf') field on the out-skirts of Moscow. The outer limit had been set at a lethal 18 paces, the opponents being allowed to approach six paces to the *barrière* before shooting. Sheremet'yev and Zavadovsky were the first to fight. At the given signal from the seconds, they advanced towards the *barrière*, Zavadovsky walking very quietly and with the utmost coolness and composure. This seemed to infuriate Sheremet'yev, who could restrain himself no longer. He fired without waiting for Zavadovsky to reach the *barrière*. The bullet flew so close that it removed part of Zavadovsky's collar. Zavadovsky exclaimed furiously, 'Ah il en voulait à ma vie, à la barrière!'[11]

Zavadovsky now had the right to get his adversary to the *barrière* to get a closer shot. He waited for Sheremet'yev to be six paces away, almost at point-blank range. The spectators, realising that the outcome was likely to be fatal, asked him loudly to spare Sheremet'yev's life. 'I will fire at his legs,' said Zavadovsky. 'I must continue, I have given my word of honour to fight.' Sheremet'yev then said, 'You must kill me, or sooner or later I will kill you,' and ordered his second to reload his pistol for a second shot. Zavadovsky could only take an honest aim. He fired. The bullet pierced Sheremet'yev in the side, going through his stomach and coming out on the other side. He fell down immediately and began flapping and plunging like a fish. 'Vot tebe i repka' ('Well, that's the end of you, little turnip'), said Kaverin sadly from his hiding place,[12] as he watched his piteous efforts to drag himself through the snow.

Yakubovich, looking at the expiring figure of Sheremet'yev, signalled to Griboyedov that under the circumstances they could not fight. Sheremet'yev must be carried home to his flat, and their duel postponed. Sheremet'yev died the following day, but, according to Dr John, he wished to see Griboyedov in his dying hours, to ask his forgiveness and be reconciled.

The story of the duel, as recounted to Smirnov by Zhandr and Dr John, took on a different aspect with the publication in 1883 of the not altogether trustworthy memoirs of a certain O. Przhetslavsky. According to Przhetslavsky, Zavadovsky had at first fired wide, intending to miss. He then proposed a reconciliation to Sheremet'yev, who at first could not make up his mind, but then refused, on Griboyedov's advice.[13] Sheremet'yev took two further shots at Zavadovsky, but the first shot failed to ignite the powder on the pan, and the second misfired altogether. Zavadovsky then took all his time to aim, misfiring once, and then fired the fatal shot.

Przhetslavsky, of course, had not been present at the duel, but he had talked to Zavadovsky. Perhaps Zavadovsky was trying to pass on some share of his guilt, and had altered the facts to show himself in a better light. Perhaps his version was the true one. It is certain that

Griboyedov blamed himself bitterly for what had happened, though this may have been because he felt responsible for bringing Istomina to Zavadovsky's flat, and for failing to dissuade Sheremet'yev from challenging him. Writing to Beguichov, who was then in Moscow, he described himself as being overwhelmed by appalling melancholy. The dying Sheremet'yev was constantly before his eyes.

In Russia, as in other countries, duelling was strictly illegal. Under Peter the Great it had been an offence punishable by death for both participants and seconds. By the time of Alexander I, the worst penalties had been abolished, though duelling remained a criminal offence. The affair had caused too great a scandal to pass unnoticed, especially as it had had a fatal outcome. An official enquiry was set up,[14] headed by the Minister of Internal Affairs, with a committee including the Governor of St Petersburg, the Chief of Police and the Colonel of Sheremet'yev's regiment. In his evidence to the court, Griboyedov played down his role, appearing only as a second to Zavadovsky, and not as a potential participant, committed to fight with Yakubovich. His friends did not give him away.

The sentences were mild. Zavadovsky was required to go abroad for a long time. Yakubovich, who was held to be chiefly responsible for inciting Sheremet'yev to fight, was transferred from the Life Guards to the fashionable Nizhegorodsky Regiment in the 'warm Siberia' of the Caucasus. Griboyedov himself received no specific punishment thanks, it was said, to the intervention of the Tsar. But he was regarded as being under a cloud, and was expected to leave the capital for a foreign post.

V

Into Exile

From the memoirs of Griboyedov's superior in the Foreign Ministry, A.S. Sturdza, we know that Griboyedov was offered the choice of two postings. The first was as a junior official in the consulate in Philadelphia, the second was as attaché to S.I. Mazarovich, just appointed head of the first permanent Russian mission to Persia. The second, more senior, post was the one preferred by the Ministry; Griboyedov had made rapid progress in his Persian studies, and had already acquired a considerable knowledge, not only of the language but of Persian history and customs. But he found the choice intensely painful. 'Never in my life,' wrote Sturdza, 'has it happened to me to be such a close witness to a decision by the man involved, agonising profoundly over the secret personal reasons for his fate'.

Griboyedov poured out his unhappiness to Beguichov.[1] 'Can you imagine where they want to exile me,' he wrote. 'To Persia, so that I should live there. However I try to wriggle out of it, nothing will help.'

He had even sought an interview with joint Foreign Minister Nesselrode:

I told him that I would not agree unless I was given a double promotion the moment I was nominated to Teheran. He screwed up his face in doubt, and I then tried to convince him in my finest French how wicked it would be to make me spend the bloom of my youth and my most creative years among wild mannered Asiatics in a kind of involuntary exile, to be separated from friends and relatives for long periods, to be denied the literary success which I was entitled to expect, and to be removed from all contact with literate people. Not only literate, but enlightened people, and sympathetic women, to whom I might myself be pleasing. In a word, it was impossible for me to sacrifice myself without some comparable compensation.

The Minister remarked drily that his gifts could be perfected in solitude. 'Not at all, your Excellency,' said Griboyedov. 'The musician and the poet need an audience and readers. They do not exist in Persia.'

Despite Griboyedov's eloquence, the appointment to Tehran was confirmed,[2] the Ministry compromising by offering him a promotion of one grade to Acting Counsellor, ninth class, as the price of his exile (see Appendix II). He was to be secretary to Mazarovich, doubling as the official interpreter. A young German official, A.K. Amburgherr, was to be head of Chancery. The mission would leave in September 1818.

Griboyedov made the best of his last months in St Petersburg, collaborating with Zhandr on a benefit piece, *Les Fausses Infidelités*, for the great actress Semyonova and writing a vaudeville skit of his own, *The Trial Interlude*. The skit poked fun at the benefit system – the custom by which the theatre's profits for one evening went to the actor or actress in whose honour the performance was given. Like Sheridan's *The Critic*, the piece was a play within a play, as the prompter and the manager of a provincial theatre cobble together a benefit for their leading actor. A new play is needed, with a new set, songs and dancing. 'The fewer words the better,' says one of the cast. They find a backcloth of a river scene. The prompter is delighted:

Here are woods and here is water
So the main work's done.
There's a river on the backcloth…
Let it be the Oka.
We even have a title
Thanks to the river's name,
'A revel on the Oka'
Or 'a jolly walk along the Oka's bank',
And let us start with songs
And end upon a dance.

The piece, which was not performed until after he left St Petersburg, was a new departure for Griboyedov, since he may have composed the music as well as the words, though the score does not survive. Music was always an essential part of Griboyedov's life.[3] We know from his contemporaries how brilliantly he could play and improvise on the piano; his favourite composers were Beethoven, Weber and Haydn. We catch a glimpse of him later at the piano in the memoirs of a sympathetic journalist, Ksenofont Polevoi, accompanying the celebrated baritone Tosi in Grech's drawing-room.[4] In another vignette from the same source we see him jumping up in his box in fury at a bad performance of *The Magic Flute*, complaining that Mozart was being atrociously mangled, and that there was not one singer worthy of the opera.

Amongst the musical figures in St Petersburg at the time were the Irish composer John Field, who, as has been suggested, may have taught Griboyedov as a child: Griboyedov may well have absorbed from him the impromptu brilliance of his roulades, a special feature in Field's playing too. Field's influence can also be seen in his two waltzes, one in E flat, one in A major. Published in a musical almanac of the 1830s, they are the only compositions of Griboyedov to survive. The pianist, Oliver Williams, comments on the second waltz as follows:

> There is a charming opening melody, a more robust middle section, and in the reprise of the melody a strikingly beautiful key-change. There is a high degree of musical craftsmanship and elegance. Hummel, Weber or John Field would have been proud to have written such a piece...Field toured Russia extensively, enjoying great popularity in Russia and I should imagine Griboyedov was thinking of his music in this waltz. One hears the singing right hand melody and flowing left hand accompaniment that are hallmarks of Field's music, particularly in his famous nocturnes.[5]

Of Griboyedov's sentimental life during his first years in St Petersburg we know little, beyond his complaint to the Minister that he would be deprived of the company of sympathetic women if he were posted to Tehran. He was certainly not rich enough to marry, or even to become the protector of, a successful actress. According to his friend Bestuzhev, he claimed that he was not interested in women, quoting Byron's remark that women were only children: 'Give them a sugar plum or a mirror and they will be perfectly happy'. 'Or so he affirmed,' wrote Bestuzhev, 'but I have reasons to doubt it.'[6] Another friend, the future Decembrist D.I. Zavalyshin, described him as being a confirmed philanderer, whose affairs with married women were the gossip of the town, but gives no names or evidence to substantiate this.[7] Beguichov, his closest intimate, describes him as leading a dissipated [*razgulnoye*] life during this period, but also gives no details. However, a letter from Griboyedov to Beguichov on leaving for the east refers to a certain 'Didon', for whom he enlisted his friend's help:

> Please make enquiries through Aksiniya, the mistress of Amlikhov [Griboyedov's servant in St Petersburg] and ask her to check up on my Didon. Ilya Ogaryov [his mother's agent] will send her money from Kostroma in your name.[8]

Didon has not been identified. She may have been a singer or an actress who had played the part of Dido on the stage – both Paisiello's opera *Didon* and Knyazhnin's play of the same name had recently played in St Petersburg. It is equally possible that he had given her the name because, like Dido, she was abandoned at his departure. What is significant about the letter is that, at a time when the dispute with the serfs at Kostroma was at its height, Griboyedov was sending money to his mistress through his mother's agent there. The story squares uncomfortably with the Soviet picture of Griboyedov as a man committed to liberal ideals and the abolition of serfdom. Under severe financial pressure, his mother was behaving as savagely as the worst serf owners of her time; at the very least, Griboyedov was turning a blind eye to where the money came from.

Griboyedov left St Petersburg at the end of August to pay a farewell visit to his family in Moscow. *Les Fausses Infidelités* had transferred there from the capital, and he duly attended a performance on arrival. The audience was full of friends wishing to greet him as the playwright of the moment. He described them privately to Beguichov as 'the local Hottentots',[9] and was equally scathing about Kokoshkin, the leading actor in the play, who 'crawlingly excused himself for the way my enchanting verses had been tortured – it was nothing to do with him'. To console himself, he drank a bottle of champagne straight off, and retired after the theatre with a splitting headache, which his mother's cold compress, soaked in eau de cologne, failed to cure. Moscow did not suit him, he complained. There was too much idleness and senseless extravagance, unlinked to the slightest taste or decency. There was no-one with whom he could discuss literary matters on an equal footing. The theatre was poor, music, once greatly appreciated, was regarded with indifference. Even the dancing of the delightful ballerina Medvedyeva in *Cinderella* did not console him, the audience was too sluggish to applaud her properly. Sympathising with complaints from Beguichov that in his military career his brother officers were also Hottentots, he grumbled that it was the fate of clever people to be thrown into such company.

Griboyedov's role as a diplomat on an important mission to Persia, which as every patriot knew was a source of constant trouble to the Tsar and Holy Mother Russia, was of far more interest to his mother's Moscow circle than his literary achievements. He told Beguichov,

> Truly no man is a prophet in his own country. My country, my family, my home are all in Moscow. Everyone there remembers me as Sasha, a nice child who has now grown up, and after various youthful escapades is old enough to be be fit for something, nominated to a mission, in time perhaps to become a government councillor: beyond that they are not interested in me. At least in St Petersburg there were some, let us say, who appreciated me more or less at my own valuation, and in the light in which I would like to be considered. In Moscow it is the very reverse. Ask Zhandr how contemptuously my mother once spoke after supper about my versifying and scribbling.[10]

At the last moment, however, he found it hard to tear himself away. There were tearful farewells and leave-takings with his mother and sister. They were so attached to him, he told Beguichov, that he would be a scoundrel if he did not repay them in the same loving coin. 'Until now I have only been a son and brother in name, when I return from Persia, I shall become so in fact, and live entirely for my family. I shall take them with me to St Petersburg.' He forgave his mother 'from the bottom of my heart' for failing to understand his literary aspirations; on his side, he would never forgive himself in future if he allowed himself to cause her pain.[11]

By mid-September 1818, he was en route for Persia and the Caucasus.[12] 'What an absurd country!' he wrote to Beguichov.[13] The latest news from the Caucasus was that a Russian convoy had been waylaid by 5000 Circassians. He had been delayed for a day in Tula, due to the unavailability of horses, with nothing to allay his boredom but the graffiti on the walls of the posting house. His travelling companion Amburgherr (the head of Chancery to the Persian mission) was a good man, very talkative and the scourge of postmasters.

> I have convinced him that being German is a very foolish part to play in life. He has already changed his name enough to sign it Amurgev, and no longer Amburgherr. His sausages infuriate me. Farewell my friend, I am already 1200 versts away from you and will soon be even further.

Griboyedov's next letter to Beguichov was written as a series of travel notes, a formula he would adopt throughout his absence in the East. As he told Beguichov, he was writing to him privately and not for publication, though he did not mind him showing his letters to a few selected friends. 'You are kind and love my gifts,' he wrote, 'do not betray me to people I despise.' Written with an immediacy and ease that a more studied treatment would have lacked, his first notes describe his journey through the mountains, along the still half-finished Georgian military highway to Tiflis, where he would join up with the other members of the mission. After the endless plains of Russia the snow-covered glaciers and peaks of the great Caucasian chain would come as a thrilling revelation to any traveller seeing them for the first time. Griboyedov, who had made his dislike of romantic exaggeration clear in his play *The Student* and in his criticisms of Zhukovsky's verse, had no intention of indulging in purple passages, least of all about nature. He warned against travellers' hyperbole: 'Words like "soul", "heart" and "feelings" are repeated much too often in those pink-bound booklets "for the beloved"'. But though his remarks were deliberately terse and laconic, they still conveyed the tremendous drama of the landscape.

As was usual in crossing the mountains, Griboyedov and his party travelled in an armed caravan, in this case of 600 men, including a complement of light artillery, reconnaissance cavalry and infantry. To the beat of the drum, the convoy moved off slowly along the fast-flowing Terek river to their first night's halt, the fortified Kabardinsky Redoubt at the foot of the mountains. Bivouacs were placed at its gates and the soldiers warmed their hands at campfires. They began to climb into the mountains the next day:

> The trail is slippery, muddy, twisting from one steep cliff to another, from hour to hour more cramped from the thickening bushes which finally turn to oak forest. A mix of seasons; it is hot and I open my jacket; then frost; on the surface of the frozen leaves the hoar frost is mixed with green.[14]

They spent the night at Kumbaleyevka, another fortified redoubt. On the third day they descended towards the plain, Griboyedov riding ahead with a party of Cossacks: 'It is cloudy... The snow, like linen, is draped over the crevasses, the mountains golden at times. The roar of the Terek, from the precipices.' They reached Vladikavkaz (literally 'Ruling the Caucasus'), the border town controlling the northern end of the passes and the military highway, that evening. Griboyedov saw pheasants, wild boar and chamois in abundance, 'but nowhere to eat them in Vladikavkaz';[15] the green kitchen gardens around the town contrasted with the dark granite peaks above it.

From Vladikavkaz, the military highway ran through Ossetia, a lawless country whose marauding tribesmen were a constant threat to travellers. On the fourth day, after passing a small Ossetian fort with conical watchtowers, Griboyedov reached the first of the string of Russian forts along the route, perched high above the Daryal Gorge. The noise of the Terek tumbling and foaming far below grew more and more menacing; he felt that the convoy could have tumbled into the gorge at any time. On leaving the gorge, he noted how huge boulders, rolled down from the peaks, made natural, almost impassable barriers. Sometimes a group of Ossetians, cooking their meal, could be glimpsed behind the boulders.

On the next day he passed the village of Kazbek, which he described as a fortress without, a prison within. He could just see its dramatic church and monastery perched on the steep slopes of Mount Kazbek, the mountain where, according to legend, Prometheus had been chained; the hawks and eagles flying overhead, he supposed, were descendants of Prometheus's tormentors. At Sioni, a few miles further on, he noticed the guard-towers nestling on the precipices. His sixth march brought him to Kobi, which he found 'frightful'. The snow and wind howling round him were awesome, as was the precipitous drop to the narrow Terek Valley. Passing only a few Ossetian refuges, as inaccessible as swallows' nests, he reached the Krestovaya Pass and the mountain of Gud Gora. As he surveyed the view before him, he felt, he wrote, like the Welsh bard in Gray's poem 'The Bard'. On several occasions he fell from sheer exhaustion. He makes no reference to the quality of his horses, but seems to have been in a *brichka* (small carriage) for much of the time. He was to spend much of his remaining life in these jolting, comfortless *brichkas*.

At the top of the Kashaur Pass the party got fresh horses and began the welcome descent into Georgia and the green beauties of the Aragvi Valley; he was reminded of the virgin world of American plantations, melons, peach and apple trees completing the feeling of an earthly paradise. The seventh day brought them past Ananuri and Dusheti. Griboyedov made no mention of the great cathedral fortress of Mtskheta, where the Georgian kings are buried, or of the gaunt sixth-century church of Dzhvari and St Nino dominating the skyline above it. His thoughts, no doubt, were already turned towards the capital. On 21 October, the eighth day of their journey, the convoy rode into Tiflis.

VI

Arrival in
Tiflis

We must assume that Griboyedov had received an extensive briefing from Sturdza and Rodofinikin on the background to his Persian mission. In Tiflis, however, he would be in touch with those who had been directly involved in the Russo–Persian War of 1804–13,[1] and the resulting Treaty of Gulistan, which governed Russo–Persian relations at the time.

Isolated between the Turkish and Persian empires, the Christian kingdom of Georgia had always been vulnerable to its Muslim neighbours.[2] In 1801, after suffering the appalling sack of Tiflis by the Persians in 1795, the Georgian ruling house had 'voluntarily' abdicated, and Georgia had become part of the Russian empire. For the Russians, the psychological and moral justification for the annexation was the defence of their fellow Orthodox Christians, and bringing them the benefits of Russian 'civilisation'; in practical terms it was a bloodless victory, moving Russia hundreds of miles closer to the strategic possibilities of controlling the Black Sea and the Caspian Sea.

Since the seventeenth century, Russia had sought to widen its territory and influence at the expense of the Persian and Ottoman empires. In 1724, Peter the Great, in a costly campaign against the Persians, had captured Astrakhan, and extended Russia's frontiers on the Caspian coast as far as Derbend and Baku. Catherine the Great, at equal cost in money and men, had conquered the Crimea as the first step towards controlling the Black Sea and making it a 'Russian lake'; she even called her second grandson Constantine, with an eye to his possible future as the ruler of Constantinople.

With the acquisition of Georgia, Russia was able to reactivate the imperialist policies of Peter and Catherine the Great. The weakening of the Ottoman empire, the humiliation of Persia, the removal of the British (to whom Persia was important as a buffer state for India), were all now possible. The control of the Caspian, and the annexation of the Central Asian khanates and kingdoms of Bokhara, Khiva and Samarkand, offered a glittering prospect in the first half of the nineteenth century. The expense of Peter and Catherine's campaigns could now be repaid. Russia's luckless hosts in Georgia could not stand for a minute in the way of Russia's exciting eastern prospects, nor would any Russian diplomat or general allow them to.[3]

For Russia, the pretext for the next war with Persia was to extend its territory southwards as far as the deltas of the Kura and the Araxes and create a *cordon sanitaire* against attack.[4] Memories of the sack of Tiflis by the first Qajar ruler, Agha Muhammed Khan, in which thousands of Georgians had been slaughtered, and thousands of young boys and girls transported to the harems and slave markets of Tabriz and Tehran were still vivid. The river frontier, in the words of Alexander I, was necessary 'to prevent the incursions of barbarian peoples'. In 1803, the tough and aggressive Russian Commander-in-Chief, General Tsitsiyanov,[5] a Georgian by descent, had invaded the Persian vassal state of Ganjeh in the eastern Caucasus, renaming its capital Elizavetpol in honour of the Alexander I's wife. He was eager to provoke a war; the Persians, seeing their vital interests in the area threatened, and fearing that other khanates would defect, were forced to respond.

The war dragged on for nine years, the diplomatic background increasingly complicated by the Napoleonic wars in Europe and Russia's changing pattern of alliances with France and Britain. The Russian army was vastly superior in manpower and firepower, but it was hampered by the difficulties of operating in an unfamiliar terrain; desertion and disease were rife; and there were appalling logistical problems for artillery and supplies crossing the snow-covered ranges in winter. The Persians, led by the Shah's favourite son, Crown Prince Abbas Mirza, had the advantage of mobility, but despite a limited subsidy from the British were desperately short of funds. In the end it was the British, having become Russia's allies since Napoleon's 1812 campaign, who helped to negotiate a peace. At the Treaty of Gulistan in 1813, the borders were redrawn in line with the position of each side's forces. The Persians ceded Talish and all the khanates north of the Araxes and the Kura, with the exception of the khanates of Erivan and Nakhichevan, which the Russians had failed to capture, and Moqri, a district on the Karabakh border. At the same time, Persia recognised Russian sovereignty over the rest of the Caucasus, including Western

Georgia, thus blocking Ottoman claims in the area. Russia could claim a limited victory, but an intentional looseness in the definition of frontiers, in particular over Talish and Balikloo and Lake Gokcheh, where it was agreed that the border should be decided by a joint commission, would later cause great difficulties between the two countries. The resolution of these frontiers would be one of the chief aims of the Russian mission to Tehran.

At the time of Griboyedov's arrival in Tiflis,[6] the Viceroy of Georgia and Commander-in-Chief of the army in the Caucasus[7] was General Alexis Petrovich Yermolov,[8] a veteran of the 1812 resistance to Napoleon. He was openly contemptuous of the Persians and all 'Asiatics' (though he kept three Muslim concubines, and would find good places for his three sons by them as officers in the Russian army). He had recently returned from a six-month embassy to Tehran, following up the clauses of the peace treaty. Whereas Alexander I would have been content to make minor territorial concessions, for instance allowing Talish to become an independent state, Yermolov had refused to give away an inch of conquered territory.[9] His intransigent attitude was compounded by his arrogant refusal to take off his boots and don the red slippers and stockings which etiquette demanded that foreign emissaries should wear in presence of the Shah. (Since the Persians used their carpets for sitting and eating on, they found it distasteful that someone should bring in dirt on their boots.) In diplomatic terms, the embassy had merely exacerbated relations between Russia and Persia, increasing the problems which Griboyedov's chief, Mazarovich, would have to deal with on his forthcoming mission.

Griboyedov would spend three months in Tiflis, absorbing the sights and sounds of a city still recovering from the devastation inflicted by the Persians over 20 years before. Though Yermolov had begun an energetic programme of rebuilding in the European style, its character was still largely 'Asiatic', with mainly low flat-roofed houses and fretted overhanging balconies; the windows were usually made of oiled paper, since glass was too expensive. On the left-hand side of the river Kura was the old city, a mass of churches, towers, domes, houses and bazaars, piled up along the foothills, with the medieval fortress of Nari-Kala at its crest. On the right was the so-called new town, with its massive barracks and military hospital. In the suburbs beyond, a colony of industrious Würtemburgers had set up farms and market gardens which provided butter, meat and vegetables to the town.

According to the French consul, Charles de Gamba, the population of Tiflis in the 1820s was some 30,000, of whom some 6000 were Russian officials and garrison troops. Set as it was halfway between the Caspian and the Black Sea, Tiflis was a natural transit point for visitors of every nationality. There was a huge traffic of Englishmen, en route from India to Europe via the Black Sea; Armenians from Erivan and Smyrna, and Uzbeks from Bokhara; silk merchants from as far away as Paris, Lyons and Leipzig. The bazaars were noisy with the sounds of many languages: Lezgian traders, with furs from the mountains; majestic Greek priests; drunken Cossacks; Ossetian porters staggering under massive loads of straw; Persian camel drivers; Russian officials, cutting their way through the crowds on prancing Karabakh stallions. As well as its importance as a strategic centre, Tiflis offered great commercial possibilities, and Yermolov, as its military commander, was not too grand to promote the development of trade by such basic measures as improving roads and communications, building new bazaars and warehouses and simplifying customs duties.

The claims of Tiflis to be 'the Paris of the East' were perhaps exaggerated, but it still had much to offer European visitors. There were fine public gardens, shaded by poplars and plane trees, sulphurous hot springs, where for a small fee you could be pummelled and massaged to within an inch of your life (an experience Pushkin underwent), a local paper, printed in three languages, a library and reading-room where the latest Russian and foreign papers were available, and an excellent French restaurant, run by a former French prisoner-of-war, Jean Paul, who provided food for all the important dinners and weddings in the town. There was also an assembly, founded under Yermolov's auspices, where mixed company was welcome, and Russian officers could mix with members of the Georgian aristocracy at dances, concerts and receptions – Yermolov, being unmarried, could not receive ladies at his headquarters.

Griboyedov would be exposed to all this, but it did not mitigate his sense of exile. Letters to and from Russia took 28 days to arrive, and he felt himself neglected by his friends. But his first meeting on arrival was a throwback to his former life: a confrontation with Yakubovich, his opposite number in the ill-fated *partie carrée* in which Sheremet'yev had been killed. Yakubovich, it will be remembered, had been exiled to the Caucasus, and Griboyedov had written to him in Karabakh, where he was stationed with his regiment. He had now come to Tiflis to settle accounts.

In the memoirs of Nicholas Muravyov-Karsky (a future hero of the Russo–Turkish War of 1829, who won his title Karsky at the siege of Kars) there is a detailed description of the duel and its surrounding circumstances.[10] As a fellow officer and friend, Muravyov had heard the whole story of the *partie carrée* and had reluctantly agreed to be Yakubovich's second. The two men went to meet Griboyedov on the evening after he arrived. He was dining at Jean Paul's restaurant.

'I found him to be an extremely clever and well read person but, I felt, excessively preoccupied with himself,' noted Muravyov.

Griboyedov had asked a certain Captain Bykov of the Life Guards Pavlovsky Regiment to be his second, and the Captain, as was his duty, did his best to reconcile the two parties. Muravyov at first refused to intervene, commenting that Yakubovich alone could know if his honour had been impugned. Bykov renewed his entreaties, pulling Muravyov into another room to tell him that he had seen Griboyedov's mother in Moscow, and that she had foreseen that her son would be unable to avoid the duel. Meanwhile Yakubovich was beginning to quarrel rather loudly with Griboyedov in the adjoining room.

Muravyov then suggested to Yakubovich that he should agree to a reconciliation. Griboyedov said directly to Yakubovich that he had never offended him. Yakubovich was forced to agree, but added that he had promised Sheremet'yev before he died that he would take revenge for him on Griboyedov and Zavadovsky. 'I respect your actions,' he told Griboyedov, 'but what has been done must now be accomplished. I must keep my word to the deceased.' 'That being so,' said Griboyedov, 'let the seconds settle the conditions.'[11]

Muravyov suggested that they should fight in Yakubovich's apartment, with a *barrière* of six paces, and one pace backward for each duellist. Griboyedov's second would not agree to this, as Yakubovich would be fighting on his own ground. It was decided that a field would be the place. They needed a light carriage and horses, and a co-operative doctor, and Amburgherr, who already knew Tiflis well, agreed to find the transport.

After a brief meal, the principals adjourned to Muravyov's apartment, both cheerful and apparently friendly, and joking that such a duel had never been fought before. The next morning, 23 April, Muravyov rose early and rode to the village of Kukito to find a suitable place for the duel. Beside the main road to Kakhetia he found a Muslim tomb, beside a ravine in which one could find good cover.

> I decided this was the place, and returned to Griboyedov, who was in an eating house with Amburgherr [who had taken Bykov's place as second], and warned them that they should leave before they had been seen. I measured out an amount of powder to them, and then found Yakubovich. I sought out Dr Miller, due to act as doctor, in the military hospital, and told him it was time to set off. I told Yakubovich to set off on foot and hide behind the Muslim tomb till I should summon him, Griboyedov and Amburgherr. I told them to ride out in the carriage with their pistols. Everyone understood their instructions except Dr Miller, who missed the site of the ravine and galloped off into the hills.

Muravyov then set up the boundaries of the *barrière*, primed the pistols and having placed the duellists, who were in their shirt sleeves, walked away a few paces. Yakubovich came up to the *barrière*, with a bold step, and awaited Griboyedov's shot. Griboyedov took two steps. They stood motionless facing each other in this way for a minute, then Yakubovich lost patience and fired, aiming at the leg since he did not wish to kill Griboyedov. The bullet hit the little finger of Griboyedov's left hand, Yakubovich apparently exclaiming, 'At least he will have to stop playing the piano'.

Griboyedov raised his bloodied hand and showed it to them, then he trained his pistol at Yakubovich. 'I could not but derive pleasure from Yakubovich's dignified conduct and courage,' wrote Muravyov. 'He looked truly magnificent as after firing his shot, he folded his arms and awaited death.'[12] Griboyedov had every right to approach closer to the *barrière*, but having seen that Yakubovich had deliberately aimed at his leg, he did not take advantage of this.[13] He moved a little and then fired. The bullet flew past Yakubovich's neck and embedded itself into the ground. It went so close that Yakubovich thought he was wounded, and felt along his neck and then looked at his hand which was bloodless. When all was over the seconds ran forward to the wounded man, who exclaimed, 'O sort injuste!' ('O unjust fate!'),[14] but did not complain or appear to be suffering.

Muravyov galloped off to find Dr Miller. He found him in the hills nearby, and when he had bandaged Griboyedov's wound, they put him in the carriage and went away. Griboyedov spent the rest of the day with Muravyov and Yakubovich, apparently on the best of terms. To cover up the fact of the duel they let it be known that they had been out hunting, and that Griboyedov's horse had trodden on his hand. The next day, Yakubovich's commanding officer, Colonel Naumov, who had been the duty officer responsible on Yermolov's staff at the relevant time, and who had heard rumours of the duel, approached Adjutant Captain Talysin to find out about the matter. 'He was only activated by curiosity,' noted Muravyov. 'He would have liked us all to have approached him with a full confession, in which case he would have played the role of our protector.' Talysin, however, stonewalled, and Naumov then sent for Yakubovich pretending he knew everything. 'If you are so well informed,' retorted Yakubovich, 'why are you asking me questions? I can tell you there was no such duel, and these rumours are unfounded.'[15]

The matter was allowed to rest, though rumours of the duel reached Yermolov himself. He deliberately turned a blind eye to the matter, and Mazarovich, Griboyedov's head of mission, obligingly followed his lead. It was the first of many debts that Griboyedov would owe to Yermolov.

VII

Yermolov and Russian Imperialism

It is a strange fact that Griboyedov, the sensitive artist in words and music, should be closely associated three times in his career with tough and ambitious military chiefs, to each of whom he made himself invaluable. The first had been General Kologrivov, the third would be his kinsman and Yermolov's successor, General Paskievich; the second and most important was Yermolov himself.

From the first, Griboyedov was accepted as one of Yermolov's inner circle; his reputation as a playwright had preceded him, and his quick intelligence and linguistic skills were further recommendations. A legendary figure in the history of the Caucasus, Yermolov combined brutality towards its subject peoples with a surprisingly enlightened attitude towards the young men on his staff. He detested the St Petersburg bureaucracy, in particular the preponderance of German civil servants and Baltic generals, and tended to follow his own line with as little reference as possible to the capital. His attitude to the Caucasus was that of a conqueror, and he pursued a ruthless and destructive policy in subduing the unruly tribes and khanates who resisted Russian rule. While the Georgians had sought to placate neighbours with bribes and concessions, Tsitsiyanov, Yermolov's predecessor, had wasted no time on diplomacy. 'I shall wash my boots in your blood' was a typical pronouncement. Yermolov, conscious that his troops were too thinly spread to patrol the border areas effectively, relied on a similar policy of fear. 'I desire that the terror of my name should guard our frontiers more potently than any fortress,' he once declared. '...Out of pure humanity I am inexorably severe.'[1]

In practice, this meant a policy little short of genocide. When Griboyedov first met him in November 1818, he had just returned from punitive expeditions in Chechnya and Daghestan, and created the new fort of Grozny (or 'Menacing') on the river Sundja; the following year, as a revenge for the destruction of another Russian fort on the same river, he sacked eight villages, killing most of the women and children (many of whom chose death rather than surrender), destroying the crops and burning all the houses to the ground. This, in the words of the Russian military historian A.V. Potto, was the essence of his system. 'He regarded all tribes, peaceable or not, inhabiting the mountains of the Caucasus as *de facto* Russian subjects, or destined to be so sooner or later, and in any case demanded from them unconditional surrender.'

It is not hard to see why Yermolov's methods would lead to Shamyl's *jihad*, or holy war, against the Russians 10 years later. Yermolov himself, in true colonialist style, regarded his mission as a civilising one. He genuinely believed that the whole of the Caucasus should become an integral part of the Russian empire, and side-by-side with his military objectives, he planned to develop the area economically. He built roads to encourage trade, completing the great Georgian military highway and building new roads on the way from Tiflis to Kutaisi and the Black Sea coast, and to Telavi and the Caspian. Much of the work was carried out by his own soldiers, who, in view of the lawless nature of the country, were established in permanent garrisons at points of strategic importance. The men were allowed to have their own families with them, and in times of war or other alarms would defend their forts as they would their own homes.

The building of the forts was all done by the men themselves. It was they who cut down the trees and hauled the timber from the nearest mountains; who quarried the stones and made the bricks and cement; who were their own carpenters and masons and painters. The soldiers of the Caucasus were labourers as well as fighting men, providing all they needed for existence; they were also military colonisers who were to 'develop and steadily improve the economy'. Since these were the days of long service, 25 years and often longer, so that fathers and sons fought side-by-side, each regiment developed its own strong loyalties; this fact, combined with continuous fighting, made them a military force of the highest class.

Yermolov was only just putting this system into practice when Griboyedov arrived in Tiflis. Later he would come to question the whole basis of Yermolov's policy in the Caucasus. But at the time he first met him he was bowled over by his grizzled charm. 'On n'est pas plus entrainant' ('he could not be more attractive')[2], he wrote in his travel notes for Beguichov, and later,

What a splendid fellow he is, it's not only that he's clever, everyone's clever nowadays, but he's capable of grasping anything, from great deeds to the smallest detail, in a totally Russian way. He is so eloquent and has such a Napoleonic gift of oratory, that one wants to write down everything he says.[3]

Yermolov at this time was in his early forties. He was tall and physically imposing, with a round face, fiery blue eyes and bristling hair: 'the head of a tiger on the torso of Hercules', as Pushkin put it.[4] Born of a family claiming descent from Genghis Khan, he had first seen action under Suvorov in Poland, winning his first St George's Cross at the age of sixteen. Since then he had fought against the Persians in the Caucasus, languished in the fortress of St Petersburg under suspicion of disloyalty under the maniacal Tsar Paul, and after a period of exile had returned to active duty in time to fight at Austerlitz. He had been at Borodino in 1812, fighting with the infantry in the blood-bath of the Rayevsky Heights, and had taken part in Kutuzov's famous council of war at Fili, when Kutuzov decided to yield Moscow to Napoleon and live to fight another day. He had been appointed Commander-in-Chief in the Caucasus four years later.

If his savagery to the native tribes were disregarded, Yermolov had many of the qualities of a military hero. He was fiercely patriotic: Count Benckendorff, Alexander's Chief of Police, once described him to the Tsar as 'the idol of Russia's patriots'. He lived frugally, sharing the hardships of his troops on campaign, and was adored by the soldiers under his command. He was also highly cultivated, an avid reader of Plutarch and Roman history, whose military heroes he modelled himself upon. He spoke excellent French, Italian and German, and was well-versed in international affairs. He liked to surround himself with competent and talented young men, who could rise to his intellectual level and banish the boredom of garrison life. It was natural that he should favour Griboyedov, sometimes spending several hours a day in his company, and inviting him to all his grand dinners. 'He seems to love me very much,' wrote Griboyedov to Beguichov, 'but with these five star personalities one can never tell'.[5] It was noticeable, according to Muravyov, that Griboyedov always listened very attentively to what Yermolov was saying, and never took up a position till he knew which way his chief would jump.

As with Kologrivov, Griboyedov had found a powerful patron, and he repaid Yermolov, like his former chief, with a panegyric in the press. Since his literary beginnings in St Petersburg he had carefully nursed his relations with the editors of the main journals there. Despite Grech's joking attacks on him in *The Puppet Theatre*, he had remained on good terms with him, as the editor of *Son of the Fatherland*, and had already published some of his work there. The city's local paper, the *Tiflis*

Record, was not sufficiently influential for his purposes. *Son of the Fatherland,* on the other hand, would be read by the St Petersburg elite, and in an article from 'our esteemed correspondent', he set about singing the praises of Yermolov's regime.

The article was dated 21 January 1819, and was printed six weeks later, but to achieve some local credibility he began it by claiming that it was nearly half a year since he had left St Petersburg to exchange it for the thundering Terek, and the sterile rocks of Tiflis, where descendants of the eagles that had tortured Prometheus wheeled overhead. All around him were the snowy peaks of the Caucasus, icebound throughout the year, and fearsome snowdrifts which would eventually be dispersed in the pure waters of the Aragvi river. After this picturesque beginning, worthy of any romantic travel writer, he went on to reproach his friends 3000 versts away for forgetting all about him. He himself was always thinking of them, and eagerly reading any news from St Petersburg. They could therefore imagine his amazement on finding in *The Russian Invalid,* between articles on hot springs in America and Napoleon's personal physician, an account of what was happening in Georgia. 'I rejoiced! Luckily, I thought, they have not all forgotten us.' But the article, written in Constantinople, and dated three months earlier, turned out to be totally untrue. It reported that there had been an insurrection in Tiflis, and that its instigator was a Tatar prince. 'This saddened and infuriated me,' he wrote. There was no such thing as a Tatar prince in Georgia, nor had there been anything like a revolt. Indeed, in place of former anarchy, everything was quiet and law-abiding, thanks to the firmness of the Russian Government. In the crowded alleyways of the bazaars, people were busy buying and selling; bearded men in long felt cloaks (*burkhas*) and fur caps were exchanging the latest gossip; local beauties showed off their rouge, 'without which they would be much more beautiful', on flat roofs nearby; and at night the rhythm of their tambourines added pleasantly to the noises of the city. 'Can all this be happening at a time when it has occurred to a Tatar prince to start a revolt?'

The only possible explanation for such confusion was that it arose from garbled rumours about Yermolov's recent expedition against the Chechens, though even here, since Yermolov's appointment as Commander-in-Chief, the 'ungovernability of the highlanders' was becoming a thing of the past. In any case, it was as ridiculous to transpose events occurring on the Caspian line to Tiflis, as to attribute what was happening in Finland to Lithuania. 'I would not take upon myself,' he concluded,

> such a thankless task as that of trying to correct misrepresentations in the papers, if it did not have a very important influence on my personal mission to a certain Asiatic power...The English in Persia are perfectly

likely to come across such a story, published in an official Russian newspaper, and to repeat it naively in Tabriz or Teheran. I leave it to everyone's imagination what the consequences might be.

Griboyedov's motives in writing this piece of special pleading and dis-information on Yermolov's behalf are easy enough to understand; it is also possible to see it as a cry for attention from his St Petersburg friends, born of loneliness and a sense of isolation. But he must have known very well that Georgia was a troubled province, still barely subdued internally, and constantly under threat from hostile neighbours; his picture of an idyllic Tiflis, devoted to trade and peacetime concerns, was a far cry from the bustling military headquarters, on a semi-permanent war footing, that it was in reality. He admitted as much in a letter to Beguichov: *The Russian Invalid* has written a lot of nonsense and I have answered with a lot of nonsense too'.[6]

Disingenuous though it was, Griboyedov's article could be expected to please not only Yermolov, but his immediate superior, Mazarovich. The mission to Persia was due to set off on 28 January 1819. 'The journey, like death, is inevitable, there's nothing I can do about it,' wrote Griboyedov to his friends the Tolstoy brothers in St Petersburg.[7] But he was cheered on the day of his departure by a friendly farewell from Yermolov, who told him jovially that he was a madcap and a prankster (perhaps in reference to his duel) but a 'splendid fellow' nonetheless.

As Griboyedov climbed into his saddle, they had one last exchange. 'I said to him,' he wrote to Beguichov, 'Do not sacrifice us, Your Excellency, by declaring war on Persia'.

Yermolov laughed, saying, 'What an odd idea!'

'It's not such an odd idea,' noted Griboyedov. 'He has the power to declare war and make peace. He may suddenly get the idea that our frontiers are not defined enough on the Persian side and decide to extend them along the Araxes. And then what will happen to us?'[8]

Amongst the numerous cavalcade that came to see the party off was Griboyedov's old opponent Yakubovich. In a way it was a fitting finale to his stay in Tiflis. 'I hope now to forgive him,' he wrote to Beguichov, 'and shall never allow such a foolish thing [a duel] to happen again...Let him shoot at others! My turn is past.'[9]

VIII

Journey to Tehran

Semyon Mazarovich, Griboyedov's chief of mission, was an experienced Persian hand. He had travelled with Yermolov on his abortive embassy in 1817, officially as the party's doctor, but in fact as Yermolov's spokesman when for one reason or another he had not wished to speak directly to the Persian ministers. He was a Roman Catholic and a foreigner (his father, a Venetian, had been a Rear Admiral in the Russian service), but he had served with Kutuzov in the 1812 campaign, and Yermolov, despite his normal xenophobia, had perfect confidence in his ability to carry out his policies.

As well as leaving the question of borders undecided, the Treaty of Gulistan had left a number of other matters in the air. The first was the repatriation of Russian deserters, so many of whom had transferred their loyalties to the Persian side that they formed an 800-strong battalion in the Persian army. This issue, an affront to Russian prestige and morale, would be one of those that Griboyedov would have to deal with directly. A second vexed question, equally galling to Russian pride, was the Persian protection of the Georgian pretender to the throne, Prince Alexander Bagration, son of the last Georgian king. He had already fomented a rising against the Russians in the Georgian province of Imeretia, and as long as he remained in Persia was a potential source of trouble. Apart from dealing with these tricky problems, the Russian mission was expected to do all it could to foster trade and Russian interests, and wherever possible to counteract the influence of the British, who were already well ensconced in Persia. On the whole, it was a relatively low-profile embassy, without the means to offer more than modest gifts to Persian officials, and with a medium-ranking civil servant rather than a grandee at its head. On the plus side for Griboyedov, it offered greater scope for individual action than a larger or more structured mission would have done.

Writing to Beguichov on the day after leaving Tiflis, Griboyedov told him that he had spent his time there on three important things: the duel, an illness (about which we know nothing) and playing cards. He knew he had been a lazy correspondent, but then so had his friends, including Beguichov himself, who seemed to have assumed that he was too busy to receive letters. Now he was on the road to Erivan, the first step on the road to Tehran.

Griboyedov had resumed his practice of sending travel notes to Beguichov on leaving Tiflis.[1] As before, he was writing 'only as to a friend'. He could thus be totally open and truthful about any third parties known to them both, as well as those he would be dealing with professionally, whether Russian officials or representatives of the Shah. Katenin, he wrote, had suggested that he should publish his notes, but quite apart from the loss of freedom this would mean, his reference books were all in trunks, and he could not achieve the standard of scholarship he would have liked.

He was travelling in tough conditions of snow and ice, often sleeping at night with the horses for warmth, with his comrades snoring around him. Sometimes a string of hunting hawks, with jingling bells, would be tethered outside: 'Watch out for them or they'll peck through your furs'. Mazarovich, cheerful and considerate, shared all the hardships of the group. The contrast with Griboyedov's earlier existence in Moscow and St Petersburg was enormous, but in a curious way he found it liberating:

> It is strange how many people in Petersburg begged me to indulge my muse, and I remained silent whereas here, where I have no readers, as they do not speak Russian, I cannot put down my pen. There is only one drawback to these lands: the paucity of facts and knowledge about them. I never imagined I would travel to the East. My thoughts never tended that way...I would give anything to have a painter here: no words can describe the mists that curl around the mountain heights at dawn; a touch of morning sunlight falls on them and they become a burning fiery sea.

On their third day of travelling the party reached Sogan Li. A ray of fleeting sun cheered the scenery, otherwise dark and overshadowed by the hills of Daghestan in the distance:

> I galloped ahead to inspect the pass on my uncomfortable Georgian saddle; I fell off my horse several times.[2] Fortunately the 'Cossack of the Escort' refreshed me with a pomegranate, and together we reached

Dermutchizana, otherwise known as Hasan-Li. We descended next to the bed of the river Khram across which was arched the most beautiful bridge.[3] It was a stunning sight and an architectural gem against the snow; it was artfully built of bricks. The river washed half of it, and not the other half, a caravansaray. Its architect was clearly a master of symmetry as the beauty of its arches proved.

They spent the night in the caravansaray. Its vaulted main hall was full of sheep, and the walls were scrawled with travellers' graffiti, but Griboyedov, with his keen eye for antiquities, was once more struck by the elegance of the architecture.[4] 'There is nothing so splendid on this side of the river Kura, the ancient Cyrus described by Strabo. It just goes to show what good taste the Safavid Shahs had.'

They set off at four the next morning, Griboyedov riding a new stallion, so sure-footed that he was able to go on singing or smoking his long pipe, even when scrambling down the steepest precipice. The party consisted of 25 travellers, not counting the men who handled the pack-horses and an armed escort of Tatars. These last were a 'very cheerful group, never shy of loosing off a shot into the fog and clouds'. The mission's servants had a number of Borzoi hounds, which they unleashed in pursuit of the odd hare – 'or rather,' wrote Griboyedov, 'the illusion of a hare, for I never saw one'.

The journey from Tiflis to Erivan[5] took seven days in all, sometimes through awesome mountain passes – in the words of Zhukovsky, 'yawning chasms, fogs and clouds' – sometimes along the foothills, on paths so overgrown that the bushes lashed their eyes. At night, in the absence of a caravansaray or mountain hut, they would unhook the pack-horses' harnesses, draping them with carpets to turn them into tents, and lighting camp fires to cook a supper of shashliks. As they approached Erivan, the distant peaks of Ararat rose up above the mist:

> Even for someone whose soul is already in awe of the sacred tales of it, the sight of this ancient mountain fills one with an inexplicable sense of wonderment. I stood motionless for a long time; my stallion, clearly not sharing the feeling of his rider, moved forward, and deposited me in a second on the wet snow; the dampness went through to my very bones. The base of Ararat had disappeared, the middle also, but the very top part hung like a cloud before us all the way to Erevan.

The capital of the khanate of Erivan (a former province of Armenia), the town was large and straggling, dominated by a formidable citadel on a huge battlement of rock, and surrounded by a double row of fortified walls and towers. Once an independent Christian kingdom, Armenia had been attacked and invaded so often – most recently by Tsitsiyanov in 1804 – that most of the city was in a ruined state, its gardens and fine Persian architecture fallen into decay and its population much reduced. But its rugged mountain setting, with the peaks of Ararat in the distance, was magnificent. 'Nothing can exceed the grandeur of these bulwarks of nature, which frequently present themselves around fortified places in these precipitous countries; their vastness, simplicity and impregnable appearance being far beyond the power of man to imitate,' wrote the English traveller Sir Robert Ker Porter, who was doing a Grand Tour of the area. A distinguished portrait painter who hoped to get commissions from the Persian court, his path would cross with Griboyedov's in both Tabriz and Tehran.

As a milestone on the way to Tabriz, the administrative centre for foreign delegations to Persia, Erivan was a sensitive area diplomatically. The Russian delegation would naturally expect to be treated with due honour, as representatives of the Tsar. To their disgust, there was no-one to greet them when they first arrived.[6] 'This drove me mad,' wrote Griboyedov, 'especially after struggling through such dreadful weather conditions and looking forward to a civilised reception. Such studied disrespect to Russian officials would have been offensive even to some-one with less self-esteem than myself.'

Eventually, as they reached the outskirts of the town, an official came galloping towards them and begged their forgiveness, saying that the adjutant who had been sent to meet them had gone on the wrong road. Accompanied by his ushers, or *ferrashes*, 'three evil smelling ruffians', he conducted them to the house of the Governor's lieutenant, Mehmed Bey. Passing through the wide outer gates, they dismounted in an inner courtyard with frozen fountains, and were conducted into a series of interconnecting halls. Fires were lit to right and left, and water pipes, the ever-present Persian *kalyans*, were offered round.

> At last the erring 'adjutant' came forward to make his bow, accompanied by a crowd of visitors. We were amused at the comicality of this title for the Sardar's lieutenant. Our host had been hunting, as his brother [the adjutant] explained. The house, its servants and all the people within it were ours to command. We immediately found an English interpreter, not a dictionary but a person who took it upon himself to interfere in everything. It seemed that he had once…been a cab driver, or else an oarsman on the Thames. With these qualifications he was teaching the Persians English military drill…A whole battalion was under him…He is desperately bored here; we did not know how to get rid of him. His importunity and restless curiosity about everything are impossible to get away from.[7]

Mehmed Bey returned from hunting in the evening. He was a jolly, bald-headed man who seemed a great admirer of the Russians. He obligingly told Mazarovich that should he wish to behead his, Mehmed Bey's, servants, or even his brother, for his entertainment, it could easily be arranged: this offer the envoy politely declined. A banquet was served, the strong drink, greasy mutton and heavily sugared sweetmeats taking Griboyedov back in imagination to one of those feasts in ancient Muscovy described in *The Travels of Olearius*.[8] He woke next morning with a splitting headache, and the prospect of a visit to the Sardar later that day.

Sardar Husayn Khan, a member of the ruling Qajar family, was one of the most powerful figures in the realm. He paid his own troops, only receiving a subsidy from the Shah in time of war, and could be relied on to hold his own against the Turks. He had already paid his compliments to the Russians by sending them a wild ram, with a shaggy fleece and horns like a stag's, from the previous day's hunting, and was now to give them an official audience.

The Sardar's quarters, in a crenellated tower, were reached through a maze of courts, full of doors and gloomy passages in which it was easy to get lost. The main reception hall had handsome patterned carpets, a decorated ceiling with 'Japanese motifs', probably lacquered, and painted friezes depicting the adventures of Rustam on the walls. Griboyedov was training his lorgnette on these when the Sardar entered, accompanied by a crowd of courtiers. His son, dressed in a red fur coat, sat on the carpet by him; the Russian party, out of courtesy, were offered chairs and tables, to avoid the embarrassment of sitting backwards on their heels. Pipes were offered, sweetmeats passed round, conventional enquiries made about Yermolov's latest expeditions in Chechnya and Daghestan, and the journeys of the Tsar to Europe in pursuit of peace. 'The Sardar confused Vienna with Venice! I cannot recall how.'

They stayed for three days in Erivan, suffering intensely from the cold. Apart from their ceremonial visit to the Sardar, wrote Griboyedov, he never strayed from the fireplace at Mehmed Bey's, though even here the supplies of firewood were woefully inadequate. 'The people of Erevan may be agreeable in summer: in winter they would happily kill you by letting you freeze to death. At the Sardar's I shivered, at Mehmed Bey's my bones rattled with the cold.'

On the day of their departure, he wrapped himself completely in a *burkha* and Caucasian hood, and let his horse ride as it willed. He could not speak, or even look, as it meant uncovering his face – one member of the party already had frost-bitten cheeks. Crossing fords was a particular ordeal, the horses slithering hopelessly through the icy roads. 'No, I am not a traveller,' he wrote despairingly.

> Only the iron hand of destiny could drive me this far, to wander in a barbarous country, at the worst possible season; had I had any choice I would never have abandoned my domestic gods. When we finally reached Devalhu [their next stop] I could not undress, or eat, or drink, and slept like a murdered man.[9]

The nightmare journey was a little relieved when their convoy joined up with a Persian grandee, on his way to pay his respects to Crown Prince Abbas Mirza at Tabriz. His servants, or *ferrashes*, rode behind him, one carrying his pipe, another with a huge tobacco pouch and portable stove strapped to his saddle, so that his master could have ever ready burning coals. 'If only all these pipe bearers and their deputies could be put to clearing the snow drifts off the roads, it would be much more sensible,' Griboyedov complained. Their new-found friend, the Khan, however, was in seventh heaven at falling in with the all-powerful Russian mission. As a result, they were drowned with compliments. 'What hyperboles!' wrote Griboyedov. 'Nobody tells such flattering lies as the people here. The words "soul", "heart", "feelings" are never off their lips.'[10]

At Tabriz, they were met by a mounted escort sent by the Governor or Kaimakam.[11] As they rode through the turreted gates, decorated with brightly coloured green and blue tiles, Griboyedov had his first sight of a city with which he would become achingly familiar over the next few years. His travel notes at the time were tantalisingly laconic.

> Tabriz[12] with its bazaar and caravansaray – meetings, honours – dinner with the English – visit to the Kaimakam – Sir Ker Porter – arrival of the Crown Prince – ceremonial visit – presence of the English – my opinion about them – our relations with Persia – the baths and climate in comparison with Tiflis – iced fruit – dancing and music.[13]

The key event of their visit, only glanced at in his notes, was their visit to the Crown Prince. Responsible for Persia's foreign policy, as well as commander of the army and governor of the prosperous province of Azherbaijan, he was the most powerful man in the kingdom after the Shah.

Abbas Mirza was twenty-six at the time of their first meeting, an impressive, black-bearded figure with pale distinguished features, whose greatest claim to fame was as a military commander and reformer. Unlike his Qajar predecessor, the sadistic Agha Muhammed Khan, responsible for the sack of Tiflis and innumerable eye gougings, beheadings and impalements, he was a civilised and moderate ruler: during the sixteen years that he was Governor of Azherbaijan, with a population of a million, he sanctioned only seven capital sentences. Intelligent and energetic, with a disinterested passion for his country, his greatest desire was to Europeanise the Persian army – for which the British provided officers and training – and to modernise the Persian state when, as heir apparent, he succeeded to the throne. He had no cause to love the Russians, and had been especially humiliated by Persia's loss of Muslim territories in the Treaty of Gulistan, but his manners were characteristically silky and urbane. 'His expressions of civility,' wrote an English visitor, 'wore that tinge of hyperbole for which the Persians were renowned.'

Although Griboyedov left no details of their meeting in his travel notes, it is probable that an article, 'Letter of a Person attached to the Russian Embassy of S.N. Mazarovich', published in the St Petersburg paper *Le Conservateur Impérial*, came from his fertile pen.[14] To some extent a public-relations exercise on behalf of Mazarovich, it described the flattering attentions they received from Abbas Mirza. It explained how they changed their shoes for the customary slippers and silk stockings: there was to be no repetition of Yermolov's rudeness. The Crown Prince received them standing, 'an honour the Turks never offer and the Russians very rarely'. He asked them to explain the advantages Persia was deriving from the Treaty of Gulistan – a question difficult to answer – and in a second interview spent nearly three hours questioning them on official attitudes to Persia in Moscow and St Petersburg. He concluded by assuring them of his love for Russia and his pleasure in greeting the mission, adding politely that he had ordered a good fire to be made for them, as he had noticed they were suffering from the cold.

Such courtesies were significant. With their arrival imminent in the capital, where the Shah himself would receive them on the occasion of Nowruz, Persian New Year, the Russians would be alive to every nuance of etiquette and honours, as reflecting the glory of their imperial master, the Tsar, and his status as the head of a military superpower whose territorial gains were enshrined in the Treaty of Gulistan.

They left Tabriz at the end of February.[15] Abbas Mirza and his party had gone on before, leaving a number of horses of 'fabulous quality' for their use. Resuming his travel notes, Griboyedov described the deep drifts in the passes, enlivened at one point by the sight of numerous foxes gambolling in the snow. For four days they battled with the drifts, their pack-horses foundering. On the fifth day, snowstorms were replaced by fog, and by the seventh the snow had disappeared. Passing through Ujan and Miana, they reached Zanjan, where there were signs of spring, music to entertain them in the evening, even a bath house. On the tenth day, they came to Qazvin, an ancient centre of poets and men of learning, where ruined mosques and *maidans* (public squares) bore witness to the town's departed splendours. From Qazvin onwards, their ride became a pleasant cavalcade; there were travellers and children riding donkeys on the road at Sultaniye, and no less than seven summer kiosks of the Shah along the way. At last they saw the summits of the Alborz mountains, with Tehran nestling in their foothills, and knew that they had reached their destination.

IX

Tabriz and the Deserters

Tehran had been promoted from a provincial capital to the capital of Persia by the first Qajar monarch, Agha Muhammed Khan, less than 50 years before.[1] Not far from the Qajar power base of Astarabad, it was ideally placed for the general surveillance of the kingdom. It had certain obvious disadvantages, namely the damp caused by the spring torrents and the excessive heat in summer: from the end of June onwards, the court and most of the richer citizens of Tehran moved to the more temperate plains of Sultaniye and Ujan.

Visitors to the city noted its deep surrounding ditches, towers and mud walls, their lines unbroken by any mosque or palace; the chief buildings and palaces were situated in a separate quarter close to the citadel. The streets were very narrow, full of mud or dust according to the season. 'When a great man goes out to take the air,' wrote Ker Porter,

> he seldom condescends to be seen on foot. Mounted on horseback, he sets forth with a train of thirty to forty ill-appointed followers on foot…Successions of such groups, loaded camels, mules, asses and royal elephants are continually passing to and fro, jamming up the streets to the hazard of life and limb.[2]

The Russian mission's stay began with a visit to the Prime Minister, the Sadr-i Azam, on the eve of the religious festival of the Bairam, a date advised by the court astronomers. A cannon was fired in their honour, and presents distributed, though Griboyedov does not specify what they were. Two days later, on the first day of the Persian New Year, they were collected by the master of ceremonies for an audience with the monarch, Fath Ali Shah.

It was a magnificent occasion,[3] in keeping with the Persian love of ceremonial and outward show. 'The arrival of a foreign embassy,' wrote Sir John Malcolm, who had visited Tehran as the representative of the East India Company,

> is deemed one of the occasions when the king ought to appear in all his grandeur. The ceremonies of the reception appear to have been substantially the same in all ages...The envoy advances with his suite and escort to one of the interior gates of the palace...When he dismounts he is conducted into a small apartment, where he is met by one of the principal officers of the government. After being seated there for some minutes the King is announced to be on his throne and the ambassador proceeds to the hall of audience. That splendid room, the floor of which is raised about eight feet from the ground, is situated in a garden intercepted by regular alleys and fountains; from the throne to the entrance of the gardens, the princes, ministers, nobles, courtiers and royal guards are ranged in their respective ranks: but the splendour of these officers, who are robed in their richest habits, is eclipsed in a moment, when the eye glances at the sovereign whose throne and dress are covered in the most precious jewels. As the ambassador advances between two officers, whose gold enamelled wands are the badges of their high stations, he is twice required to make an obeisance. When near the throne the lord of requests (the Eshik aghasi bashi) pronounces his name, and that of the sovereign by whom he is sent. The King then says, in reply, 'You are welcome', and the envoy proceeds to take his seat in the same room, but at some distance from the king. After the ceremony of delivering the letter of credentials is past, the monarch repeats that he is welcome, and generally enters into a conversation calculated to make the visitor feel at ease and to substitute more pleasing impressions for those which the imposing pomp of the scene had inspired.

Griboyedov, in attendance on Mazarovich, would have been present at just such a scene. His notes add further details: the three salvos of light cannon fired to greet them, the royal elephant bearing presents of money, the mullahs pronouncing poems in their honour, trumpets, presentations, more poems and, irritatingly for the Russians, a band striking up with 'God Save The King'.[4]

His article for *Le Conservateur Impérial*, in which he had already described the mission's interviews with Abbas Mirza, gave a deliberately anodyne picture of their reception. He described how affably the Shah had spoken to Mazarovich and the other members of the mission, 'conceding on this a point of etiquette whereby a great distance should be preserved between the rulers and the ruled'. 'Such intimacies,' he concluded, 'confirm the excellent relations between our two powers.'

There was no mention of more controversial issues, such as the return of the deserters or the border question. It was one more example of Griboyedov's readiness to sweeten the truth in the interests of pleasing his superiors.

Griboyedov complained in his travel notes of the 'diplomatic monastery'[5] to which he was condemned in Tehran. But he had too much intellectual curiosity to be bored. He was pursuing his Persian studies, and had made friends with the Shah's court poet, Feth Ali Khan, a gentle talkative man of about sixty: one of his odes had pleased the Shah so much that he had filled his mouth with diamonds.

In July, when the heat in Tehran became unbearable, the Russian mission moved with the court to tented summer quarters in the ruined city of Sultaniye. Griboyedov would rise early to enjoy the coolness and freshness of the dawn. The sound of the early morning call to prayer was 'pittoresque'; less pleasant were the cries of the faithful as they inflicted ritual floggings on each other. Whenever he could, he broke away from the rest of his party to sit by a running stream, 'surrounded by a mass of turtles', and read Tom Moore.[6]

In August, the Russian mission divided forces. Mazarovich, as its most senior figure, was to represent the Tsar at the court of the Shah; Griboyedov was to return to Tabriz as acting Chargé d'Affaires.

It was an important post. Tabriz was the diplomatic capital of Persia, to which all foreign missions were accredited. As Russian representative to Abbas Mirza, Griboyedov could try to match the influence of the British, who already had a full mission there, and whose activities he regarded with a suspicious eye. Without going too deeply into Britain's intentions in Persia and its attitudes to Russian expansion in the Caucasus, it is possible to see the Great Game as beginning not, as is commonly assumed, in Central Asia in the 1850s, but in the Persia of the 1820s. London still considered Persia as the insurmountable bastion for the defence of India.

It is certainly true that Griboyedov, as a Russian patriot, was eager to promote his country's interests at Britain's expense. In the early stages of the Russo–Persian War, the British had been active in training and subsidising the Persian army. But their responsibilities had decreased with their alliance to Russia in 1812; moreover, the Government in London was eager to reduce expenses. By the time Griboyedov arrived in Tiflis, only a handful of British instructors was left to train the Persian army – no doubt they were of better quality than the cab driver in Erivan.

Griboyedov's instinctive suspicions of the British led him to begin his mission in Tabriz with a diplomatic gaffe. The return of the Russian deserters in Persia was high on his agenda; the fact that they formed a battalion in Tabriz was a running grievance.[7] He was therefore indignant when he learned that Captain Edward Willock, the brother of Henry Willock, the British Chargé d'Affaires, had personally escorted two Russian deserters from the Caucasus to Tehran.[8] In a formal note to Henry Willock, dated 14 August 1819, he protested at his brother's conduct. He was sure that it stemmed from a temporary aberration, but he must ask that British officers travelling to Georgia did not repeat the offence. It was intolerable that the British should suborn Russian subjects from their duty to the Tsar, as well as providing an appalling example to their Persian hosts of bad faith between two ostensibly friendly powers.

Henry Willock, a far more experienced diplomat than Griboyedov, responded to this arrogant protest by despatching two members of his mission with a letter in reply and instructions to negotiate with Griboyedov for the withdrawal of his note. The Russians, he explained, had merely been hired as coachmen for the journey, for which Abbas Mirza himself had provided a guide, or *mehmendar*; if Griboyedov had spoken to him personally, the matter could have been cleared up far more easily.

Griboyedov refused to retract his accusations against Edward Willock, repeating them in a second letter. Willock wisely decided not to continue the exchanges. In a letter to the British Foreign Secretary, Castlereagh, he put the episode down to Griboyedov's inexperience, and the bad feelings it was calculated to produce, which he, as an older hand, was 'desirous of avoiding'. Griboyedov, he wrote, was 'a young man of little experience and no prudence'; he had been led into error by his hasty and intemperate disposition.

Griboyedov reported his tough line to Yermolov, who wrote congratulating him: 'I must judge you as deserving rightful praise'.[9] Despite this, he realised he had gone too far with Willock, and the affair was eventually patched up with a half apology on his side. Meanwhile, the far more serious question of Russian deserters serving in the Persian army had to be addressed.

The Russian deserters were much valued by the Persians. Well trained by their former masters, they were particularly useful in cases of internal disorder or religious dispute, in which they could be relied on not to take sides. As a consequence, they were usually better and more regularly paid than the native Persian troops. They had been led to desert originally by the harsh discipline of the knout in the Russian army, and the appalling living conditions, both during campaigns and periods of peace. Though many of them were now homesick, and would have returned to their duties if they could, they were deterred by the prospect of the hideous punishment for deserters from the Russian army. This involved the torture of running the gauntlet through three thousand men, each of whom struck the victim's naked back with a rod. It was a punishment that almost invariably led to death, unless some humanely disposed officer arranged with his troops to soften the blows.

If Griboyedov were to persuade the deserters to return, it could only be by promising them an amnesty, or bribing them with some hope of money, and in any event assuring them that they would not be flogged to death, or taken in chains to Siberia the moment they arrived in Tiflis. It was not a promise he, or even Mazarovich, could give. Yermolov had recently left on a campaign. Mazarovich therefore turned to his Chief of Staff, and deputy in his absence, General Velyaminov, for a decision on the matter, and seems to have been given a guarantee that the men would be pardoned. However, as he later admitted, the whole affair was dealt with very hurriedly. Griboyedov, in his eagerness to get the matter settled, and to further his own career, was pressing ahead, and had already persuaded a number of the deserters (about 70) to consider returning.

He then sought an audience with Abbas Mirza. The Crown Prince was not pleased at the idea of losing some of his best soldiers. However, he was committed to abide by the terms of the Treaty of Gulistan, although, as his interview with Griboyedov made clear, he did his best to make it difficult for Griboyedov to communicate with them. Griboyedov recorded their exchanges in his travel notes. His first complaint was that the soldiers he had hoped to bring back were being deliberately kept out of sight. Here is the transcript of the debate:[10]

> Griboyedov: Your Highness, please let me go to the soldiers so I can hear how your civil servants are interrogating them.
>
> Crown Prince: My officials are doing what they have to do, you have no need to approach them.
>
> Griboyedov: I strongly suspect that whatever they are doing is not being done straightforwardly. When your officials found them at the mission, they began to ply them with offers of debauchery, girls and drunkenness; when we appeared they ran away in shame. Meanwhile we could not go into the maidan and talk to them about returning to the Fatherland. Then you ordered that...certain soldiers from the battalion who had been arrested leaving my quarters should be brought to you. I have a list of all their names, but they never re-appeared even if you ordered it...Your four officials are doing their best to talk them into Lord knows what, and I am not even allowed to approach them.

The Crown Prince made it clear that he would not pay the departing soldiers any of their back pay: 'No, no, no. Why should I? It would be different if they were continuing in my employment...Let Mazarovich now pay them, they are his'. Then, switching tack, he asked Griboyedov why he was so insistent that the deserters should return. 'You see this water channel. It loses little if a few drops escape, and the same is true about my Russians as far as Russia is concerned.' 'But what if the drops wished to return to the fountain?' asked Griboyedov.

The conversation grew more acrimonious, Griboyedov accusing the Crown Prince of bribing the Russians not to leave, Abbas Mirza complaining that the Russians were spreading false rumours and trying to stir up his people. 'Why do you not behave like the English?' he concluded. 'They are quiet and obedient. I am very pleased with them.' To this irritating question, Griboyedov gave a delphic answer: 'They may, or may not be, an example for us to copy'.

The Crown Prince then called forward Samson Makintsev, a former Russian officer, the commanding officer of the Russian battalion. 'I could not restrain myself on seeing such a swine included amongst my immediate companions,' wrote Griboyedov. Abbas Mirza defended him: 'He is my "Nuker" [adjutant]'.

'Even if he were your general,' said Griboyedov, 'he is still canaille and a swine, and I should not have to see him.'

'The Crown Prince became rather angry at this,' he wrote, 'and wished to have nothing more to do with me; we parted.'

Writing to Castlereagh shortly after, Willock reported on the interview. Griboyedov had burnt his boats with the very man to whom he was accredited, and with whom he should remain on diplomatic terms. Upon seeing Makintsev, he had 'used such improper language to the Prince that the latter ordered him from his presence, asserting that he would complain to Mazarovich, and request he might never again be charged with any communication to him or his ministers'. Had this happened, it would have been the kiss of death for Griboyedov's diplomatic career; luckily Abbas Mirza did not carry out his threat.

By the end of August, Griboyedov's obstinacy had borne fruit, and some 70 deserters[11] (see Notes on the text on the continuing debate about the numbers) had agreed to return to Tiflis with him. He seems to have trusted Mazarovich's half promises on their behalf. 'I have put my neck on the line for my unfortunate fellow countrymen,' he wrote. 'The men sing sentimental folk songs such as "There is a little hamlet on the other side of the river; there is a path in the field". My eyes involuntarily fill with tears.'[12]

The journey back to Tiflis took two months. Amburgherr, the useful if somewhat stolid German attaché, shared the task of shepherding the tragic band. Obligingly, despite his fury at Griboyedov's stubborn rudeness, Abbas Mirza provided six horses and two escorting officers to guide them. He had spoken movingly to the men before they left, telling them to serve the Tsar as well as they had served him, and instructing

Griboyedov to see that they were well treated in Russia. One soldier even deserted back to Abbas Mirza at the last minute, flinging himself at his knees and crying that he did not know how he had ever forsworn his duty to him. 'I could cut him to pieces,' wrote Griboyedov.

Griboyedov needed all the determination he could muster to bring his party safely back. The *mehmendar* he had been given turned out to be a broken reed, and he was in a constant state of anxiety as to whether they were following the right road through the mountains. Added to this, there was always a possibility of trouble from hostile Persian khans, or the Georgian pretender Prince Alexander, who was known to be lurking somewhere near Tabriz. There were outbreaks of drunkenness, and signs of backsliding among the soldiers; he had to keep them in line by bluffing them with threats of punishment, and even flourishing a pistol. It was with intense relief that he reached the summit of the pass which marked the Georgian border, and knew that he was on Russian soil.

The march to Tiflis was delayed by foraging problems, to solve which he was forced to pay 300 roubles out of his own pocket, but it was only when he reached the capital that his real troubles began. Despite the assurances from Velyaminov, Griboyedov's promises to the deserters had always had an element of wishful thinking about them.[13] During their long journey he had grown to know and sympathise with the men he was bringing back, and to feel responsible for them. Now, to his intense mortification, he found that the military establishment was not prepared to honour the amnesty he had been promised. Mazarovich had been as much deceived as he.[14] According to Griboyedov's biographer Meshcheryakov – who, however, gives no source – he had even received a guarantee from Yermolov: 'I can assure you the people returned to freedom thanks to your great hearted intervention will obtain not only a pardon but a very friendly reception, and if necessary some financial support'.

There is absolutely no evidence of this leniency. Military discipline was inexorable, and it is clear from an exchange of letters between Griboyedov and Mazarovich that somebody, possibly the Tsar himself, had overridden their pledges to the miserable men. Griboyedov felt his responsibility bitterly. 'Me voici dupe et trompeur,'[15] he wrote to Mazarovich. General Velyaminov had been doing all he could to help him, but behind him were the ranks of *les barbus* (the bearded ones), old-fashioned army men who insisted on the full penalty being exacted. 'They are as obstinate and stupid as ever,' Griboyedov told Mazarovich. 'Please keep up the pressure so as to bring them round and bully them into line.'

In the end, a compromise seems to have been reached. In a some-what embarrassed letter to Griboyedov, Mazarovich was forced to confess that he been misled by his enthusiasm into giving promises that he could not deliver. Griboyedov's concern for the 70 men, he told him, showed that he had 'a noble soul'. However, the soldiers could take comfort from the fact that a decent solution had been found, and that the army, after adopting a 'stern paternal tone' had commuted it to a more sensitive one. They would have to accept the necessity of some reparation; on the other hand, they would be genuinely pardoned, and could receive their rights as citizens with a peaceful conscience. 'My dear Griboyedov, I see no harm done except that I was unable to obtain for your men all the welfare which I tried to obtain for them...One is never completely happy on this earth.'

At a distance of nearly 200 years, it is impossible to discover the meaning of this patronising homily without knowing what fate had been decided for the men.[16] It is possible that they were spared the horrors of physical punishment, though the Soviet scholar Nechkina writes grimly, 'From his [Griboyedov's] inability to keep his promises, it is apparent that their fate in Russia was very much more severe than that agreed initially'. It is a controversial episode in which at worst Griboyedov could be accused of gambling with the deserters' lives in order to further his own career, and at best of naivety in believing the promises he had been given. An entry in his travel notes while he was still in Tabriz seems to show he knew the risks involved: 'The return of the prisoners; negotiations about the prisoners; madness and sorrow'.

X

Diplomatic Diversions

Having delivered his band of deserters, for better or worse, to the authorities in Tiflis, Griboyedov reported to Yermolov at his campaign headquarters in Grozny.[1] The Commander-in-Chief received him amiably, not only writing an official note to Mazarovich approving his actions, but recommending him to the Foreign Ministry for a decoration. St Petersburg thought differently: Griboyedov was later reproved for leaving his post to escort the prisoners, for antagonising Abbas Mirza in the first place, and for engaging in undiplomatic activities. Meanwhile, however, Griboyedov took the opportunity to ask Yermolov to transfer him to a post in Tiflis, either as a teacher – Yermolov was planning to set up an academy of Eastern languages – or as a legal expert, working on the amalgamation of Georgian and Russian law.[2] (It should not be forgotten that Griboyedov had obtained a law degree at Moscow University.) The request was refused, though Griboyedov continued to hope that Yermolov would change his mind.

Back in Tiflis for a few short weeks, Griboyedov was able to catch up with the St Petersburg newspapers, and perhaps read reviews of his vaudeville skit, *The Trial Interlude*, written a year earlier, which had had its first performance on 10 November. He also made a new friend, Nikolai Alexandrovich Kakhovsky, an officer in the 7th Carabiniers and a nephew of Yermolov. Kakhovsky was only eighteen, six years younger than Griboyedov, but he was obviously a kindred spirit, to whom Griboyedov wrote some of his most revealing letters when he returned to Tabriz. Larded with indiscretions about his Persian hosts, they would have done his diplomatic career no good had they been intercepted.[3] On the other hand, he may not have been unwilling for Kakhovsky to pass on his comments to his uncle: 'All without exception respect Alexis Petrovich [Yermolov],' he wrote on one occasion, 'and regard the slightest word from him as a reward'.

Griboyedov returned to Tabriz with mixed feelings, at one moment seeing his future there as a desert of boredom, at another as an opportunity to distinguish himself by his zeal in furthering Russian interests. He was no longer acting head of the Russian mission there, for Mazarovich had arrived from Tehran while he was away. An imposing new residence had been built for him at great expense; Griboyedov contrasted the splendours of this 'palais de Russie' with his own small house nearby. It was large enough, however, for him to give card parties; with his books and piano lost somewhere en route from St Petersburg, *vingt et un* was one of his chief distractions.

Apart from the various diplomatic missions accredited to Abbas Mirza, there was a fair-sized European community in Tabriz: soldiers, military instructors, traders, adventurous travellers like Ker Porter. One of the most interesting figures from Griboyedov's point of view was Madame de la Marinière, governess to the Crown Prince's children. The wife of a doctor in Tabriz, she had served in the mini-court of Napoleon's sister, the Duchess of Piombino, in Lucca, had travelled widely in Europe, and known Madame de Staël. There were other more accessible ladies, among them a certain Mademoiselle de la Fosse, the daughter of the former military doctor there. Griboyedov, displaying something of that specifically Russian quality known as *vranyo* – or outrageous boasting – claimed that she was on the brink of granting him her favours, though Mazarovich was competing for them too.

A tone of disrespect was creeping into Griboyedov's references to Mazarovich.[4] He owed him a debt of gratitude for following Yermolov's lead in overlooking his duel with Yakubovich; had Mazarovich made an issue of it, his career would have ended before it began. He had found him genial and good company to start with, not given to standing on his dignity, and with a gaiety that had lightened the hardships of their journeys. Disenchantment had probably begun with the question of the deserters, and Mazarovich's failure to honour his promises about their treatment, but there were basic differences in attitude between them. Fiercely patriotic, Griboyedov was far more hawkish in his outlook than Mazarovich. He was influenced perhaps by Yermolov's aggressive attitudes; Mazarovich's milder approach was closer to that of the Foreign Ministry in St Petersburg, which wanted no trouble with the British, more interested in peaceful relations with Persia than in asserting Russia's military supremacy. The Russian mission in Persia had a difficult brief in following the contradictory policies emanating from St Petersburg and Tiflis.

Mazarovich's foreign background – he did not become a naturalised Russian till 1836 – and fervent Catholicism were further sticks for Griboyedov to beat him with. As an Orthodox believer, for whom the Russian church was synonymous with Russian patriotism, he was irritated by Mazarovich's ostentatious parade of Catholic piety. 'A priest has appeared as a house magician alongside Mazarovich, a certain Kaplan, a Catholic bishop from the Chaldees...' he complained to Kakhovsky.[5] 'The Crown Prince appears to have given him to Mazarovich. He and his brother Osip go jointly to confess to him.' Griboyedov had been forced to escape from the influence of Mazarovich's Latin missals by galloping off into the plains.

Even Griboyedov was not tactless enough to show his feelings about Mazarovich openly, confining himself to disloyal remarks in his letters to Kakhovsky and other friends. Mazarovich was his official superior, and it was in his interest to work with him, especially in the all important area of trade. The Russo–Persian War, by interrupting British trade routes from India, had done much to take away commercial advantages that country had previously enjoyed. The Treaty of Gulistan, following on the Russian annexation of Georgia, had opened up new opportunities for Russian trade with Persia, the balance of profit being very much on the Russian side. Exports of cotton, furs, raw silk and brocades from Persia fell far short of the quantities of paper, glass, leather and cloth coming from Tiflis and Astrakhan. Mazarovich, as head of the mission, was officially in charge of furthering commercial relations with Persia, but he and his brother Osip were also busily engaged in trading on their own account. Amburgherr accused them sourly of abusing their privileged status by 'dragging themselves around the bazaars'.

Griboyedov might have criticised them too, but he had his own hopes of cashing in on any trading opportunities available. His financial situation was as dire as ever. His civil servant's salary scarcely covered his expenses, his mother's unsavoury dealings at Kostroma had left her with little to spare. Soon after his return to Tabriz, he had made the acquaintance of a former French army officer, Théodore Ettier,[6] who had come to seek his fortune in Persia, and had just been enrolled as an instructor in Abbas Mirza's army. Ettier, who had lived in England, was immediately welcomed by the French and English colonies in Tabriz, and it was at the house of Dr de la Fosse that he first met Griboyedov. He described him in his memoirs as a young man full of talents and amiability; 'from then on,' he wrote, 'we became very close'. Their friendship was based on mutual interest. Ettier's position as a member of Abbas Mirza's military staff made him a useful informant professionally.

It seems likely that Griboyedov recruited Ettier as an unofficial agent; this was perfectly normal at the time, when almost all fortune-seeking Europeans in Persia had a secondary activity, working either for the British or the Russians as well as their Persian employers. More important for both of them, however, was the idea of setting up in business together, and of making their fortunes, as the *nabobs* of the British East India Company had done the previous century.

Neither Ettier nor Griboyedov had any capital to float the venture, but Griboyedov was able to call in the help of his rich friends Alexander and Nikita Vsevolozhsky, whom he had first met at Moscow University. (Alexander, the elder, was the founder of the Green Lamp Society.) The Vsevolozhsky brothers had a wide variety of financial and trading interests: iron smelting in the province of Perm, river transport on the Volga, fish smoking in Astrakhan. Griboyedov put Ettier in touch with Alexander, and in the summer of 1823, when Griboyedov was on leave in Moscow, the three young men met to set up their plan for a 'trading enterprise between Russia and Persia'. Griboyedov's mother, surprisingly, was to be another partner in the enterprise. Financed by Vsevolozhsky, Ettier set out on a fact-finding mission round Persia to gather intelligence on prices, notably of arms, and potential business, armed with introductory letters to local governors and grandees from Griboyedov and Mazarovich. Mazarovich saw no conflict of interest between the roles of diplomat and entrepreneur.

By early 1825, the arrangements for the trading company were in place, but Vsevolozhsky, when the moment came, found himself unable to realise sufficient capital without damaging his existing business. The project had to be temporarily shelved, and before it could be revived the twin blows of the Decembrist catastrophe and the second Russo–Persian War of 1826 put an end to the whole idea. By the time the war was over, Griboyedov's aims had changed, and another company was proposed in place of the one he and Ettier had been unable to develop.

Griboyedov's hopes of finding a Persian Eldorado had failed, but he had learnt from the experience. Vsevolozhsky had lost money in financing what was in practice a feasibility study of trading conditions between Russia and Persia. But it had been a study with a difference, in that the Russian Government, through Griboyedov and Mazarovich, had extended protection to it. For Griboyedov, it had provided a wealth of useful information, holding out hopes of a far more ambitious project in the future. It had also taught him that private finance was unreliable. Someone else should take the risk of launching a trading venture, on a suitably colossal scale. Should this not be the Russian Government itself? His restless intelligence now turned to the problem of making his own financial interests coincide with those of the state.

Griboyedov's plans to form what would be in essence a Russian version of the East India Company belong to another chapter. In 1820 and 1821, he was still marooned in Tabriz, involved in the first stages of his unsuccessful joint venture with Ettier, and bemoaning the boredom of his exile. 'What a life!' he wrote to a friend, A.I. Rykhlevsky, on 25 June 1820, '...Perish the day when I first donned the uniform of a diplomat!'

Despite his complaints, however, there were diplomatic excitements afoot, in which he would play a leading part. The Greek movement for independence, leading to a general insurrection in 1821, had placed the Tsar in a difficult position. On the one hand, as an upholder of the status quo in Europe, he was bound to treat the Sultan as the legitimate sovereign of the Greeks. On the other, opinion in Russia demanded that fellow Orthodox Christians should be supported in their struggle against the Turks. Military common sense dictated that any distraction that would tie up the Turkish army away from the Balkans would not only help the Greek cause, but also further Russian interests of an expansionist character in northern Persia. Would Russia launch a 'just war' against the Sultan? Would Yermolov, as the Russian Commander-in-Chief become the 'saviour of Hellas'?

Tsar Alexander vacillated about these grave questions, and weakly recalled his envoy from Constantinople. Yermolov, who had accompanied him to the Congress of Laibach, was aware of his doubts, but saw no harm in fomenting trouble between the Persians and the Turks. The excuses for conflict were already there. A high-ranking Turk from Baghdad, who had been persecuted by the government there, had fled to Persia for refuge. He had been kidnapped back across the border by the Turks, together with a number of Abbas Mirza's officers, and had later been beheaded. There had also been complaints that a number of Persian (Shiite) pilgrims to Mecca had been insulted by the (Sunni) Turks, and that their women had been mistreated. Encouraged by Russian assurances that the Tsar would turn a blind eye if the Persians acquired a few extra provinces from the Turks, Abbas Mirza decided that he had sufficient pretext for launching a campaign against Turkey.[7] Crossing the frontier with an army of 40,000 men, he attacked the town of Yeni Bayazid. The Turks responded by seizing all Persian property in Turkey, and by besieging a former Turkish fortress in Erivan, which had been captured by the Persians some years previously.

The war continued for two years, pursued with only moderate enthusiasm by both sides. Abbas Mirza was chronically short of money, and his appeals to the Shah for help rebounded when the Shah responded by ordering 15,000 men, under one of his chief officers, Allah Yar Khan, to march to his assistance. 'This was a species of aid by no means to the Prince's taste,' wrote James Baillie Fraser, an English traveller returning from Bombay who witnessed the campaign, 'and he is said to have inveighed bitterly against his royal father, for making use of such a *ruse de guerre*, and choosing a moment of so great necessity to quarter upon him a large body of worthless troops, who would only plunder and impoverish the country.'

The Russians, spurred on by Yermolov, paid the British the supreme compliment of copying their policies of financial leverage. An order from the Russian Finance Minister, Guryev, countersigned by Nesselrode himself, transferred the sum of 1,000,000 silver roubles to Abbas Mirza towards the costs of the campaign. Meanwhile, Griboyedov, who despite his earlier differences with Abbas Mirza seems to have to got back on good terms with him, did his best to strengthen his resolve with assurances of Russia's sympathy, even suggesting that the Tsar himself might go to war with the Turks if their persecution of the Greeks continued. In this he was echoing Yermolov, who had written to Mazarovich in August 1821, saying that the Russian Government 'might be compelled to resort to force in order to curb the violent and bestial frenzies of the Turks, who were slaughtering innocent Christians for no reason whatsoever'.

Griboyedov's active encouragement of Abbas Mirza during the Turkish–Persian War earned him the gratitude of the Persians,[8] who awarded him the Order of the Lion and the Sun, second class. Mazarovich, who had played a more passive role throughout, received no such award. To some extent the two men's positions reflected the differing policies of the Foreign Ministry in St Petersburg and Yermolov in Tiflis. In 1828, describing the part he had played during the war, Griboyedov wrote to a friend, 'I prosecuted this very successfully, receiving a reprimand from Nesselrode, though I was fully supported by Yermolov'.

The war ended in June 1823, in what was virtually a stalemate. The frontiers remained unchanged, though there were a few minor concessions on each side. Abbas Mirza's army had been ravaged by cholera in the last stages of the campaign, but he chose to regard the operation as worthwhile. Persian honour, he told Yermolov, had been vindicated, which had been his only aim in going to war. From the Russians' point of view, the episode had been highly satisfactory, tying down the Turks in an important eastern diversion from the Greek war of independence. It had also helped to counter the influence of the British, disrupting their trade and undermining their position as Abbas Mirza's chief paymaster.

For Griboyedov, the war had been a chance to distinguish himself in Yermolov's eyes. In November 1821, he had come to Tiflis on leave to have treatment for a broken arm, and had so impressed the Commander-in-Chief by his grasp of the Persian situation that Yermolov had intervened with Nesselrode to have Griboyedov seconded from the Persian mission:[9]

1. ABOVE. Pushkin meeting Griboyedov's corpse at Gergery between Tehran and Tiflis, 1829. Lithograph, P. Borel, 1892.

2. RIGHT. Sketch of Griboyedov by Pushkin which appears on one of Pushkin's drafts for *Eugene Onegin*. R.G. Juikova, *The Portrait Drawings of Pushkin*, Petropolis, St Petersburg, 1996.

3. Lt General A.P. Yermolov (1777–1861), commander-in-chief of the Independent Caucasian Corps. Replaced in 1827 by Paskievich. 'The head of a tiger; the torso of Hercules' (Pushkin). George Dawe, after 1812. Military Gallery, the Hermitage, St Petersburg.

4. A.I. Yakubovich (1792–1845). Cornet Uhlan Guards Regiment, 1817. This painting shows him as a Decembrist prisoner in Siberia. N.A. Bestuzhev, 1831.

5. Nina Chavchavadze before marriage. Watercolour, belonging to her sister, later the reigning Princess Dadiani of Mingrelia. Artist unknown, Palace Museum, Zugdidi.

6. ABOVE. Griboyedov's mother's house on the Novinsky Boulevard, Moscow. Photo early twentieth century.

7. BELOW. Khmelita. Priscilla Roosevelt, *Life on the Russian Country Estate*, courtesy of Yale University Press, 1995, and Professor Roosevelt.

8. N.M. Karamzin (1766–1826), author of *History of the State of Russia* and the sentimental novel *Poor Lisa*. 'A great writer and ... an honest man' (Pushkin). Karamzin was an influence on Griboyedov's generation. Engraving, N. Utkin, 1819.

9. P.Ya. Chaadayev (1794–1856), the most original and perhaps the cleverest of Griboyedov's contemporaries at Moscow University. Chaadayev knew most of the Decembrists, and was a sympathiser, although not an active participant. From *The Major Works of P.Ya. Chaadayev*, tr. R.T. McNally, London, 1969.

10. RIGHT. General A.S. Kologrivov (1776–1818), commander of cavalry reserves based at Brest-Litovsk. He commanded the 49th Jaegers during the campaigns of 1812, including Borodino and Malo-Yaroslavets. Griboyedov acted as his adjutant.

11. ABOVE. S.N. Beguichov (1785–1859), adjutant to Kologrivov in Brest-Litovsk and Griboyedov's closest friend after 1813. After the war, he joined the Chevalier Guards, and was later cleared of Decembrist involvement.

12. RIGHT. A.V.I. Istomina (1799–1848), ballerina and mistress of Sheremet'yev. Gouache on bone, Winterhalder. Courtesy of Pushkin Museum, Moscow.

13. LEFT. Prince A.A. Shakhovskoy (1777–1846), playwright and theatre director, poet, theatrical tutor to Griboyedov, and host of 'garret' evenings. Sketch by Pushkin, 1821, showing him with donkey ears. R.G. Juikova, *The Portrait Drawings of Pushkin*, Petropolis, St Petersburg, 1996.

14. ABOVE. P.A. Karatygin (1805–79), actor and close friend of Griboyedov in Shakhovskoy's circle. He was an accomplished artist, and painted the miniature of Griboyedov that was later used by I.N. Kramskoi as the basis for his painting. Courtesy of Pushkin Museum, Moscow.

15. LEFT. V.A. Karatygin (1802–53), tragic actor and also a close friend of Griboyedov in Shakhovskoy's circle.

16. TOP LEFT. F.F. Kokoshkin (1773–1838), Moscow actor who played in Griboyedov's *Les Fausses Infidelités*. From 1823, he was Shakhovskoy's opposite number in Moscow, responsible for all the theatres. Watercolour caricature, Dmitrovsky Provincial Museum. *Portraits of Pushkin's Contemporaries*, Representative Art, Moscow, 1975.

17. TOP RIGHT. P.A. Katenin (1792–1853), literary critic, playwright and early Decembrist, co-author with Griboyedov of the play *The Student* in 1817. An assiduous frequenter of Shakhovskoy's 'garret'. Griboyedov defended his translation of Bürger's 'Leonore' in *Son of the Fatherland*.

18. ABOVE. A.A. Zhandr (1789–1873), close friend of and theatrical collaborator with Griboyedov, especially on their joint vaudeville *The Trial Interlude*. Photograph, Piksanov Collection, Pushkin House.

19. RIGHT. W. Küchelbecker (1797–1846). Poet and close friend of Griboyedov, particularly in Tiflis during work on *Woe from Wit*. Later exiled to Siberia as a Decembrist. Caricature, P.L. Yakovlev, 1820.

20. LEFT. Count Nesselrode (1780–1862), Foreign Minister during Griboyedov's life as a diplomat. Caricature, N. Boranov, courtesy of Pushkin Museum, Moscow.

21. BELOW. K.K. Rodofinikin (1760–1838), under secretary in charge of Asiatic Affairs (Griboyedov's superior). Caricature, P.J. Tchelitshchev, 1820s. Courtesy of A.V. Kornilova.

'Knowing as I do his splendid capabilities, and wishing to make use of his knowledge of the Persian language, I have the honour to request that he should be transferred to me as a secretary for my diplomatic chancery'.[10] From Tiflis, Griboyedov continued to carry out Yermolov's hawkish policies, keeping in close touch with Abbas Mirza, the Georgian Prince Sevarsamidze, the Russians' liaison officer with the Persian army, and provincial governors like the Sardar of Erivan.

Mazarovich had been happy to let Griboyedov go to Tiflis, seeing the advantages of having a spokesman who could report directly to Yermolov. In fact, far from being a loyal supporter, Griboyedov may well have been part of a whispering campaign against him for failing to uphold Russian dignity and for being too subservient to Abbas Mirza. It was headed by the belligerent Muravyov-Karsky (the witness at Griboyedov's duel with Yakubovich), who had been specially indignant at a story that Mazarovich had kissed Abbas Mirza's hand in gratitude for his decision to go to war. 'Good God!' he exclaimed. 'What an act worthy of a foreigner, a hireling in our service!' As Muravyov could not have been present at this interview, it is likely that Griboyedov was its source. If so, it was a shabby ending to Griboyedov's relationship with a kindly and tolerant superior who had not only overlooked his indiscretions, but given him the opportunity to shine in his first diplomatic post.

Griboyedov's two years in Persia, 'this gloomy kingdom where one learns nothing and worse still, loses the very memory of what one knew',[11] had done much to further his career. He had arrived in Georgia under a serious cloud because of his role in the Sheremet'yev duel, and had promptly engaged in another. Yermolov had ignored this officially criminal act, but it had needed hard work to live down the two duels. In Tabriz, as Mazarovich's second-in-command, he had been able to deal directly with the Crown Prince and had felt the intoxication of power politics in tempting him into the war. The affair of the deserters had perhaps caused him moral suffering, but had done him good in his superiors' eyes. Few diplomats at such a young age had enjoyed so much responsibility, or achieved their objectives so successfully. His recall to Yermolov's staff was a sign that he had worked his passage back, as it were, and that the follies of the past were forgotten.

On a deeper level, the years of exile had been invaluable too. Drawing up the balance sheet in his notes on Griboyedov (as taken down by D.A. Smirnov), Beguichov commented on the benefits of his enforced isolation.[12] His character had been tested and strengthened by the challenges he had encountered, and his long periods of leisure had given him the opportunity to study deeply, in particular to add to his already dazzling array of languages. He had learnt Persian thoroughly, and studied Persian poetry, even attempting some Persian verses of his own, and had also begun to learn Arabic, Sanskrit and Turkish. Above all, it was in Persia that *Woe from Wit* began to take shape.[13]

According to Beguichov, Griboyedov first conceived the plot of the play in St Petersburg in about 1816. 'But I know,' he wrote, 'that he changed many scenes in Persia and Georgia, excluding for instance the provision of a wife for Famusov, a grande dame with a sentimental manner (false sentimentality was very much the fashion amongst Moscow ladies of the time).' There is no such character in any existing manuscript of the play, so Beguichov must have seen a draft which has now been lost.

Another friend who heard some early extracts from the play was the Georgian Cornet Prince Bebutov of the Narva Dragoons. A sympathetic, liberal-minded figure who had abolished the instruments of corporal punishment in his squadron, he was a friend of Griboyedov's from his time on Kologrivov's staff in Brest-Litovsk. In 1819, on his way home to Georgia, he met Griboyedov, who had just left Yermolov in Grozny, where Bebutov's brother was stationed. Griboyedov was able to give him news about him, and the two young men rode from Mozdok to Tiflis together, pausing to call on Bebutov's parents; since Bebutov's father could not speak Russian, he and Griboyedov communicated 'quite freely' in Persian. Bebutov claimed that Griboyedov read him his verses during their journey, including some from *Woe from Wit*, which was then only in a preliminary stage.[14]

Beguichov and Bebutov provide the only evidence about the early sketches of the play, but it was in Persia that Griboyedov's ideas for it took final shape. He was inspired, so it is said, by a prophetic dream. There are two versions of what happened. Bulgarin, in his *Memoir of our Unforgettable Friend, A.S. Griboyedov*, describes how Griboyedov, alone one evening, was thinking sadly of the theatre and his absent family and friends, and fell asleep in a kiosk in his garden. He dreamed that he was once more back among the people he loved best, and that he was describing to them a comedy that he was going to write, and even reading extracts from it to them. On waking he seized a pencil and wrote down some scenes from the first act, and the concept of the whole play.[15]

Griboyedov's own version of the story, in a letter to an unknown prince (probably Shakhovskoy) dated 20 November 1820, is longer and more detailed. He dreamed, he wrote, that he was entering a house where he had never been before, where a grand party was in full swing. The host and hostess received him at the door. Going through a number of brilliantly lit rooms, he saw a number of familiar faces, including that of his uncle. In the last room, the guests were conversing and dining.

You [Shakhovskoy] were sitting in a corner leaning towards someone and whispering; your lady was next to you. A delightful feeling overcame me. Somebody came towards me and said, 'Is that you Alexander Sergeyevich? How you have changed!' It was impossible to recognise him. You came with me into a long adjoining gallery and put your head so close to my cheek that I blushed. You bent over to touch my face... and asked me questions for a long time. 'Was I writing anything?' You forced out of me a confession that I had no inspiration and no wit, and no desire to write. I was avoiding the challenge; my heart was not in it. You bewailed this state of things: 'Make me a promise that you will write?'

'What would you like?'

'You know yourself. When will it be ready?'

'Within a year. I solemnly promise.'

At this moment a small person, whom short-sightedly I had not noticed, said very distinctly, 'Idleness destroys talent.' You said, 'Look who is here'. I looked round and who was it? His head jerked up and he threw himself round my neck with a cry, hugging me warmly. It was Katenin. I then woke up and tried to forget such a pleasing dream. I went out to refresh myself; what a splendid night! Nowhere do the stars shine so brightly as in this dreary Persia. As the hour was just after midnight the muezzin began to chant the dawn prayer from the nearest minaret. All the other mosques picked up the chant; a cool night breeze blew and vividly recalling my promise I sat down to write. What was given in a dream must be achieved in the cold light of day.

It would be nearly four years, not one, before the promise in the dream was fulfilled. But the commitment had been made. By the time that Griboyedov left Tabriz, he had already begun a new draft of the play.

X I

Return to Tiflis

On returning to Tiflis,[1] Griboyedov found his intellectual solitude lightened by the presence of a St Petersburg friend and colleague, Wilhelm
Küchelbecker. Küchelbecker (nicknamed Kukliya), who had joined the
Foreign Ministry on the same day as Griboyedov, and was now attached
to Yermolov's staff, belonged to the same literary world as Griboyedov
and his friends; his name appears in almost all the literary memoirs of
the time. A classmate and close friend of Pushkin's, he had studied at
the Lycée at Tsarskoye Selo, where he had imbibed the free thinking of
the period. His radical views had been strengthened when in 1820 he
went abroad as secretary to A.L. Naryshkin, and witnessed the turbulent
liberalism of Italy in Naples and Sicily, and, from Nice, the revolution
in Piedmont. These experiences, together with the growing call for the
liberation of Greece, led him inevitably to consider the state of Russia.

In November 1820, he met Goethe in Weimar; they had several
meetings devoted to poetry and its state in Russia. In Paris, still crusading
for Russian literature, he met Benjamin Constant, who arranged for him
to lecture at the Athenée Royale des Arts. His lectures, addressed to high-
minded progressives in France on behalf of their Russian counterparts,
struck such a radical note that the French police forbade them and the
Russian embassy took alarm. He returned to Russia in semi-disgrace,
and to get him away from St Petersburg was sent to Tiflis as a member
of Yermolov's staff.

Küchelbecker stayed in Tiflis only a few months before being dismissed
by Yermolov as the result of a foolish and unnecessary duel.[2] But before

their intimacy was broken off, he and Griboyedov had ample time to establish a lifelong friendship. Küchelbecker was twenty-three, two years younger than Griboyedov, ungainly and myopic, with a drooping moustache and heavy German accent – his father, a Saxon noblemen, had been in the service of Tsar Paul and been rewarded with a property in Estonia. Already a rising literary figure, Küchelbecker hero-worshipped Griboyedov, addressing several perfervid poems to him. Two typical stanzas give their tone:

> Ah, but you…you will soar above the singing of the crowd!
> The hand of fate has accorded you, Troubadour,
> A lively spirit, the flame of feeling,
> A sparkling gaiety, the quietude of love,
> The golden mysteries of art
> And blood that leaps within your veins!

> Oh! when I descend to the dim shores of Lethe
> A mute and nameless shade,
> Then let my image, illumined by your soul,
> Glimpse the day one final time!
> Obedient to your call I shall fly from the grave,
> Unfold my pinioned wings,
> Rise to the gilded sun –
> And ardently plunge into the eternal dawn!

Recalling their friendship later, Küchelbecker wrote how Griboyedov had opened his eyes to Shakespeare (who, he insisted, should only be read in the original); how he detested ridicule or sarcasm about the beliefs of other races, while remaining devoted to his own deep Orthodox faith; how he had inspired him with love for the beauties of the Slavonic bible: 'I read today the first thirty chapters of the prophet Isaiah,' he wrote in 1832:

> the fiery strength of his writing is unequalled by any other prophet. The first five chapters are so inspired they amount to an ode, and were loved as such by my dear departed Griboyedov. He read them to me in Tiflis in 1821, and literally forced me to read them too, which is how I came to know them.[3]

For Griboyedov, after the intellectual starvation of Tabriz, it was a joy to find a friend who could share his interests and ideals. At last he had a committed listener, someone from his own literary circle, on whom he could test out his verses. He gained inspiration from his audience. According to Küchelbecker, 'Griboyedov wrote *Woe from Wit* almost before my eyes; at the very least he read each separate scene directly after its composition'. However, he may not have heard the play in its entirety, at least not in its final version. Beguichov claims that only the first two acts were completed when Griboyedov left Georgia, and that the rest was written in the garden of his country house. What probably happened was that, having been plunged back into the realities of Moscow society, particularly as portrayed in the climactic ballroom scene, Griboyedov rewrote the final acts whilst staying with Beguichov.

In May 1821, Küchelbecker's ill-judged duel brought his creative association with Griboyedov to an end. Karsky, in his memoirs, suggests that Griboyedov had a hand in furthering the duel; certainly he acted as a second to his friend. The circumstances are obscure, but it seems that Küchelbecker thought he been insulted by a certain Nikolai Nikolayevich Pokhvisnyev, a nephew of Yermolov's, also on his staff. When Pokhvisnyev refused to accept his challenge, Küchelbecker had slapped him twice on the face, making a duel inevitable. The duel was fortunately inconclusive, with neither side being hurt, but Yermolov, who had only accepted Küchelbecker on sufferance, used the excuse to dismiss him from his staff and send him to rusticate on his sister's estate at Zakup in central Russia.

Griboyedov may well have supported Küchelbecker in what he thought to be a matter of honour, but he was heartbroken to see his friend depart. Writing to him a few months later, he complained that in Küchelbecker's absence he could only communicate his poetic inspirations to the walls. 'From time to time I read them verses by myself or others; but to people I read nothing; there is no-one.'[4] To Küchelbecker's sister, Madame Glinka, he wrote touchingly of the perfect knowledge that his friend had of his character, recalling his trusting, open-hearted nature and deploring the bad luck and misunderstandings which had dogged him. He could not foresee how mild these would seem when, in the wake of the Decembrist rising, Küchelbecker, a tragic victim of his liberal ideals, was led off in chains to spend the last 20 years of his life in imprisonment and exile.

The Decembrist catastrophe lay three years ahead, but already the movement to which the rising gave its name was taking shape. In Europe, liberal passions were erupting with armed uprisings in Naples, Piedmont, Spain and Greece. In Russia, the ferocious suppression of a so-called mutiny in the Semyonovsky Guards – whose men had risen in protest against a sadistic senior officer and the continuing horrors of the agricultural colonies, with their brutal military regimes – had heightened disillusion in the army. In 1821, the Union of Welfare (descended from the smaller Union of Salvation) gave way to two conspiratorial societies, the Northern Society in St Petersburg and the Southern Society in Tulchin, the headquarters of the Russian army in the Ukraine. Their aims were not identical. The Northern Society was in favour of a constitutional monarchy, the Southern Society committed to establishing a republic, if necessary by assassinating the Tsar. But both were united in condemning serfdom and passionately opposed to the repressive policies of the Tsar and his sinister henchman Arakcheyev; both too were encouraged by events in Europe.

It was a matter of debate whether there was a third conspiratorial society in the Caucasus – the investigative commission after the uprising came to the conclusion there was none. But there were certainly a number of future Decembrists in Tiflis, among them Yakubovich, Griboyedov's old opponent, a brooding dissident figure on the fringes of Yermolov's court whose reputation as a daredevil frondeur and duellist made him a role model for the whole Caucasian corps. Yermolov himself had no taste for radical politics, though he loathed Arakcheyev and had little respect for the German bureaucrats who dominated the court and civil service. Outspoken and independent-minded, he did not discourage independent thinking in those around him, and two of his senior adjutants, P.Kh. Grabbe and M.A. Fonvizin, were future Decembrists.

Griboyedov, as will be seen, was officially cleared of any complicity in the Decembrist plot. On the question of abolishing serfdom, a key issue for both the Northern and Southern Societies, he had already shown himself a broken reed. But he knew very well what was going on in Tiflis and later in St Petersburg, and was bound by links of sympathy and friendship to many of its leading members. Debarred by poverty and necessity from the idealism of his friends, he would survive the débâcle by the skin of his teeth.

Meanwhile, for the rest of 1822 and early 1823 he was combining work on his play with his duties as Yermolov's acting head of chancery; he had recently been promoted to the rank of 'collegiate assessor', eighth class (equivalent to a major in the army), in line with his new role. The Commander-in-Chief had departed on a punitive mission to Kabarda, where he wasted all the province 'till no more than 10,000 remained', leaving Griboyedov behind in Tiflis to continue to encourage Abbas Mirza in his war against the Turks, and to plot the trading venture which he hoped would solve his ever present money problems.

The departure of Küchelbecker had left a spiritual vacuum, but he found some consolation in widening his acquaintance among the Georgian aristocracy: the Orbeliani brothers, whose mother had been the daughter of Irakli III, the last Georgian king, and whose town house adjoined his rented quarters in Exarch Square; the soldier-poet Prince Alexander Chavchavadze, whose rambling country estate at Tsinondali was the focus of many pleasant riding expeditions; Solomon Dadashvili, editor of the *Tiflis News*, a graduate of St Petersburg University who taught logic and philosophy at the Tiflis Gymnasium.

Ever since coming to Tiflis, Yermolov had done his best to win the leading Georgian families to him, dealing out ranks and orders to the sons of the nobility who joined the Russian army, presiding genially at the Club, and encouraging local grandees to beautify the town, in the certainty that Tiflis was no longer in danger from marauding Turks or Persians. Not all the aristocracy were so easily won. Historians tracing the ramifications of the Decembrist movement in Griboyedov's life have established the existence of a major conspiracy brewing in Georgian society in the 1820s. It had no links with the St Petersburg or Moscow societies. It would have come to a head in 1832 – three years after Griboyedov's death – but was unmasked beforehand, leading to 145 arrests. Its adherents were aristocratic nationalists seeking independence from Russia, but its aims were divided between those wishing to regain their feudal privileges by restoring the Bagration monarchy and those of liberal, or Decembrist, sympathies, whose views mirrored those of their contemporaries in St Petersburg. Griboyedov's friends, including Chavchavadze, belonged to this second group.

An interesting visitor to Tiflis, in the summer of 1822, was a Scottish doctor, Charles Lyall. Born in Edinburgh, he had been unsuccessful in his profession there, and according to the *Dictionary of National Biography*, 'took the low road to find a career in Russia…where he passed some of the best years of his life'. As well as being doctor to a number of distinguished Russian families he was an indefatigable traveller, whose *Travels in Russia, the Crimea, the Caucasus and Georgia* would be published three years later. From Tiflis, he planned to visit the Georgian province of Kakhetia. Since all foreigners, especially when British and travelling in sensitive areas, were regarded as potential spies, Griboyedov was tactfully assigned to travel with him as an unofficial guide.[5] Lyall's description of their journey gives an enchanting picture of the Georgian countryside, with its wooded hills and vineyards rising to the cloud-capped backdrop of the great Caucasian mountain chain. Their party, he wrote, consisted of Griboyedov (whose name, he explained in a footnote, derived from the Russian words *grib*, or mushroom, and *yest*, to eat, thus 'mushroom-eater'), various Russian officers, a native prince as interpreter, and an armed cavalcade of Cossacks and Georgians. They travelled for a week, spending the night at military stations or country estates on the way, where they indulged in 'liberal potations' of the excellent Kakhetian wine, which was stored in stone jars buried deep in the earth, and which they drank from silver ladles, or silver-mounted drinking horns. The Georgian aristocracy, noted Lyall, were much given to display, spending lavishly on horses, clothes and entertainment, while their houses were often no better than second-class farms. Most had adapted to wearing European dress, though their wives for the most part led a secluded, 'quasi-Asiatic' existence, and did not mix with visitors.

Griboyedov's travel notes make no mention of the expedition, but a poem retrieved from his notebooks by D.A. Smirnov after his death evokes the memory of the river Alazan, as it winds through the vineyards of Kakhetia:

> There where the Alazan meanders,
> And moist breezes blow coolly over the land,
> Where the purple grape is gathered in the vineyards...
> It's a country which has never known the plough,
> Where the bright flowers are luxuriant,
> And the gardener offers golden tinted fruit...[6]

But the poet's mood is not in tune with his idyllic surroundings. 'Oh wanderer,' it asks, 'do you know love?...Do you know how terrifying dreams can be under feverish, burning skies? What is fate? Separation and death.' We have no clues to the emotional context of the poem – perhaps it was triggered by the departure of Küchelbecker, Griboyedov's only real confidant in Georgia. But its inspiration clearly comes from his travels in Kakhetia, either with Lyall, or some other time that summer. As his biographer Piksanov writes, the poem 'belongs entirely to the time of Griboyedov's residence in Georgia...it is linked so obviously to its nature and his impressions of it, that the verses cannot be attributed to any date later than 1822'.

The months in Tiflis passed slowly. Writing to Küchelbecker in January 1823,[7] Griboyedov confessed that he was suffering from an 'inexplicable gloom and melancholy', which no distractions could alleviate. The death from cholera of his favourite servant, Amlikh, who had been with him for 15 years, was a further cause for depression. A friend who had arrived from Persia, a certain Shcherbatov, was another victim of the disease; he died a few hours after Griboyedov had left his bedside. Griboyedov forecast grimly that there would be an epidemic by the spring. The one bright spot on the horizon was the fact that Yermolov had promised him four months leave in March. Griboyedov told Küchelbecker to contact him at his mother's house in Novinsky Boulevard in Moscow as soon as he arrived.

XII

Theatrical Campaigns, Moscow

Griboyedov's leave would last nearly two years – a commentary perhaps on the fact that Yermolov, though he liked him personally, no longer found his services essential. He arrived in Moscow at the end of March 1823. Almost his first engagement there was as best man to his old friend Beguichov, who was marrying an heiress, Alexandra Baryshnykova. The wedding took place in April, with Griboyedov in a giddy and irresponsible mood. He whispered to Beguichov during the sermon, and could not help laughing out loud as he held the wedding crown over him. Suddenly his face changed. 'His hands shook,' wrote Beguichov. 'I saw he was as white as a sheet and his eyes were filled with tears. After the service, I asked him what had happened. "Such foolishness," he said, "I imagined you were being buried and hymned at a funeral service."'[1]

'I did not see too much of him afterwards,' wrote Beguichov, 'as he was frequenting all Moscow's balls, picnics and assemblies and was engulfed in a social whirl. When I commented on his changed way of life, he replied, "Have no fears, I am not wasting my time".'

As well as renewing his acquaintance with Moscow society, whose follies and prejudices would feature so vividly in *Woe from Wit*, Griboyedov was able to catch up on what had been happening in literature during his absence.[2] To some extent he had been able to follow this through the literary journals he received in Tiflis, and had been brought up-to-date with wider European trends through his conversations with Küchelbecker. In poetry, the most important development was the

88

growing primacy of Pushkin over older poets such as Zhukovsky. Pushkin's narrative poem 'Ruslan and Lyudmila', published in 1820, with its use of popular ballads, folk songs and fairy tales, had given a new impulse to Russian literature. The same desire to return to national roots was evidenced by the poet and historian Nicholas Karamzin. The first eight volumes of his *History of the Russian State* had been published in 1818, the next in 1821; two more would appear in 1824. His 'rediscovery' of Russian history would have an enormous influence on his contemporaries, inspiring both playwrights and historical novelists, most importantly Pushkin in his *Boris Godunov*. For Griboyedov, these trends were nothing new. He had preached their merits six years before, in his essay on Katenin's 'Leonore', with its insistence that inspiration should be sought in the everyday rhythms of Russian life and speech, and had put his theories into practice in his collaborations for the theatre with Katenin and Shakhovskoy.

Parallel to this search for national identity – *narodnost* as it was called – was the contemporary craze for Byronism, both as a literary fashion and a social pose. Zhukovsky's translation of 'The Prisoner of Chillon' had had an enormous effect when it was published in 1821. Pushkin's 'Prisoner of the Caucasus', published the same year, had echoed the Byronic note. For Griboyedov, Pushkin's poem covered well-known ground, both in its setting and its theme: the capture of a Russian soldier by Caucasian tribesmen, his imprisonment in a remote mountain hideaway, and his liberation by a local girl, who dies in saving him. It is interesting in this context to read the critical comments of Karamzin's brother-in-law, Prince P.A. Vyazemsky, on Pushkin's apparent admiration for Russian colonial policies in the Caucasus.[3] 'What sort of heroes are Kotlyarevsky [a general under Tsitsiyanov] and Yermolov?' he wrote in a letter to A.I. Turgeniev in September 1822.

> What is so good about the fact that he
> Destroyed and annihilated the tribes
> Like a black plague?

> The blood freezes in one's veins and one's hair stands on end at this kind of boasting. If we educated the tribes, then there would be something to celebrate. Poetry is not the ally of executioners; politically they may be necessary and then it's for the court of history to judge whether they can be justified or not, but a poet's hymns should never glorify slaughter.

A close friend of Pushkin's, Vyazemsky would also become a friend and literary collaborator of Griboyedov's. His splendid estate, Ostafyievo, on the outskirts of the city, boasting a library of 22,000 volumes (today the core of the old Lenin library), was one of the centres of Moscow's intellectual life. A moderate liberal who had advocated the abolition of serfdom, he was already under police surveillance, but was protected by his wealth and a position at court from further annoyance. It was the first time since he had fallen under the spell of Yermolov that Griboyedov was able to listen to home truths about his idol from someone he respected as an intellectual equal and to whom he could speak freely. In the small world of Yermolov's court in Tiflis, any criticisms of his 'pacifying' policies would have been unthinkable.

After two or three months in Moscow, presumably staying with his mother, Griboyedov went to spend the summer with Beguichov and his new wife at their country estate at Yefremovskoye, in the province of Tulsk. It was here, according to Beguichov, that the last acts of *Woe from Wit* were written in the summerhouse in their garden:

> He would rise with the sun, appearing only for dinner and then not staying long, re-appearing later for evening tea to read us the scenes which he had just written, a moment which we always awaited eagerly. He wanted me to have the manuscript as a souvenir, but only had the patience to tidy up two acts, leaving the rest to the mercies of a copyist. In September [1823] we all returned to Moscow.[4]

Griboyedov spent the winter of 1823–4 at Beguichov's house in Moscow. Perhaps he found life with his mother, as usual harassed by financial worries and unsympathetic to his literary aims, oppressive; perhaps he simply wished to be independent. Beguichov was well-off and deeply admiring of his friend, who enlivened their long winter evenings with reminiscences of his travels. 'He was so well informed and erudite', wrote Beguichov, 'so lively and fascinating about everything. I heard all his plans. He would often describe the Persian court, with its strange manners and customs and elegant public ceremonies. Yermolov was another inexhaustible topic.'[5]

One of the joys for Griboyedov on returning to Moscow was the chance to take up the piano once again. Fortunately, the injury to his little finger in his duel with Yakubovich had not permanently impaired his playing. Beguichov's fourteen-year-old niece, Lisa Sokovnina, who was staying in the house at the time, described his ravishing improvisations on the grand piano in the evenings. He dedicated one of his two waltzes to her, and allowed her the free run of his study while he was playing, a privilege, she wrote, of which she took maximum advantage.

Generous and hospitable – he was famous for keeping a good table – Beguichov kept open house for a wide circle of friends. They included Küchelbecker,[6] now returned from temporary banishment on his sister's estate, and busy promoting a literary anthology, *Mnemosina*; the composer Verstovsky, famous for his song 'The Black Shawl', which he would sing with great feeling after dinner, accompanied by Griboyedov on the piano; the dashing poet and cavalry General Denis Davydov, a cousin of Yermolov's, already known to Griboyedov; the young Prince Vladimir Fyodorovich Odoyevsky, who had first come to Griboyedov's attention through a series of articles in the *Herald of Europe* the previous year, and whose ideas on German philosophy, in particular the romantic idealism of Schelling, were of special interest to him. (Griboyedov would take a copy of Schelling's works on his last journey to Tehran.)

Throughout his stay with Beguichov in Moscow, Griboyedov was putting the finishing touches to his play. But he was also involved in a number of other literary activities. In January 1824, his poem 'David' was published side-by-side with works by Pushkin and Odoyevsky in Küchelbecker's *Mnemosina*. Lisa Sokovnina would recall how Griboyedov would read the Psalms with her, in order to show her their poetic beauties; 'David', deliberately archaic in its language, reflected his continuing preoccupation with the Bible as a source of inspiration.

Another literary project was a pageant to celebrate the opening of the new Bolohoi Theatre, an imposing classical building on the site of the old Imperial Theatre on Petrovsky Square. Its theme was the genius of Russia arising from the ashes of the past, and the accompanying triumph of the muses. Griboyedov took as his hero the towering figure of Mikhail Lomonosov, son of a poor fisherman, born in the early eighteenth century, and generally regarded as the father of modern Russian literature and science. Griboyedov's verses have been lost, but Beguichov kept a paraphrase:[7]

> The youthful fisherman, Lomonosov, sleeping by the shore of the Arctic Ocean, is seduced by a marvellous dream. At first he sees miraculous beings who arouse him, eventually, to show him the complete company of Parnassus in all its splendour. Dazzled and wonder-struck, he awakes in a daze; he cannot shake off the memory of his vision. It follows him across the seas to deserted islands where, with other fishermen, he pursues a humdrum working life. But his soul has been woken to a thirst for the unimaginable, and a longing for the knowledge of higher truths. He flees the paternal home...

Griboyedov did not complete the pageant, though he gave readings from it to his friends. But either his heart was not in it or the management refused it, for the commission was given to an older writer, M.A. Dmitriyev, and the opening celebrations, including a full-scale ballet and singing by the celebrated Italian soprano Catalani, took place without him. It must have been a wounding episode, but the opening of the new theatre, under its musical director Verstovsky, offered other exciting opportunities, and he was soon embarked on a collaboration with Vyazemsky on the libretto for a vaudeville operetta by Verstovsky, *Who is the Brother? Who is the Sister?*[8]

Griboyedov was already friendly with Verstovsky, whom he had known as a very young man in the days of Shakhovskoy's garret in St Petersburg. Now one of the most popular composers of the day, Verstovsky was fully committed to the reaction against imported French theatre, and the mood of national renewal following 1812. For this reason, Moscow, with its tradition of popular festivals and carnivals, appealed to him, and he had responded to an invitation to take over the musical direction of the new Bolshoi Theatre, where for many years he contributed an annual vaudeville, along with cantatas, ballads and incidental music of all kinds.

The idea of writing the libretto for Verstovsky's operetta had been Vyazemsky's. That such a senior figure in Moscow's social and intellectual life should be involved in so frivolous an undertaking is best explained by his passion for the theatre. In his memoirs he describes how the Bolshoi's actor-manager Kokoshkin had asked him to write 'something' for the benefit of the actress Lvova Sinyetskaya. Vyazemsky had modestly denied having any special theatrical gifts, but he was prepared to have a try at writing the lyrics for the vaudeville, the plot of which could be concocted by another. 'Having met Griboyedov at this time,' he wrote, 'I proposed that we should collaborate over Kokoshkin's request. He eagerly agreed. He would write everything in prose, settle the order of the scenes, and create the dialogues. I would write all the pieces to be sung in verse.'

Griboyedov began the project enthusiastically. In December 1823, we find him writing to Verstovsky, 'I do not doubt the beauty of your music and congratulate myself prematurely upon it'; another note describes how Verstovsky's music had kept him at home with his piano 'in company with a bottle of champagne'.[9]

The theme of the operetta had come from Vyazemsky, who had recently returned from Warsaw, and suggested giving it a Polish setting and a Polish heroine; for Verstovsky it would be a chance to introduce the rhythms of dances like the mazurka and the polonaise into the score.

In view of the joint talents involved, it may be worth summarising the plot. The action takes place in an isolated post-house in a small village, somewhere between St Petersburg and Moscow. A young Hussar officer, Roslavyev, has recently married a Polish beauty, Julia. Meanwhile, his elder brother, who hates womankind, is hurrying through there on his way to St Petersburg to prevent the marriage. Julia disguises herself as a young Hussar, supposedly the brother of Julia herself, while Roslavyev poses as a disagreeable old invalid, whom Julia is trying to marry. After various complications, in which a crafty innkeeper, supported by his two young daughters, plays a leading part, Julia discloses her deceit, the elder brother is won round and all ends happily.

It was a light-hearted piece, 'no better and no worse than other vaudevilles,' wrote Vyazemsky, but though all went well at rehearsals, the first night was a flop. Kokoshkin, whom Griboyedov had already accused of torturing his verses in 1819 when *Les Fausses Infidelités* was performed in Moscow, seems to have been chiefly responsible. 'He suddenly changed everything,' wrote Vyazemsky, 'what had been lively, cheerful and attractive was slowed down and so to speak congealed by the sluggish performances of the actors, many of whom appeared in it unwillingly.' A further disadvantage was the average Russian's prejudice against the Poles, habitually portrayed as arrogant or ridiculous on stage; the first night audience, it seemed, was not disposed to accept the virtues of a Polish heroine.

Griboyedov seems to have been prepared for a hostile reception. 'On the opening night,' wrote Vyazemsky,

> Griboyedov dined with me and some friends. One of these was Denis Davydov. 'My dear fellow,' he said to Griboyedov, 'you must admit that your heart is missing a few beats in anticipation of the performance.' 'It is beating so steadily,' Griboyedov answered in a cool detached way, 'that I may skip the performance completely and not go to the theatre at all.' We set off without him. At the end a few voices clamoured from the parterre for the author. I sat tight and did not step forward. One of the actors appeared on stage and explained that there were two authors, one of whom was absent from the theatre.[10]

The operetta had only four performances in Moscow and two in St Petersburg. Vyazemsky ascribed its failure to backstage intrigues. The young playwright Alexander Pisarev, the leading writer of vaudevilles at the time, was furiously jealous of any competition, while Zagoskin, the theatre's leading playwright, had not forgotten Griboyedov's satire of him in *The Puppet Theatre*. Both were on the best of terms with Kokoshkin, which may have explained the sluggish performance, and both attacked it in the press. Pisarev fired the opening shot in what became known as the 'War of Epigrams', in an article criticising both the authors in the *Herald of Europe*. Griboyedov and Vyazemsky responded in the *Moscow Telegraph*. Matters quickly became personal, Pisarev characterising Vyazemsky as Mephistopheles and Griboyedov as Gribus, 'who hides his snake-like stare behind his spectacles'.[11] Dmitriyev, Griboyedov's successful rival in the pageant episode, joined in; Griboyedov and Vyazemsky counter-attacked with verses dismissing him and Pisarev as liars and paid hacks of the *Herald*. In the end, more than 30 epigrams were exchanged, Pisarev reserving his fiercest sallies for Griboyedov:

> There is no call to praise him,
> Since he is his own panegyrist.

His rendering of David
Is more frightful than Goliath...[12]

Vyazemsky, thanks to his wealth and great position, could afford to ignore the sniping of Pisarev's clique. Griboyedov was more exposed. The attacks on his contribution to the operetta were a cover for more serious literary jealousies. Since his return from Persia, he had been regarded as something of a celebrity, aureoled in his fame as a diplomat, a fascinating conversationalist, a many gifted writer and musician. Above all, he was becoming known as the author of a brilliant new play, already famous while still in manuscript. At first known only to a chosen few, the news of it got out, apparently, when the musical amateur, Count Vyel'gorsky, whilst leafing through the scores on his sister's piano, came on some pages of the play in Griboyedov's hand. 'Griboyedov,' noted Beguichov, 'was extremely careless and insouciant, writing wherever the fancy took him, and never making any effort to arrange his papers.'[13] Griboyedov's sister tried to evade his enquiries by dismissing them as 'Alexander's follies', but the count was not to be put off, and carried them off despite her. The 'follies', in fact, were part of *Woe from Wit*, and before long extracts from the new play were beginning to circulate round Moscow. Griboyedov, meanwhile, began to give readings from it amongst his friends, while at the same time continuing to make changes to the text.

XIII

Woe from Wit

To reach a wider public it was necessary that the play should pass the censors, and in order to ease its way with the authorities involved, Griboyedov decided to take it to St Petersburg himself. Yermolov had obligingly extended his leave, even agreeing to a request that he should be allowed to travel abroad on grounds of ill health. His first hope was that, after a brief stay in the capital to launch his play, he would travel to France and Italy, returning to Tiflis via Constantinople and the Black Sea coast of Georgia. But he had reckoned without the censors, whose delays and obstructions would keep him in St Petersburg for nearly a year.

He arrived there in June,[1] having been delayed by heavy snowdrifts on the way, and made his first headquarters in Demuth's Hotel. Situated on the corner of the Nevsky Prospekt and the Moika Canal, Demuth's was one of the best-known hotels of the day, much frequented by literary figures,[2] and remarkably good value. Griboyedov, as usual, was in financial difficulties; he had borrowed from Beguichov, and had pawned his Persian Order of the Lion and the Sun in order to raise money. But he was received in St Petersburg as a hero, and almost immediately began to publicise his play. The censors could delay publication, but they could not prevent him from showing the manuscript around, or 'scattering its sparks', as he expressed it, in private readings to his friends. In this way, the play became known to most of literary and theatrical St Petersburg.[3] Writing to Beguichov in July, Griboyedov described how he had already given 12 readings to audiences including Krylov, Khmel'nitsky, Shakhovskoy, the actor Karatygin and the publishers

Grech and Bulgarin: 'Each caused a sensation, exaltation, curiosity, wonder and delight – there is no end to it!'

Amongst the early enthusiasts for *Woe from Wit* was a young Guards officer, Alexander Bestuzhev[4] (best known under his pen-name Marlinsky as one of the most popular novelists of the 1830s, a kind of Russian Walter Scott). Then in his early twenties, he had long avoided meeting Griboyedov because of his role in the Sheremet'yev duel – whether this was due to stories spread by Yakubovich that, as Zavadovsky's second, he had prevented him from seeking a reconciliation with Sheremet'yev is impossible to tell. But he had begun to change his views when they met by chance at the bedside of a sick friend, where Griboyedov's genuine sympathy for the invalid had been apparent, and had swung round completely when Bulgarin allowed him to read some extracts from the play. He devoured them eagerly, warming to the hero Chatsky's invective, and deciding there and then that 'whoever had penned these verses was a noble and honourable being'. Taking his hat, he rushed round to see Griboyedov, and to ask to make his acquaintance properly. He would have done so long before, he told him, but had been warned against him because of Sheremet'yev's death. 'All these slanders,' he told him, 'melt away before the verses of your comedy. The heart which composed them could never be cold or indifferent.' The two men shook hands. 'I am delighted,' said Griboyedov, 'this is how friendships should be made between people who understand each other.'[5] Bestuzhev asked him for a full copy of his manuscript, but Griboyedov had none at hand, and asked him instead to dinner with a mutual friend, where he was to give a reading the next day.

'I was there punctually at six,' wrote Bestuzhev. 'Griboyedov was an excellent reader. He could give variety to every character and shade, every felicitous expression. I was in ecstasy...From then on we were no longer strangers to each other.' The relationship developed rapidly. First and foremost, wrote Bestuzhev, was the similarity of their characters. Neither could stand the bland superficiality of meaningless social dinners, obsessed with the values of rank, or the glittering formal evenings where so-called grand society showed itself off. Both were blazingly sincere and intolerant of hypocrisy. Griboyedov's satire on the follies and foibles of polite society, thought Bestuzhev, was 'wonderful...a superb breath of fresh air'.

As a co-editor of the literary journal the *Northern Star*, Bestuzhev was in the thick of the literary debates of the day. He had contributed to the nationalist movement with a passionately argued essay entitled 'The Antiquity and Superiority of the Russian Language over other Languages'. He was also an avowed romantic, and thus a fanatical admirer of Byron, about whom Griboyedov remained cooler. But both shared a love for Shakespeare – one of Griboyedov's projects at this time was a translation of *Romeo and Juliet*,[6] which failed because his collaborator, Zhandr, did not know English: 'I would be working from the original,' wrote Griboyedov, 'and he from a bad translation; cutting up Shakespeare is a bold undertaking...In any case I prefer to write a tragedy of my own, and shall certainly do so once I have left here.'

Despite Yermolov's good nature in extending his leave, Griboyedov knew that his time in St Petersburg was limited. This made his frustrations with the censors still harder to bear. He had begun his negotiations with high hopes. He called several times on Admiral Shishkov, the head of literary censorship at the Ministry of Education, and on Lanskoy, the Minister of the Interior, in charge of licensing theatrical performances, who assured him politely that the matter was being studied. But as the summer turned into the autumn, with no decision from the censors, he grew increasingly desperate. After a meeting with Baron von Fock, head of chancery in the Ministry of the Interior, he was driven to such fury by his intransigence that he rushed back to the flat he was sharing with Vladimir Odoyevsky's cousin Alexander and tore up every scrap of his writing in sight.[7]

His irritability and frustration could be taken out on others. 'There is something wild and farouche about his egotism,' noted Vyazemsky. 'He flies off the handle at the slightest provocation.' On one particular occasion, described by the actor Karatygin, he pulverised a fellow guest at a lunch party given by Khmel'nitsky before a reading from his play:

> Lunch was luxurious, cheerful and noisy; suddenly over coffee and cigars, Griboyedov placed the manuscript of his comedy on a chair. Everyone moved their chairs nearer in order not to miss a word. One of the guests, a certain Vassily Mikhailovich Fyodorov, the author of a play called *Lisa*, a nice, rather simple man with pretensions to wit...leant forward and seized the manuscript, which was written in rather sprawling writing, while Griboyedov was smoking his cigar. Waving it about, he cried with a naive, good-natured smile, 'Oh, how heavy it is is – it's worth as much as my *Lisa*.
>
> Griboyedov glared at him from under his glasses and said through his teeth, 'I do not write rubbish [or 'vulgarisms', or 'commonplaces', in Russian, *poshlosti*]'. This unexpected reply naturally took Fyodorov aback, and trying to show that he took it all as a joke, he smiled and hastened to add, 'Nobody doubts that, Alexander Sergeyevich; not only did I not wish to offend you but I can honestly say that I am the first to laugh at my own work'. 'You may laugh at your own work as much as you wish,' said Griboyedov, 'but I will let no-one ridicule mine.' 'You must understand I was not speaking of the quality of our respective plays but only of the number of sheets.' 'The quality of my comedy you cannot yet know, but the quality of your plays has long been known to everyone.' 'Really, you've no call to say that; I repeat, I had no wish to offend you.'

'Oh, I'm quite sure you spoke without thinking [said Griboyedov], and as for offending me I am afraid that is something you will never do.' Their host, who was on the very edge of his chair while listening to this barbed exchange, attempted to pour oil on troubled waters. He took Fyodorov by the shoulders, and said to him with a laugh, 'As a punishment we'll have to put you in the back row of the stalls.'

Griboyedov, who had been walking up and down the drawing room smoking his cigar, said to Khmel'nitsky, 'You may put him wherever you wish, but I will not read my play in his presence'.

The wretched Fyodorov seized his hat and as he left had a last word with Griboyedov to explain that he was leaving in order not to embarrass his host any more. Griboyedov coldly wished him a safe journey.[8]

It is a revealing episode, if only to show how touchy and thin-skinned Griboyedov had become. In November 1824, however, he had a glimmer of encouragement. Thanks to the efforts of his would-be publisher, Bulgarin, and the excision of some so-called doubtful passages, the Ministry of Education agreed to the publication of four scenes from the first act and the whole of the third act in the literary almanac, the *Russian Thalia*.[9] The extracts would be published in January 1825. At the same time, Karatygin, at the risk of his career, persuaded Bok, the director of the Imperial Theatrical School, to stage a performance of the authorised fragments by his pupils, with Karatygin in the main role. 'In a week they all knew their parts,' wrote Karatygin.

> Griboyedov came to the rehearsals and threw himself into teaching us, his applause bearing witness to his joy at seeing his play performed in our childish theatre...We were finally ready for the first night, but alas! all our hopes and negotiations collapsed like a bubble. At the very last rehearsal Bok appeared, bearing the dreaded firman of Count Miloradovich [the Military Governor of St Petersburg, responsible for public order in the theatre], advising us...that the play was not approved for acting by the censors, even in a school...and letting it be known that our imprudence might well lead to our being locked up in the Peter and Paul fortress. We set off to tell Griboyedov who was deeply saddened by the news.[10]

Griboyedov's play was not to receive a stage performance till 1831, two years after his death, and then only in a much truncated form. (It would not be played in its entirety until the 1860s.) Meanwhile, however, his friends had taken the law into their own hands. Appalled at Griboyedov's carelessness about his manuscripts, some of them so heavily corrected as to be almost indecipherable, his fellow playwright Zhandr had begged him to let him take copies of the play. 'With the utmost insouciance', Griboyedov agreed, and at Zhandr's initiative a whole chancery of clerks and copyists were set to work.[11] Young officers on leave would join the group, taking their copies with them when they left for the provinces. The process snowballed, copies were copied and re-copied, until by 1830, according to Bulgarin, there was scarcely a small town in Russia, or a literary household, which did not have a handwritten version of the play.[12] One estimate puts the number of manuscripts of the play in circulation at 40,000, a form of *samizdat* unequalled until Soviet times. In defiance of the censorship, *Woe from Wit* had become public property.

One of Griboyedov's earliest readers in the provinces was Pushkin,[13] in exile since 1820 for writing supposedly subversive verses, and now under house arrest at his family estate, Mikhailovskoye. The arrival of his friend, Ivan Pushchin, bearing a copy of *Woe from Wit*, on a snowy morning in January 1825, was a red-letter day for the exiled poet. In a letter to Bestuzhev shortly after, Pushkin gave his reactions to the play in what is probably the best known of all critiques of *Woe from Wit*. We shall return to his comments in more detail later; suffice it to say at this stage that he made the prediction that half the lines in the play would become proverbs. No prophecy could have been truer. Scores of quotations have acquired the status of popular sayings. They have been used by innumerable writers, from Pushkin himself to Pasternak and Nabokov, sometimes, as with Shakespeare, becoming so much a part of everyday speech that their actual origin is forgotten. Professor Karlinsky, in the chapter on Griboyedov in his *Russian Drama*, calculates that, line for line, *Woe from Wit* is the most quoted work in Russian literature.

It is strange that a play so familiar to Russian audiences should be so comparatively little known in other countries. In one way this is because of the extreme complexity and difficulty of the language. To quote Karlinsky,

> A blend of uproarious humour and hauntingly subtle verbal music in the original Russian, [*Woe from Wit*] is the ultimate proof that the art of literature is on its basic level the art of words. Griboyedov's art is addressed to those who can understand his words instantly in all their finest shadings and ambiguities. Some knowledge of Russian is no help at all: students at Western universities who know enough of the language to read Turgenev and Akhmatova in the original shrug their shoulders at lines and passages that make native speakers gasp in awed wonder or slap their thighs in mirth. Nor has there yet been a translation into any language that can convey to people in other countries why this play is such a miracle of wit and verbal precision.

Even the title of the play, *Gore ot Uma* in Russian, is virtually untranslatable. English versions vary: *The Misfortune of Being Clever*, *'Tis Folly to be Wise*, *Brains Hurt*, or *Woe From Wit*. Anthony Burgess, in his translation of the play, gave up the struggle and simply called it by the name of its hero, Chatsky. There is a good argument for doing so.

Chatsky is one of the great parts in the Russian theatre, comparable to playing Hamlet for a Russian actor. As with Hamlet, his character is open to a variety of interpretations. At first sight there is a resemblance to Alceste, the hero of Molière's *Le Misanthrope*.[14] Like Alceste, Chatsky is a young man at odds with the hypocrisy of the society in which he lives. For Griboyedov, Molière had always been the greatest of satirists, whose comedies had provided an essential safety valve in the autocratic France of Louis XIV. Chatsky shares Alceste's brutal honesty, but he is moodier, wittier, more romantic and uncertain than his French ancestor. And although, as in *Le Misanthrope*, the action of the play takes place in 24 hours, Griboyedov's verse, in rhyming lines of varying length, is more flexible than the French alexandrine, and its framework is looser and less confined. In the third act, 23 characters are crammed onto stage in a grotesque Gogolian extravaganza unthinkable in the classical theatre. There is a sense of limitless horizons outside the stifling world of Moscow, of the vast open spaces through which Chatsky has travelled,

> More than seven hundred leagues without a moment's rest,
> Stumbling on through wind and storms, like a man possessed.[15]

The story of *Woe from Wit* is relatively simple; the drama is far more one of character, of discovery and self-discovery, than of plot. Chatsky, a young nobleman, steeped in post-Napoleonic *ennui*, returns to Moscow after an absence of three years to find that his beloved Sophie has fallen in love with her father's secretary, the toadying Molchalin. He is further disillusioned by the ignorance, smugness and corruption of Moscow society, epitomised above all by Sophie's father, Famusov, a venal bureaucrat whose surface joviality conceals an underlying menace: at the end of the last act, he threatens his servant with forced labour in Siberia.

The action takes place in Famusov's house. The scene opens at daybreak, to the sound of a flute and piano off stage. Liza, the maid, is yawning outside Sophie's room, where Sophie and Molchalin have stayed up all night, supposedly to play duets. Famusov comes in and almost catches them, but is fobbed off by Sophie's story of a romantic dream from which she has just awoken, full of 'devils and love, flowers and fear'.[16] He goes off suspiciously with Molchalin, leaving the maid and mistress to laugh at their narrow escape. Sophie sings Molchalin's praises, but Liza reminds her of Chatsky, and his tears when they said goodbye. It was true that they had loved one another since childhood, says Sophie, but this had not prevented him from leaving her; even before he left Moscow, his visits to their household had become less frequent:

> Oh, if you love someone with a love that's true,
> Why go off seeking learning and disappear into the blue?[17]

Chatsky's return, to throw himself at Sophie's feet, leaves the question open. Does he truly love her, or does he love the idealised image he has made of her? He cannot believe that Sophie could prefer an unworthy figure like Molchalin, but his jibes against her favourite only serve to turn Sophie against him. It is she who in the third act starts the rumour that Chatsky is mad. The story spreads like wildfire round a ballroom crowded with characteristic Moscow types: the Blimpish Colonel Skalozoop, the rascally Zagoretsky, the hen-pecked Platon Mikhailovich, the prince and princess with six twittering daughters, the elderly countess with a granddaughter in tow. Even Repetilov,[18] the club-room radical, with his talk of secret meetings, 'parliament, jury service, Byron',[19] is eventually convinced his friend is insane.

By the end of the play, Chatsky, discredited, calumniated, and cut to the heart by Sophie's betrayal, can only shake the dust of Moscow from his feet. Sophie, equally disillusioned, finds that Molchalin's love for her is no more than a sycophantic ruse; it is Liza, the pertly pretty maid, that he prefers. The final scene reveals the truth to both her and Chatsky. Sophie, creeping downstairs to meet Molchalin, overhears him making advances to Liza; he had only gone along with Sophie to please his boss's daughter, and is secretly terrified that Famusov will find out. Sophie steps forward to denounce him, threatening to tell her father the whole story, unless he leaves the house immediately. Her humiliation is complete when she finds that Chatsky, who has been hidden behind a pillar, has overheard everything. Molchalin cravenly hides in his room, but Chatsky has scarcely time to express his scorn and wounded feelings before Famusov, who has been disturbed by the noise, bursts in with a crowd of servants. Instantly jumping to the conclusion that Chatsky has been his daughter's secret lover, he threatens her with banishment to the country, and orders him to leave the house. Chatsky is only too ready to do so, but not before he has delivered a final diatribe against Sophie, her father and the iniquities of Moscow in general:

> The people I've been with! What a place I've been thrown to by fate!
> A tormenting crowd that curses and pursues!
> Treacherous in love, implacable in hate,
> Raconteurs who endlessly narrate,
> Incoherent clever fellows, simpletons full of guile,
> Malignant old crones,
> Old men aging in their bones,
> Obsessed with nonsense and crumbling all the while –
> Like a chorus you've all proclaimed me mad.
> You're right, anyone who spends a day among your kind
> And so much as sniffs an air so bad
> And still retains his balance of mind
> Could pass through fire and still not burn –

I've had it with Moscow, I'll never return.
I'll fly from here with never a backwards glance,
I'll search on earth to see if there's a chance
Of finding a corner where outraged feeling can go to ground![20]

He rushes out, calling for his carriage, leaving Famusov to wring his hands at the prospect of social disaster:

Well! You see! He's really off his head!
Seriously he's mad, all those stupid things he said!
Sycophant! Father-in-law! And about Moscow what severity!
And you've decided to be the death of me!
My life's in such a sorry way,
Oh God! What will Princess Mariya Alexeyevna say![21]

Let us return to Pushkin's reactions to the play. In his letter to Bestuzhev already mentioned,[22] he jotted down his first impressions:

One must judge a dramatic writer by the laws which he acknowledges for himself. Consequently I do not condemn the plot, the exciting force or the proprieties in Griboyedov's comedy. His aim is in the characters and the sharp picture of manners he gives. In this respect Famusov and Skalozoop are superb. Sophie is not sketched clearly; she is not exactly a whore, nor exactly a Moscow female cousin. Molchalin is not glaringly base enough; couldn't he have been made a coward too? ...Les propos de bal, gossip, Repetilov's tale about the club, Zagoretsky, who is known by all as an inveterate scoundrel and yet received everywhere – here are the traits of a truly comic genius. Now a question. In the comedy *Woe from Wit*, who is the most intelligent character? The answer: Griboyedov. And do you know who Chatsky is? A fiery, noble and fine fellow who has spent some time with a very intelligent man (namely Griboyedov) and has become steeped in his ideas, witticisms, satirical observations. Everything he says is very intelligent. But to whom does he say all this. To Famusov? To Skalozoop? To Moscow grandmothers at a ball? To Molchalin? That is unpardonable. The first mark of an intelligent man is to know at first glance whom he is dealing with and not to cast pearls before Repetilovs and the like ...

In this last comment, Pushkin touches the most questionable aspect of the play. Why does Chatsky, unlike Griboyedov, whose friends were among the best and brightest of his generation, waste his anger on such unworthy targets? The answer is perhaps that Chatsky is not Griboyedov, that he is a man possessed by two overriding passions, his detestation of hypocrisy and his love for Sophie. Borne along by his own feelings, he cares less with whom he speaks than about expressing what he feels, and his eloquence and conviction carry his audience with him. Even Pushkin admitted that he had suspended his judgement until afterwards: 'While I was listening to his comedy I was not criticising; I was revelling in it'.

We have no record of Griboyedov's reaction to Pushkin's comments, though Pushkin had asked Bestuzhev to show them to him, 'written directly, without any beating about the bush, as to a real master'. But in a letter to Katenin, his former collaborator on *The Student*, and one of the few men whose literary judgement he respected, he gave a revealing summary of the play.[23] 'I got your letter yesterday,' he wrote in January 1825,

> and locked myself up with it all day, remembering those good old days we spent together. Your critique is absolutely wicked and unjust, all the same its candour brought me real pleasure...You find the chief weakness lies in the plot. It seems to me that it is very clear and simple in its aim and execution. A young girl, herself not stupid, prefers a fool to a clever man...And this person, it is clear is in opposition to the society round him. Nobody understands him, no one makes allowances for him, for which he stands a little higher than the rest. At first he is cheerful, and this is a mistake. He is always making jokes, and showing up the eccentricities of his old acquaintances. What can you do about it? His humorous sallies are relatively mild until he is driven mad, but as they have not the slightest trace of nobility in their characters, they talk about him as follows. 'He is not a human being, he is a snake' [Sophie], and later when their vanity is piqued by his remarks, 'He likes to belittle people and makes caustic comments – he is envious, he is proud and evil'. He cannot endure baseness and mean tricks: 'Oh, my God he's one of the Carbonari!' Someone, out of malice invents the story that he had gone mad. Nobody believes it and everyone repeats it. The general ill will towards him, and the absence of that girl's love, which was the only reason why he came to Moscow, explains everything to him. Then he spits in her face and everybody else's, and that's how it was.

Griboyedov went on to answer specific criticisms.

> 'The scenes are connected arbitrarily': just as in nature, events occur in random order, whether small or important. The more unexpectedly they follow each the more they arouse our curiosity. I write for those who feel like me, and when in the first scene I can guess what will happen in the tenth, I begin to yawn and flee the theatre. 'The characters are portraits': I may not have the talent of Molière,[24] but at least I am truer to nature than he is. Portraits and only portraits deserve a place in tragedy or comedy...I loathe caricatures – you will not find one in my picture. This is the essence of my poetic art...

It is this ability to breathe life into his characters, so that they exist not as types, but as genuine individuals, that is one of the miracles of the play. Even before extracts were published in the papers, those who had read the play in *samizdat* were talking of Famusov, Skalozoop and Molchalin as though they were real people. Like Shylock or Mr Micawber, the characters have a universal quality which transcends their period and makes them points of reference for all time. They are also marvellously playable, down to the smallest part. As Karlinsky points out, stage careers have been launched in the almost wordless role of Prince Tugokhovsky (the hard-of-hearing father of six twittering daughters), and Chekhov's widow, Olga Knipper, at the height of her fame did not disdain the part of the countess-grandmother in the ballroom scene.

Apart from the servants, the only two characters who are not treated satirically are those of Sophie and Chatsky himself, and it is they who give the play the melancholy, half-romantic quality that is its special charm. It is strange that Griboyedov, on record as saying (quoting Byron to Bestuzhev) that women were like children, happy with sugar plums or a mirror, should give such a sympathetic picture of Sophie. Misguided as she is in her love for Molchalin, she shows real dignity and spirit when the scales fall from her eyes. One feels that she will go on developing as a person, and that her passion and sincerity will not be crushed by social pressures. As for Chatsky, doomed to failure in his conflict with society, he is in one sense the archetypal 'superfluous man'. The alienated hero was not a new figure in literature, though Chatsky is surely the wittiest. His scintillating diatribes may be misplaced, the targets of his indignation vague, but it is he, in the words of Prince Mirsky, who is the play's 'imaginative and emotional focus, its yeast and its zest'.

Generations of critics have sought to analyse his character. For Byelinsky, writing in the 1830s, Chatsky's protests against society were futile and quixotic; his precipitate flight from Moscow would lead to an 'impotent exile, which in practice is a form of non-commitment, possible only for a *barin* [a member of the gentry] living off the the unearned income derived from his estates and serfs'. In this, he agreed with Griboyedov's twentieth-century biographer Piksanov, who saw *Woe from Wit* as essentially a *barskaya* play, shot through with the values of the minor gentry: Chatsky, riding away in his carriage at the end, remained a landowner.

Herzen, in *My Past and Thoughts*, was the first to propagate the idea that Chatsky, 'melancholy, ironic, quivering with indignation and replete with dreamy ideals, appearing as he does in the last moments of Alexander's reign on the eve of the disturbances in Senate Square', was the incarnation of the Decembrist type in literature.[25] He compared the impact of the play to the searing indictment of Russian society in Chaadayev's *Philosophical Letter* of 1836: 'It was a shot that rang out in the dark night... There had been nothing written since *Woe from Wit* which made so powerful an impression. Between that play and the letter there had been ten years of silence, the fourteenth of December… gallows, penal servitude, Nicholas.'[26] (It has been suggested that the character of Chatsky, whose name has the same first letters, owes something to that of Chaadayev.)

For Goncharov, writing many years later in the *Herald of Europe* in 1872, Chatsky was equally a prophetic figure, 'the warrior in the front line, the sharpshooter', who though defeated by society deals it a mortal blow. 'Chatsky is the victor in the duel with Moscow society, even if also its victim; Famusov and his crowd can brand him as a madman, but their world is doomed and they know it.'

It was left to Soviet propagandists to sanctify Chatsky fully as a forerunner of the Decembrist movement, and hence by association of the Russian Revolution. The high priestess of this theory, Nechkina, took this idea to its furthest limit in her book *Griboyedov and the Decembrists*, which with great erudition and ingenuity showed Griboyedov as a Marxist propagandist, and Chatsky as his spokesman.'[27] Written in the late 1930s, at the height of the Stalinist terror, her conclusions, though not her scholarship, were inevitably distorted by the ideological pressures of the time.

In the spring of 1825, the failed uprising of December, which would colour so many subsequent reactions to the play,[28] still lay ahead. Griboyedov, through his friendships and sympathies, belonged to that doomed generation, and Nechkina, in tracing his many links with the leading figures of the Decembrist movement, shows how inextricably he was involved with them. But *Woe from Wit* was not a Decembrist manifesto. On one of the Decembrists' most specific issues, the question of serfdom, Griboyedov, as we have seen, was in no position to take a moral line. It is true that he criticises the institution indirectly. Famusov threatens his porter with Siberia, and Liza with relegation to the poultry yard. Chatsky, in a monologue against the hypocrisies of his elders, gives the example of two Moscow worthies, the one a roistering ne'er-do-well whose band of faithful servants had frequently saved his life in drunken escapades, 'Until suddenly he swapped them for three Borzoi hounds',

> The other, who for our great delight
> Herded into his corps de ballet the edifying sight
> Of children torn from their fathers and their mothers.
> By having them act as zephyrs and as lovers,
> He made all Moscow marvel at their grace,
> But he couldn't keep his creditors at bay,
> So all his zephyrs fair of face
> One by one he had to sell away.[29]

But even here, it is the excesses of the system, rather than the system itself, that he attacks. Chatsky's disgust is the disgust of any generous-spirited and idealistic young man against the smugness and hypocrisy of society, and the growing realisation that his beloved Sophie is a product of its values. Wounded in his love as well as his ideals, he needs no political agenda to underline his disillusion.[30] The play is a satire, not a revolutionary tract, and as such, in the words of Goncharov, gives 'an unsurpassed picture of Moscow society about 1820, with its easy hospitality, serf ballets, foreign tutors, governesses, nepotism and careerism, veneer of French customs and culture and fear of new ideas'.

The part publication of *Woe from Wit* in Bulgarin's almanac, the *Russian Thalia*, made printed discussion of the play acceptable for the first time. (Most critics had probably read it in manuscript, but the fiction of reviewing extracts was preserved.) For the last few months of Griboyedov's stay in St Petersburg, it was hotly debated in the literary journals. Byelinsky recalled the storm of hatred it generated amongst the older generation, above all in Moscow. Griboyedov, who had once called Moscow 'my country, my family, my home',[31] had betrayed his clan, and perhaps it is possible to hear in Chatsky's indignation some echo of the humiliations he had endured as a poor relation, and the son of a drunken father, in his childhood. At the same time, the originality of the play, with its loosely connected structure, irregular verse form and lack of a conventional denouement, gave offence to the literary establishment. 'When Griboyedov composed his play French classicism was dying amongst us,' wrote Byelinsky. 'He wrote it in irregular verse, a medium reserved for fables…Literary scribblers could not forgive him for mocking the whole of their society. His satire pulverised the eighteenth century, whose spirit was still about in the early nineteenth century.'[32]

Griboyedov's contemporaries, on the other hand, were overwhelmingly enthusiastic. Led by Bestuzhev in the *Northern Star*, they welcomed the play as a landmark in Russian drama, unrivalled in its richness of language, boldness of characterisation and brilliance in painting social scenes and situations. Meanwhile, its growing fame in manuscript, and the interest it aroused, established him amongst the leading poets of the day. He was feted on all sides, reacting, like Chatsky, with a certain mordant cynicism. 'Last night I dined with all the local literary swine,'[33] he wrote to Beguichov, on the day of his birthday, 5 January 1825. 'I can't complain, obeisances on every side, praise rising like incense, but also a sated feeling from their tomfoolery, their scandal-mongering, their tinsel talents and tiny souls. Don't despair, noble friend, I haven't quite sunk into this kingdom of mire. I'll be gone soon, and that for a long time.' Yermolov and the Caucasus awaited him.

XIV

Love and Politics, St Petersburg

Griboyedov left St Petersburg in May 1825. He had spent almost a year there, keeping a small flat of his own but staying for much of the time with Prince Alexander Odoyevsky,[1] a distant cousin, in his spacious eight-roomed apartment overlooking Saint Isaac's Cathedral. It was here that the team of young officers and copyists had gathered to produce the first copies of *Woe from Wit*, working under the very eyes of its creator, who would intervene to settle unclear words or phrases.

Alexander Odoyevsky was twenty-one when Griboyedov first met him, and newly commissioned as a Cornet in the Horse Life Guards. It is clear from pictures painted later in his Siberian prison by Alexander Bestuzhev's brother Nicholas that he was astonishingly good-looking, with blue eyes, a straight nose and curly chestnut hair; another Decembrist, Lorer, who met him in the Caucasus, thought him one of the handsomest men he had ever seen. There was a child-like quality about him which was irresistibly appealing, allied to a passionate love of poetry and an ardent patriotism. 'Do you remember how I was before I left for Persia,' wrote Griboyedov to V.F. Odoyevsky, asking him to look after Sasha on a visit to Moscow. 'He is almost comparable, but with a number of splendid qualities most of which I never had.' Odoyevsky, he continued, was his pupil and his foster-child, 'l'enfant de mon choix'.[2]

Odoyevsky in his turn was devoted to Griboyedov. Quite apart from offering him his hospitality, he had apparently saved his life – alas, we have no details of exactly how – in the great flood of November 1824,

107

immortalised in Pushkin's *The Bronze Horseman*. He also turned to him in his emotional difficulties, having become involved with a certain 'V.N.T.',[3] a married woman with children, somewhat older than himself. In a letter to Zhandr, written after he had left the capital, Griboyedov writes of his worries for his friend:

> Do not let him become too overwhelmed by this relationship, as I know from my own experience how dangerous such things can be, but perhaps with my miserable reservations I am harming Alexander. I plead guilty, it is forgivable to assume in others those weaknesses which have ruined my life.

No more is known of this mysterious love affair, but it casts an interesting light on Griboyedov's own experiences, confirming his friend Zavalyshin's remark that his affairs with married women were notorious.

Quite apart from his trials and frustrations over *Woe from Wit*, Griboyedov was, as ever, passionately interested in the theatre during his stay in St Petersburg. His greatest delight, recalled Zhandr, was to hang about backstage, and to take part in its intrigues. Even at this level, the theatre could be a dangerous place: Katenin had recently been exiled to the provinces for causing a disturbance by hissing during a performance. Griboyedov, according to Zhandr, might well have been dragged into a similar adventure and ended up in the Peter and Paul Fortress, had it not been for his 'guardian angel' Odoyevsky, who never left him alone in the theatre: 'He was worse than a nanny, and often pulled him out by force, seizing him by the arm'.[4] After performances, the two young men would go on to dine with Zhandr and his mistress Varvara Miklashevich, who loved them both like 'her own sons'. 'Griboyedov would smile and turn to Odoyevsky, saying, 'Undo your bag and give us a story', which would always be something terrifically amusing.'

In September 1824, Griboyedov had had the pleasure of seeing his operetta *Who is the Brother? Who is the Sister?* performed in St Petersburg. This time the piece was a success, thanks to the actress Byelichkina, who chose it for her benefit, with Griboyedov's great friend Karatygin playing the hero. Karatygin's memoirs, published long after Griboyedov's death, give vivid glimpses of Griboyedov during this period. We see him, for instance, at the piano, playing a rondo by Field, or holding his audience spellbound with his brilliant improvisations.

> I said to him,' wrote Karatygin, 'Ah, Alexander Sergeyevich, how many talents God has endowed you with! You are a poet, a musician, a skilled and experienced horseman, and finally an excellent linguist!' He smiled, and, looking at me from under his glasses, replied: 'Believe me, Petrushka, I may have many gifts, but he who has many talents is master of none of them'.[5]

From Karatygin too comes an attractive picture of Griboyedov's relation-ship with his serf servant, and probably half-brother, Gribov.[6] (It will be recalled that Griboyedov's previous servant, Amlikh, had died in Tiflis.) The two men were inseparable, Gribov playing something of a Leporello role to his master's Don Giovanni. Griboyedov loved to tease him, on one occasion insisting that he played the piano in front of Karatygin, then making fun of his performance, saying he would be better at playing bowls or knucklebones. On another, when Griboyedov had gone out early, Gribov went out himself, locking the door of the flat behind him. He was still not back when Griboyedov returned at two in the morning and, after knocking and ringing vainly Griboyedov went to find a bed with Zhandr, who lived close by. On return the next day, he was met by Gribov.

'Sasha, where did you go yesterday?' asked Griboyedov.
'I was asked out to friends,' said Gribov.
'But I returned at two a.m. and you were not there.'
'How could I know that you would return so early?'
'What time did you return yourself?'
'Almost exactly three.'
'You are right,' said his master, 'you could not possibly have opened up to me at such an early hour.'

The story had its epilogue a few days later.[7] Griboyedov was writing in his study when Gribov appeared to ask permission to visit friends for a few hours. As soon as he had left, Griboyedov put on his best coat, locked the flat and, taking the key, went to spend the night with Zhandr once more. At one o'clock, Gribov returned. He knocked, cried and tried to get back in, but all in vain. Luckily it was summer, so, realising that he had nowhere else to go, he lay down on the ground and fell asleep in the doorway. At dawn, Griboyedov returned, to find his loyal servant stretched out across the porch like a household dog. Awakening him, he exclaimed, 'I have now got my own back on you, you old carousing dog. If I had not had a good friend nearby, I would have had to do the same last week.'

With Karatygin, Griboyedov visited Shakhovskoy's garret, though he had largely outgrown his old mentor, who was secretly hurt by his neglect. But it was here that he met and briefly fell in love with the beautiful ballerina Ekaterina Aleksandrovna Teleshova.[8] Twenty years old, and barely graduated, she still had no official protector, but was being pursued by the Military Governor of St Petersburg, General Count Miloradovich, the man who had earlier banned performance of the extracts of Griboyedov's play. A much bemedalled hero of the 1812 campaign, involved with the theatre through his duty to keep public order in the capital, Miloradovich, according to Herzen, 'was one of those military men who occupied the most senior positions in civilian life, with not the slightest idea about public affairs, signing all official documents as Governor General of St Petersburg without ever reading them'.[9] He had a great reputation for gallantry amongst the ladies, and and was commonly nicknamed Bayard, after the famous 'Chevalier sans peur et sans reproche'; Griboyedov christened him 'le Chevalier bavard' ('the garrulous knight'). He was too short of money to be a long-term rival to the General, and in any case was due to leave St Petersburg, but Teleshova, it appears, fell madly in love with the bespectacled playwright, and he with her. Writing to Beguichov in January 1825, Griboyedov described their short affair.

> For three or four evenings T. drove me out of my mind, all the more so since she too, for the first time, was at ease with the feeling which all my sinful life has burned me black as pitch. And what tempted me was that my rival was Miloradovich, that boastful idiot whom Shakhovskoy grovels to and idolises. They are both cattle. I drove that Chevalier Bavard crazy every day, and whipped up the whole household into a fever of indignation... T. meanwhile, during the three weeks of our attachment, had such a success with her dancing that every one here was amazed, demanding to know the reasons for such a marvellous transformation, such perfection. And I stood there in the wings triumphant.

He celebrated their love with a poem for 'The Son of the Fatherland'. Graceful and slightly conventional, it had none of the sparkle of Pushkin's verses on Istomina in *Eugene Onegin*, perhaps, as Griboyedov told Beguichov, because from the moment he wrote it his rhymes took over from his feelings. 'Can you believe it, from that day on my ardour cooled, and I see her more rarely, so as not to be disappointed. Or maybe what has knocked me off course is that now everything is in the open, the veil has been pulled aside. I have trumpeted my secret to the whole town, and my rapture has lost its edge.'[10]

Miloradovich seems to have borne Griboyedov no grudge; indeed he may well have been pleased to see his future mistress praised by such a celebrated writer. Zhandr, in his conversations with D.A. Smirnov, described how Griboyedov accompanied Miloradovich to the worst-hit parts of St Petersburg after the flood of 1824. 'How could that be?' asked Smirnov naively. 'I assumed they were sworn enemies.' 'No,' said Zhandr, 'they were only competitors.' By January 1825, Miloradovich had replaced Griboyedov as Teleshova's lover. It was a shrewd career move from her point of view, since as his official mistress she would be promoted over the heads of more senior dancers. But she was not to enjoy her position for long. The gallant General was killed on the Senate Square by Peter Kakhovsky on 14 December, 1825.

When Griboyedov left St Petersburg, the fatal date was still seven months away. But throughout his stay there he had been mixing on an

22. RIGHT. I.A. Krylov (1768–1844), teller of fairy tales, 'Russia's La Fontaine'. Painting K.P. Bryullov (end 1830s). *Alexander Pushkin and His Time in the Fine Arts of the First Half of the Nineteenth Century*, Khudojnik, RSFSR, Leningrad, 1985.

23. BELOW. N.V. Vsevolozhsky (1799–1862), friend of Griboyedov, rich theatrical producer, founder of 'Green Lamp' thespian circle. Oil, Desearno, courtesy of Pushkin Museum, Moscow.

24. TOP LEFT. S.I. Muravyov-Apostol (1796–1886), radical thinker and Decembrist, hanged for his part in the uprising. Watercolour, N. Utkin.

25. ABOVE. P.I. Pestel' (1793–1826), Decembrist leader of the Southern Society, hanged for his involvement in the uprising. Watercolour, N. Bestuzhev.

26. LEFT. I.D. Yakushkin (1793–1857), retired captain and Decembrist: fully informed about the property speculations of Griboyedov's mother and the serf mutinies. Drawing, Sokokov after Utkin.

27. A.A. Bestuzhev (1797–1837), nicknamed 'Marlinsky', literary critic and popular novelist. With his tales of the Caucasus, he was Russia's Walter Scott in the 1830s. A Decembrist, he edited, with Ryleyev, the *Northern Star*. After a shaky start, his intimacy with Griboyedov developed only in 1823–4. Bestuzhev was something of a role model to the young poet Lermontov. Watercolour, 1823–4.

28. K.F. Ryleyev (1795–1826), hanged as a leading Decembrist, Ryleyev denied that he had accepted Griboyedov in the Northern Society. He admitted that 'they had had conversations about improving the government of Russia'.

29. Arrival in the Caucasus through the mountains: the Daryal Gorge. N.G. Tchernetsov, *c.* 1832.
Courtesy of Sotheby's.

30. The Georgian military highway, between Lars and Vladikavkaz, the road travelled by Griboyedov's convoy in 1817. Mount Kazbek is in the background. N.G. Tchernetsov, 1805. Courtesy of Sotheby's.

31. N.N. Muravyov (1792-1866), who acted as Yakubovich's second in the duel with Griboyedov, and was later Viceroy of the Caucasus and GOC Independent Caucasian Corps.

32. General A.A. Velyaminov (1771-1837), Yermolov's Chief of Staff in the Caucasus, in practice Yermolov's deputy as ruler of Georgia. George Dawe, courtesy of Hermitage Museum, St. Petersburg.

33. ABOVE. Metekhi Church, Tiflis. N.G. Tchernetsov, 1839. Rumyantsev Museum. *Alexander Pushkin and His Time in the Fine Arts of the First Half of the Nineteenth Century*, Khudojnik, RSFSR, Leningrad, 1985. Courtesy of the State Russian Museum, St Petersburg.

34. BELOW. Tiflis and the river Kura. Oil, M.Yu. Lermontov, 1837. Pushkin Literary Museum, St Petersburg.

35. Scenes of Georgian life, near the Sioni Cathedral, Tiflis by Prince G. Gagarin, pub. 1840. Georgian girls dancing the 'Lezginka'. One of the figures may be Maiko Orbeliani, cousin of Nina Chavchavadze.

almost daily basis with the future plotters. Odoyevsky's apartment was one of the main meeting places for the Northern Society, whose members included many of Griboyedov's closest friends:[11] Küchelbecker, Bestuzhev, his brothers Nicholas and Mikhail, Kakhovsky, known to Griboyedov from his Smolensk childhood, Prince Evgeny Obolensky, Pushchin, Muravyov and Kondraty Ryleyev, Bestuzhev's co-editor on the *Northern Star*. Ryleyev's flat on the Moika Canal was another centre of activity, where on certain days he would offer the conspirators a puritanical 'Russian breakfast', consisting of rye bread, raw cabbage and vodka, a far cry from the normal champagne diet of the young officers and dandies of the group. Together with Muravyov, who drew up the society's draft constitution, Ryleyev, a radical poet whose fervour and idealism complemented Muravyov's cooler judgement, was the leader of the Northern Society. Bestuzhev, who was inducted into the inner circle of the group in April 1825, a month before Griboyedov's departure, played a key role in recruiting new members and co-ordination with the leaders of the Southern Society.

Living as he was with Odoyevsky, and in constant touch with Bestuzhev, in an atmosphere of warm friendships, literary enthusiasms and shared ideals, Griboyedov could not fail to know of his friends' involvement in the conspiracy. But at the time he left St Petersburg, the Northern and Southern Societies were far from certain of their aims, Muravyov still envisaging a constitutional monarchy, the Southern branch, led by Pestel', in favour of a republic and the assassination of the imperial family. (The idea of political assassination was nothing new; it should be remembered that Alexander I's father had been murdered, probably with his son's connivance, and that Catherine the Great, Alexander's grandmother, had been privy to the murder of her husband, Peter III.) There was vague talk of concerted action by the two societies, tentatively fixed for the summer of 1826, but nothing firm had been arranged; nor, apparently, did Griboyedov become a member of the Northern Society. His cold sceptical brain was not in tune with their exalted idealism, and he had none of the craving for action of those who had fought in the 1812 campaign. His family background, lack of funds and dependence on a civil-service career did not allow him the emotional freedom of the rich young men who thronged Odoyevsky's drawing-room. Sympathetic though he might be to their aims, he had no faith in their ability to carry them out. 'A hundred second lieutenants,'[12] he once remarked, 'cannot transform the whole governing structure of Russia'; on another occasion, when they were quarrelling over their definitions of programmes and constitutions, he told them frankly they were fools. The Decembrist Dmitri Zavalyshin, a young naval officer who got to know him during this period, gives a vivid picture of Griboyedov at mornings in Odoyevsky's flat, sipping tea in his dressing gown and assailing the young idealists with his sarcasms at their parroting of liberal slogans. As Chatsky said to Repetilov,

> You all make a lot of noise –
> And to little effect.[13]

Summing up Griboyedov's attitudes in relation to the Decembrist movement, his biographer Professor Piksanov describes them as 'liberalism, scepticism and nationalism'.[14] Griboyedov, he wrote, had declared himself in his own way through his writing, using the weapons of satire, not political action, to point up abuses in society. His friends, who had made the circulation of his play a rallying point, did not press him to go further. They recognised his genius and wished to spare him. In his evidence to the interrogatory commission after the rising, Bestuzhev made a revealing statement:

> As far as Alexander Griboyedov is concerned, as a freethinking intelligence and personality, I frequently talked over my dreams of reforming Russia with him; I even hinted at the fact that there were people aiming or striving towards this aim...I cannot at all recall anything specific. I know that as a poet he desired these ends: freedom of the press and publishing and the wearing of traditional Russian dress. But I did not accept him as a member, firstly because he was older and cleverer than me, and secondly because I wished to divert any danger from a man of such talent. Ryleyev agreed with me on this, and gave him absolutely no assignments when he left Moscow.[15]

Ryleyev and Muravyov, testifying independently, both confirmed Bestuzhev's statement that Griboyedov had not been drawn into the conspiracy, as if its outcome were unsuccessful, they did not wish to compromise a man whose talents could bring glory to Russia. Ryleyev, however, admitted that he had held wide-ranging conversations with him on the condition of Russia and the possibility of political reform. Contradicting these disclaimers is the view of Zhandr, who in conversation with Smirnov years later told him that Griboyedov was fully involved in the conspiracy; even if he mocked their methods as impractical, he believed in the necessity of the Decembrists' aims. Corroborating this, Obolensky and Sergei Trubetskoy told the interrogatory commission that they had been told that Griboyedov had joined the Northern Society shortly before leaving St Petersburg, though neither had been present at the time. A further, less reliable, piece of evidence comes from the memoirs of a certain Polina Nikolayevna Lavrent'yeva,[16] the illegitimate daughter of Count A.I. Tchernyshev, and a close friend of Odoyevsky and Obolensky. Ignored by Nechkina and other sober-minded literary historians, it reflects such a Russian response to a critical event that it deserves quotation:

Griboyedov was accepted into the [Northern] society by Ryleyev and Obolensky. All his friends were overjoyed at the event. Sasha Odoyevsky gave a terrific party to celebrate it. Griboyedov and A. Bestuzhev led the frenzied dancing. At the end all those present smashed up all the crockery. I did not expect this from Griboyedov. Clearly one should not judge by exterior appearances, inside all might be ice, outside hot. All this I learnt from Odoyevsky.[17]

Whatever the truth of the matter, it is clear that by the time Griboyedov left St Petersburg he had few illusions about the extent of the conspiracy. In a letter to Beguichov, now the father of a child, he warned him against being drawn into it by the hot-headed Bestuzhev. He himself was returning to Georgia by way of the Ukraine and the Crimea, and would soon be out of range of what was going on.

It is possible, however, that even though he was physically taking leave of his Decembrist friends, he had not altogether detached himself from their concerns. The outline of a tragedy, *Radamist and Zenobia*,[18] left behind in a notebook with Beguichov in 1828, before his last journey to Persia, shows how deeply the themes of conspiracy and the overthrow of tyranny had entered his mind. Opinions vary as to when the sketch was written.[19] Nechkina, pursuing her Decembrist thesis, considers the most probable date to be the summer of 1826, in the aftermath of the failure of the uprising. Professor S.A. Fomichev and the late V.E. Vatsuro, today's leading experts on the subject, propose the period of Griboyedov's stay in St Petersburg in 1824–5 as an alternative. They argue that it would be unthinkable that Griboyedov, severely shocked at the execution or exile of so many of his friends, would wish to compromise them further by drawing parallels from Tacitus. It is far more likely that the sketch – covering only eight pages in his notebook – was written immediately after he had finished *Woe from Wit* and was looking for a change of theme. He had not long come from Tiflis, where he had lived in creative intimacy with Küchelbecker. The latter had also written a tragedy based on a classical theme, *The Achaeans*, and had sent a dedicated copy to his hero. Griboyedov's own sketch may well have been the libretto for an *opera seria*; his friendships with the leading musical figures in Moscow and St Petersburg would have made a collaboration easy. By a strange coincidence, Handel's first *opera seria* for the Royal Academy of Music in 1719, *Radamisto*, was based on the same sources, though it is more likely that Griboyedov found his inspiration in Crébillon's play *Radamiste et Zénobie*, first played in Russia in 1809, or from its original in Tacitus's *Annals*.

For Griboyedov, freshly returned from Tabriz and Tiflis, the juxtaposition of Rome with the exotic East would have made the theme especially apt. His version, full of oriental colour, begins with an operatic flourish to the roll of drums, the sound of horns and the bark of hunting dogs as Radamist, the tyrant of Armenia, and murderer of Mithridates, King of Armenia, receives the Roman envoy, Kasperius. He is not convinced by Kasperius's boasts that the Roman legions are invincible. The Emperors of the East and their peoples, he tells him, may yet be a match for the Romans; then, scornfully calling for his horse, he goes off to resume his tiger hunt.

The next scene, with stage directions calling for an avenue of cypresses, shows the courtiers gathered at the entry to the harem, to await Radamist's return. Prompted by Armasilius, a friend of the murdered Mithridates, they voice their complaints against the oppressor, whose appointment of foreign officials to senior positions in the army affronts their national pride. (We need only recall Yermolov's hatred and contempt for the German Generals around the Tsar to trace the pedigree of this prejudice.) Their anger is fuelled when another courtier, Ashod, rushes in calling for revenge on Radamist, who has just killed his brother. The Holy Fool interrupts them to forecast success for the conspirators. They are uncertain whether or not he is a spy. Is he only feigning madness, or does his sanctity invest their plot with sacred purpose? Armasilius is inclined to trust him, and urges them to do the deed at night when the tyrant is asleep. Ashod, impatient at the delay, calls upon evil spirits to curse the cruel Emperor.

Radamist returns from the hunt and, having distributed the bag among his courtiers, goes to the harem, where his favourite wife Zenobia, daughter of Mithridates, awaits him. Zenobia is devoted to Radamist, despite the stern reminders of her handmaiden, who urges her to revenge her father. But she cannot shake off a feeling of foreboding, which checks the loving words on her lips. Disappointed, Radamist suspects her of infidelity. He leaves her, in a state of uncertainty and agitation. More conspirators gather for secret consultations, Ashod burning to murder the tyrant immediately, Armasilius urging him not to destroy the rest of them through his impatience. His last instruction is that they should all meet that night, and draw their daggers against the tyrant together.

The next act begins with a riot of the populace offstage against the hated foreigners. Meanwhile, Radamist has been warned that many of his courtiers are disloyal. He despises such petty opponents. He longs for a chance to display his exceptional powers of leadership, and for enemies worthy of his heroic gifts. Left alone to reflect on these matters, he hears stealthy footsteps and prepares to defend himself. Ashod creeps up behind him, but is foiled in his attempt to overpower him. Radamist disarms him, but is wounded in the hand. Under severe interrogation, Ashod reveals the conspiracy.

The draft of the tragedy is unfinished. Reconstituting the rest of the story, Fomichev and Vatsuro suggest that Griboyedov intended to show how Radamist suppressed the conspiracy, then had to give in to a rising of the populace. Radamist and Zenobia are forced to flee; in the last act, returning to Tacitus as a source, Radamist would have killed Zenobia as a sacrificial victim and thrown her body into the Araxes.

There was a wealth of operatic and dramatic precedents for Griboyedov's borrowings from classical history. He could have brought his own experience of the orient to the theme, but the character of Radamist was drawn far more from literary sources – Byron's daemonic heroes, Shakespeare's *Richard III* – than from the contemporary Russian scene. It is easy to see why he would have abandoned the project after the Decembrist rising, when the theme of a failed conspiracy became so agonisingly relevant, but less so to date it, as Nechkina did, as being written after the event. It remains a tantalising fragment, one of the many might-have-beens in Griboyedov's literary life.

XV

Crimea and the Northern Caucasus

Although there is no record of him doing so, it is probable that Griboyedov stopped in Moscow to pay a farewell visit to his mother after leaving St Petersburg. If so, the meeting must have been unsatisfactory. 'I am virtually convinced,'[1] he wrote to Odoyevsky on 10 June 1824, 'that the true artist must be a person without family ties. It is a fine thing to support one's parents at critical moments, but continuous attention to their needs, which are frequently trivial and pointless, stifles the living fire and freedom of the creative gift.' It was no coincidence that he had spent most of his leave away from his mother and the family circle.

Griboyedov had prepared for his visit to the Ukraine and Crimea with characteristic thoroughness and scholarship.[2] A series of notes in the notebook left behind with Beguichov in 1828 show the breadth of his interest in the history, geography and archaeology of the area. Studded with the names of medieval and eighteenth-century authorities, they were almost certainly made at the end of his stay in St Petersburg in 1824–5, when the sources would have been readily available to him. Apart from his understandable desire as a patriot to see the cradle of Russian history in Kiev and the Ukraine, and the intellectual curiosity which any new country inspired in him, the journey was a logical route for his return to the northern Caucasus, where Yermolov was currently campaigning.

Griboyedov arrived in Kiev at the beginning of June 1825, taking a room at the Green Inn, close to the ancient Lavra monastery. He was enthralled by the city's heroic past. In his letter to Odoyevsky, he described himself as living amongst ghosts.[3] 'The Vladimirs and the Iasyaslavy have possessed my imagination, virtually crowding out the present generation; what the local Russian officials and Polish landlords are thinking or doing, Heaven knows.' The impact of Christianity as seen in the great cathedral of Saint Sophia and the rock monasteries impressed him deeply; the sunlight irradiating the vines and poplars, after the gloom of the sanctuaries, was in dazzling contrast to the north. 'Nature is majestic and wonderful here, especially from the high banks of the Dniepr.'

There was no word in his letter of the romantic young revolutionaries of the Southern Society, but inevitably Griboyedov came in contact with some of its leaders during his stay. Mikhail Bestuzhev-Ryumin (later hanged for his role in the conspiracy) called on him at his inn, and despatched a messenger to bring Sergei Muravyov to join them from his regimental base at Vasilkov, four hours ride away. Prince Sergei Trubetskoy, an old friend from Moscow, was also in Kiev, as were the Muravyov brothers, Artamon and Alexander, cousins of the Northern Society leader Nikita Muravyov. All were members of the so-called Vasilkov cell, and at the time that Griboyedov met them were in the thick of a plan to assassinate the Tsar, who would be visiting the Ukraine for a grand review of the army later that summer.

The murder would have taken place at Belaya Tserkov' ('White Church'), the house of a Countess Branitska, where the Tsar was expected to stay. It would have been followed by two proclamations, one for the military, one for civilians, after which the Third Corps of the army would have marched on Moscow, attracting other disaffected units as it marched. In Moscow, they would force the Senate to effect reforms of the Government. Remaining units in the area would seize Kiev. The Northern Society would mobilise the Guards and the fleet and reinforce the Third Corps' pressure on the Senate. At a discussion of this proposal in January 1825, Pestel' had strongly opposed the plan as being ill-prepared and over-estimating the strengths of the Southern Society. Pestel' thought armed revolt would only succeed if it was launched in St Petersburg, and all the organs of power seized at once. Despite his opposition, members of the cell continued to nurse the plan, with Trubetskoy as the leader of those who opposed Pestel'. In the event, the Tsar was warned of the possibility of an assassination attempt by an informer, and the review was postponed, but the very fact that it was being discussed while Griboyedov was in Kiev brought him dangerously close to the conspirators. He would later insist that his meetings had been only chance encounters, so casual that he left Kiev without taking proper leave of them, while they in their turn made it clear that he had not been asked to join them. Their reasons, according to Bestuzhev-Ryumin's evidence to the interrogatory commission, were as follows:

1. Griboyedov, being attached to Yermolov, was too far away to be of use to us.
2. We did not know his real ideas, nor his character.
3. He might have proselytised for Yermolov, and caused trouble by forming a splinter group.
4. He was to be protected, as a literary talent needed for the future of Russia.

This was certainly the best construction to be placed on Griboyedov's position, as far as the commission was concerned. It was confirmed by Trubetskoy, who stated in his evidence that he had told Ryleyev that although the conspirators had at first intended to enrol Griboyedov, they had not done so, 'as they did not find in him that cast of mind which they were seeking'. Ryleyev, apparently, had made no comment on this; however, according to Trubetskoy, he had been heard to say in an earlier conversation, 'He is ours [*on nash*]'.[4] As has been seen, the evidence on this is contradictory. One explanation, as suggested by another Decembrist, Prince Dolgorukov, is that Griboyedov was regarded as a sleeping supporter, or *affilié*, who had never signed up formally but could play an important role if the rising were successful. In this case, his influence with Yermolov to bring in the Caucasian army on the rebels' side would be crucial.

Griboyedov stayed only a few days in Kiev, and must have left it with divided feelings. On the one hand, he was a sworn diplomatic servant of the Tsar, who had recently promoted him, and whose representative (Yermolov) had overlooked his second duel. The White Church plot, had he known of it, can only have deepened his scepticism about the impracticality of the Decembrists' plans. On the other, he was standing on the sidelines while his comrades were preparing to risk their lives. It was a humiliatingly unheroic role.

By mid-June,[5] he was drowning his moral confusions with an energetic exploration of the Crimean peninsula, accompanied by the faithful Gribov as valet and groom. We can trace his journey in his travel notes. On 24 June, we learn, he followed the ridge of the Salgyr range on horseback, enchanted by everything about him: gardens, minarets, poplars, gravestones and ice-cold waterfalls under which he was quick to strip off and cool himself. His road led lazily to Aiyan and then Temiridji, finally reaching the village of Thovki, next to Alushta on the bay of Kyzyl Kobe. Here he spent the night relaxing and listening to gypsy music, 'a mixture of Tatar, Polish and Southern Ukrainian,' he decided.[6]

On 25 June, he retraced his steps through the woods to Buyuk Dzhanskoy and reached the source of the river Alma, which began on the mountain of Chatyr-Dag. From here he could see the white heights of Sabli, and beyond them the hills of Bakhchisaray. Occasionally he halted in a sheepfold, for a snack of *shashlyk* and shepherds' bread. He tried to size up the shepherds' ethnic origin from their faces. The learned authority Pallas had suggested they might be descended from the ancient Greeks or from Italians from Liguria. They were neither Mongolian nor Turkish, he thought; their features were more northern, possibly from Ossetia in the Caucasus. Soon clouds blotted his view completely. He emerged from them at the mountain top to find sub-alpine conditions of summer pasturage, enlivened by the occasional mountain hare. A rosy sunset gave him the illusion that a boat at Alushta far below was flying through the air. The evening chill made him shiver, and he bivouacked for the night, using his saddle as a pillow, his only serenade the dialogue of sheep and goats. Rising in the middle of the night, he saw the moon turning the sea between two headlands into a silver streak; the stars twinkled above black clouds.

The next day was clear enough to see the panorama from the summit, his sweep including Sebastopol and the valley of Balaklava (where the charge of the Light Brigade would later astound the Russians and the world) to the west, and Ak Mechet', today Simferopol', to the east. Eagles were hovering above him, soon lost in the mist as he descended, and a torrential downpour obliterated the view. The wind was so strong it almost blew him away. Throughout his notes, Griboyedov conveys a sense of wonder at nature in the mountains, together with an appreciation of its dangers – which he exaggerated picturesquely on occasion. The risk of getting lost was very high, with landslides and hostile weather a further threat. But he came down safely to Alushta, a Tatar village huddled on a flank of the mountain. He was attracted by its gardens, streams and ruined castle, and paused for a time on the shore to exchange impressions with a Turkish sea captain loading wood.

For the next few weeks, he explored the rocky Crimean coastline. He noted the miserable poverty of the Tatar villages and the way that, as in all of Asia, their corn was threshed by being trampled under horses' hooves. He was struck by the profusion of the vegetation, wild ivy, ash trees, weeping willows, maples, walnuts, pomegranates, fig trees, acacias and wild grapes, and was pleased to discover a plant he knew from Shirvan in Persian Azherbaijan, the Rhus Delphinus. Sometimes there was a glimpse of a ruined fortress or the remnants of a classical ruin – this was the ancient coast of Tabriz, where, according to legend, Iphigenia, having escaped sacrifice at Aulis, was priestess of Diana's temple. Following Pallas, Griboyedov located the sacrificial site on the immensely dramatic flat space below the monastery of St George at Balaklava.[7] With its sheer drop of hundreds of feet into the sea near

Cape Fiolente, it was easy to imagine how a corpse could be thrown into the kingdom of Poseidon.

There were few country estates. The coast had not yet been colonised by those grand dukes and super-rich aristocrats who would build their Gothic or Moorish palaces there later in the century. But he called at Partenit, the house of a Polish friend, the exiled Count Olizar, set amid cypresses and pomegranate trees, and visited the empty palace of Gursuf at Ayu-Dagh ('Bear Mountain') nearby. Originally built as a summer villa for the Duc de Richelieu, Governor General of New Russia (which included the Crimea) under Catherine the Great, it had been used by General Rayevsky, the hero of the 1812 campaign, with his family in 1820. Here Pushkin had joined them, in the course of a leisurely tour of the Crimea, and had spent what he described as the happiest three weeks of his life. A number of his most beautiful lyrics were composed here; his poem 'Nereid' was directly inspired by Gursuf's incomparable setting, the sparkling foam of the waves, the oriental beauty of the dark, minaret-like cypresses, the sun playing on the bear-like promontory of Ayu-Dag stretching far out into the sea. By 1826, most of these poems had been published, and would have been known to Griboyedov, adding to the interest of his visit there. He must have found some guardian to show him round the house, for he refers to the 'view from the gallery',[8] the cypresses and the impressive promontory beyond. Even today, the journey along the coastline, through almost impenetrable woods inhabited only by deer, or the boulder-strewn chaos of the Yayla cliffs, is something of an adventure, and one can only salute his horsemanship in getting there.

At Balaklava and Inkerman, his greatest interest was in the earliest traces of Christianity and the great umbilical cord that linked the Slavs to the Byzantines of Constantinople. He sketched the chief monuments and reproached himself for being an 'appalling barbarian' in knowing so little about them. Had he found the church built by Saint Vladimir?[9] Was he standing on the same place as the legendary Grand Duke of Kiev? Were the huge stones, standing as silent witnesses to antiquity, indeed attributable to the times of the Cyclops?

More purely eastern was the little town of Bakhchisaray, with its fountains, mosques and poplar trees. He spent the night here, dining at a coffee house, the evening enlivened by the sound of music and fountains; a Tatar galloped by on a horse, its hooves striking sparks in the darkness. The next day he climbed the minaret of the Khan's palace for a better view, noting the monastery, with its stairs and balconies and cells splayed across the beetling rock face of Chufut-Kale, and the six octagonal mausoleums, with their marble cornices. He makes no actual mention of Pushkin's poem 'The Fountain of Bakhchisaray', with its legend of the grieving Sultan and his Polish princess, but refers to the tomb of 'the Georgian', the murdering wife who features so passionately in Pushkin's story.

At various moments in his journey, Griboyedov was accompanied by the nineteen-year-old poet Andrei Muravyov, one of the many members of the Muravyov clan.[10] They had first met in Kiev, where they were staying at the same inn. Muravyov, who had been warned that Griboyedov was difficult with strangers, engineered their meeting by pretending that he had had a nightmare, and rushing out of his room screaming. Griboyedov, who had a room on the same floor, came out calm him down. Later, Muravyov had joined him on his ascent of Chatyr-Dag. 'We stood together in the clouds,' wrote Muravyov. '...An involuntary ecstasy seized me. I was carried out of myself; he understood me, and our intimacy was born.' They met up again at Bakhchisaray, where they climbed the crags of Chufut-Kale by moonlight. Inspired by the romantic setting, Muravyov poured out his poetic ambitions and recited two of his poems. Griboyedov encouraged him, saying 'For God's sake create; do not translate'. When Muravyov explained his intention of writing a poem on Vladimir, Kiev's first great ruler, Griboyedov confided his own idea of writing a tragedy based on the same subject. The tragedy never materialised, but Muravyov's collection of Crimean poems entitled *Tavrida (Tabriz)*[11] were published in 1827. They attracted no great interest, but for Muravyov a dream had been realised. 'In 1825,' he wrote in his memoir of the tour, 'my dearest wish was accomplished, I saw the Crimea and became a poet'.[12]

Griboyedov, as a successful writer, might have smiled at Muravyov's enthusiasm. But he was already tortured by the idea of his literary sterility. Could it be that he was a man of only one play, that after *Woe from Wit* his creativity had burnt itself out? After his superhuman efforts to get his play accepted and performed, the bitter knowledge that it would remain unpublished must have added to his sense of frustration. He had been feted at St Petersburg, and even on his Crimean journey, where his fame had gone before him, but it was more an irritation than a solace. 'I spend my life in trying to find some corner where I can be alone,' he complained to Beguichov on 12 September,

> and can find it nowhere. I arrive somewhere, I see no-one, know no-one, and wish to know no-one. It never lasts more than a day...People burst in on me, cover me with compliments, and the little town becomes even more insufferable than St Petersburg...I've already spent almost three months in the Tauride (Crimea). Result: zero. I have written nothing. I don't know why, perhaps I ask too much of myself. Am I able to write? It's truly an enigma for me. I know what I want to say, and more than necessary, I assure you, so why am I silent? As silent as the tomb.

The letter to Beguichov seems to have marked a crisis in his life:

> For some time I have been gloomy in the extreme. It is time to die. I
> cannot think why my existence is so long drawn out. My melancholy is
> bottomless. If it tortures me much longer, I am not inclined to go on
> being patient. Can you imagine it, the hypochondria which drove me out
> of Georgia has come back again. But it's now so intensified that I've
> never experienced anything like it before…Stepan, you love me like a
> brother. You are wiser, older and more experienced; do me the great
> favour of advising me how I can escape from either madness or the
> pistol. I feel that either one or the other await me in the future.[13]

It has been suggested the sense of moral confusion created by his
loyalty to his friends, about to risk their lives on an enterprise which he
regarded as doomed to failure, added a further dimension to his
despairing mood. In the course of his Crimean journey, he had had
chance encounters with several members of the Southern Society, writing
of one of them to Bestuzhev: 'Did Orzhritsky tell you of our meeting in
the Crimea? We thought of you and Ryleyev. Please embrace him from me,
in a truly republican manner.'[14] Even if he was not directly involved, he
was fully aware of the relations between his friends in St Petersburg and
the Ukraine, and conscious of the republican aims of the Southern Society.

Griboyedov left the Crimea in mid-September, making the dreary
journey across the steppes of Kerch to the Kuban', and thence to Kabarda
in the northern Caucasus.[15] On 4 October, he met with Yermolov's
second-in-command and Chief of Staff, General Velyaminov, at the
Stone Bridge Fort on the river Malka. Yermolov himself was at Grozny
on a 'pacifying mission' against the Chechens, whose opposition to the
Russians had now reached the dimensions of a religious war. Only two
months earlier, two of his most brutal Generals, Grekov and Lissanievich,
had been murdered when a Chechen Imam, held for questioning, had
snatched a hidden *kinjal* (Caucasian dagger) from his clothing and
stabbed them both; 300 Chechen captives had been killed as a reprisal.

Griboyedov was plunged into activity straight away, spending the
first half of October with Velyaminov on a tour of inspection of the forts
along the Line. He was back in the saddle, straight from his camp bed
every morning, with no time for idleness or introspection. The vast
panorama of snowy peaks and gorges lifted his imagination, the sharp
autumn dawns and invigorating climate helped dispel his mood of
spleen and writers' block. 'I have begun something poetic here; it pleases
me,' he told Bestuzhev.

The work in question was a poem, 'The Brigands of the Chegem',[16]
based on a recent happening on the Line. Five days before Griboyedov's
arrival at the fort, a raiding party of 2000 Karbardin and Chechen
horsemen had fallen on a nearby Cossack settlement, killing 10 people

and kidnapping over a hundred more. After driving off all the cattle and horses, they had set fire to the village, retreating with their captives to the impenetrable fastness of Chegem, close to Mount Alborz. In destroying a key link in the Russian line, they were doing no more than paying the Russians in their own coin, but the Russians were naturally indignant at their impudence. Griboyedov rode out with Velyaminov to survey the smoking village, and to try in vain to catch up with the perpetrators, but it is clear from the tone of the poem that his sympathies were largely on the raiders' side.

Written in short staccato couplets, the poem is a thrilling despatch from the front line. It describes the return ride of the tribesmen through the misty invisibility of treacherous valley paths and precipices, catching their feelings of defiance as they stumble through rocks and ravines, rolling away obstructive stones into the tumbling river below. 'These stones and cliffs are ours! O Russians, why do you struggle to acquire these age-old heights?' The cry is not only rhetorical, but conclusive in its certainty that the Russians will not win. Their lust for power will be defeated by the local weapons. For a moment they will think they have won, then their enemy will melt away again, to snipe at them from the mist. Where is the Russians' target? Invisible, as nature comes to the tribesmen's aid.

Griboyedov's language is full of local colour: he evokes the stallions, the moonless nights, the sound of the river, the whistle of blizzards, the roar of the waterfalls, the massive glaciers, the golden-fleeced sheep and roaming boars and wolves who share the raiders' bivouac. The final scenes of the poem, after the perilous return journey to Chegem has been negotiated, show a grand feast in their mountain stronghold, where they celebrate their victory and divide the spoils. Griboyedov reveals a close knowledge of the raiders' psychology and customs in describing the division. The youngest girls would go to the bravest cavaliers, the boys would be re-educated by the Holy Men (kadis) and thus, in due course, provide the tribe with further warriors and leaders (uzdens). As for the rest, they would either become slaves, or be ransomed for the best price. Any jewellery or precious stones would go to the wives, the horses and cattle would be shared amongst the warriors.

It was a vivid picture of a tribal triumph, similar in its way to Repin's famous painting of the Zaporozh'ye Cossacks writing their defiant letter to the Sultan. Despite its questioning of Russia's civilising mission in the Caucasus, and its glorification of men normally treated as criminals, the poem passed the censors and was published in Bulgarin's paper the Northern Bee in November 1826. In an enthusiastic editorial note, Bulgarin praised his protegé's description of the untamed Caucasus and its wild inhabitants, but took care to add a reference to the Russian eagles, who would soon avenge the insult of the raid.

Griboyedov accepted the necessity of securing Russia's frontiers in the Caucasus, and of subduing the clans which threatened them. But his travels with Velyaminov had brought him in touch with the day-to-day realities of the Yermolovian policies of terror; for the first time, he saw them in practice for himself. An episode which especially shocked him is described in a letter to Küchelbecker on 27 November:[17]

Kuchuk Dzhangotov is the most important feudal overlord from Chechnya to Abkhazia. He is considered loyal to us and no subject dares molest his stallions. His son, Dzhambulat, was a favourite of Alexis Petrovich [Yermolov] and went with him on his Persian embassy of 1817. He did not share his father's predilection for Russia; in the last irruption of raiders from beyond the Kuban he was on their side. He is generally considered the finest shot and best rider of all the young aristocrats; he would undertake any exploit if only the Kabardan maidens would praise him in their songs around the Aouls [villages]. The order went out to capture and arrest him. Accompanied by his father he appeared voluntarily at the Fort of Nalchik. I was standing by the window as I saw the old man in his turban, evidence of his pilgrimages to Mecca and Medina, appear with his son. Slaves followed on foot. Dzhambulat was in a magnificent costume, a coloured surcoat over his armour. He carried his *kinjal* and a short sword, a rich saddle and over his shoulder a bow with a quiver. In the reception room, we heard the GOC's orders. Arrest in this context did not just mean surrendering his weapons and by doing so losing his honour, it meant craving forgiveness and an admission of guilt which he determinedly refused to give. His father urged him not to destroy himself and all those subject to him. The older men pleaded with Velyaminov not to use force on the bold youth. Sentries were ordered to patrol the room containing the rebel. Any attempt at flight was to be met with shots.

I covered my window so that the old man, his father, should not see what was happening in the house opposite.

Suddenly a shot rang out. Kuchuk Dzhangotov started and raised his eyes to the sky. I looked around. Dzhambulat had fired from the window which he had kicked in, then he had lifted his arm with a kinzhal to stave off the people around him, leaning his head and breast from the window; at that moment a rifle shot and bayonet straight in the neck had thrown him to the ground; after this several further bullets put an end to him. His companion who had jumped behind him in the middle of the yard was likewise shot point blank several times; he fell on his knees, but they were shattered to bits, leant on his left arm and with his right just managed to raise his pistol, but missed and was instantly shot dead.

Farewell, my friend. I have been so interrupted that I have not been able to describe this bloody event properly to you. It happened a month ago and I have not been able to banish it from my memory. I was sorry not so much for those who fell so gloriously, but for the father. He has not been seen since.

Despite this tragedy, which 'at one blow removed the two supports of a courageous, noble people', Griboyedov admired Velyaminov as a first-class soldier and a 'supremely worthy and impressive man'. He accompanied him to Ekaterinengrad at the end of October, spending two months there on a further tour of inspection. He shared a hut with his former diplomatic superior Mazarovich, who had arrived there for consultations with Yermolov, whiling away the evenings by reading him extracts from *Woe from Wit*. Yermolov arrived there on 22 November, in order to prepare for his next punitive expedition to Chechnya. Writing to Beguichov on 7 December, Griboyedov told him that Yermolov did not want him on the expedition, saying that he should be in Tiflis to catch up on Persian and diplomatic paperwork. Even so, he had talked him into letting him accompany him, to see 'the fight for the mountains and forests', and to 'bring freedom and enlightenment to the roll of drums and the whistle of Congreve rockets'.[18] Defiantly, Griboyedov justified the unjustifiable with a memorable forecast: 'We shall hang them [the Chechens], and forgive them, and spit on the verdict of history'.

Griboyedov's renewed involvement with Yermolov may well have encouraged this bellicose stance, so out of tune with the tone of 'The Brigands of the Chegem'. Once again he had fallen under Yermolov's spell.[19]

> I must tell you, he is cleverer than I ever found him before. The pleasure of his company banishes the boredom of attending him during games of whist, which is unavoidable due to our confined quarters. He is unbelievably talkative and friendly and original until the early hours. I cannot admire his physical and moral qualities enough.

He went on to praise Velyaminov and to regret the absence of General Davydov, who might have lightened Yermolov's responsibilities; it was a palpable mistake of the Government to refuse him a Caucasian command.[20]

> Other generals such as Stahl are fools, Gorchakov is a cardboard soldier, Shulgin is no better, a decisive, warlike and clever soldier is needed here! Davydov could put right many of Yermolov's mistakes, he cannot be everywhere at the same time. Now I have known many local leaders, Princes and Uzdens. Two were shot under my very eyes, others were hanged in chains, others flogged through the ranks, another hung over the river where he swings gently in the wind. But to impose order by alternating terror and generosity requires time. Let us see how the next punitive expedition works out against the Chechens; they have been stirred up by their Imam...To Chechnya! To Chechnya is the cry. The main obstacle is that war here has a special character, you have to smoke the enemy out of impenetrable forests and caves; to kill him off means nothing.[21]

Stimulated by the prospect of action, his spirits soared. 'You cannot believe what a cheerful state of mind I am in,' he told his friend.' He made no excuses for his inconsistency. 'People are not like clocks, they are not always the same. Where will you find a book without contradictions?'

The expedition to Chechnya, at this stage only one of several border skirmishes, was planned for the end of December. But meanwhile history had taken a hand. On 19 November 1825, Tsar Alexander died unexpectedly at the age of forty-eight, whilst taking a cure in the little town of Taganrog. Since he was childless, his expected successor was his brother Constantine, at that time Commander-in-Chief of the Polish army and Viceroy there in all but name. Three years previously, however, Constantine had renounced his right to the throne. Married to a Polish commoner, and traumatised by memories of his father's murder, he preferred to govern in Poland rather than risk assassination as the Tsar. Alexander had accepted his renunciation, and nominated his younger brother Nicholas in his place. But he had kept his decision secret, even from Nicholas, and it was only a few days after this death that the document became known. By this time, the Government and the army had sworn loyalty to Constantine as the new heir. A period of confusion followed, Constantine refusing either to leave Warsaw or to renounce the throne; Nicholas, dithering on the sidelines, reluctant to seem to be usurping his brother's place. For a fortnight, the Government of the country ground to a standstill.

Yermolov had received the news of Alexander's death at Ekaterinengrad on 9 December, and had taken the oath of allegiance to Constantine that same day. In St Petersburg, however, the question of the succession had already been resolved in favour of Nicholas, his brother having formally renounced the crown on 6 December. The ceremony in which the Senate, State Council and Guards swore allegiance to the new Tsar was arranged for 14 December.

For the conspirators of the Northern Society, the uncertainties over the succession seemed to present the ideal opportunity to strike; a rising in St Petersburg was fixed for the day of the ceremony. We do not know how much Griboyedov knew of their intentions. Yermolov, it seems, had no foreknowledge of them, though he referred to 'strange rumours' in a letter he sent to a fellow officer in Taganrog. Griboyedov, according to one anecdote, seems to have known much more. Yermolov had a close friend in the North Caucasus, a wealthy sheep farmer, Aleksei Fyodorovich Rebrov. The story comes from General Davydov, who had heard it either from Yermolov or direct from Rebrov himself. He tells us that in mid-December in Ekaterinengrad, where Generals Yermolov and Velyaminov, Griboyedov and Rebrov were gathered round a card-table in the house of some Cossack general, Griboyedov turned to Rebrov and said, 'At this very moment in St Petersburg, an appalling blood-letting is taking place'. Rebrov was greatly struck by this remark, which he recounted to Yermolov two years later.[22]

The story gains its interest from the date. If, as Davydov relates, it took place in mid-December, before the news of the uprising of 14 December in St Petersburg could possibly have reached them, it would prove that Griboyedov had advance warning of what was happening. If it took place later, when the news was generally known, such a remark would have no significance.

It was not until 25 December that a *feld jaeger*, or government courier, arrived with official confirmation that Constantine had abdicated and that Nicholas was Emperor. By this time the conspiracy had collapsed in ruins, and most of Griboyedov's friends in St Petersburg had been arrested.

XVI

The Decembrist Débacle

On the evening of 13 December 1825, there was a noisy meeting in Ryleyev's flat at which the decision to stage the coup for the following day was confirmed.[1] For some weeks previously, the plotters had been stirring up dissension within the various regiments in which they served. The abdication of Constantine, a far more liberal figure than Nicholas, gave them the chance to claim that Nicholas had usurped the throne, and to rally the troops under the twin slogan of 'Constantine and the constitution'; many of the soldiers who followed them thought that the word *constitutsiya* ('constitution') was the name of Constantine's wife. It was planned that the troops should gather on the Senate Square on the following morning and then march to the Winter Palace and arrest the Tsar. A few of those present thought the uprising was premature, but most agreed that things had already gone too far to turn back. 'We were so utterly determined either to succeed or die that we did not come to the least agreement in the event of failure,' wrote Bestuzhev years later. 'We shall die, oh, how gloriously we shall die!' cried Odoyevsky, exalted by Ryleyev's eloquence and the prospect of action at last.[2]

Prince Sergei Trubetskoy, the senior army officer amongst the conspirators, had been elected as leader of the military operation. On the morning of 14 December, however, he lost his nerve completely and slipped away to swear allegiance to the new Tsar, spending the rest of the day in hiding in the Austrian embassy. Yakubovich, who had recently arrived from the Caucasus, full of ardour for the revolutionary cause, was another who betrayed it on the day. He had been intended to lead the Marine Guards in capturing the Winter Palace; at six in the morning, after a sleepless night of doubt and indecision, he told Ryleyev and Bestuzhev that he refused to carry out the plan.

The two defections were symptomatic of the day's confusion. Of the sixteen regiments stationed in St Petersburg, only parts of three of them gathered in the Senate Square – some 3000 men in all. For five hours they stood in the freezing cold, with no clear leadership or direction; Ryleyev, a civilian, having tried vainly to whip up his officer associates, finally returned home in despair. Nicholas, at first terrified of provoking a full-scale insurrection, gathered courage as the day went on. The gallant Miloradovich, who had tried to harangue the troops into surrendering peacefully, was shot down by Kakhovsky. By three o'clock, the Tsar had overcome his fears and scruples about using force, and had mobilised 12,000 troops. Reluctant to shed blood on the day of his accession, he twice countermanded his own orders before he finally ordered his cannon to fire on the mutineers. Within moments, the serried ranks of soldiers had turned into a fleeing, panic-stricken mob; great numbers lay dead and wounded on the square behind them. Throughout the night and over the next few days, the leading conspirators were rounded up, to be interrogated singly by the Tsar before being taken off in irons to the Fortress of St Peter and St Paul. Trubetskoy, who had given himself up to the police, provided most of the basic information about the chief members of both the Southern and Northern Societies. Couriers were despatched throughout Russia to arrest suspects.

The same confusion that had destroyed the revolution's chances in St Petersburg reigned among the members of the Southern Society. The day before the uprising, Pestel' had been arrested, following a police enquiry begun before Alexander's death. Deprived of his leadership, many of his followers panicked. Muravyov-Apostol, on hearing the news of the failed uprising in the capital (which reached the Southern Decembrists on 23 December), at first contemplated suicide, then embarked on a last desperate throw, rallying 800 members of his regiment to march on Kiev, in the hopes that other disaffected troops would join him. No reinforcements were forthcoming. On 3 January, the rebels were defeated by government forces, and Apostol, severely wounded, was taken back to St Petersburg for interrogation.

Yermolov was encamped at Chervlennaya on the river Terek, preparatory to leaving for Chechnya, when the threefold news of Constantine's abdication, Nicholas's accession as Tsar, and the failure of the St Petersburg uprising reached him on 25 December. It was a bright sunny day, recalled one of his aides, and a parade had been planned in honour of the Commander-in-Chief as part of the Christmas festivities; all the camp gossip was of the forthcoming expedition against the Chechens. Suddenly a troika came galloping up to the Commander-in-Chief's hut and its passenger, Feld Jaeger Damish, emerged, carrying a stout brown envelope.

Yermolov, off duty, and dressed in an unbuttoned frock coat, was playing patience when Damish came in.[3] 'Well,' he said, 'read us the news.' He continued playing cards as Damish read out the official announcement of the Tsar's accession to the throne. When it came to the passage stating that Nicholas would 'follow in the footsteps of Alexander the Blessed', he remarked sarcastically that he was very grateful to hear it. The casual tone of this remark, and his unceremonious reception of the imperial emissary would be duly reported back to Nicholas, already suspicious of Yermolov as a possible Decembrist sympathiser. In the immediate aftermath of the rising, the fear that he might raise the Caucasian corps against him seemed very real.

After he had finished reading the official announcement, and had handed it over to the Commander-in-Chief, Damish began to speak about the uprising. Griboyedov, who had been present as a trusted member of Yermolov's staff, stood nearby. His hands were so tightly clenched together, noted Yermolov's aide Liprandi (later to be involved as a General in the charge of the Light Brigade), that the knuckles were white. Then he smiled and, with a sweeping movement of his arms, exclaimed, 'Now, stand by for a real stir, and watch the sparks fly in St Petersburg! How will it all end?'[4]

There are differing accounts as to how soon Yermolov's troops took the oath of allegiance to the new Tsar. According to his own memoirs, he ordered those stationed at Chervlennaya to take it at once and despatched his Chief of Staff to Tiflis to deal with any remaining troops and the civilian population. However, there seems to have been a delay of two days before the troops on the spot took the oath, perhaps because there was no priest available to administer it. To the ever-suspicious Tsar, it may well have appeared that Yermolov had postponed the ceremony till he knew for certain that the conspiracy had failed.

For Griboyedov, the news that his friends in St Petersburg were facing trial and possible execution must have been shattering enough. But he does not seem to have felt that he himself was in danger. He was intent on taking part in Yermolov's expedition to Chechnya, and had been attached to the First Battalion of the Shirvan Regiment, which were supplemented by Cossacks and some horse-drawn artillery. The expedition set out for Grozny early in January. Already, however, the question of Griboyedov's implication in the plot was being raised in St Petersburg. On 17 December, the first session of the Secret Committee Appointed by his Majesty for the Purpose of Investigating Members of Subversive Societies took place. Its purpose was to find out the full extent of the conspiracy in which members of some of the noblest families in the land were implicated. How far had the rot spread? The Tsar took a personal hand in questioning the chief suspects. Trubetskoy, now a broken man, was one of those who put forward Griboyedov's name as a possible member of the Northern Society. Bestuzhev and Ryleyev, on the other hand, staunchly denied that he had ever joined it, though they admitted having had discussions with him on the state of Russia; other friends under arrest, such as Küchelbecker and Odoyevsky, avoided mentioning his name altogether. Despite this, there was sufficient suspicion against Griboyedov to justify issuing a warrant for his arrest. On 22 January, a courier from the Ministry of War, Feld Jaeger Uklonsky, arrived in Grozny with a letter to Yermolov from the Chief of Staff in St Petersburg, General Dibich, ordering him to place Griboyedov under arrest.

In his letter, Dibich had specifically instructed Yermolov to see that Griboyedov had no time to destroy any papers. It was typical of Griboyedov's recklessness or self-confidence that during the period between receiving the news of the uprising and Uklonsky's arrival, he had made no attempt to do so. Fortunately, the travelling trunks containing his papers were being pulled by the Shirvan regimental bullocks, and were not drawn up next to his sleeping quarters. On receiving Dibich's letter, Yermolov immediately sent a message to Griboyedov, warning him that his trunks were about to be searched.[5] With just an hour in hand, the faithful manservant Gribov (who, it was said, knew everything about Griboyedov's affairs) was able to drag his cart from the column, open the trunks and burn the papers they contained on his cooking stove; only the manuscript of *Woe from Wit* escaped the pyre. He then brought them to the hut which Griboyedov shared with a fellow officer, Shimanovsky, where they were placed at the head of his bed to await the arrival of Uklonsky.

'As usual I was having an argument with Griboyedov about Moscow,' recalled Shimanovsky,

> I was defending it, while he covered it with sarcasms. Suddenly the door opened and Colonel Mishchenko, his commanding officer, came in together with Talyzin [Yermolov's adjutant] – immediately behind him was the Feld Jaeger Uklonsky. Mishchenko went up to Griboyedov and said 'Alexander Sergeyevich, it is the wish of the Emperor that we should arrest you. Where are your things and your papers?' Griboyedov nonchalantly showed him the trunks, which were dragged into the middle of the room. They began to sort out his linen, and finally at the bottom of one of them they came on a fairly thick notebook, which was the manuscript of *Woe from Wit*. They asked if he had any more papers, to which he replied that there were none, that all his property was in the

trunks. Mishchenko had his trunks bound up and sealed. Griboyedov was then transferred to other quarters with a sentry at each window and the door.[6]

Griboyedov spent the night under arrest. He did not get undressed; other young officers, including Yermolov's nephew Sergei Yermolov, and Talysin, as duty officer, looked in on him from time to time, perhaps to wish him luck or say goodbye. The next morning the trunks were officially re-opened and inspected by Colonel Mishchenko, and Talysin, representing Yermolov. Feld Jaeger Uklonsky then took over the sealed chests.

In his letter to Dibich, to be delivered with the prisoner in St Petersburg, Yermolov assured the German General (whom he detested) that Griboyedov had been arrested 'in such a way that he could not destroy any papers'. He added a note of commendation: 'I must tell Your Excellency, Mr Griboyedov whilst serving attached to our Persian Mission, and then attached to me, distinguished himself by the probity and exemplary morality of his conduct, as well as in many other admirable qualities.'[7]

Yermolov had done his best for the young man who, according to one witness, he 'regarded almost as a son'. As Dibich later wrote to the Tsar, 'Yermolov loves Griboyedov, especially his unusual mind, fanatical honesty, the diversity of his learning, and his amiability as a colleague'. It was no surprise that the two men were on first-name terms, or that Yermolov had tried to protect him. It may well be too that Yermolov feared that some of the letters that were destroyed might have compromised him personally. He had always been an outspoken critic of the St Petersburg bureaucracy whose views could have been quoted by Griboyedov's friends. The correspondence in the trunks almost certainly included letters from friends such as Bestuzhev, Küchelbecker, and Alexander Odoyevsky, all now under arrest, as well as being scattered with the names of other prominent Decembrists. Griboyedov would have had a lot of explaining to do about his friendships, apparently so intimate and warm, with so many of the leading conspirators. In the opinion of Zavalyshin (himself arrested after the plot), Griboyedov derived an important advantage during his interrogation from Yermolov's generosity in giving him time to burn his papers: 'Quite a few of these would have been highly dangerous'. He added that a number of other senior figures had given similar chances to suspected Decembrists.[8]

Griboyedov had left two other trunks containing papers in the care of a Major Ogaryov at Vladikavkaz. These had to be retrieved and brought to Ekaterinengrad by Uklonsky before leaving for St Petersburg, thus delaying their departure until 30 January. Griboyedov showed no undue alarm at this; however, on arrival at Ekaterinengrad, he managed to extract a number of letters from under the very eyes of the officer on duty in the guard-house, and prevailed on a suspect about to be released (a certain M.S. Alekseyev) to smuggle them out.

Relieved of the most damning evidence against him, Griboyedov could spend the journey to St Petersburg turning over his line of defence before the commission. Travelling on sledges, in appalling conditions of frost and heavy snow, he and Uklonsky reached Moscow early on 6 February, where they stopped over for the day with Beguichov's brother Dmitri. Stepan Beguichov was rapidly alerted, and rushed to see his friend, whom he found eating at table with his brother and a third, white-haired figure in the uniform of a *feld jaeger.*

'Why are you staring at him,' asked Griboyedov jokingly. 'Don't imagine this is just a simple courier. My good friend, the person you see is not just a courier, he comes from a distinguished family, he is a grandee of Spain, Don Lysko-Pleshivos-di-Parichentsa [or, roughly translated, "Don Balding, the Hairless One"]'. [9]

'Such humour,' wrote Beguichov, 'showed me Griboyedov's relation ship with his jailer. Griboyedov was cheerful after dinner; he turned to his bodyguard, saying, 'Surely you have beloved relatives here, shouldn't you go and visit them?' The jailer was delighted to be liberated in this way, and left.'

By 2a.m. they were on their way again, Griboyedov having probably received a full briefing from Beguichov. Almost all of his St Petersburg acquaintance had been rounded up. Zhandr had been arrested and then released on 31 January. Küchelbecker had fled to Warsaw, and was picked up there on 10 January, one of the last of the Northern Society to be arrested.

The charges on which the leading Decembrists were tried were serious – attempted murder of the Tsar and his brothers the grand dukes. (Pestel' had wanted 'a gallows large enough to hang the whole Imperial family'.)[10] There was also incitement to riot and armed mutiny, conflicting with their oath of loyalty, and their declared intention of sweeping away the autocracy in favour of a constitutional monarchy or a republic. Witnesses before the commission therefore had to answer firstly whether a given individual was a member of the conspiracy through one or other of its secret societies, and secondly if he had known of its treasonable aims and programme. In view of his long-standing friendships and daily contact with so many of the leading Decembrists, it was not surprising that Griboyedov should be included in the list of suspects.

Fortunately, there were a number of helpful circumstances on his side. His mother, whose first reaction to his arrest was one of disapproval – according to Beguichov, she described her son as 'one of those Carbonari'[11] – was soon doing all she could behind the scenes. One of her trump cards was the fact that her brother's daughter, Elizaveta Alekseyevna, was married to General Paskievich, one of Nicholas's most trusted generals and a member of the commission. Another circumstance in Griboyedov's favour was the fact that Nicholas, though suspicious of Yermolov, was reluctant to move against him openly. He knew him to be popular with his troops, and had no wish to precipitate a mutiny by removing him from his post; Griboyedov, as Yermolov's diplomatic adviser, was to some extent protected by Nicholas's cautious attitude towards his chief.

Griboyedov was lucky not to be imprisoned in the grim Fortress of St Peter and St Paul, where most of the leading Decembrists were incarcerated. The fortress was gravely overcrowded,[12] and the headquarters of the general staff was being used as a kind of holding pen for surplus prisoners. Here conditions were far better than in the gloomy, dripping cells of the fortress, where darkness and loneliness played their part in breaking down the resistance of the accused. In the guard-room of the staff headquarters, Griboyedov could mix with other prisoners, and receive books and newspapers from friends outside.[13] Security was comparatively relaxed. He was allowed to visit Laredo's tearooms, adjoining the general staff building on the corner of Admiralty Square, a fashionable establishment deservedly famous for its ices, where customers could peruse the latest newspapers at leisure. There was a piano in a separate room. Here Griboyedov entertained his security officer, Captain Zhukovsky – a passionate musical amateur – by playing the piano; his fellow prisoner Zavalyshin would read the papers while Griboyedov beguiled his attentive listener with Mozart and Rossini.

Griboyedov was the two-hundred-and-twenty-fourth person to be cross-examined by the commission. The first session took place shortly after his arrival on 11 February, in the cellars of the Hermitage. Zavalyshin recalls how a fellow prisoner, a certain Colonel Lyubimov, came up to Griboyedov in the guard-house while he was preparing his defence. 'Whatever you are writing has nothing to do with me,' said Lyubimov. 'I have no contacts at all with you, so please accept that advice as utterly impersonal and unbiased.' He warned him to say as little as possible about himself and his friends. 'Much better stick to the old Russian saying: "I have absolutely no idea, I know nothing".'[14]

It was sound advice. During his first interrogation, conducted by Adjutant-General Levashov, Griboyedov denied any knowledge of the conspiracy. Levashov noted down his answer:

> I did not belong to the secret society and I did not suspect its existence. When I came back from Persia to St Petersburg, I became acquainted with Bestuzhev, Ryleyev and Odoyevsky through the literary interests we shared; I was already linked with Küchelbecker from our time

together in Georgia. From all these people I heard nothing which could have given me the slightest idea about the secret society. In conversation with them we often exchanged bold judgements about the government in which I took part. Where I thought things were harmful, I wished for improvements. There were no other acts on my part which could possibly have brought me into suspicion. As to why such suspicion has fallen on me, I can neither comment nor elaborate.[15]

Levashov was impressed by Griboyedov's seeming frankness, and led him to understand that he would soon be released. But the commission did not intend to let him get away so easily. On 14 February, some of the leading figures of the conspiracy, including Ryleyev, Nikita Muravyov, Odoyevsky, Bestuzhev, Trubetskoy and Obolensky, were formally asked whether Griboyedov had ever been enrolled in the Northern Society. All but the last two denied that he had ever been a member, and did their best to minimise his involvement. Trubetskoy, backtracking, admitted that his evidence was only based on hearsay. The most damning statement came from Obolensky, who claimed that Griboyedov had been received as a member a few days before leaving St Petersburg, though he himself had not been present. Two other minor figures, Briggen and Orzhritsky, also claimed that they had heard him mentioned as a member.

Griboyedov, probably unaware of these interviews, wrote a personal appeal to the Tsar the following day.[16] He pleaded his innocence, the injustice of the suspicions which had led to his being dragged 3000 versts from Grozny, and the effect which the news of his tragic situation would have on his mother, who might well lose her reason on hearing it. He had been totally frank with Levashov, who had promised him a speedy release, but the days had gone by and he was still incarcerated. 'All-merciful Sovereign...be good enough to give me back my freedom, the loss of which my conduct in no way deserves, or allow me to confront my accusers face to face, so that I may refute their lies and slanders.'

The letter, with its tone of injured innocence, did nothing to advance his cause: 'One does not write to the Sovereign in such a manner,' noted Dibich drily. On the evening of 24 February, his eyes blindfolded, Griboyedov was led across the ice of the Neva to the Fortress of St Peter and St Paul for a full-scale interrogation. This time he faced the whole commission, including his cousin by marriage Paskievich, the War Minister, Tatishchev, Grand Duke Michael and the Tsar's new head of security, Count Benckendorff. Unlike his fellow prisoners, broken down by questioning and the prospect of death or forced labour in Siberia, he remained cool-headed and composed throughout the interview. His attitude was typified in a note to Bulgarin (to whom he wrote a note from prison, asking for a copy of *Childe Harold*): 'To fear people is to indulge them or to flatter them'.[17]

He freely admitted his acquaintance with five of the most active figures of the December uprising, Bestuzhev, Ryleyev, Obolensky, Küchelbecker and Odoyevsky; their role on the fateful day he already knew through chance conversations in the Caucasus, Moscow and the Guard House. He agreed that he had discussed general questions of reform with them, but denied that he had any knowledge of the conspiracy. Trubetskoy and others were mistaken in believing that he shared their views. 'Just because I agreed with them in certain judgements about morals, literature and new ideas, it does not prove that I agreed with them politically.'[18] As for Obolensky's allegation that he had joined the Northern Society just before leaving St Petersburg in May 1825, he dismissed it completely. The Prince must have confused it with the fact that he had joined the Society of Lovers of Russian Literature, a few days before leaving the capital; he had always considered his membership of the society, which enjoyed imperial patronage, as one of the consolations of his life.

In this, as in many of his answers, Griboyedov was dealing in half-truths. In fact, as the records of the Academy of Sciences show, he joined the Society of Lovers of Russian Literature five months, not two or three days, before leaving St Petersburg, so it was hardly likely that such a confusion would have arisen. His interrogators never cross-checked this, or other statements. A group of well-bred, sometimes bumbling, senior military men, they were scarcely the stuff of which Fouquier-Tinvilles or Vyshinskys are made.

Griboyedov had made a good impression on the commission, who recommended his release the following day. The Tsar refused. He was still suspicious of Griboyedov's intimacy with Yermolov, and the possibility that he might have joined the Southern Society, with the aim of recruiting in the Caucasus. The question of possible subversion, even a branch of the society, existing in the Caucasian corps of Yermolov's army was not yet settled in his mind: he wanted further exploration of the possibility. As with the Northern Society, some leading members of the Southern Society, Bestuzhev-Ryumin and the Muravyovs, were formally interrogated on Griboyedov's involvement with the rising. All made it clear that he had not been asked to join them, that they did not know him well enough, and that there had been no intention of creating a splinter movement in the Caucasus.[19] The Tsar remained unconvinced, still brooding over Yermolov's possible disloyalty. It was not until the end of May, when he had received a report from his special envoy to the Shah, Prince Menshikov, stating positively that there was no evidence of any disaffection amongst Yermolov's officers, and that his troops were overwhelmingly loyal, that he was forced to abandon his suspicions.[20]

In the interval, Griboyedov had undergone a series of further inter-rogations, through which he had managed not only to evade or deflect difficult questions, but also to avoid drawing anyone else into trouble. For instance, in describing his educational influences, he refrained from mentioning his tutor Dr John, but concentrated on Bühle, who was already dead. He was never confronted with his friends from the Northern Society who, with the exception of Trubetskoy and Obolensky, had always played down his relations with them, nor did the commission follow up the inconsistencies in their evidence. He was fortunate in the support of General Tatishchev, to whom Yermolov had written interceding for him, and of Paskievich, whom he later called 'my benefactor'. He was also helped by the civil servant in charge of the committee's paper work, a certain A.A. Ivanovsky, who admired him as one of the hopes of Russian literature, and may well have adapted or omitted unfavourable evidence. On 31 May 1826, on the advice of the commission, his file was finally minuted by the Tsar: 'Release him with a certificate of innocence'.[21] On the same day, Tatishchev sent a formal note to Yermolov to tell him that Griboyedov was freed of all suspicion, and had been granted the necessary funds to rejoin his post, namely the chancery of the GOC in Tiflis, where he had the honour to serve as diplomatic secretary.

XVII

The Persian Campaign

Griboyedov was officially released on 2 June 1826. A week later, he was promoted to the rank of College Counsellor, seventh class (equivalent to Lieutenant-Colonel), with a corresponding rise in salary. As a further mark of favour, he was granted an audience with the Tsar, together with a number of other well-connected prisoners who had also been exonerated. The Tsar was 'most affable to us,' Griboyedov told Varvara Miklashevich; 'he was clever, wise and kind, and spoke with an adroitness and skill only equalled in my experience by Yermolov'.[1]

Still reeling from his narrow escape, Griboyedov could only express gratitude to the imperial autocrat whose towering presence and terrifying 'pewter eyes'[2] had reduced so many of the Decembrists to grovelling remorse. The Tsar had insisted on interrogating the major conspirators himself. Far more punitive and vengeful than the commission, he was determined to make an example of the plotters, ignoring the advice of those who pleaded for a more lenient approach. The conspiracy, after all, had failed; its tentacles had reached into almost all the country's leading families. It might have been politic as well as generous for the emperor to propitiate them by beginning his reign in a spirit of magnanimity. It was not in his character to do so.

There was no death penalty as such in Russia, though the punishment of flogging in the army came to the same. But the guilt of the leading five conspirators was considered so great that they were sentenced to be hanged, drawn and quartered. In the spirit of modern enlightenment, the Tsar had commuted the sentence to hanging only.

138

On 12 July, Ryleyev, Nikita Muravyov, Kakhovsky, Pestel' and Bestuzhev-Ryumin were hanged on a common gallows in the courtyard of the Fortress of St Peter and St Paul. At two in the morning the following day, more than 100 former officers were led from their cells into the same courtyard, where detachments from all the regiments in St Petersburg to which they belonged were gathered. One by one they were made to kneel down before their respective regiments, while their epaulettes and decorations were stripped from them, and their swords broken over their heads. They were then led back to their cells, to await the long journey in chains to forced labour in Siberia, or to serve in the ranks in the 'warm Siberia' of the Caucasus.

Almost all of Griboyedov's circle had been gathered up. Obolensky and Trubetskoy were sentenced to hard labour for life, Küchelbecker and Odoyevsky to 12 years, Bestuzhev to five; all were deprived of their nobility and rank. Pushkin, still exiled on his country estate, was one of the few who escaped the frightful reckoning, but his grim sketch of the five hanged men, scribbled in one of his notebooks, summed up the horror of the situation. Of the soldiers who had blindly followed their officers onto Senate Square, more than 200 had been killed, others would be flogged to death or reassigned to the front line in the Caucasus, where the chance of surviving the tribesmen's bullets was very small.

Griboyedov had been extraordinarily lucky to escape. Even if it was true that he had never joined either of the societies, it is inconceivable that he had not been aware of their aims. To have had foreknowledge of the conspiracy without revealing it was an offence in itself. He had survived thanks to his own coolness under questioning and the support of influential friends. But the psychological toll must have been very great. Granted leave before returning to the Caucasus, he spent two months recovering in the country with Bulgarin.[3]

Since 1825, Bulgarin and Grech had been editors of a new literary journal, the *Northern Bee*. Even before the Decembrist catastrophe, it had been notably conservative in its outlook, and for the next 30 years the paper would be one of the leading upholders of government policy. Bulgarin himself was on close terms with Count Benckendorff, the new head of government security, and was a political informer on occasion. However, he had only narrowly escaped arrest that winter owing to the malice of a journalistic rival, and he had shown considerable courage in sending books to Griboyedov while he was in prison. He was an ardent admirer of Griboyedov, whom he had first met in St Petersburg two years before. 'I was fonder of Griboyedov than any other human being... perhaps I even loved him more than my children; this was something holier and more precious than anything else in the world. His spirit was paradise, his mind was the sun.' One is reminded of the passionate devotion Griboyedov inspired in Küchelbecker, and indeed in other friends, such as Beguichov and Bestuzhev.

Griboyedov's mood during his stay with Bulgarin was sombre in the extreme.[4] 'He only saw those close to him, passing his time in reading, conversation, walking and playing the piano...his improvisations were impregnated with a deep feeling of melancholy.' Two poems probably dating from this time were found in his notebook after his death. The first, entitled 'Liberation', was a lyrical evocation of the woods, blue skies and silken lawns to which he had been restored. But freedom was meaningless – he was alone. 'Our lips are sealed with grief, our hands bear heavy chains.' The second, dedicated to 'O', almost certainly Alexander Odoyevsky, was a lament for their friendship:

> Your gifts inspired my verses and my thoughts.
> I loved you with my very soul.
> O God, my Creator, I reproach you
> For so pitilessly cutting short our dawning century.

The world as Griboyedov had known it before 1826 had been shattered irretrievably, and he had to come to terms with the new one being fashioned under Nicholas I. His association with Bulgarin, a comparatively venal figure when contrasted with the blazing idealism of his martyred friends, was a sign of things to come.[5] Henceforth he must conform to the suffocating ideals of the new regime: Orthodoxy, autocracy and nationalism. Under Alexander I there had been no official ideology as such. With the suppression of the Decembrists, and the very different character of Nicholas I, a military autocrat rather than a civilian Hamlet, it could truly be said that the rules of the game had been changed. Confirmed in his hatred of everything that threatened the status quo, the Tsar saw his mission as an absolute ruler as a sacred obligation. A rigid bureaucracy would replace the nobility as a ruling class; free speech and the expression of political opinions would become taboo. Romantic liberalism, even the heedless babble of drawing-room radicals like Repetilov, had no place in the new order. Griboyedov's university contemporary Chaadayev, who had been abroad during the Decembrist tragedy,[6] would sound a solitary note of protest when he published the first of his *Philosophical Letters*, with its drastic indictment of Russian history and culture, in 1836. The Government's response was to declare him officially insane; Chatsky's fate in *Woe from Wit*, where his diatribes against society are taken as a sign of madness, had been prophetic.

For Griboyedov, there was no longer any room for the Chatsky side of his character or the luxury of denouncing society's hypocrisies. The time had come for survival. As a newly promoted Counsellor, it was the role of Molchalin, the assiduous civil servant, that he must now adopt. Beset by chronic financial problems, he required his miserable state salary. He had none of the 'arrogance of riches' enjoyed by those of independent means; he knew he had no choice but to conform. (In fact, as he admitted to Bulgarin,[7] he was broke: 'I haven't a single kopeck.') Reflecting his new-found resignation, he advised Beguichov to read Plutarch, since history at least was safe. Republican heroes were unthinkable in the new present. 'I have stopped being clever,' he confided.[8]

Friends of the past, now exiled or in prison, would always acknowledge that Chatsky, through his fiery eloquence, had expressed his generation's aspirations and ideals. No Decembrist ever accused Griboyedov – who had not only escaped a prison sentence, but been promoted on release – of being traitor to their cause. Only Griboyedov could ask himself, in his innermost conscience, whether in escaping the martyrdom of so many of his friends he had played an ignoble role. For the rest of his life he would do his utmost to mitigate the fate of his friends, borrowing money to help Küchelbecker, pleading with Paskievich for Odoyevsky and Bestuzhev, as former officers, to be transferred from Siberia to the Caucasus. But the knowledge that he had survived where others had not, must have always been with him, driving him on perhaps towards a different kind of expiation.

For the time being, his duties in Georgia called him, and in the middle of August, after a short stay with Beguichov and a farewell visit to his mother, he set out on the long dusty ride towards the Caucasus.[9] At Vladikavkaz he met up with his old friend General Davydov, now re-appointed to active service commanding a cavalry brigade on Yermolov's staff. The two men travelled to Tiflis together, riding ahead of the slow-moving convoy in a light two-wheeled *droshky*; during their conversations together Griboyedov was able to recount the story of Yermolov's generosity in forewarning him.

They arrived in Georgia to find the country at war.[10] In July 1826, exasperated by Yermolov's failure to make concessions over disputed border areas (Balikloo and Lake Gokcheh), and urged on by his Shiite clerics, Abbas Mirza had launched an attack on Karabakh. War had been brewing for some time. Abbas Mirza had long resented the refusal of the Russians to accept him as the Shah's official heir; the Russians favoured the claims of one of his brothers, who was more likely to go along with their demands. The news of the Decembrist rising had at first spread the idea that Russia was on the brink of a civil war, and thus in a poor position to defend itself. Even when it was dispelled by Nicholas's official envoy, Prince Menshikov, who had arrived in Persia to bring the news of his accession as Tsar, the situation between the two countries did not improve.[11] Menshikov, although the official envoy, was not allowed to override Yermolov's policies.[12] Yermolov was spoiling for a fight. Not only did he refuse to discuss disputed borders, but he had also moved Russian troops into two tracts of Persian territory at Gokcheh and Balikloo firmly believed by the Shah and the British to be Persian according to the Treaty of Gulistan. This violation was supposedly to prevent incursions from Muslim tribes. Despite this, he was taken by surprise by Abbas Mirza's attack, and the subsequent invasion of Georgia's southwestern border provinces by troops from Erivan. The Russian army, thinly spread over vast areas of country, was unable to stem the Persian advance; Karabakh was devastated, and only the gallant defence of Shusha, during a six-week siege, saved Georgia itself from being overrun.

At this moment of crisis, Yermolov, the man of action, played a curiously passive role. Disregarding orders from the Tsar that he should use the 15,000 troops already in Georgia to occupy Erivan, he insisted that it was impossible to do so until Karabakh, and the safety of Georgia itself, had been secured. His call for reinforcements had only been partially met. Neither the Tsar nor Foreign Minister Nesselrode – Capodistrias had retired in 1820 – had wished for war with Persia, and Menshikov had still been in Persia when Abbas Mirza had invaded Karabakh. Yermolov was offered a compromise involving concessions near Talish against the Gokcheh/Balikloo infringements, but killed it off. (Prince Menshikov had only been able to get home thanks to the good offices of the British.) Having done everything to provoke the war by his intransigent attitudes, Yermolov now seemed incapable of dealing with it;[13] he later claimed that his energies had been paralysed by the knowledge of the Tsar's distrust. For the Tsar, who did indeed suspect him, it was a further confirmation of his views. He still did not dare to dismiss him, but he appointed the loyal Adjutant-General Paskievich as his commander in the field, under direct orders from himself, thus effectively bypassing Yermolov's authority as Commander-in-Chief. Arriving in Tiflis at the end of August, Paskievich rapidly justified the Emperor's faith in him by routing the main Persian army on the banks of the Akistafa near Elizavetpol on 14 September; the tide of Russian defeats had been turned.

Paskievich had won the battle in the teeth of furious opposition from Yermolov and Madatov, even to the extent of denying him troops and supplies. Griboyedov, on his return to Tiflis, found the two men at daggers drawn. 'My life here is miserable!' he complained to Beguichov.

> I did not get to the seat of war as Alexis Petrovich [Yermolov] did not get
> there and now we have another war [between the generals]. If two elderly

36. Mirza Abul Hassan Khan (1776–1846), envoy extraordinary from the Shah to George III, 1810. Abul Hassan Khan accepted a pension from the East India Company for many years, and was Persia's Foreign Minister at the time of the Treaty of Turkmanchai and Griboyedov's murder. Sir William Beechey, 1810, commissioned by the East India Company. Courtesy of Oriental and India Office Library.

37. Crown Prince Abbas Mirza (1792–1833). Sir Robert Ker Porter, from *Travels in Persia, Armenia, Ancient Babylonia During the Years 1817–1820* (2 vols, 1821).

38. ABOVE. Persian meal inside
caravansaray; Griboyedov often
found himself having to share
such facilities. From Colonel
G. Drouville, *Voyage en Perse
faite en 1812 et 1813*, Paris,
1825.

39. Persian in court dress. From
Colonel G. Drouville, *Voyage en
Perse faite en 1812 et 1813*, Paris,
1825.

40. ABOVE. Persian musicians. Griboyedov complained that he found Persian music barbaric, but could not stop himself listening to it. From James Morier, *A Second Journey Through Persia, Armenia and Asia Minor to Constantinople* (1818).

41. LEFT. Fath Ali Shah (1762–1834). Mihr Ali, 1809–10. Hermitage Museum, St Petersburg. A.T. Adamova (ed.), *Persian Paintings in Hermitage*, Slaviya, St Petersburg, 1996.

42. Fath Ali Shah receiving the homage of his son, Abbas Mirza, at a 'military review'. The picture was
a bold attempt to convince father and son that Western military reforms would be effective against
Russia. General Kotlyarevsky's victory, leading to the humiliating Treaty of Gulistan in 1813, told a
different story. The very sight of the picture infuriated Yermolov during his 1817 embassy. Oil. Picture
Gallery, Hermitage Museum, St Petersburg. A.T. Adamova (ed.), *Persian Paintings in the Hermitage*,
Slaviya, St Petersburg, 1996. Courtesy of Hermitage Museum, St Petersburg.

43. LEFT. Prince P.A. Vyazemsky (1792–1878), owner of Ostafyievo, near Moscow and Pushkin's great friend and correspondent. He collaborated with Griboyedov on the vaudeville *Who is the Brother? Who is the Sister?* Oil, O.A. Kiprensky. *Alexander Pushkin and His Time in the Fine Arts of the First Half of the Nineteenth Century,* Khudojnik, RSFSR, Leningrad, 1985.

44. RIGHT. F.V. Bulgarin, editor of *The Northern Bee,* friend and financial benefactor of Griboyedov. He was said to be a stylish dancer, especially of the mazurka (he was Polish). Caricature by Stepanov.

45. LEFT. N.I. Grech (1787–1847), editor of *Son of the Fatherland,* close colleague of Bulgarin. Profile, Thomas Wright, 1820s.

46. A.I. Odoyevsky (1802–39), Decembrist and Griboyedov's flatmate in St Petersburg. Watercolour, N.A. Bestuzhev. I.S. Zilbershtein, *The Artist Decembrist, Nicholas Bestuzhev*, Representative Art, Moscow, 1977.

47. E.A. Teleshova (1804–57), as Luisa in the Ballet *The Deserter*. Oil, Kiprensky. Courtesy of the State Tretyakov Gallery, Moscow.

48. LEFT. Bear Promontory,
near Gursuf, Yalta, Black Sea.
Oil on canvas, Boglyubov.
Courtesy of G. Putnikov,
Moscow.

49. BELOW. Griboyedov
explores the ancient Crimean
palace of the Khans at Bakchi-
Saray Emelyan. M. Korneyev,
courtesy of Pushkin Museum,
Moscow.

generals fight, the feathers fly from the coats of their subordinates; my former friendship with A.P. [Yermolov] has rather chilled.

Griboyedov was in an embarrassing position.[14] Before leaving Moscow, his mother had extorted a promise from him that he should do his utmost to serve under Paskievich, seeing the appointment of a powerful kinsman as an ideal opportunity to re-establish his career. At the same time Griboyedov was deeply indebted to Yermolov, and there were those, such as Davydov and Muravyov-Karsky, who did not hesitate to accuse him of ingratitude. In his memoirs, Muravyov reminds us how much Griboyedov owed to Yermolov: he had turned a blind eye to his second duel, he had recommended him (unsuccessfully) for a decoration for repatriating the deserters, he had promoted him to his diplomatic chancery, above all he had given him an opportunity to destroy any compromising papers before his arrest in 1825, and had written to Dibich on his behalf.

Griboyedov had still been fascinated and impressed by Yermolov in the months before his arrest, but his poem 'The Brigands of the Chegem' showed that he was beginning to have doubts about Russia's 'civilising' mission in the Caucasus as preached by Yermolov; his conversations with enlightened figures like Prince Vyazemsky may also have helped to change his perspectives. There had been too many hangings and floggings, too many bodies swinging in the wind. On a pragmatic basis too, it was becoming clear that Yermolov's policies of terror were not working. His oppressive treatment of the Muslims in the former Persian provinces had been one of the factors in inflaming religious opinion against the Russians; when the war came, his punitive campaigns against the tribesmen of Chechnya and Daghestan proved to have been counterproductive, tying down so many troops on garrison duty that he had not enough to fight elsewhere.

The process of detachment started slowly.[15] In private, Griboyedov's first reactions to Paskievich were disrespectful, even hostile. Davydov reports him as saying to him and Shimanovsky, one of Yermolov's ADCs, 'How could you wish to see this idiot triumph over one of the cleverest and best intentioned men in Russia? Be sure, our man will prevail, and Paskievich who has crept into this situation, will remove himself in a hurry.' He added that Paskievich was 'an unbearable ass, gifted only with the cunning of a Ukrainian', and that all his successes were due to the excellence of Yermolov's soldiers, and the skills of Generals Velyaminov and Madatov.

Paskievich, in fact, was an experienced soldier who had fought in all the main campaigns of the war of 1812, and later commanded the Guards Infantry Division, in which the Tsar, then Grand Duke Nicholas, had served under him. As a result, the Tsar referred to him affectionately as 'my father, my commanding officer',[16] and trusted him completely. A rich man whose grandfather had made money from a monopoly of salt in the Crimea under Catherine the Great, he had only recently married Griboyedov's cousin. She would later hold court with great magnificence as the Governor's wife in Tiflis; one English visitor (Captain Mignan) described her later as festooned with pearls the size of peas.

The struggle for power between Yermolov and Paskievich continued until the spring of 1827. Paskievich, driven to distraction by Yermolov's obstructive policies, laid all the blame for the war and the lamentable situation in the Caucasus on Yermolov,[17] and finally declared that either he or Yermolov must go. The Emperor, still playing for time, sent Dibich to investigate the situation, but gave him authority to choose between the two commanders. Dibich, after several weeks of hesitation, came down on the side of Paskievich. Yermolov was forced to resign, his humiliation compounded by an official reprimand, and on 27 March Paskievich was appointed as Supreme Commander in the Caucasus. Yermolov left Tiflis a few days later, never to return. At Taganrog, he turned aside to visit the spot where Alexander I had died – 'with whom was buried all my good fortune'.[18]

It is hard to believe that Griboyedov saw the departure of his old patron without a feeling of pity and regret. But in the meantime he had learned to work with Paskievich, and found his new role in many ways more interesting than the old. Not only was Paskievich favourably disposed towards him as a relative, but he was far more ready to make use of him. Unlike Yermolov, who delegated as little as possible, even in the writing of reports, Paskievich was inexperienced in dealing with the Byzantine ways of the St Petersburg bureaucracy, and needed secretarial help. Involved as he was with the war, he was content to delegate all he could to Griboyedov's tirelessly fluent pen. For the first time in his working life, Griboyedov had a taste of real administrative power; Paskievich, delighted to be relieved of bureaucratic detail, came to rely on his clever subordinate more and more. 'Do not expect any poetry from me,' Griboyedov wrote to Bulgarin.[19] 'The highlanders, the Persians, the Turks, the needs of the administration, and the huge volume of paper generated by my present superior, overwhelm me and demand all my activity.'

Griboyedov spent six months in Tiflis, keeping his head down while the rival commanders jostled for position, renewing his acquaintances among the Georgian gentry. There were visits to the Chavchavadzes and their neighbour Praskovya Nikolayevna Akhverdova, the widow of a former artillery general and the guardian of a clutch of marriageable girls. Prince Chavchavadze, as a serving soldier, had entrusted his wife and family to Madame Akhverdova's care; they lived in a wing of her house in Tiflis, a wooden mansion in a leafy park above the town. Other members of the household included her ward, Alexandrina Perfileyeva, her step-daughter Sofiya, and her own two children. Griboyedov had first been introduced to the family by Muravyov, who was officially courting Sofiya, but also had an eye on Chavchavadze's fourteen-year-old daughter Nina, a dark-eyed beauty who was already causing a flutter amongst the young officers of Tiflis. After the stresses and intrigues of the general staff guard-room, it was delightful for Griboyedov to escape to this enchanting world of *jeunes filles en fleur*, with their accommodating chaperones and their light-hearted round of picnics, balls and supper parties. He would call there almost daily, holding them spellbound with his exquisite piano playing and giving piano lessons to the girls.

Paskievich's appointment as Commander-in-Chief brought this pleasurable interlude to an end. For the rest of the war, Griboyedov was in constant attendance on him, accompanying him on his military campaigns and acting as his chief adviser on diplomatic matters. Never before had he worked so close to the centre of power. Paskievich, serving in the Caucasus for the first time, found Griboyedov's experience of local conditions and topography invaluable; his knowledge of languages, in particular his fluency in Persian, was a further asset.[20] Writing to his brother Alexander in June 1827, Griboyedov's old friend Nikita Vsevolozhsky seized the essence of the situation when he described him as Paskievich's 'factotum':[21] 'What he says becomes holy writ. This is confirmed by Denis Davydov, who I see every day'.

The departure of Yermolov meant that a whole range of his hard-line policies could be reversed. Peaceful intervention and respect for Muslim laws and institutions could replace his tactics of scorched earth and terror; local potentates could be wooed into becoming allies rather than beaten into submission. The new approach coincided with the views of Nicholas I. Dedicated to the principle of legitimacy in the Middle Eastern cockpit, as elsewhere, he did not wish to see the Shah or Abbas Mirza entirely overthrown; the same applied to a lesser extent to those khans with a hereditary title to rule.

Throughout the campaign, Paskievich would back up his military efforts with a series of side deals with local tribes, avoiding conflict wherever possible and ensuring the continuity of his supplies. His most notable success was regaining the key province of Karabakh, thus securing Georgia's eastern flank, by the time-honoured weapon of bribing the ruler, Mehdi Kuli Khan, with an annual subsidy, and the promise that he would carry out no military operations there. Griboyedov acted as Paskievich's adviser and interpreter in the negotiations, and dealt with the ensuing mass of paper. He was helped by a trusted colleague, Abbas Kuli Agha Balikhanov, an Azherbaijani whom he had first met with Yermolov in 1819. Clever and well-read, Balikhanov could teach Griboyedov much about the ethnic background and culture of the area, and frequently pitched his campaign tent next to his. Paskievich was soon induced to share Griboyedov's faith in his 'Asiatic' mentor.

Paskievich would never acquire Yermolov's legendary status as a great pro-consul, but in many ways he was a better commander in the field. His first move after Yermolov's departure was to carry out the strategic instructions set by St Petersburg to capture Erivan.[22] Early in May, he moved off with his staff to join up with General Benckendorff, a brother of Nicholas's head of security, who was leapfrogging his way southwards, via the venerable Monastery of Etchmiadzin, in order to besiege the capital of Armenia. After replacing Benckendorff's exhausted troops at Erivan with a fresh force under General Krasovsky, he then turned south to attack the khanate of Nakhichevan, thus securing his rear against any interference by Abbas Mirza from Tabriz. He took the provincial capital unopposed on 26 June, then moved on to besiege the fortress of Abbas Abad, controlling the crossing of the river Araxes; the fort was commanded by a brother-in-law of Abbas Mirza, with a garrison of 2700.

Griboyedov, as a civilian, was delighted that some of the military glories of the campaign could rub off on him. Writing to Madame Akhverdova, he describes the searing heat and dusty winds, the excitement of coming under fire in a dawn raid with the Cossacks, the sporadic sound of cannonades, the dramatic sight of Benckendorff's cavalry as they fought their way across the Araxes to seize the dominating heights opposite, the beauty of the laboriously cultivated river valley and its wild backdrop of hills and mountain ranges, culminating in the snowy peak of Mount Ararat on the horizon. Joining the other young bloods round their tents, Griboyedov was forced to beat a retreat when no less than seven cannonballs whizzed past. 'All this makes life more cheerful!' he exclaimed.[23]

After a short siege and discreet approaches from the Russians, the garrison commander of Abbas Abad decided to capitulate; Abbas Mirza's troops had failed to relieve the fortress, and Paskievich's assurances, through Griboyedov, that there would be no looting or reprisals were enough to clinch the matter. On 7 July, the garrison surrendered, and the whole province of Nakhichevan passed into Russian hands, thus opening the way to Tabriz. But for sickness in his army and delays in his provision trains, Paskievich would have marched on Tabriz straight away. As it was, he decided to withdraw his troops to cooler conditions in the mountains near Karababa to regroup.

XVIII

Armistice Negotiations

Abbas Mirza's *blitzkrieg* of early victories had given way to a series of defections and disasters, culminating in the threat to his own capital. Paskievich had let it be known, through the former Governor of Abbas Abad, that he was ready to receive an official from the Persians to discuss an armistice. Abbas Mirza seized the olive branch, sending one of his most trusted officials, an English-educated Persian named Mirza Saleh, to open negotiations. Mirza Saleh's journal, preserved in the India Office, gives a vivid picture of his visit to the Russian camp and his subsequent exchanges. He describes his 'gracious and hospitable reception' by Griboyedov, Amburgherr and a certain Prince Dolgorukov, all previously known to him in Tabriz. But he found Paskievich in no mood to make concessions. When he suggested that the Shah was ready to make peace along the lines of the Treaty of Gulistan, Paskievich brushed his overtures aside.[1] 'Come, come,' he said, 'let us have no shuffling, but let us know what sacrifices you are prepared to make. The offers must come from you, not from me, as I now hold the key of Azherbaijan [the newly captured fortress of Abbas Abad] in my hands.' He went on to demand the formal cession of the provinces of Nakhichevan and Erivan, the full cost of the war and a substantial indemnity for the ravages of the Persian troops: if not, he threatened, he would dictate his terms beneath the walls of Tabriz or Tehran.

Since Mirza Saleh was not entitled to discuss such major questions, it was agreed that he should return to Abbas Mirza, accompanied by an official from the Russian side. Paskievich chose Griboyedov for the role, and on 7 August he and Mirza Saleh set off for the Persian camp. Griboyedov was received with every courtesy. 'Accommodation was prepared for him in the garden of Karaziadin,' wrote Saleh. 'Fifty soldiers were assigned to him as an honorary guard. Mirza Muhammad Ali [Abbas Mirza's Secretary of State] delivered a complimentary message from his Royal Highness.'

Griboyedov met Abbas Mirza the following morning. He reiterated the Russian demands in their entirety, allowing just a hint of flexibility by suggesting that they might be open to discussion in St Petersburg; meanwhile Abbas Mirza suggested a five-week armistice, and evaded all the main demands, causing Griboyedov to remark that his answers bore no reference to the Russian proposals, and counter-proposed an armistice of ten months rather than five weeks. This was a question for Paskievich, and Griboyedov returned with Mirza Saleh to the Russian camp. They reached the picket lines at midnight. Paskievich and his Chief of Staff, General Shablovsky, rode out to meet them. They rejected the request for an armistice of ten months without even dismounting, Paskievich arguing that he could not possibly provision his army over such a length of time, Shablovsky saying bluntly, 'You may tell your government that no prevarication will be tolerated. You shall have neither an armistice nor peace till you agree to our conditions.' Mirza Saleh, privately aware of the half-starving state of the Persian army, was hard put to find an adequate reply.

Mirza Saleh returned to Abbas Mirza with a letter from Paskievich, repeating his answer in somewhat more diplomatic terms, then went on to inform the Shah of his discussions. After these preliminary exchanges, in which Griboyedov had been little more than a messenger (though he probably drafted Paskievich's letter), it was agreed that formal negotiations should begin. Despite the presence of a diplomatic adviser from St Petersburg, State Counsellor A.M. Obreskov, on his staff, Paskievich nominated Griboyedov to conduct the talks.[2] It was a singular tribute to his abilities, offering him a unique opportunity to show off his patriotism and grasp of Russia's essential interests. It was also a chance to justify the trust Paskievich had placed in him and his knowledge of the Persian character. His despatch, when approved by Paskievich, would be forwarded to Nesselrode in St Petersburg, who in turn would show it to the Emperor. He could thus be sure that all those whose judgements could affect his career and promotion would see it. It was only a year since he had emerged from prison; in a startling reversal of his fate, his prospects now looked more promising than they had ever been.

Griboyedov's despatch to Paskievich, written at the conclusion of his talks, is worth quoting at some length, if only to show the confrontation between two opposing cultures, one Eastern and almost medieval, the other Western and colonialist. Griboyedov was outspoken to the point of brusqueness, Abbas Mirza flattering, evasive and silkily polite: 'All the courtesies were observed, even to excess,' remarked Griboyedov. But behind their very different manners the outlines of the situation were clear: the Russians held the upper hand, the Persians were desperate to minimise their losses.

After politely recalling their earlier acquaintance in Tabriz, Abbas Mirza opened the talks by blaming Yermolov's arrogance and incursions into Persian territory for the outbreak of the war. Griboyedov replied that the presence of Prince Menshikov, as the new Tsar's ambassador to the Shah, was evidence that Russia had been prepared to listen reasonably to the Persian point of view. 'Your Royal Highness took matters into your own hands by the use of force,' he said, adding rather tactlessly in view of Russia's recent military successes, 'One never knows where the use of force will end'. He referred to the fall of Abbas Abad, provoking Abbas Mirza to exclaim that his brother-in-law was 'a coward and a woman, nay indeed, worse than a woman!'

Griboyedov then invoked the name of his Sovereign and August Master, who expected some reasonable response to Russia's demands from the Persians, based on military realities. 'It is my duty,' he continued, 'to outline to you, if you will hear them, our conditions'. But Abbas Mirza, postponing the evil moment with a lengthy diatribe, explained how he had always sought a peaceful accommodation with the Russian Emperor. The more he insisted on his admiration for the new Tsar, the more Griboyedov reproached him for the Shah's behaviour to his envoy Menshikov, who had been held against his will in Tehran, in violation of every diplomatic convention. 'Sovereigns have their honour, as much as their people!' exclaimed the wily young diplomat. Abbas Mirza then played into his hands. How much was the Tsar prepared to delegate? Griboyedov answered firmly that the Tsar's conditions were not negotiable: 'The Sovereign's will is not open to modification by his subjects'.

With a meaningful gesture towards the curtain where Allah Yar Khan, the military commander of Tabriz, was hidden, the Crown Prince stated:

> We too have only one will. But in St Petersburg they pronounced one policy and Yermolov another. If Paskievich will not modify these conditions, we will have to conclude an armistice with him. I and my son will then come to your camp and ask him to direct us to your Sovereign and leave for St Petersburg where we will lie prostrate at the foot of the throne. We have offended him and ask his forgiveness. He is all-powerful and seeks our provinces and our fortune. I will seek the protection of the Russian Tsar.

Griboyedov replied that these praiseworthy intentions would have been better carried out 'last year during the Coronation in Moscow. Instead the Crown Prince had seized his sword to attack us'. Abbas Mirza returned again and again to the theme that he had insulted the Tsar, and now wished to make amends and throw himself upon the Emperor's generosity. 'If we cede the provinces and pay you,' he continued,

> what do we get in exchange? At the last Treaty we ceded vast provinces and territories to you, indeed all that you demanded. The English can witness that. Thereafter what happened? More and more demands. Peace has been a hundred times worse than war! I have endured so many humiliations over the last decade. I, or my son and heir must travel to St Petersburg and be received by the Emperor.

'Next,' wrote Griboyedov,

> he insisted that I should guarantee that he would be received by the Emperor. I countered by saying that such proposals could not be accepted in wartime. The Persian practice of trying to turn affairs of state into cosy talks, conducted as it were in the relaxed atmosphere of a harem, was unacceptable.

The Crown Prince ignored this comment, and reverted to the proposal of an armistice lasting four to six weeks, time enough for his views to reach St Petersburg, and a substantive reply to arrive. When Griboyedov attempted to bring the talk back to the working arrangements for an armistice, Abbas Mirza proposed that the Russians should evacuate the province of Nakhichevan, to be treated as neutral, excepting Abbas Abad, whose garrison he undertook to provision. He himself would retire to Tabriz.

'We appeared to agree on most points,' Griboyedov reported. 'I asked for a break to retire and prepare a draft.' However, the Crown Prince disagreed. 'We must take decisions now. I do not want a letter. You will be inflexible later about each word.'

Griboyedov then stated the Russian conditions and proposals, Abbas Mirza showering him with incessant compliments throughout his exposition. 'This lasted for about six hours,' wrote Griboyedov. 'In all my time in Tabriz, I have never seen him so ready to reach agreement, or to be in such a heat of repentance and contrition.'

By 22 July, the written draft of the Russian terms was ready for agreement. Meanwhile Griboyedov had received a visit from Mirza Muhammad Ali to explain the difficulties of Abbas Mirza's position vis-à-vis the Shah, and the weaknesses of the Persian army. All their proud pretensions had evaporated. Griboyedov hinted to Mirza Muhammad Ali that he was concerned at Abbas's unenviable future position in the context of the succession once Azherbaijan, his power-base, was ours, lost by his rashness. If the war were to continue Abbas Mirza would be blamed for all the troubles affecting Persia. This might affect his role as Heir to the throne. Mirza Muhammed Ali promised to pass this poisoned message on to Abbas Mirza.

I was due to appear before Abbas Mirza the next day, but in the heat of 47 degrees Reaumur, I fell ill with a fever and took to my bed. I received every kind of Persian honour, demonstrating their duplicity at this parlous moment of their affairs: the Chief Master of Ceremonies, Muhammad Husayn Khan, followed by a huge suite and bearers of every kind of delicacy handed me a *ferman*, sealed by Abbas, congratulating the Emperor and the late Emperor's widow on the Feast day of her patron saint. I believe Mirza Saleh is responsible as I had mentioned this solemnity to him.

Meanwhile the Shah, encamped at Chur, not far away, had received the Russian draft proposals, and had sent back his officials with an alternative version, using 'all the dialectic of the thirteenth century,' and contradicting most of what had been agreed. The Russians were asked to abandon the two conquered provinces and the request for a ten-month armistice was renewed.

'Considering the uselessness of the talks,' wrote Griboyedov, 'I requested permission to leave.' It had been the Persians, he insisted, who had asked for an armistice; the Russians had no need for it. He went on to issue an ultimatum: 'Take them [the Russian proposals] freely or leave them'. He pointed out that Azherbaijan was so rich that once captured it could support an occupying militia of 20,000 men. 'Russia would then be permanently installed there. She would have no political relations with Persia in the future; such a country could not honour its treaties; they would be treated as non-persons in the same category as the Afghans and other remote peoples lost in Asia.'

Griboyedov had arranged to leave the Persian camp on 25 July. On the morning of that day, he was received by Abbas Mirza, flanked by two of his brothers, the Princes of Qazvin and Urmia, Allah Yar Khan and the brother of the Sardar of Erivan, a hardliner, who had intervened with the Shah to reject the Russian conditions. Griboyedov had assumed that before such a distinguished audience his terms would either be accepted or negotiated. It was not to be. The Crown Prince renewed his request for an armistice of ten months, Griboyedov again refused: 'How could we justify this loss of time, so much at odds with our military success!' Stung to the quick, Abbas Mirza retorted that he would indeed sign all the proposals of the Emperor if he put them to him, or his son, in person. He would present his son to Paskievich as a hostage, and in addition two of his brothers would set off to his camp. Griboyedov could not accept these suggestions, but the pleading and humble tone in which they were offered made a curt reply impossible. Instead he repeated his advice that the Persians should accept the inevitable, rather than invite further misfortunes. He also instanced recent diplomatic successes, such as the defection of the ruler of Karabakh, to show that those seeking Russian protection would be fairly treated. Abbas Mirza picked this up and commented,

> Without doubt one of General Paskievich's most effective weapons is to establish a policy of fair and even-handed justice towards the Muslims, both his and ours. We know how he acted towards the nomadic tribes of Erevan and Nakhichevan [a policy proposed by Griboyedov himself]. His troops never harmed them and treated them equitably...General Yermolov, in contrast, was a latterday Genghis Khan, who would have revenged himself by depopulating these provinces and utterly destroying them.

The talks finished on this self-justifying note, and Griboyedov was offered a farewell feast of the greatest luxury and distinction. No terms had been agreed, but during his stay there he had noted the relative weakness of the Persian forces, and had included valuable intelligence on the numbers of men and guns in his report. 'I left the Persian camp,' he wrote, 'with the encouraging impression that the enemy do not have the stomach for war. Their cumulative setbacks have been both frightening and damaging to their morale, which is destroyed and dejected.'[3] He added that the Kurds who escorted him back to the Russian lines had indicated that they were ready to defect. The Shah had caused great anger locally by paying only one toman for a standard measure of bread, instead of the market price of five.

'It is clear from the Crown Prince's humble tone,' concluded Griboyedov,

> that he does not find himself militarily to be our equal. It would be unrealistic to find him ready to pay the price of our conditions immediately. We must be tough and resolute about this. In the counsels of the Crown Prince the predominating voices are still those of the hardliners such as Allah Yar Khan and the Sardar and his brother, who are against making peace. The Sardar fears very much that he and his brother will be ousted with the cession of the province of Erevan. Only after the fall of Erevan will the Persians really feel threatened as far as the capital of Azherbaijan, i.e Tabriz. These events will allow us to conclude peace on our own terms.

XIX

The Treaty of Turkmanchai

Griboyedov's prediction that the Persians would not come to terms before Erivan had fallen was well-founded, but he had underestimated Abbas Mirza's will to fight. While Paskievich and the bulk of his troops remained inactive at Karababa, Krasovsky, further north, had been forced by the heat and lack of supplies to abandon the siege of Erivan till reinforcements came. He retired to the mountains beyond Etchmiadzin, leaving only a small garrison to guard the monastery. Abbas Mirza seized his opportunity. In early August, only days after Griboyedov's departure, he moved his troops northward and attacked the monastery with an overwhelming force. His plan was to capture Etchmiadzin, then march on Tiflis through Gumri, devastate the capital and return through Karabakh. Only the outstanding courage of Krasovsky, who fought his way back to the monastery through the mountains, with some 2000 troops against 30,000, prevented him from succeeding. The monastery was saved, though at a heavy cost, and the Persians, losing heart, retired to Azherbaijan. It was several weeks before Paskievich, 100 miles away, with communications interrupted by the Persian army, heard the news. Immediately postponing all thoughts of marching on Tabriz, he hurried to reinforce the depleted garrison at Etchmiadzin, then moved on to resume the siege of Erivan. On 23 September, after heavy fighting at the fortified village of Sardar Abad, his troops drew up beneath the lowering walls of the city, and the siege of Erivan began in earnest.

The capture of Erivan, which would earn Paskievich the title of Prince Paskievich Erevansky,[1] was the first great military victory of

Nicholas I's reign; after the bloodstained events of his accession and the humiliation of the Decembrist revolt, it was greeted with delight in faraway St Petersburg. Ironically, much of the success of the siege was due to the skills of Pushkin's friend Ivan Pushchin, a former engineer who had been reduced to the ranks after the Decembrist rising, and who directed the batteries breaching the walls. (The Tsar, usually implacable towards those he called 'mes amis du quatorze', agreed to his promotion to the rank of ensign.) The city which had resisted so many Russian attacks fell in only six days, and it was to Paskievich's credit that there were no reprisals nor looting afterwards. Nonetheless, the destruction had been appalling, 'an inferno of bombardment the whole time,' Griboyedov wrote to Madame Akhverdova. He went on to describe the grand parade held immediately after the town had fallen, at which the Te Deum was sung outside the main breach in the city's walls.[2] 'I suddenly saw old Simonich (later Minister in Teheran) appear on his crutches, followed by all his officers. I was moved to tears, not only by the holy hymns but by the sight of his injuries.'

In the heady days after the victory, Griboyedov enjoyed a rare pleasure when the officers of the 7th Carabiniers, later to be renamed the Erivan Regiment, decided to celebrate by staging a production of *Woe from Wit*,[3] aided by the sage counsels of the author. It was a historic occasion, the first full performance of the banned play, already familiar to most of those present from the thousands of handwritten copies circulating throughout Russia. The palace of the Sardar of Erivan, where Griboyedov had shivered in the winter of 1819, was adapted for the occasion, and we can only assume that Paskievich, despite his normal concern for keeping on the right side of authority, turned a Nelsonian blind eye to the distractions of his victorious regiment. Krasovsky went so far as to send an account of the performance to the *Tiflis News*.

For Griboyedov, the performance was a sign of the regard in which he was held by his military colleagues. Although a civilian, he had shown consistent courage during the campaign: according to Paskievich he was so short-sighted, 'almost blind', that he never knew when to stop, and always went too far forward under fire. There may have been a conscious element in this. Talking to the journalist Y. Polevoi in St Petersburg the following year, he described how he had overcome his fear in battle by the exercise of willpower.[4] 'For instance,' he said,

> I was with Prince Suvorov during the last Persian campaign, when a hostile cannon ball landed near him, throwing up a cloud of earth which covered him. At first I thought he had been killed. I began to shake and shiver. The Prince was only lightly bruised. I was dismayed at my show of weakness; was I indeed a coward at heart? I decided quite deliberately I had to master my fears and placed myself in situations of maximum

danger and exposure, where I could indeed count the number of shots exploding round me. After this experiment I never again felt such weakness. If you surrender to fear, it grows and becomes stronger.

Before marching northwards to Etchmiadzin and Erivan, Paskievich had left a small force to garrison Nakhichevan under General Prince Eristov, with Nikita Muravyov as his second-in-command. Eristov was a dashing cavalry officer, Muravyov was no less of a daredevil, and despite their strict instructions to play a purely defensive role, they determined to win glory by capturing Tabriz. On 2 October, the day that Paskievich made his triumphal entry into Erivan, Eristov took the fortress of Marand, an essential stepping-stone on the way to Tabriz; nine days later, in clear contravention of their orders, he and Muravyov marched their troops towards the capital.[5] 'The matter was decided,' wrote Muravyov later to his father, 'my honour demanded it.' Abbas Mirza's troops, who had been thoroughly demoralised by the fall of Erivan, were routed when they tried to cut them off, and the Crown Prince retired defeated to the province of Khoi. On 13 October, the Russian advance guard under Muravyov arrived outside Tabriz to find that the garrison troops had fled. The Commander-in-Chief, Allah Yar Khan, had tried in vain to rally them, but had been overridden by the *mujtahid*, the senior Imam, Agha Mir Futta, who took the view that resistance would led to the unnecessary loss of Muslim lives.

Muravyov, to his amazement, saw the enormous citadel of Tabriz, with its many cannon and crowds of hostile people inside it, await his arrival in silence. With two-and-a-half battalions of infantry and six guns he marched through the Istanbul gate and occupied the city without opposition, Eristov arriving a few hours later with the main body of his troops. One of his officers, Edward Brimmer, gives a vivid description of his entry in his memoirs: Eristov at the head of his cavalry, closely followed by a Persian escort on richly caparisoned horses, receiving the keys of the city from the humiliated Beglerbeg; the sound of Russian bands and drums and the downhearted Persian cries of 'Allah' as he cantered past; the primitive sight of innumerable sheep being sacrificed as propitiatory offerings along the way.

Paskievich marched into Tabriz three days later, consolidating its capture with a garrison of 14,000 men. Russian officers strolled about the streets, greeting new arrivals 'as casually as though we were in Kaluga,' wrote Brimmer. Among them was Griboyedov, who, sighting Eristov surrounded by a cheerful group of Generals, remarked with a touch of sarcasm to Brimmer that following the capture of Tabriz Eristov considered himself greater than Caesar. Brimmer, knowing that Eristov had officially disobeyed Paskievich's instructions, asked him what he thought his reaction would be. 'I don't know,' said Griboyedov, 'we shall see.' 'Never mind, my friend,' cried Brimmer, 'Tabriz is captured, the Crown Prince in flight! My dear chap, what do you think they'll say in Europe?' 'Ah,' said Griboyedov drily, 'Europe is not Katerina Akakiyevna [the wife of a Russian colonel in Tiflis]. It has other things besides the capture of Tabriz to think about.'[6]

Paskievich installed himself in Abbas Mirza's palace. One of his first concerns was to pay his respects to the wife of the British Chargé, whose husband, Sir John Macdonald, was away, and to allay the fears of other Europeans.[7] 'Parties were held every evening,' reported one of his officers, 'and it proved the gayest season ever known at Tabriz amongst the English residents.' But behind their gaiety the Russians were in deadly earnest. Paskievich had an important peace treaty to negotiate with the Persians, confirming Russia's recent territorial gains and settling the question of reparations. The matter was the more urgent since Russia was contemplating war with Turkey, which was threatening Georgia's western borders. Troops and money would be needed elsewhere, and the Government was eager to bring the war with Persia to a speedy conclusion.

After a one-month armistice had been agreed, peace talks began at the village of Deh Kurgan (Dei-Kargan) on 6 November.[8] They included, on the Russian side: the Commander-in-Chief, Paskievich; State Counsellor Obreskov for the Ministry of Foreign Affairs; and, responsible for the drafting the minutes of the conference, Griboyedov, assisted by Amburgherr and Kiselyov. The chief interpreter was Balikhanov. On the Persian side were: the Crown Prince, Abbas Mirza; Kaimakam (Prime Minister) Mirza Abul-Kasim; the Beglerbeg of Tabriz, Fath Ali Khan; and Abbas Mirza's Secretary of State, Mirza Muhammad Ali. Their interpreter was called Mirza Masud.

The Russian demands for the khanates of Erivan and Nakhichevan were agreed by the Persians at the first meeting; given that the Russians were already in possession, there was little else they could do. The royal province of Azherbaijan, Abbas Mirza's own province, was to be returned to Persia upon the payment of a financial indemnity. The question of this indemnity, both the amount and the manner of its payment, would be the crux of all their subsequent negotiations. The Shah, secretly hoping that Russia's impending war with Turkey would weaken her position, insisted that he had no money, and did his best to postpone a decision. The Russians were determined to extract all they could from him, but though they threatened to carry the war to Tehran if they got no satisfaction, they were reluctant to embark on another major campaign.

At a distance of nearly two centuries, it is not possible to get more than an approximate idea of the sums of money involved. The Russians' preliminary demand was for 12 kurors, later dropped to 10; the term 'kuror', borrowed from the Indian word 'crore', represented about 500,000 tomans in the Persian currency, roughly 2,000,000 Russian silver roubles, or some £3,000,000 sterling. The British figure is relevant since it soon became clear that without the mediation of the British, in the persons of Macdonald in Tabriz and McNeill, First Secretary in Tehran, the negotiations would reach a stalemate. (Macdonald had replaced the British envoy, Willock, one year previously). In 1826, Macdonald and McNeill had been against the war, foreseeing that it would end badly for Persia and undermine its position as a buffer state for India. But funds for the British mission had been drastically reduced, and they had not been prepared to support the Persians in a military sense. However, the possibility that Azherbaijan, Persia's largest and most prosperous province, might fall into Russian hands, and that Persia might be broken up altogether, put a different complexion on things. It was in Britain's interests as well as Persia's to ensure its preservation as an independent kingdom, and to bolster up the tottering Qajar dynasty.

In the complex negotiations over money, the British had one trump card to play. They were bound by an called treaty, the Treaty of Tehran, to pay an annual subsidy of 200,000 tomans in the event of Persia being invaded,[9] but had so far avoided paying it, somewhat disingenuously and dishonestly on the thin excuse that Persia had opened hostilities while the Russian plenipotentiary (Prince Menshikov) was still at the Persian court. From the Persian point of view, the British owed them 400,000 tomans for two years of war; the British, on the other hand were eager to annul the Treaty altogether. By offering to pay half a kuror (later reduced to 200,000 tomans) in return for annulling the treaty,[10] and by personally guaranteeing another 500,000 tomans (one kuror) Macdonald hoped to break the deadlock between the Russians and the Persians, as well as ending Britain's own commitments.

It took some time to bring the two parties to a compromise.[11] The Russians, with Paskievich and Griboyedov as hardliners – Obreskov, who wanted to return to St Petersburg, was more flexible – refused to modify their demands; the Shah, pleading poverty and the exhaustion of his country, sought every ruse to avoid disgorging the money. The one-month armistice came to an end before any conclusion was reached, and Paskievich resumed military operations. He was in no hurry to march on Tehran, as a letter from Macdonald to McNeill[12] makes clear: 'The General has promised me to move in slow marches, in order to give time to his Majesty [the Shah] to reflect more maturely on the immensity of the danger with which he is menaced'. But the Persian delays gave him the chance to capture more territory in Azherbaijan, and to seize the ancient town of Ardebil, on whose library of priceless manuscripts the Russians had long had their eye.[13]

It was a friend of Griboyedov's, the orientalist Osip Senkovsky, who had alerted the Tsar to the importance of the Ardebil collection. Even before the armistice had lapsed, Dibich had written to Paskievich instructing him that though the acquisition of the library could not be included in the formal list of points for the peace treaty, it should not be lost sight of in the negotiations. 'Instead of conventional presents from the Shah at the conclusion of the talks, his Highness would prefer manuscripts, a description of which I shall forward to you shortly; for this exercise his Imperial Highness deems it appropriate to use Griboyedov.' The library was attached to the shrine of Sheikh Seffi ed-Din, a famous sufi whose tomb, together with that of the founder of the Safavid dynasty, Shah Ismail Sophy, was housed there. Abbas Mirza, well aware of its religious and scholarly importance, at first did his best to prevaricate.[14] 'For the love of Allah,' he said to Griboyedov, 'why does your Tsar need these books? I can assure you they are unbelievably boring and heavy, and written in the dreariest style. Should the Tsar need such writings, I will commission some elegant new histories in the best contemporary prose.'

The Russians were not to be deterred, though they did not wish to cause unrest by seeming to desecrate the shrine. The commander, General Sukhtelen, accordingly summoned the spiritual leaders of the community. The Tsar, he told them, wished to know more about the religion of his many Muslim subjects, but lacked sufficient authorities; if they would agree to the library being taken to St Petersburg, copies of the manuscripts could be made and the originals then returned. After some discussion, the leaders agreed to this request, which was accompanied by a lavish distribution of gold coins. Griboyedov then arranged for the library's removal, insisting that it went to Senkovsky at the Academy of Sciences, rather than the Imperial Collection, 'where they are all illiterate'.[15] Needless to say, it was never returned, and today forms the core of the superb oriental collection in the Russian National Library in St Petersburg.

With the loss of Ardebil, the Persians realised that further resistance was useless. McNeill in Tehran, where his position as court physician gave him a special influence, and Macdonald in Tabriz were actively working to bring about peace. The two men were trusted on both sides, the Shah insisting that he would only accept the Russian terms if they were guaranteed by Macdonald. At the earnest request of Paskievich, Macdonald agreed to guarantee the treaty. Thanks to this pledge and McNeill's persuasion, the Shah, who had hitherto refused to make any payment before the Russian troops left Azherbaijan, agreed to the immediate release of five of the ten kurors of the indemnity. Peace talks were begun in the village of Turkmanchai, where on 6 February 1828 the first five kurors were delivered by a train of 1600 mules. The war artist V.I. Moshkov made a vivid picture of the weighing of the bullion: we see Griboyedov in his white diplomatic trousers leaning nonchalantly against the open window while his Russian colleagues check the weight; one of the Persian officials sees that the makeshift scales do not over-balance; a Russian officer busily packs up the moneys (which were to be lodged with McNeill for safekeeping) while a Russian sentry guards the access to the strongroom.

The final terms of the treaty, differing very little from those suggested at Deh Kurgan, were quickly concluded. The Persian party was joined by Allah Yar Khan, the former military commander of Tabriz, the Foreign Secretary, Abul Hassan Khan, and the Shah's Chief Treasurer and Eunuch, Manuchehr Khan, according to Macdonald 'the man of the greatest influence at Court'. Griboyedov, as Paskievich's closest political adviser, responsible for drafting the treaty and the paperwork involved, was worked off his feet. Obreskov, though officially Griboyedov's superior, played a largely passive role.[16]

The preparation of the documents took until 9 February. The signing was to be at midnight on the night of 9–10 February, a favourable moment selected by Abbas Mirza's astrologer. Moshkov was once more present to record the scene. Paskievich, in full uniform, epauletted and bestarred, sits next to Abbas Mirza at a long candlelit table strewn with papers. Eight bearded and bonnetted Persians, in the poses of respectful courtiers before Darius at Persepolis, wait to whisper their views to Abbas Mirza. Griboyedov sits attentively on the edge of his chair. He is just recognisable thanks to his spectacles, and has exchanged his thin white trousers for heavier blue ones. No stoves are visible within the freezing tent.

The principal clauses of the treaty were the cession to Russia of the provinces of Erivan and Nakhichevan, and territories north of the river Araxes; confirmation of the occupation of the khanates previously taken by Russia, and the establishment of the frontier of Talish; the payment of 20 million silver roubles, or ten kurors, in reparations. In addition, Russia was to have the exclusive right to trade and navigation on the Caspian, including maintaining a navy; Russian consulates were to be opened up to protect her traders and merchants; the Persians were to remain neutral in the event of war with Turkey; and the Shah was to guarantee the free emigration of Persian citizens, Armenian Christians in particular, who wished to settle in the new Russian territories, as well as the repatriation of all prisoners-of-war and Russian citizens held against their will in Persia. The only concessions to Persia were the recognition of Abbas Mirza as heir to the throne – putting an end to the long-standing Russian refusal to acknowledge him – and the withdrawal of Russian troops from Azherbaijan following the payment of the first five kurors. (The Russians would leave a garrison in Khoi till three more kurors had been paid; the last two kurors were to be paid in 1830.)

Throughout the bargaining involved, the British had acted as honest brokers, a fact much appreciated by both sides. The Shah presented Macdonald with the Order of the Lion and the Sun for his help in saving his throne; the Tsar followed suit with the Order of St Anne, first class, for Macdonald and the Order of St Anne, second class, for McNeill. Both Abbas Mirza and Paskievich wrote fulsome letters of gratitude to Macdonald – Paskievich's letter, written in exquisitely elegant French, was almost certainly the work of Griboyedov, a past master of such refinements. The British themselves were well pleased by the results. In a letter to a George Swinton at Fort William, for the attention of the Governor General of India, Macdonald summed up the benefits of the treaty:

> Though the terms of the compact be of a nature sufficiently humiliating to the Shah, who has dearly paid the price of his temerity, in rashly plunging into a war with a power against which the weakness and inefficiency of his government rendered him altogether unable to compete, I must yet consider the conclusion of the peace to be of inestimable importance not only to Persia, but to England. This has saved the former from impending destruction as an independent kingdom, and us from all the hazard of that collision with the court of Petersburg into which we might otherwise have been dragged by a sense of the danger attending the further success of the imperial arms.[17]

The importance of the Treaty of Turkmanchai, both as a major Russian triumph and as releasing much-needed troops for the impending war with Turkey, was fully recognised in St Petersburg. The imperial dreams of Peter, Catherine and Alexander I of controlling the Black Sea and the Caspian had finally been fulfilled. By conquering all the khanates beyond Georgia, from Erivan to Baku, and placing the Russian frontier along the Araxes river, the Russians had secured the country's southern borders against invasion; the frontiers established at the treaty were to hold good until the break-up of the Soviet empire. Britain had been replaced by Russia as the major power in Persia, and would be forced to seek new buffer zones for India in Afghanistan and the Punjab.

The Tsar was generous with his rewards. Paskievich, as well as having been made Prince Paskievich Erevansky, received a grant of a million roubles. Obreskov, second in seniority, received 300,000 roubles. Griboyedov, whose mother's financial affairs, according to Beguichov, were in 'the most serious disorder', was given 40,000 roubles, together with promotion to the rank of Counsellor General, equivalent to that of a Brigadier, and the Order of St Anne, second class, with a diamond star. He was also nominated by Paskievich for the honour of carrying the Treaty to St Petersburg, where, according to the cumbersome procedures of the day, it would have to be ratified by the Emperor and the Ministry of Foreign Affairs, and then brought back to Persia to be exchanged for the copy of the Treaty ratified by the Shah. In his accompanying letter to Nesselrode, Paskievich, usually grudging in his praise for others, recommended Griboyedov in the highest terms:

> I am trusting the Despatch and Treaty to Griboyedov as a major contributor to the recent negotiations. Your Excellency can learn from him every detail. He, better than any other, can explain to you all the complications and problems encountered. May I recommend Griboyedov to your Excellency as a first-class, totally dedicated and experienced official in these matters. He entirely deserved the confidence of his Imperial Majesty. On your recommendation depends his reputation and further happy progress in the service. I most humbly request on his behalf that he should receive recognition from our generous sovereign... for his sincere and dedicated services.[18]

Armed with this letter and the treaty, Griboyedov set out for St Petersburg, receiving a hero's welcome on his way through Georgia. Only six months before, Tiflis itself had been threatened with invasion, and perhaps a second sack as terrible as that of 1795. Now a lasting peace had been secured. It was no wonder that he was greeted by salvos of rockets, fired from the citadel of Metekhi in honour of the treaty, as he rode into Tiflis. It was a heady foretaste of his reception in St Petersburg.

XX

A Hero's Return

Griboyedov broke his journey to St Petersburg in Moscow, where he called on his old friend Beguichov and probably spent a few nights with his mother. On his way there, he made a detour to Orel,[1] where the disgraced Yermolov, now fifty-six years old, was living in retirement. He would later describe his visit as a 'serious gaffe'. Yermolov, still smarting from his dismissal, could hardly be expected to rejoice in the triumphs of his former protégé. In his fictionalised account of Griboyedov's last 11 months, *The Death of the Vazir Mukhtar*, written in the 1920s,[2] the novelist and critic Yuri Tynianov gives an imaginary description of their meeting. Yermolov is coldly polite, addressing Griboyedov with the formal 'vy' instead of the familiar 'ty' of earlier days. He implies that Griboyedov has changed, that he has become the creature of Paskievich. He warns him that the terms exacted from the Persians are too harsh – 'one should not ruin conquered peoples'. Griboyedov reminds him that he has always said that ruts should be cut deep, that the Persians only respect a show of strength. 'Ruts are one thing,' Yermolov replies, 'this is war or cash. "Your money or your life!"'

On arriving in Moscow, Griboyedov was to find his mother's affairs in a predictably disastrous state.[3] 'The fact is,' writes Tynianov, 'Nastasiya Fyodorovna Griboyedova was broke. Spendthrift? No, tight-fisted. But in spite of that the money slipped through her fingers like sand; once again the walls were cracking, the house was in need of repair, the very air breathed ruin.' It must have been galling for Griboyedov to see his plans for his prize money – horses, books, a carriage or a new piano – endangered by her fecklessness and greed.

But St Petersburg awaited him with a triumphant reception as the bearer of the Treaty of Turkmanchai.[4] An announcement in the *Northern Bee* of 14 March 1828 recorded his arrival:

> At three o'clock this afternoon a volley of cannon at the Peter and Paul Fortress informed the inhabitants of the capital of the conclusion of the Peace with Persia. The news of this event and the actual treaty were brought to the capital today from the headquarters of the Russian Armies in Persia by Mr Griboyedov, College Counsellor of the State College of Foreign Affairs. The guns fired two hundred and one rounds.

The next morning, after spending the night at Demuth's Hotel, Griboyedov donned his best uniform to call at the Foreign Ministry, where he handed the Treaty to Nesselrode before going on with him to be received in audience by the Tsar. We have no official record of the interview, at which he was decorated with the diamond star of the Order of St Anne (second class) as well as a campaign medal for the Persian War – 'worth a hundred times more to me than the Order of St Anne,'[5] as he reported to Paskievich. But both the Tsar and Nesselrode were well pleased with the Treaty, and with his contribution to it. Writing to Paskievich shortly after, Nesselrode praised the 'scrupulous exactitude' with which it had been drafted, and forecast that 'this young man will be invaluable in our future relations with Persia'.

Griboyedov's future role was yet to be defined. Meanwhile, he was feted as a hero in St Petersburg. In a letter to his wife, a few days after Griboyedov's arrival, Vyazemsky described him as 'l'homme du jour',[6] though unchanged from the friend of yesterday. 'Without doubt he was the chief architect of the peace, in the first place because he is a hundred times cleverer than the rest. He knew the Persian people inside out. I am delighted at his success.'

To Griboyedov, his diplomatic achievements counted little beside his desire to write. 'Everything which I have been doing up to now is of secondary importance as far as I am concerned,' he wrote to Beguichov. 'My vocation is at my desk, my head is full of ideas and I feel the need to write.' But he made the most of his new-found favour with authority to plead for his Decembrist friends, above all Alexander Odoyevsky. From a letter written to Paskievich we learn that on his last night at Turkmanchai he had flung himself on his knees before him and begged him with tears to use his influence to transfer Odoyevsky (a distant cousin of Paskievich's wife)[7] to the Caucasus. In St Petersburg he went further. According to Bestuzhev's memoirs, he even dared to intervene with the Tsar on behalf of 'those very names which made the Autocrat blanch'. The Tsar remained implacable, but Griboyedov was able to use his influence with

Benckendorff – whose brother was serving under Paskievich – to obtain permission to send books and a letter to Odoyevsky in Siberia.

Griboyedov's closest literary friends – Odoyevsky, Bestuzhev, Küchelbecker – had been swept away by the Decembrist tragedy. But others were eager to welcome him back. The young journalist Y. Polevoi, who first met him at this time, gives a picture of the admiration he inspired:

> How delighted I was when P.P. Svinin [a well-known journalist] told me, in inviting me to dinner, that Griboyedov, just returned from Persia, would be there...Beside other great personages there were present, one could say, the flower of our literature: Krylov, Pushkin, Grech and others. Griboyedov arrived with Pushkin, who held him in the highest esteem, and who had said of him a few days before, 'He is the cleverest man in Russia; you will be fascinated to hear him'. But on this first occasion I was disappointed. He seemed irritable and unhappy, contributing only sarcastic remarks to the general conversation.[8]

Dining with Grech a few days later, Polevoi was able to revise his first impressions. He found Griboyedov seated at a grand piano, accompanying two singers. When the music was over, his friends, who had held back in order not to interrupt him, crowded round to greet him.

> What gentleness and good nature, what sincerity he showed amongst these dear friends. I realised then how charming he could be. Some congratulated him on his successes, so glitteringly revealed by the orders on his chest, others wanted to know about his life in Persia. 'I grew old there,' he replied. 'Not only did I become tanned by the sun, and almost bald, but in my soul I feel my youth has gone.' One could hear a note of melancholy in his words.

On 17 May, Griboyedov attended a stary literary event at which Pushkin read extracts from his *Boris Godunov* to everyone who mattered in literary St Petersburg.[9] Besides a number of young men, 'all listening in dramatic attitudes,' those present included the bluestocking German wife of the Grand Duke Michael, Princess Odoyevskaya Lanskaya, and the poet and embodiment of the Polish romantic movement, Adam Mickiewicz. Griboyedov had taken a close interest in *Boris Godunov*, of which he had read extracts while he was still in Tiflis, though the play would not be published until after his death. His increasing intimacy with Pushkin, whom he had last met as a boy in Shakhovskoy's garret, was one of the most fruitful products of his stay in St Petersburg. We read of them going on a cruise together on the new Neva steam launch (*Piroskaf*) between St Petersburg and Kronstadt, accompanied by Krylov and Zhukovsky, and of their plans for a European tour to London and Paris:[10]

> We'll take the town by storm! Four dedicated Russian men of letters are no mean thing! The papers will surely write us up!

On another occasion at the Olenins's house, recorded in the diaries of the composer Glinka, Griboyedov [whom Glinka described as 'a first-class composer and musician'] provided the tune for a Georgian love song, for which Pushkin wrote the words:

Sing not O beauteous one to me
Your melancholy Georgian strains...[11]

Pushkin was fascinated by Griboyedov's character, and would make him one of the leading figures in the draft for his novel *The Russian Pelham*. Named after Bulwer Lytton's popular novel *Pelham, or the Adventures of a Gentleman*, it covered Griboyedov's early years in St Petersburg, culminating in the ill-fated duel – his notes use the actual names involved – and setting him against the effervescent political and literary background of those pre-Decembrist days. The novel, written after Griboyedov's death, remained in note form only, perhaps because its subject matter was too risky.

Any hopes Griboyedov may have had that *Woe from Wit* could be published and performed on his return from Persia were soon dispelled. The censors under Nicholas I were stricter than ever, though the fact that so many copies were in circulation made their veto largely irrelevant. He gave readings from it to selected listeners, together with extracts from his new tragedy, *The Georgian Night*,[12] begun in Tiflis but set aside in the hectic circumstances of the war. Based on a Georgian legend, it told the story of a Georgian prince who exchanges an oriental slave boy for a favourite horse, and of the revenge exacted by the young man's mother, the prince's former nurse, who invokes the spirits of the forest (the *delis*) to destroy him. Only a resumé of the plot, recorded by Bulgarin and a few fragments of verse – the invocation of the spirits, the dialogue between the prince and his nurse – survive. But the play was highly praised by his contemporaries. 'Even the coldest hearts were touched by the pleas of the mother,' wrote Bulgarin, while Grech, after hearing him read from it, declared: 'Griboyedov was only testing his powers in *Woe from Wit*. He will reach heights in literature which none of us have yet approached.'

However much his heart might be in literary matters, Griboyedov had many other concerns during his stay in St Petersburg. Something had to be done to sort out his family's finances. His earlier project for a Russian version of the East India Company, in which he and his mother would be shareholders, had been shelved in the wake of the Decembrist rising and the Russo–Persian War. He now decided to revive the plan on a far larger scale, envisaging nothing less than a government-backed Russo–Transcaucasian Trading Company,[13] in which he himself would play a leading role. Designed to exploit the commercial advantages of

Russia's new dominance in Persia, such a corporation would provide capital to develop plantations and factories in Georgia and the Caucasus, and thus supply Russia with a wide range of semi-tropical products hitherto only imported from abroad. It would also involve the building of new roads, the import of skilled labour and its own port on the Black Sea. He was helped in drawing up his plan by the Vice-Governor of Tiflis, Peter Zavileisky, an able and ambitious Pole who was staying in St Petersburg at the time. They knew that the ultimate success or failure of the project would rest with Paskievich, as Viceroy of the Caucasus and Georgia, rather than the civil servants in St Petersburg, but meanwhile were keen to create a favourable climate for their ideas.

Griboyedov was also in demand at the Foreign Ministry,[14] to draft the instructions for a future envoy to Persia, who would enforce the terms of the Treaty of Turkmanchai. The draft, in his neat handwriting, with pencilled corrections by Rodofinikin, Secretary for Asiatic Affairs, can still be seen in the Russian Foreign Ministry archives. The first objective of the brief was to consolidate the peace with Persia, by 'mildness and leniency' towards the conquered power. The next was the active prosecution of Persian neutrality in the impending war with Turkey; should Abbas Mirza decide to wage war against the Turks himself, he would be certain to demand a share of Russia's spoils. The third important issue was that of reparations, with the suggestion by Griboyedov that the envoy should have some discretion in remitting the full amount if Abbas Mirza had difficulty in paying. (This last proposal was firmly vetoed by Rodofinikin; the payment must be extracted to the last kuror.) Other points touched on included the establishment of trade relations, the definition of frontiers, and expenses sufficient to keep up the honour of the Russian envoy at an Asiatic court.

In drafting these instructions, Griboyedov had been writing not for himself but for some putative envoy to Persia. But Mazarovich, who would have been the obvious candidate, had retired, and the best-qualified man to succeed him was Griboyedov himself. He fought against the appointment as best he could. 'The Minister [Nesselrode] first proposed sending me as a Chargé d'Affaires,' he told Beguichov.

> I replied that Russia should have a full Ambassador Plenipotentiary in order not to be inferior to the British Ambassador. The Minister smiled and fell silent, assuming that I desired the role of Ambassador out of ambition. I felt the menacing cloud had passed and that some higher ranking civil servant would be picked, but some days later the Minister sent for me and informed me that in consequence of an imperial decision I was to be Ambassador Plenipotentiary. There was nothing for it, to turn this down after so many imperial favours would have appeared as the blackest ingratitude. I can foresee I shall not return alive from Persia.[15]

The appointment, when announced, was scaled down to that of Resident Minister Plenipotentiary to the Persian court. Even so, it was a dazzling promotion, though Griboyedov's feelings of foreboding remained. But his new rank and prospects gave him the possibility of contemplating marriage for the first time. He already had a bride in mind, and while he was in St Petersburg had confided in Bulgarin and a few 'true friends' that he was in love. The girl in question, he told them, was one of a household in Tiflis where he was treated as a member of the family, where he had known her as a child and was accustomed to treating her as a younger sister. He did not know what her feelings towards him were; one moment when he saw her would settle all. She was, of course, Princess Nina Chavchavadze, whose father, now commanding the conquered provinces of Erivan and Nakhichevan, was an old acquaintance of Griboyedov's. As well as being a highly cultivated man, who had translated Racine, Corneille and the French romantic poets, he belonged to one of Georgia's oldest and most distinguished families. Tynianov suggests that in making the match Griboyedov would have been guided by motives of self-interest rather than love, but there is no reason to suppose that this was so. Nina was now sixteen, and already much sought-after, as his letters from Madame Akhverdova would have told him. He had seen enough of St Petersburg under the regimented rule of its new Tsar to feel the attractions of the freer, more exotic atmosphere of Georgia. Marriage to Nina, beautiful and accomplished, might well have reconciled him to a life of study and retirement there, once his mission to Persia was accomplished.

Griboyedov was scheduled to leave St Petersburg in early June. Before that he had to assemble the members of his new mission.[16] His First Secretary was to be Ivan Mal'tzov, a personal nomination of the Tsar's. Twelve years younger than Griboyedov, he was described as a 'cheerful, resourceful and practical fellow'; he was also very rich. The Second Secretary was Karl Adelung, son of the historian and bibliophile Friedrich Adelung, Director of the Institute of Eastern Languages under the Ministry of Foreign Affairs. Amburgherr, Griboyedov's previous colleague in Tabriz, was promoted to Consul General in Tabriz, with an assistant called Ivanov. Griboyedov was also anxious to have a doctor as a member of the party, not only to counteract the 'harem diplomacy' practised by Dr McNeill, but to provide skilled help against the frequent illnesses, particularly cholera, the mission was likely to encounter. Initially the Government dragged its feet, but eventually a military doctor called Malmberg was found to join the mission as it entered Persia.[17] Accustomed as he was to the rough necessities of army life, it was hardly possible to imagine a less suitable figure to deal with the confidences and gynaecological problems of the Shah's ladies.

As well as assembling his party, Griboyedov had to supervise the choice of presents from the Tsar to the Shah and his courtiers. These were to include malachite vases, textiles of every hue and quality, especially velvets and brocades, jewel-encrusted clocks (which had to be checked lest they were carved with nude goddesses or nymphs which might offend the Muslim ruler), telescopes, dinner services and a hundred pounds of rare rose tea. At the same time, he had to make his own preparations for departure.[18] Bulgarin, to whom he had entrusted his prize money to invest for him, acted as his banker for a wide variety of purchases: silver, wine, crockery, even an up-to-date map of Persia. Despite his insistence in his brief for the Foreign Ministry that the Russian envoy should be given suitable expenses, the Government proved slow and niggardly in providing them, and he was forced to draw on his own resources.

Bulgarin's stewardship of Griboyedov's prize money was entirely disinterested. Griboyedov, high-handed in financial matters, had always been happy to use him as a factotum. He borrowed money from him shamelessly, and when in the East had relied on him to send him books and journals and to look after his literary interests. An unpleasant sequel to his death took place when Griboyedov's mother, who had found his receipt for the money in her son's papers, demanded that it should be returned to her in full. Bulgarin appealed to Benckendorff to arbitrate, noting indignantly that apart from the injustice of her claim, she had completely ignored the interests of Griboyedov's widow and sister. Fortunately, he was able to produce evidence of the many unpaid bills Griboyedov had left behind him, proving that not only had the prize money been spent, and more; he had been forced to arrange credit with the various tradesmen against Griboyedov's future salary, and had also lent him money of his own. It is pleasing to record that on leaving St Petersburg, Griboyedov showed his gratitude and friendship for Bulgarin by giving him his autographed manuscript of *Woe from Wit*.[19] It is inscribed: 'I entrust my copy of *Woe from Wit* to Bulgarin; from a true friend'.

On 6 June 1828, having made sure that the seven horses to which he was entitled by his rank would be ready at every post station on his journey, Griboyedov left St Petersburg. Zhandr threw a final luncheon for him,[20] and after the other guests had left in a cloud of cigar smoke, he and Alexander Vsevolozhsky accompanied him to Tsarskoye Selo to see him off. The three friends rode in silence, overcome with melancholy. Griboyedov suggested as a last gesture that, as evening was coming on, they should all share a bottle of good burgundy, some champagne and something to eat. He then installed himself in his carriage, and Zhandr and Vsevolozhsky went back sadly to St Petersburg.

Griboyedov stayed two nights with his mother in Moscow. Passing through the province of Tula, he made a farewell call on Beguichov on his estate,[21] leaving him his working notebook, including the notes from his two tragedies, *Radamist and Zenobia* and *The Georgian Night*. He confessed that he could write no more comedies, 'as my cheerfulness has disappeared'. The whole time he was with him, wrote Beguichov, he was in an exceptionally gloomy mood.

> Taking me by the arm, he said, 'Farewell, brother Stepan, I shall see you no more.' 'Why this gloom?' I asked. 'You have been through the wars, and God has spared you!' 'I know, but the Persians and Allah Yar Khan regard me as a personal enemy. He is out to get me. He will not allow me to enjoy the peace we have concluded with them.'

Also living in the province of Tula were Griboyedov's sister Mariya and her husband. He was able to spend two days with them, and to be the godfather at the christening of their baby son. Then it was time to move on, meeting Mal'tzov and Adelung at Stavropol'. Cursing the road, he wrote to Zhandr, 'Nothing but flies, dust and heat. I have done this calvary twenty times.'[22] By early July, they arrived in Tiflis, where the whole party put up at the Viceroy's palace. War against Turkey had been declared three months earlier, and Paskievich was away campaigning. It was difficult to know where to find him in the midst of his highly successful military operations; he had already captured Anapa from the Turks and had taken Kars by storm. Griboyedov would have to see him in order to receive instructions before setting out for Persia, but cholera had broken out in the army, and travelling was temporarily forbidden. Meanwhile, there were old friends to revisit, amongst them Madame Akhverdova and the young ladies of her household.

XXI

Courtship and Marriage

It was only in Tiflis that Griboyedov was able to savour the sweetness of his new rank and honours to the full. 'The further I am from Petersburg, the more importance I derive from my peacock title,'[1] he had written to Bulgarin. From the letters of his Second Secretary, Karl Adelung, we know that he made the most of his position as Minister Plenipotentiary. He was invited as a guest of honour by all the local dignitaries, and entertained freely himself. He employed a first-class chef, and kept a table worthy of his new status even amongst his intimates and staff,[2] offering champagne, pineapples and ice cream as a matter of course. He had always believed, as had Yermolov, that 'face' and prestige were immensely important in the East.

His thoughts could now turn to the prize he had dreamt of in St Petersburg. His rank and future prospects in the Tsar's service were ample compensation for his usual state of indebtedness, but his personal happiness depended on his marriage to Nina Chavchavadze. Since Griboyedov's last visit to Tiflis,[3] bearing the Treaty of Turkmanchai, Nina had been besieged by suitors. They included an elderly Cossack general; Sergei Yermolov, a nephew of the former Viceroy, who nearly fought a duel with Griboyedov for her sake; and most persistent of all, Nicholas Senyavin, the son of a distinguished Russian Admiral, and a Colonel in the Jaeger Life Guards regiment. 'I see her every day, either in the street or in the assembly, where her beauty overwhelms me totally,' Senyavin wrote to a friend. 'I suffer, I am dying! I fear my angel is indifferent to me.' He wanted to propose to her, but Nina had no fortune and his parents refused their consent. Nina, in any case, had already given her heart to Griboyedov, revealing later that she had long felt a spiritual affinity with him and desired him as a husband.

The cholera epidemic in the Russian camp had been contained by mid-July, and Griboyedov was due to join Paskievich on the seventeenth. The day before, he lunched with Madame Akhverdova. Nina sat across the table. 'I kept looking at her,' he wrote to Bulgarin,

> my heart was pounding faster, I was feeling a perturbation quite unlike that felt on military duty, but now exceptionally important and demanding. I was suddenly overwhelmed by a feeling of unaccustomed decisiveness, and taking her by the hand I said to her in French: 'Venez avec moi, j'ai quelque chose a vous dire'. She obeyed me, probably thinking that I would sit her down at the piano, as usually happened between us. We wandered along to her mother's apartments and in a room there, with my cheeks burning, holding my breath, I began to mutter something to her. In the end it all poured out faster and faster, she cried and laughed. I kissed her, then we went to her mother and grandmother, and to her second mother, Praskoviya Akhverdova. I hung on her lips all night and the whole of the next day, when we sent a courier to her father in Erevan, with our letters and those of her family. Meanwhile trunks and mules and packhorses were all ready for our departure to the theatre of war. I left the next night.

On his way to join Paskievich, Griboyedov and his party stopped at Gumri,[4] where Nina's father was stationed. Here he received the Prince's approval and blessing. 'He was overjoyed,' Griboyedov told Bulgarin. '...Do not tell Rodofinikin. He will imagine love has banished my sense of duty. Rubbish! I shall take even greater pains for myself and for her sake. I shall labour for the Tsar to feed my children.'

Griboyedov caught up with Paskievich outside the fort of Akhalkalaki, which for decades had underpinned the Turks' control of Western Georgia, Mingrelia, and Imeretia. Now manned by a garrison of little more than 1000 men, it was to fall to the Russians on 24 July. The Commander-in-Chief was naturally much occupied, but he was eager to see Griboyedov. Since the payment of the first five kurors, the Persians had paid two further kurors of their indemnity. But by the terms of the Treaty of Turkmanchai they were to pay an eighth kuror before the Russian garrison, numbering 25,000 troops, could leave Khoi. Paskievich urgently needed both the money and the troops: the sooner Griboyedov left Tiflis to put pressure on the Persians to pay the eighth kuror the better.

Griboyedov also brought with him his grand economic plan for Georgia and the Caucasus, to which he and Zavileisky had just put the finishing touches. Far-ranging as it was, its most controversial suggestion was that the new factories and plantations should be manned by indentured labour – displaced Armenians moving to the new Russian territories, or Russian serfs – who would obtain their freedom after 50 years of working there. The argument that such a proposal would 'free the *muzhiks* from serfdom' is hard to square with Griboyedov's purportedly liberal ideals. As Colonel Burtsov, whom Paskievich appointed to examine the plan, minuted sarcastically, 'Who will live long enough to obtain the state of final freedom from the indenture?' Burtsov, briefly arrested as a Decembrist sympathiser, and now chief of Paskievich's artillery, would make a detailed appraisal of the plan before giving it the thumbs down. His chief objection, and the one most likely to impress Paskievich, was that it would reduce the authority of the Viceroy, and create a state within a state. Though Zavileisky continued to press for it, the plan was more or less abandoned once Griboyedov left for Persia. 'It seemed to me,' wrote Muravyov, 'that Griboyedov having become Minister in Persia, and enjoying all the advantages attendant upon that position became more relaxed about this project, if not indifferent to it.'[5]

Muravyov, who was also at Akhalkalaki, had welcomed Griboyedov's new appointment.[6]

> Our Sovereign could not make a better choice than that of Griboyedov, who, knowing Persian well, and also being cheerful, clever, adroit and courageous, had all the qualities necessarily required to deal with Orientals. He is without question the right man in the right place, by his very presence substituting himself for a 20,000 strong division.

He was less pleased at the news of Griboyedov's engagement. Now married to Madame Akhverdova's step-daughter, Sofiya, he felt that Griboyedov's choice was the result of calculation, that he had chosen such a beautiful and inexperienced bride as a diversion and a plaything rather than an equal partner. He also surmised that Madame Akhverdova had encouraged the match because the connection with Paskievich, Griboyedov's cousin by marriage, would be advantageous to her family. There may have been a touch of sour grapes in his comments; it had been Nina he originally preferred to Sofiya.

Griboyedov returned to Tiflis on 4 August. He had scarcely arrived, in the blistering, boiling heat of its hottest month – he compared it to being boiled in a samovar – when he fell seriously ill. He took to his bed, and in a letter to Bulgarin announced that he had jaundice, and was suffering from violent shivering fits, yellow as a parchment and very weak. Only the devotion of Nina, who, casting conventions to the wind, refused to leave his bedside, helped console him.

So precarious was his health that he was barely able to fix his wedding date. Even after he recovered, he continued to be overwhelmed by feverish attacks, and on his wedding day itself underwent a violent fit of shivering[7] when the traditional veil was placed on his head. But the wedding, on 22 August, was a splendid affair. It took place in the Sion Cathedral, and was followed by a wedding breakfast in Griboyedov's rooms. In the evening, General Sipyagin gave a ball to celebrate the new Tsar's coronation and the victories of Kars and Akhalkalaki, where the guests of honour were Griboyedov and his bride. The General gallantly led Nina out in the first dance, a polonaise. The ball went on till one o'clock, with an interval for fireworks. Nina, wrote Adelung, was as enchanting as any beauty from St Petersburg. 'All Tiflis loves and cherishes the groom and bride; she is almost a child, being only sixteen.' The guests included the Chief Mufti,[8] formerly Mujtahid of Tabriz, of all the Shiites living in Russia, dressed in the Persian style with richly encrusted sword and scabbard, and wearing the portrait of Tsar on his neck. 'He drank as much wine as he could,' noted Adelung, 'and called it sherbet.'

Griboyedov was now under pressure to leave for Persia as soon as possible. His letters of credence to the Shah had still not been signed by the Tsar, who was campaigning against the Turks on the Danube; his presents for the Shah and his court had been held up by an administrative muddle in Astrakhan; and he was desperately short of official funds. (Even his previous month's salary, he complained to Bulgarin, had not been paid by that 'little mannikin' Rodofinikin.) Irritating though they were, they were not sufficient reasons for delaying any longer.[9] On 9 September, to the sound of regimental music, Griboyedov, Nina and his embassy left Tiflis, accompanied by a Cossack guard of honour, and a train of 110 pack-horses. His immediate entourage included his diplomatic secretaries Mal'tzov and Adelung, Mirza Narriman, the interpreter and quartermaster in charge of the escort, and Vatsenko, another skilled interpreter with a long experience of Persia, where he had served as a consular official. Nina's mother, Princess Salome, also joined them; she planned to meet her husband, Prince Chavchavadze, in Erivan.

During his leisure moments on the journey Griboyedov found time to write to Zhandr's mistress, Varvara Miklashevich; he had not done so earlier, he explained jokingly, because it was difficult to write to another woman under the possessive eyes of his pretty young bride:

My Ninushka is delightful, playful and amused. We are greeted everywhere by cavalry displays 500 strong, who throw up dust storms when they dismount. 'We shall live to be a hundred, we shall be immortal!' is the forecast of my sixteen-year-old...I am surprised how I have slipped again into the hands of Fortune, and begun a new life at the mercy of an arbitrary Fate. INDEPENDENCE, which I used to cherish so passionately, has now probably disappeared for ever! My consolation is that I share this loss with a being who is so comforting and serene. The future which is a mystery may offer a darker contrast. It is indeed uncertain! Will my happiness be constant? Every night when the moon appears I feel a transformation has taken place within me I never anticipated or imagined.[10]

On 20 September, Griboyedov and his party reached Erivan. In a letter to his father, Adelung described the proud moment of their entry. Griboyedov, seated motionless in his saddle, received the homage of the assembled khans and grandees of the province, accompanied by a prancing cavalcade of 500 horsemen. The embassy then cantered forward to be greeted by the city's leaders and a short speech of welcome in stilted Russian by the Russian-appointed town commandant. Ceremonial salvos followed, blinding them with powder smoke. As they crossed the numerous irrigation channels at the foot of the citadel, the Russian uniforms, thick with dust, became soaked, changing their colour from yellow to a dampish grey. The Armenian and Russian clergy, in full canonicals, greeted them on the bridge across the Zanga river with candles, icons and smoking censers.

That evening, dressed in formal uniforms, the Russian party attended a formal banquet given by the Sardar of Erivan. In deference to European custom, it was a seated dinner around a table, with the garrison officers joining in. Adelung reported that there were 30 different courses, handed round on enormous trays, together with champagne and Kakhetian wine. Dolmas and stewed rice pilaffs swimming in thick mutton grease put the young diplomat from St Petersburg completely off his dinner, which he roundly described as 'disgusting!'[11]

Adelung met the distinguished Major General Prince Chavchavadze the next day, remarking, somewhat patronisingly, that 'there was no trace of a Georgian in him'.[12] The Prince had been campaigning in the Turkish *pashalik* of Bayazid, having stormed the fortress of that name a few weeks earlier. He had only a few days to entertain his daughter and new son-in-law, and to introduce them to Dr Malmberg, the head of the military hospital in Erivan, who would be accompanying them to Persia. On 25 September, after a further round of ceremonies and banquets, the mission set off for Tabriz, the Prince and his wife accompanying them in their carriage for the first few miles.

The weather had grown colder, and their route through wintry mountain passes was a tough one. Nina was now in the first stages of pregnancy, and Adelung commented on the ordeal the journey meant for her. He noted the discomfort of the freezing windowless huts in which they stayed and the problems of eating in the open air when the party stopped for meals. To make matters worse, their steward (the scapegrace Gribov) had broken most of their glass and china, which

50. RIGHT. Tsar Nicholas I (1796–1855), succeeded Alexander I in December 1825. Oil on canvas, F. Krüger. Courtesy of Sotheby's.

51. BELOW. 'The Rising on 14 December 1825': Tsar Nicholas orders artillery to fire on the insurgents in Senate Square, decimating them with grapeshot. The remainder flee and collapse or die. Watercolour, K.I. Kollman. State History Museum. *Alexander Pushkin and His Time in the Fine Arts of the First Half of the Nineteenth Century,* Khudojnik, RSFSR, Leningrad, 1985.

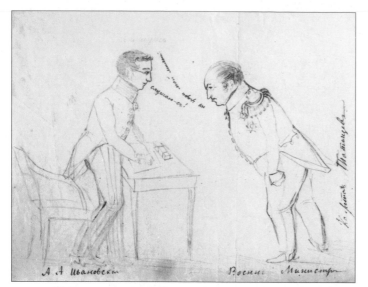

52. The interrogation of
Decembrists at the Peter and
Paul Fortress. War Minister
Tatishchev gives a prisoner a
hard time. Sketch, A.A.
Ivanovsky, 1826. Courtesy of
Pushkin House, St Petersburg.

53. Field Marshal General I.A.
Ivan Paskievich (1782–1856),
Commander-in-Chief
Russo–Persian War of 1827,
Viceroy of the Caucasus. Oil,
F. Krüger. Courtesy of
Sotheby's.

54. ABOVE. Paskievich halts Abbas Mirza's drive to Tiflis at Elizavetpol, early 1826. Original, V.I. Moshkov (Paskievich's war artist); engraving, K. Beggrov.

55. BELOW. The Russians cross the Araxes. Original, V.I. Moshkov; engraving, K. Beggrov.

56. ABOVE. Paskievich arrives at Tabriz to consolidate the victory of Generals Eristov and Muravyov, 1827. (The picture may be of Erivan, not Tabriz, because Mount Ararat is visible on the left-hand side.) R. Fraehn, 1843. Courtesy of Sotheby's.

57. BELOW. Peace treaty talks at Turkmanchai. Abbas Mirza receives Paskievich and his chief negotiators (Griboyedov in white trousers). Original, V.I. Moshkov; engraving, K. Beggrov.

58. ABOVE. Russian guards watch the mule train carrying the Shah's indemnity winding through the Kaflan-Ku passes between Tehran to Qazvin, where McNeill took it into safe custody. Original, V.I. Moshkov; engraving, K. Beggrov.

59. BELOW. Griboyedov (by the window in white trousers) casually watches the weighing of the indemnity bullion at Turkmanchai. Original, V.I. Moshkov; engraving, K. Beggrov.

60. LEFT. Sir John McNeill (1795–1883), a key player in Anglo–Persian relations. Doctor to the British mission in Tabriz and key figure in the Treaty of Turkmanchai negotiations.

61. BELOW. Abbas Mirza and Paskievich signing the Treaty of Turkmanchai: Persia's humiliation and Russia's triumph. Griboyedov is at the end of the table on the right, with spectacles. Original, V.I. Moshkov; engraving, K. Beggrov.

62. RIGHT. I. Mal'tzev (1807–80), the only survivor of the massacre, whose report was accepted as the official version.

63. BELOW. The enforced repatriation of up to 40,000 Armenians from Azerbaijan in 1828 under the Treaty of Turkmanchai, under the chaotic management of Colonel Lazarev and Griboyedov. Original, V.I. Moshkov; engraving, K. Beggrov.

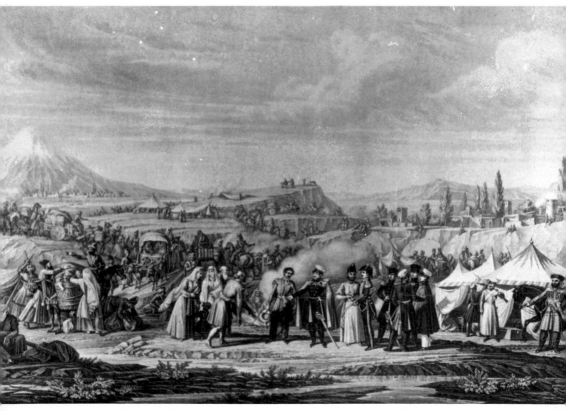

64. A.S. Griboyedov. Drawing, A.S. Pushkin.

65. Cover of catalogue of State Literary Museum exhibition celebrating the two-hundredth anniversary of Griboyedov's birth, 1995. Silhouette of Griboyedov, N.Ya. Simanovitch, 1929.

would take an inordinate length of time to replace. Meanwhile Nina was suffering from toothache and was often sick. She was faced, too, with the prospect of separation from her husband, for she would have to stay behind in Tabriz, with only the wives from the English mission for company, when he went on to Tehran. In her pregnant condition it would be too dangerous for her to accompany him.

As he travelled to Tabriz, Griboyedov kept his eye on the main issues that awaited him. Writing to Amburgherr, already installed there as Russian consul, he told him that the various delays en route had suited him. He knew that Abbas Mirza would try to put off paying the eighth kuror.[13]

> He may imagine that as I am coming from our Sovereign I will be able to make concessions. You must make it clear to Abbas Mirza that I find it indecent and dishonourable to approach him whilst a fundamental Article of the Treaty is unfulfilled. As this kuror has to be in cash, it is different in importance from the other Articles, such as the return of prisoners, or the property of the repatriated Armenians. If this is not dealt with…the Tsar has expressed the following resolution: 'If the Persians prevaricate further, let them be, and ignore them till military circumstances allow me to take care of them'. I have this in a despatch from the Vice Chancellor [Nesselrode].

On 7 November, Griboyedov arrived in Tabriz, where he formally handed over the ratified copy of the treaty with the Tsar's signature to Abbas Mirza.[14] As he had expected, the Crown Prince was making difficulties over the eighth kuror. The Shah had flatly refused to help him further, pleading that his treasury was exhausted by the war. However, Abbas Mirza was eager to recover his province of Khoi, which was a relatively prosperous one, and had already made a downpayment of 300,000 tomans in cash to the commander there; a painting by Moshkov depicts the convoy with the Persian gold wending its way across the mountains towards Russia. He now wished to be released from paying the final 200,000 tomans, or at least to reopen bargaining on the matter.

It was Griboyedov's unpleasant task to insist, under the veiled threat of military action, that no negotiations were acceptable: the Russian troops would not withdraw till payment had been made in full.[15] Fortunately, the British, who were as interested as the Crown Prince in getting the Russians out of Azherbaijan, came forward to act as bankers for half the amount. 100,000 tomans would be paid in promissory notes, secured against future taxes in the province. The remaining 100,000 tomans were to be raised from Abbas Mirza's treasury, jewels, gold plate, candelabras, his golden throne, even his wives' rings and the jewelled buttons from their dresses. They would be stored in the citadel, to be shipped to Russia the following spring, unless the Shah could be persuaded to redeem them.

It was one thing to drive a hard bargain from St Petersburg, another to enforce it down to seizing ladies' buttons on the spot. It was no wonder that Griboyedov's letters to Paskievich increasingly refer to the 'accursed contribution', or that his other discussions with Abbas Mirza were poisoned by the subject. Of the remaining questions arising from the Treaty, the most immediate was the repatriation of former prisoners-of-war and Christians held against their will in Persia. A number of these had already attached themselves to Griboyedov's party, adding greatly to the expenses of the mission. A further, more wide-ranging, question was the agreed evacuation of some 40,000 Christian Armenians from Azherbaijan to Georgia and the new Russian territories of Erivan and Nakhichevan. For Abbas Mirza, the removal of a valuable part of his labour force, mostly farmers and small tradesmen, seriously affected the income-producing capacity of Azherbaijan, and as such was highly unwelcome.[16] For Griboyedov, besieged night and day with the problems of their transfer, the operation was an administrative nightmare. Not only were they being transported through the mountains in appalling winter conditions, but the funds to resettle them were often delayed. Between badgering Paskievich for money to alleviate their plight and dealing with their demands for compensation for their property, Griboyedov, as he informed Rodofinikin angrily, was reduced to being 'a common, scribbling, low-grade clerk'. The problem would be compounded by huge numbers of Armenians from Turkish territories following Paskievich's conquests there.

In the midst of these complications, Griboyedov was still desperately short of funds. The mission's accommodation left everything to be desired. 'We are so poorly lodged here that all my staff are ill,' he wrote to Nesselrode.[17]

> Any or every English officer is better housed than I am. Indeed, numerous prisoners and their relatives are thronging my own premises, as they have no other shelter but our mission's quarters. My ten Cossack guards are in detestable accommodation, whose owners have been ejected. It is not Abbas Mirza's fault, his own palace is in the most appalling condition. I am principally concerned with the health of my staff.

Cholera and the plague were raging in the area, and Griboyedov was still very weak from his Tiflis fevers.[18] He had arrived in Tabriz, as he confessed only 'half alive'. A further concern was Nina's health; she was suffering from frequent bouts of sickness, and would have been in a still worse state but for the kindly ministrations of Macdonald's wife. Griboyedov's fury at his situation was compounded by the fact that his salary and allowances had still not been paid, so that he was subsidising the mission out of his own pocket. Rodofinikin, he wrote privately to Bulgarin, was 'a swine'.[19]

Harassed and frustrated on all sides, Griboyedov found his greatest comfort in Nina's company. In a letter to Varvara Miklashevich, he writes how 'after a fretful and alarming day I return to the privacy of my harem where I find my sister, wife and daughter, all united in one adorable little face'.[20] If Varvara wanted to know what she looked like, she should go to see the Murillo painting of the Virgin as a shepherdess, 'hanging in the Malmaison Gallery in the Hermitage, on the right just as you enter'.[21] He knew that he must leave her soon, that he was already being criticised for lingering in Tabriz too long. 'I have been married for two months and love my wife boundlessly,'[22] he wrote to Rodofinikin. 'I shall have to abandon her alone in order to hurry to the Shah, in Teheran or Isphahan, where he is presently destined.'

Writing at the same time to Paskievich, Griboyedov declared openly that he had no ambition, and could expect little further from his diplomatic career, which had ceased to be his dominant passion. Once his mission was over, he hoped to retire to Kakhetia and the beautiful estate at Tsinondali, where Nina had been brought up. Moscow and his mother's family home were out of the question. He had just received a 'perfectly poisonous letter' from his mother, instead of expressions of pleasure and congratulations on his marriage.[23]

By the beginning of December, the payment of the eighth kuror had been completed and 400,000 tomans had been sent to Russia. The remaining 100,000 tomans worth of jewels and treasure was stored in the citadel in Tabriz, though Griboyedov still hoped to persuade the 'miserly Shah' to redeem them for his bankrupt son. With his main task in Tabriz accomplished, it was time for Griboyedov to present his credentials (now duly signed) in Tehran; the Shah had been quelling an uprising in the provinces, and was expected there the following month. Macdonald had offered to care for Nina in the British embassy while he was away, evidence of the close personal relations existing between them. Although the British were opposed to the Russian war with Turkey, fearing it would destabilise the Ottoman empire, the two great powers remained on good terms in Persia, as a letter from Macdonald to his masters in the Foreign Office makes clear:

> I learn from Mr Grebayedof that the most friendly and confidential relations continue to subsist between the Courts of London and St Petersburg, and he has in consequence been instructed by the Count de Nesselrode to cultivate the best understanding with the British Mission. In this, I apprehend, he will experience little difficulty, since his Excellency and myself have long been on terms of personal intimacy, and so far as my knowledge of his character enables me to judge there are few men who have less of that jealousy usually to be found amongst the Russian functionaries than Mr Grebayedof.[24]

On 9 December, after bidding a sad farewell to Nina and leaving his final instructions with Amburgherr, Griboyedov left Tabriz for Tehran. The journey, in difficult winter conditions, was expected to take just over a month. The Tsar's presents for the Shah had still not caught up with him, but he hoped he would find them when he got to Tehran; he was taking the calculated risk of incurring the Shah's displeasure by arriving without them. Neither he nor Macdonald expected the visit to be more than a purely ceremonial one. 'I almost lament I did not accompany Griboycdov to Teheran,' Macdonald commented later,

> as I am disposed to think my presence and mediation might have been attended with good effect, in preventing matters from going to extremity, but as his Excellency went to court with the sole purpose of presenting his credentials and with a fixed resolution of immediately returning to Tabreez when he had seen the King, I was reluctant to quit Abbas Mirza.[25]

Griboyedov himself seemed to have shed his earlier forebodings, though he warned Rodofinikin to expect no diplomatic triumphs from the mission. His chief object was to go through with it as quickly as possible and return to Nina in Tabriz.

XXII

Tabriz to Tehran

Griboyedov left Tabriz with a numerous convoy. Accompanying him at the head of his departing cavalcade were his diplomatic secretaries, Mal'tzov and Adelung, the doctor, Malmberg, and two Georgian managers, called Dadash-Bek and Rustem-Bek, in charge of administration and supplies. They were followed by 16 Kuban Cossacks and 30 servants of miscellaneous origins: Muslims, Russians, Georgians and Armenians. Also attached to the mission was a *mehmendar*, or 'adviser', called Nazar Ali Khan, an experienced senior officer appointed by Abbas Mirza as his special representative. A secretary, described as 'a scribe and accountant to the Mehmendar', was to join him from Tehran.

The name of this secretary is not recorded, but his description of the journey and its sequel, later translated and published in *Blackwood's Edinburgh Magazine* of September 1830,[1] under the title 'Narrative of the proceedings of the Russian mission from its departure from Tabreez on 14th Jummade (6 December 1828) until its destruction on Wednesday the 6th of Shaban (30 January 1829)' is one of the two main eye-witness accounts of Griboyedov's final weeks. The other is the official report of the only surviving member of the mission, Ivan Mal'tzov. Some Russian historians, both Soviet and otherwise, cast doubt on the secretary's so-called narrative. They claim that it has been 'edited', or even rewritten, probably by McNeill and George Willock, to suit British and Persian perspectives; they also point out its similarities with the official Persian version, which places the chief blame for the destruction of the mission on Griboyedov's mishandling of the local

179

populace. However, the narrative contains sufficient circumstantial detail to suggest that, even if written from a Persian viewpoint, it is based on first-hand experience, and as such is an invaluable record of events.

The secretary met up with the Russian mission a few miles outside Tabriz, despite the icy conditions, snowdrifts and heavy snowstorms which had hampered his progress along the largely buried roads. From the first, his impressions of the mission were unfavourable. He spoke highly of Griboyedov, praising his impartiality and desire to behave fairly towards the local population. The problem lay with his followers. 'I must emphasise,' he wrote, 'the mission's servants were unruly and disorderly, and not subject to adequate discipline, especially the Georgians and Armenians, whose conduct gave rise to many complaints from my countrymen. The obligations of a Mehmendar were onerous and unpleasant'.

The mission was expected to live off the land, collecting supplies from the villages along the route. A day's requirement, according to the secretary, included one ox, one calf, 30 fowls, 200 eggs, 84lbs of rice, 5 sheep, 240lbs of bread, 360lbs of wood and logs, 120lbs of charcoal and 300 bottles of wines and spirits. It was estimated that all this would cost 60 tomans, or 75 Dutch florins, daily. Obtaining all this was well beyond the potential of the villages in winter time, and the Georgian manager, Rustem-Bek, had taken to demanding money instead, sometimes receiving as much as 15 tomans as a substitute for goods. 'We could not approve his conduct,' wrote the secretary,

> and assumed Griboyedov knew about it, turning a blind eye to these irregularities and depredations. The Persians described the journey as a series of 'tortures' and 'dangers'. Griboyedov used to canter ahead in the snowdrifts escorted by only two Cossacks and very often lost his convoy till they met late in the evening. We considered him to be a 'novice' in his role as envoy.

Quite apart from Rustem-Bek's extortions as a quartermaster, Griboyedov's choice of him as an administrative officer showed a curious lack of judgement.[2] Only a year before, at the time of the Russian capture of Tabriz, Rustem-Bek had played an active role in arresting and humiliating the military commander Allah Yar Khan. The episode is described by Muravyov-Karsky, who with Prince Eristov had been responsible for taking Tabriz. Allah Yar Khan, who had let the city go without a fight, was intending to escape to Tehran, but was betrayed by a compatriot, who told the Russians of his hiding-place nearby.

'We reported this to Eristov,' wrote Muravyov-Karsky,

> and we gathered up a a 'Sotnya', a Don Cossack squadron of about 25 lancers...and went off to arrest Yar Allah. The Armenian [sic] Rustem accompanied us at dead of night. He enjoyed the title of diplomatic courier, and had asked to join me on the march to Tabriz...At two a.m.

the soldiers returned with their capture. The officer commanding the Cossacks had found a small house which Rustem was the first to enter. Allah Yar Khan was not expecting such unwelcome visitors, and dashing up a small staircase he reached the roof, from which he hoped to make his escape. Initially pinned down by the lances and pikes of the Cossacks he then beat a retreat down the stairs, with his pistol at the ready, and meeting Rustem, he cocked it. The pistol misfired. Rustem, a very tall man, strong and enterprising, seized him with both hands, which prevented him from causing any further trouble. Allah Yar Khan had to surrender, and gave up his pistol (as well as a dagger, heavily encrusted with jewels) which he carried on his belt.[3]

Allah Yar Khan had been released in time to take part in the signing of the Treaty, and had returned to Tehran, where, as the Shah's son-in-law and a senior member of the Qajar family, he was an important figure at the court. As one of the leading instigators of the war, he hated the Russians, and Griboyedov personally, for the humiliations inflicted on Persia at the Treaty of Turkmanchai. The last person he would wish to see as a member of the Russian mission would be his former captor, Rustem-Bek.

Meanwhile, on the journey itself, Rustem-Bek's high-handed actions had been stirring up further trouble. Griboyedov had brought with him a list of men and women alleged to have been captured or abducted by the Persians from Russian possessions; a great number of Georgians who hoped to see their friends or relatives freed through his intervention had joined him en route. Rustem-Bek was the chief agent in charge of these 'slave searches' in the towns and villages through which they passed.

Matters came to a head in Qazvin, where the mission at first met with a friendly reception. They were greeted by a senior minister, Mirza Nabi Khan. He offered them five 'running footmen' and ten *ferrashes* as tent-pitchers, and presented them with horses from the Prince's stables, equipped with sumptuous saddlecloths. (The mission was always short of serviceable horses, frequently commandeering them from passers-by.) When the question of freeing captives arose, it was discovered that a young German girl had been brought to Qazvin by one of the servants of Husayn Khan, the former ruler of Erivan. Rustem-Bek insisted on her being produced. The servant stated that he had sold her to a merchant of the town; the latter, under interrogation, declared that he had surrendered her to a certain Sayyid (or descendant of the Prophet), Abul al Aziz, a cousin of the town's chief judge. She was now the Sayyid's second wife and had had two children by him. Rustem-Bek had the Sayyid hauled before him by two Cossacks and two *ferrashes*, and taken to the main square in front of the envoy's house. He demanded that the Sayyid should release his wife. When he refused to do so, despite repeated threats, he ordered him to be flogged with the knout, to teach him 'obedience and compliance'. The square was full of bystanders, who had been attending a wedding, and who quickly manifested their displeasure.[4] Alarmed by their cries, Mirza Nabi Khan ordered Rustem to cease his torture of the Sayyid, as he could no longer control the people's fury.

While the *mehmendar*, Nazar Ali Khan, hurried off to inform Griboyedov of what was happening, Mirza Nabi got the Sayyid to send for his wife. She was taken before Griboyedov, with her two children. The Sayyid stood by with his hand on his *kinjal*, swearing that he would cut himself to pieces if his wife were removed by force. If she wished to leave he would relinquish her without regrets. Griboyedov had a lengthy consultation with the woman, and asked her if she wished to return or stay in Persia. She replied that she preferred not to separate herself from her husband and her children. On hearing this, Griboyedov ordered that she should be returned to the Sayyid. 'This manifestation of justice,'[5] wrote the secretary, 'produced a great impression on all the bystanders, who had expected a decree of separation. Mirza Nabi invited Griboyedov to dinner that evening, and expressed his gratitude on behalf of the townspeople.'

Rustem-Bek showed no signs of having learnt his lesson. A few days later, at Rassiabad, a village near Qazvin, he was continuing his usual practice of seeking money instead of provisions. His asking figure was 11 tomans, and when a village elder offered him only seven instead, he flew into a fury and wildly hit him on the head. The elder's cries were heard by Griboyedov, who emerged from his house to demand an explanation, and appeared very surprised at the behaviour of his representative. It was the first time, he said, that he had heard of such occurrences, and he reproached the *mehmendar* for not reporting them to him. The *mehmendar* replied that he supposed 'his Excellency' knew about it,[6] as since the beginning of the journey the secretary had accounted for sums amounting to 160 tomans. Griboyedov then announced that all the money thus extorted would be returned when they rode back to Tabriz. The *mehmendar,* according to the secretary, said how pleased he was at such an undertaking, adding that he had no confidence in Rustem-Bek, who was an 'evil man'. To this, Griboyedov listened equably, and promised that on return to Tabriz he would dismiss his quartermasters, but for the present he needed their services.

Riding with him later, the secretary took the opportunity to say that the British, with whom he had served at different times, clearly understood the need for internal 'house' discipline, and always ensured that their people behaved with respect towards other people. Griboyedov may well have understood the point; he knew that he was unpopular, and that his nickname among the Persians was 'Sakht-tir' or, as he translated it himself, 'un coeur dur'. In a letter to Varvara Miklashevich before leaving Tabriz, he wrote that the Persians found him 'menacing and threatening', an unusual confession in one committed to impose the Treaty regardless of local opinion. But overwhelmed as he was by the administrative and emotional problems of the Armenian families to be repatriated, the situation was already slipping out of his control.

'The prisoners [he meant the candidates for repatriation] have driven me mad,' he wrote to Nina from Qazvin on 24 December. 'Some will not give themselves up, others will not return of their own desire. I have been here in vain and am completely irrelevant!'[7]

In four days' time, he told her, he was leaving for Tehran. 'Now I really feel I know what it is to love, the further I am from you the worse it becomes.'[8] He described a wedding feast of Mirza Nabi's, which reminded him of his own courtship,

> how we exchanged kisses for the very first time, brooking no delay, how we came together so sincerely and forever, and I held you in my arms in the corner of the window seat, and how we kissed each other more and more passionately, you blushing furiously. And then I fell ill, and you came to see me in the camp, my darling!...When will I return? I am terrified for your sake...I hope that Derejan [the maid] will sleep with you at night and will not abandon you. Perhaps next year we can travel this road together and I can show you the mosques, bazaars and caravansarays. I am sleepless, the doctor says it is from coffee, but I believe it is from a completely different cause. I kiss you on the lips, bosom, hands, and feet from top to toe.

Griboyedov had undertaken his journey at a lightning pace, driven perhaps by his impatience to accomplish his mission and return to Nina, but also by the weather. 'To begin with,' he wrote to Macdonald,

> the cold was unbearable, I galloped, I trotted, I ran at full speed from one station to another. My Mehmendar Nazar Ali Khan pointed out in a friendly manner that this was not the custom in Iran, where the envoy of a great sovereign must go slowly and with solemnity, even if he should die of the cold.[9]

On 30 December, he reached Tehran. His ceremonial entry was marred by two ominous coincidences. The first, of which Griboyedov had been warned by his own *mehmendar*, was that, according to Persian astrologers, the sun would cross the path of Scorpio around the date of his arrival. It was a highly unpropitious sign, but the Persians had not pressed the point, agreeing amongst themselves that it would be a waste of breath trying to convince such heathens as the Russians.

The second, and symbolically the more important, was that Griboyedov's arrival took place at the time of the annual re-enactment of the mystery play in which the Shiites mourned the assassination of the holy Imams Hasan and Husayn, sons of Ali, flagellating themselves till they drew blood, and cursing the name of his murderer, Yazid. In the play, Yazid was always mounted on a coal-black stallion. At the last moment before his entry, Griboyedov too chose a black stallion, belonging to one of his Cossacks, on which to head the procession. Tynianov, who deploys great scholarship and skill in describing the latent fanaticism of the streets and bazaars of Tehran during the four weeks Griboyedov spent there, lays particular emphasis on this want of tact, and the ominous cries of 'Ya Hasan! Ya Husayn!' which greeted him as he rode into Tehran.

Despite these unfortunate omens, the mission's first reception in the capital was a glorious affair. 'Our envoy was received with such honours as had never before been vouchsafed to any European in Teheran,' wrote Mal'tzov.[10] They were met outside the town by grooms leading horses with the richest trappings, and a vast body of mounted tribesmen, led by their chieftain, Muhammad Vali Khan, who had been sent by the Shah to greet them. In contrast to their miserable lodgings in Tabriz, they were housed in the spacious mansion of a recently deceased grandee, close to the Shah's palace, with buildings disposed around several courtyards and its own adjoining baths. A profusion of fruit and sweetmeats awaited them on their arrival, and they were shown to their various apartments by the nephew of the Foreign Minister, who was acting as an honorary *mehmendar*. Outside the embassy, a guard of honour of some 80 men, and 15 of the Shah's *ferrashes*, stood ready to repel intruders.

Griboyedov's first official meeting, with the Foreign Minister, took place the next day, and passed off, according to the narrative, 'with great decorum'. Two days later, he presented his credentials to the Shah. He was taken to the palace by the master of ceremonies, accompanied by a numerous suite, and riding on a horse provided from the royal stables. 'As the procession moved slowly along the extensive bazaars,' wrote the secretary,

> the shopkeepers stood erect, saluting the envoy in the Feringhee [European] style by doffing their caps. Whilst moving along the passages and courts of the palace previously to reaching the glass-saloon, where his majesty was seated in state, every demonstration of respect was shewn by the Shah's servants in attendance.
>
> I could only follow the envoy to the door of the garden of the glass-saloon,' the secretary continued. 'Full fifty minutes elapsed ere the envoy re-appeared. I gathered from reports... that the ceremony was completed to the utmost satisfaction of all parties. It was, indeed, whispered that M. Grebayedoff remained too long seated in the presence,

in the chair placed for his accommodation. The Shah had on his crown and was arrayed in his finest jewellery; their weight was so oppressive that, after the envoy retired, his Majesty was speedily obliged to cast off the ensigns of royalty.[11]

During the opening stages of Griboyedov's stay, the grandees of the court vied with one another in entertaining the Russian mission, with banquets, fireworks and torch-lit processions. He himself paid ceremonial visits to the Governor and other notables, but committed various diplomatic solecisms, first in failing to call on them in their proper order of precedence, an elementary breach of protocol duly noted by the secretary, second in omitting to call on two key figures altogether. Since one of these was the embittered Allah Yar Khan, the mistake was particularly unfortunate. But he continued to be treated with every honour until his second audience with the Shah, some 12 or 14 days after his arrival. This time the interview did not go well. Griboyedov produced a ratified copy of the Treaty of Turkmanchai, a document which could have given little pleasure to the Shah, and may also have raised the question of a loan to bail out Abbas Mirza. Availing himself of a diplomatic privilege agreed in the Treaty, he once again stayed seated in the Shah's presence, but sat so long that the Shah, weighed down with his ceremonial robes, grew irritated, and uttered the words 'dastur i murajaat' ('you have my permission to return [to Russia]'), to signify that the audience was at an end. Griboyedov chose to regard this as an affront to both himself and his imperial master, and sent a strongly worded note to the Foreign Minister to this effect. The Foreign Minister did his best to smooth things down, explaining that the phrase was one in general usage, with no discourtesy attached to it. However, he also pointed out that Griboyedov had omitted to give the Shah his traditional titles of 'King of Kings' and 'Protector of the World' in his note, and referred to him simply as 'the Shah'.

These nuances led to a certain coolness towards the mission and its envoy.[12] From that time onward, wrote the secretary, 'I perceived that the anxiety to please was gradually, though almost imperceptibly, diminished'. Lower down the social scale there were episodes involving the mission's servants and the townspeople. There were frequent complaints of the Russians' drunkenness and insolence in the streets. Gribov was seriously beaten up when a merchant reported him for allegedly stealing his goods; on another occasion, a bottle of vodka belonging to a Cossack was smashed in the bazaar. Meanwhile the precious cargo of gifts for the Shah and his chief ministers, which might have helped to calm resentments, had still not arrived.[13] The author of the narrative makes it clear what a catalogue of misfortunes had befallen them:

Dadash-Bek had been sent from Tabreez to the seaport of Anzellee [on the Caspian], to superintend the transport of the Emperor's presents... These by rights should have reached Teheran before the envoy. But by some accident they had suffered detention at Astrakhan or elsewhere; and I did learn that the vessel in which they were embarked had appeared at Lankeroun; but from circumstances unknown to me, had landed the package of presents at Saree Poochtah. Though unavoidable, it was unfortunate that the arrival of the presents was thus retarded. They would have kept the Shah and his ministers in good-humour; at least would have diverted their attention from other trifling circumstances.

Since Griboyedov was eager to return to Tabriz as soon as possible, it was decided that Mal'tzov and the interpreter Mirza Narriman would remain behind in Tehran to present the gifts when they arrived. Having accomplished his main objective in presenting his credentials and delivering the treaty, Griboyedov now made plans for his departure. The date was fixed for the last day of January. Compounding the Russians' embarrassment at being empty-handed, the Shah gave lavish farewell presents to all the members of the embassy. Those for Griboyedov included the Order of the Lion and the Sun, first class, in diamonds, with a gold enamelled collar, eight handsome shawls, and a horse with a gold bridle studded with precious stones and a saddle covered with thin plates of gold. There were shawls and diamond Orders of the Lion and the Sun, second class, for the Russian secretaries, and gold and silver medals for the Cossacks. Dadash-Bek, as administrator to the mission, received a decoration and a cashmere shawl, to the fury of Rustem-Bek, who though of equal rank was offered nothing.

Towards the end of January, the final audience with the Shah took place, the Russians proudly wearing their new decorations. Everything seemed set fair for the embassy's departure a few days later. The baggage oxen had been hired, Griboyedov had arranged to distribute farewell gifts of money to his Persian guards and *mehmendars*. 'All was gladness, all was sunshine,' wrote the secretary. 'The envoy's countenance beamed with delight at the thought of rejoining his beloved and beautiful bride, the Georgian princess.[14] She was frequently the theme of his conversation. Yet suddenly our atmosphere became darkened, even as that of the most dreary winter's night.' The last act of the drama was about to begin.

XXIII

Countdown to the Massacre

Griboyedov's last surviving letter, written eight days before his proposed departure, gives no inkling of troubles ahead. Writing in French to Macdonald in Tabriz, he thanks him and Lady Macdonald for their kindness and hospitality to his wife. He quotes Nesselrode as saying that diplomatic relations between England and Russia have never been better, and describes himself as being delighted at the fact. His reception in Tehran, he continues, has gone very well on the whole, despite the abominable weather and dinners 'five times more than my digestion can take'.[1] His tone is urbane and relaxed, and it is true to say that nothing that had happened until then – neither the unruliness of his servants nor his tactlessness towards the Shah – could have led him to foresee the hurricane of hatred which was shortly to engulf him.

The storm blew up, almost out of a clear sky, on the evening of Griboyedov's farewell audience with the Shah. Till then, the question of repatriation of former Christian prisoners, though unpopular, had caused no major problems. That evening, however, one of the Shah's leading eunuchs, Mirza Yakub, arrived at the embassy and claimed the Ambassador's protection.[2] An Armenian Christian, who had been captured during Tsitsiyanov's siege of Erivan in 1804, and had subsequently converted to Islam, he had risen to be the personal treasurer of the Shah, in charge of his harem's jewellery and accounts. The Persians in the mission were quick to see the dangers of the situation. The secretary wrote:

> We, who knew the feelings of our countrymen towards this class of persons...were fearfully alarmed at the consequences that must

inevitably ensue from his [Mirza Yakub's] reception by the envoy...We knew that by the late treaty the Russian minister had the right to afford his protection to persons desiring to return into the Russian territories; yet by no arguments could we reconcile ourselves to suppose that the pride of the King of Kings, and the suspicion with which all are regarded who are in attendance on the harem, would permit his Majesty patiently to submit to a circumstance so completely at variance with his sentiments of propriety and so likely to debase him in the eyes of his subjects. It would be to him humiliation of the deepest tinge; already from the result of the last war, the King had sunk low in their estimation, he had lately delivered (it might be said with his own hands) a vast portion of his hoarded wealth, and now he was called upon to resign his rights over a servant, whose duties in his household were of the most delicate nature; one who was intimately acquainted with all his domestic concerns; one who could afford the minutest information regarding his treasure and valuables of every description.

Griboyedov was slower to see the seriousness of the problem. There was certainly no gain in receiving such a person in the embassy, and his first reaction, when he heard of Mirza Yakub's arrival, had been that he would receive no-one who came in the night like a thief. However, he conceded that if Mirza Yakub was of the same mind next morning he should return to the embassy, and when Mirza Yakub duly reappeared the following day, he felt bound by the treaty to receive him.

As soon as the news of Mirza Yakub's defection became public, there was a flurry of protests from the Shah's chief ministers at the impropriety of harbouring one of his most confidential servants in the embassy. Griboyedov himself did his best to persuade Mirza Yakub to go back to his duties, and the Persian ministers promised him a pardon if he did so. But Mirza Yakub was adamant in his determination to return to his native Erivan, and at his insistence the first secretary, Mal'tzov, and the interpreter, Mirza Narriman, took him to the house of Manuchehr Khan, the chief eunuch, to declare his intentions officially. They left him with the chief eunuch, vainly hoping that he would be more successful in persuading him to change his mind. Mirza Yakub, however, merely collected his most important household possessions from his former quarters and returned to settle in the embassy.

The next day, wrote the secretary, the plot seemed to thicken. Mirza Yakub's house was sealed by order of the Shah; when Rustem-Bek tried to enter it that evening to collect the remainder of the eunuch's property, he was driven off with threats and curses by the guards. Meanwhile Griboyedov was informed that the fugitive had left the Shah's service with some 30–40,000 tomans unaccounted for. Mirza Yakub hotly denied the charges. Griboyedov, however, was anxious to satisfy the Persians as far as was compatible with his obligations under the Treaty.

He arranged that Mirza Yakub should go with Mal'tzov and Mirza Narriman to Manuchehr Khan's house for questioning. The Foreign Minister and the Treasurer would also be present. On their way through the passages of the chief eunuch's house, Mirza Yakub was reviled and spat on by his servants. On arriving before Manuchehr Khan, Mirza Yakub reacted so indignantly that the chief eunuch, feeling there was nothing to be gained while tempers were high, ordered one of the Shah's servants to escort him back to the embassy. Griboyedov was furious when he heard of the insults which had been offered to Mirza Yakub at a time when he was under Russian protection. 'It is not on Mirza Yakub they have spat; they have, I consider, spat upon the Emperor in the first place, then spat upon me. Such conduct is beyond endurance!'[3]

After this episode, wrote the secretary, there was little hope of coming to a friendly accommodation. Mirza Yakub swore that he would be killed if he returned to the Shah. To the suggestion that the matter should be referred to the religious court, he argued that according to Muslim tenets a person who had renounced Islam had no rights, but was considered by that act to have committed a crime punishable by death. Despite this, a meeting with the head of the clergy, the Mujtahid (Mushtekhid, or Senior Imam), Mirza Mesikh, was arranged, under the auspices of Mal'tzov and Mirza Narriman. However, on hearing of his arrival the Mujtahid refused to see him, feigning illness. The secretary learned later that he had been afraid of precipitating a situation in which Mirza Yakub would have been condemned as an apostate; had this happened, the populace would have felt authorised to stone him on the spot.

Mirza Yakub did nothing to make things easier for Griboyedov. Not only did he talk frequently and indiscreetly about the Shah's domestic life, a fact that was certainly reported back, but he did everything to encourage the search for further captives who might wish to return to Russian territory. In this he was abetted by Rustem-Bek, who, having been, as he thought, snubbed by the Shah, was out to make trouble for the Persians. As ill-luck would have it, the slaves with the most justifiable claim to be repatriated were two young Armenian women (one only fourteen) belonging to Allah Yar Khan. When Allah Yar Khan reluctantly allowed them to go to the embassy for questioning, both insisted they did not wish to leave Tehran. But Rustem-Bek persuaded Griboyedov to keep them for a few days, to see if they would change their mind. They were therefore lodged in strict seclusion under the care of Mirza Yakub, to the fury of Allah Yar Khan and his servants, who felt that they had been tricked into letting them go.

Sensing the growing perils of the situation, Mal'tzov did his best to persuade Griboyedov to return the women, at least until further discussions had been held. The Foreign Minister, with equal earnestness, tried to make a face-saving arrangement over Mirza Yakub, offering him immunity in a nearby mosque till he could be safely moved to Tabriz. In both cases they were rebuffed; despite every warning to the contrary, Griboyedov was determined to stick to the letter of the Treaty. 'He could not believe,'[4] wrote Mal'tzov later, that 'a government which had paid so dearly for peace with Russia, would dare to insult such a powerful state in the person of its envoy.'

Griboyedov had reckoned without the mob. While negotiations with the Shah and his ministers continued, public opinion was becoming increasingly inflamed. The final straw came on 29 January, when the two Armenian women (who had now decided to seek asylum)[5] were taken to the baths adjoining the embassy, on the orders of Rustem-Bek. 'No step could have been more injudicious,' wrote the secretary. 'The bath, or bathing is one of the most important ceremonies before a Mahommaden marriage.' This apparent profanation of their honour (it implied they were about to be seduced or worse) was an insult to Allah Yar Khan, whose servants made an unsuccessful attempt to seize them on their way back. Griboyedov, who had known nothing of the matter, was alerted by the scuffle. He was furious at Rustem-Bek's behaviour, and denounced him for making the mission's position still more difficult. It was too late. Reports were spreading through the city like wildfire: the Russians were holding two Muslim women by force, they were trying to make them abjure their faith, Mirza Yakub was betraying Islam. The Shah's chief adviser, deeply anxious, as he expressed it, 'to prevent a rupture between two mighty powers…on account of a miserable creature like Mirza Yakub and two unfortunate women',[6] made an urgent request for an appointment with Griboyedov the next day. But matters were already out of the Government's control. That evening the mullahs instructed the people to shut the bazaars, and to resort to the mosques the following day. A huge mob gathered at the chief mosque the next morning, where the mullahs pronounced the sentence of the court against Mirza Yakub, and urged them to proceed to the Russian quarters and seize him and the two women, either by force or otherwise. Two Georgian merchants, who were staying at a nearby caravansaray, rushed to the embassy to tell Griboyedov of the proposed attack. At the same time, Manuchehr Khan, on the order of the Shah, sent his nephew, Mirza Selliman, to warn him the in plainest possible language of the state of public feeling, and to persuade him to hand over the three fugitives.

There are various, differing, accounts of what happened next: the secretary's first-hand narrative is the fullest and most circumstantial. He tells us that by the time Mirza Selliman arrived, a crowd of four or five hundred people, waving clubs and swords, had already gathered outside the embassy, and he only got through it with the greatest difficulty. His warning had come too late; Griboyedov, in any case, refused to give up the three in question. When Mirza Selliman tried to leave, he found it impossible to do so, and was forced back into the envoy's apartments on the third, or inner courtyard, where Griboyedov, with the doctor, Adelung, Rustem-Bek, Mirza Narriman, as well as the secretary himself, were assembled.

> Showers of stones now descended into the [outer] court; the voices of the mob were from time to time raised in a general shout. We listened in dread, uncertain of what violence would next occur ... Every moment the uproar became more vehement; several guns were fired, and suddenly we were conscious of a rush of people into the adjoining court. I heard a voice exclaim, 'Take Mirza Yakub, and begone!' It was, I afterwards learnt, that of Mirza Hajji-Bek, who endeavoured to appease the mob, by delivering up to them a victim. The unhappy creature clung to his garments for protection; he was dragged to slaughter, and fell under numerous wounds, cruelties and indignities. Allah Yar Khan's servants were no less active in carrying off the two females.[7]

In the calm that succeeded these acts of violence, the mission counted their losses. Beside Mirza Yakub, Dadash-Bek (who had arrived only the night before with the long-delayed cargo of presents), a Cossack and one or two servants had been killed. Several of the Persian attackers were also dead. Their bodies were carried off to a nearby mosque, and served to exasperate the mob still further; meanwhile the Persian soldiers who had been set to guard the embassy had fled. At this moment, a neighbour, a confectioner by trade, who had been sent by Manuchehr Khan to rescue his nephew, arrived in great haste, and begged to escort him secretly to his house next door. He made the same offer to Griboyedov, but both refused to listen to his entreaties. The interpreter, Mirza Narriman, declared that no-one would venture to touch the person of the Emperor's representative. 'The noise of your guns,' he said, 'does not startle us: Have we not heard them at Ganjeh, Abbas Abad and Erevan?'[8]

After a lull of an hour-and-a-half, during which Griboyedov ordered his Cossacks to man the roof and bolt the doors, the mob appeared outside the embassy in far greater numbers than before. This time many of them carried firearms, the shopkeepers and ragamuffins of the earlier attack having been joined by groups of tribal mercenaries. For a moment, the mullahs held them back, despite the taunts of the Russian soldiers, who were drinking and gesturing on the roof; but an unlucky pistol shot from one of the Cossacks (whom Griboyedov had ordered not to fire) killed one of the crowd, a youth of about sixteen. The body was borne to the mosque, where the mullahs, urged on by the crowd, pronounced a *jihad* against the entire Russian mission. It was the signal for a general onslaught on the gates, which were quickly broken down as the mob surged into the outer courtyards.

> Yells loud and frenzied rent the air, and the showers of stones were so thick and incessant that we were obliged to keep ourselves close within the right-hand room of the [inner] court, which was M. Griboyedov's sleeping apartment. Vain attempts were made by M. Griboyedov to address the populace. No mortal voice could have quelled a tumult so furious. The order then given to the Cossacks to fire their pieces with powder, was alike unavailing. Death was at our portal; its victims herded together, helpless, panic-struck, and struggled to avoid their fate, like sheep beset by wolves, fierce and ravenous.[9]

The Cossacks fought desperately to clear the courtyard, but were hopelessly outnumbered; meanwhile the attackers had scaled the walls of the Ambassador's apartments, and were shooting from above. They next began battering at the bedroom roof, smashing holes in the ceiling through which they could fire. One of the first shots killed Gribov. Griboyedov exclaimed, 'Look! Look! They have have killed Alexander!'[10] in grief-stricken tones. But the mob was breaking into the bedroom, killing two more people, and the defenders were forced into the adjoining saloon. It was too exposed to shelter them for long. Griboyedov, with arms crossed, paced the floor. His face was bloody from a blow he had received on the temple, and from time to time he passed his hands through his hair. 'They will kill us, Mirza – they will kill us,' he said to the secretary, who could only agree. 'The last words I heard him utter,' he wrote, 'were "Fath Ali Shah! Fath Ali Shah! J'enfoutre, j'enfoutre (je m'en fous)[11] or some such expression".' His prophecy to Pushkin had come true.

The end came quickly. As the mob burst into the saloon from the doorway and windows, yelling and brandishing swords and daggers, the Russians could only resolve to sell their lives as dearly as possible. The doctor, Malmberg, who had rushed into the courtyard with his sabre at the first attack, lost his left hand; gaining the saloon, he paused only to wrap a curtain round his injured limb before plunging back into the fray till he was cut to pieces. Griboyedov too was last seen fighting desperately, though there were no witnesses to the moment of his death. The secretary had managed to save himself by mingling with the attackers. After an interval he was pushed back by the crowd into the saloon, where he saw Griboyedov's body, pierced by repeated knife blows through the breast; at his feet lay the body of the head Cossack, who had tried to shield him to the last. The bodies of 16 of their companions lay close by. Terrified and half-fainting, the secretary watched as the mob fell upon the corpses, stripping them bare and tossing them through the window, one on top of the other.

'Almighty God!' he wrote, 'Can these acts go unpunished? I never supposed the human frame contained so much liquid. The blood had gushed in streams from their bodies, covered the floor deeply, then found its way in a torrent into the court.'[12]

Saved by the fact that he was wearing Persian dress, the secretary eventually found his way back to his quarters on the first courtyard. Since the apartments there were supposed to be occupied only by Muslims, the building had been spared by the rioters. In fact Mal'tzov, the First Secretary, had his rooms there, and had been cut off from the rest of the mission when the crowd burst through the gates for the second time. Within minutes, the fighting in the courtyard was raging so fiercely that it was impossible to join the envoy, and he had hidden in an upstairs room, having bribed some *ferrashes* to say that it belonged to the *mehmendar*, Nazar Ali Khan. For three hours he had cowered there, 'in imminent expectation of a cruel death',[13] till the shouting and firing gradually subsided. He was the only European of the mission to survive.

The mangled body of Mirza Yakub, and that of a man mistakenly supposed to be Griboyedov, were dragged through the streets and bazaars of the city.[14] 'A frantic mob formed the retinue,' wrote the secretary, 'and at intervals voices exclaimed – "Make way, oh citizens! for the Russian ambassador on his way to visit the Shah! Stand up, out of respect; salute him in the Feringhee style, by taking off your hats. He is thirsty for the love you bear his master the Imperator – spit freely in his face!"'

Throughout the day, the Persian Government had done nothing to intervene. It had stood by powerless while the mission was attacked, though at the first outbreak of violence, the Governor, Mirza Ali Shah, and various other princes had gathered what forces they could to disperse the multitude. They soon realised their own lives were in danger, and were forced to seek refuge in the citadel, where the royal palace was situated. The Governor had been pelted and reviled when he attempted to reason with the crowd. 'Go,' they shouted, 'pander your wives to the Russians! It is worthy of your long beard on which you sprinkle so much rose-water. Your brother, Abbas Mirza, has sold himself body and soul to the Emperor! – Begone, or we will make mincemeat of you.'

It was not until evening that the Shah was able to send a column of infantry to take over the looted embassy, and Mal'tzov, disguised as a Persian soldier, was spirited over to the safety of the citadel. Forty-four members of the Russian mission had been killed. The fury of the mob had even extended to the stables of the neighbouring British embassy, where some five or six of the Russian grooms were lodged. They too were promptly slaughtered; had any other Europeans been present, as Macdonald noted later, they would certainly have been included in the massacre.

The next day, the tumult round the embassy had died down sufficiently for the bodies to be removed. According to one account,
Griboyedov's corpse was so badly mutilated that it was only identified
by the scar on his finger from his duel with Yakubovich; the secretary,
however (who may have wished to spare the family), insisted that his
features were clearly recognisable, and that his body had not been
subjected to any indignities. After funeral rites had been performed,
Griboyedov's body was placed in an Armenian church outside the city;
his fellow Russians were buried in the churchyard, and the rest of the
victims in a common pit nearby.

It was four days before order could be restored in the city, during
which the Shah and his court were virtually prisoners behind the locked
gates of the citadel. At the end of that time, the people, having neither
leaders nor objective, began to weary of insurrection. The Shah was
then able to send out his guards, who killed all those found bearing
arms on the spot; other known ringleaders were arrested and executed,
or had their eyes put out; five of the heads of districts were decapitated;
the rest of the population was subdued and terrified into submission. It
was now time to contemplate the full enormity of what had happened,
and to wonder fearfully what the reckoning would be.

Mal'tzov, closely guarded in the citadel, knew his life hung by a
thread. As the sole surviving European witness, his testimony could be
severely damaging to the Shah. Tynianov's novel includes a scene in which
Mal'tzov is secretly warned by a *ferrash* that he is to be entertained with
every possible honour, sent on his way to Russia – and killed en route.
If not true, it at least reflects the reality of the situation. Mal'tzov's one
hope of safety lay in absolving the Persian Government of all blame, and
in putting the responsibility on the uncontrollable fanaticism of the mob,
and on Griboyedov's mistakes of judgement. It was only by sticking to
this line, which was duly formalised in his official report, that he was
released some three weeks later and allowed to return to Tabriz. By then
the task of damage limitation had begun.

XXIV

Diplomatic Repercussions

The destruction of the Russian mission would be endlessly examined and discussed,[1] both in its immediate aftermath and in years to come. According to Yermolov, who read all the various accounts of the disaster closely, and who knew as much as anyone about the realities of the Persian scene, the account by the unknown secretary, published in *Blackwood's*, came closest to the truth of what had happened; he recommended it as such to Zhandr. A number of questions remained. How much did the Shah know beforehand? Mal'tzov's official report, not surprisingly, gives no suggestion of his complicity. In private, however, he was convinced that the Shah was determined to destroy Mirza Yakub, because of his intimate knowledge of his financial and domestic affairs. He knew that he could not seize him by force without violating the Treaty which had already cost him eight kurors; nor could he kill him secretly as long as the Russian Ambassador was alive. Once every other means of getting Mirza Yakub back had failed, he could let the fanatics of the mob do their work, and claim that he was unable to control them. Mal'tzov was certain this was the true explanation, and Griboyedov's final denunciation of the Shah – 'Fath Ali Shah! Fath Ali Shah! Je m'en fous' – suggests that he felt the same.

A number of other explanations have been put forward.[2] Allah Yar Khan, who hated the Russians and despised the weakness of the Shah, may have had a hand in inciting the mob; if the Qajar dynasty could be unseated by a further war with Russia, he might well become the Shah himself. It has also been suggested that rumours of a delivery of bullion to the mission, for salaries and expenses, had excited the greed of the mob, providing a further incentive to attack the mission. However, Mal'tzov, who would have known of any such delivery, makes no mention of the matter in his report. A further explanation, scarcely mentioned at the time, but later much favoured by Cold War Soviet historians, was that the British, jealous of Russian influence in Persia, had deliberately fomented the uprising. There is not a shred of evidence in either the British or Russian archives (see Appendix I) to support this view. As has been seen, it was completely contrary to British interests to put the stability of Persia at risk.

In retrospect, it is clear that Griboyedov had been given an impossible remit by his masters in St Petersburg, or set himself an unrealistic list of aims. The harshness of the terms he had to impose made him a hated figure from the start. He had been given no leeway in negotiating the payment of the indemnity, or in dealing with the demands for repatriation of those who claimed to be Russian subjects. Intensely proud of his position as the personal representative of the Tsar, he regarded it as a sacred duty to enforce the terms of the Treaty, however dangerous in practice. Perhaps, too, as a survivor of the Decembrist tragedy, he felt a moral debt to his friends who had been executed or imprisoned, and was determined to make no compromises where his country's honour was at stake. In support of this theory, it is worth considering his refusal to consider any of the rescue options offered by the Persians: the suggestion by the Foreign Minister that Mirza Yakub should be sheltered in a mosque, the request by the Shah's chief adviser (which came too late) for an urgent meeting on the morning of the uprising, the confectioner's offer to spirit him away to his shop next door. Whatever Griboyedov's failings, he was a passionate and committed Russian patriot. It is appropriate, in this context, to quote Pushkin's epitaph: 'I do not know of anything more enviable than the final years of his stormy life. Even his death which befell him in the midst of a valiant, unequal battle held nothing terrible, nothing agonising for Griboyedov. It was instantaneous and beautiful.'[3]

Pushkin's was a poet's judgement. But in the political and diplomatic re-evaluations that took place after the destruction of the mission, it became convenient to cast Griboyedov not as a hero but a scapegoat, whose 'excess of zeal' in carrying out his duties had helped to trigger the catastrophe. It was in everyone's interests to play down what had happened. The Shah, having achieved his aim in destroying Mirza Yakub, was desperate to avoid the resumption of the war which had already all but ruined his country. He would do everything to blame the massacre on the mullahs and the religious fanaticism provoked by Griboyedov's mistakes; and as far as was possible with words and self-abasement, would do his utmost to placate the Russians. The British, concerned to preserve the Qajar dynasty, and to save Persia from dismemberment, were equally eager to temper the Russian fury, and would do their best to act as intermediaries and peacemakers. As for the Russians, in the midst of their campaign against the Turks, the last thing they wanted was a war on two fronts. Paskievich had neither the troops nor the inclination to hold down a hostile Persian population; provided Russian face could be saved, and the Persians showed themselves sufficiently contrite, Russia was ready, if not to overlook, at least to accept the Persian explanation of the tragedy.

Certainly nothing could seem more heartfelt and remorseful than the way that Abbas Mirza broke the news to Sir John Macdonald in Tabriz. (Amburgherr, the Russian consul, was at that moment in Nakhichevan). Macdonald tells the story in his report to the political secretary of the East India Company, dated 19 February 1829:

> At a late hour of the night on the 18th inst., I received through one of the confidential servants of the harem, an intimation that his Royal Highness the Prince Abbas Mirza wished to speak to me without delay on a matter of the first importance.
>
> In obedience to these commands I repaired on the instant to the palace, where I found his Highness and the Kaimakam closeted together and impatiently awaiting my arrival. Both appeared to be in a state of the utmost consternation. The Prince was in tears, and marks of sorrow were strongly depicted on his countenance. He was indeed so greatly agitated that for some moments after I had entered the apartment, he could only repeat, 'La ilah ila' llah', there is no God but one God, am I, alas! doomed never to know a moment's repose? The waters of the Danube would not wash away our crimes...' Continuing bitterly to bewail his own misfortunes, and the unspeakable calamities impending over his house, he was for some time, either unable or reluctant to communicate to me, what had occurred nor could I define the cause of his distress, until he desired, or rather made a sign to his minister, to read aloud certain letters, which had just arrived from Teheran, and which I deeply lament to say, announced the appalling intelligence that M. Griboyedov the Envoy Extraordinary and Minister Plenipotentiary of his Imperial Majesty, the Emperor of Russia, had together with nearly the whole of his suite, been massacred by the inhabitants of the capital, during a popular commotion which took place in that city.[4]

After describing the events that had occurred, Macdonald expressed his conviction that neither the Shah, nor any member of his Government had in any way been responsible for the catastrophe, which were solely to be ascribed, he thought,

> to a sudden and irresistible ebullition of popular frenzy, caused by the treatment experienced by the women, the haughty demeanour of those attached to the mission, the deaths of several citizens, and in an over

zealous invasion of those customs, which more than anything else, is calculated to rouse the prejudices, and inflame the wild and ungovernable passions of a Mahomedan mob, prone to fanaticism, adverse to any encroachment of their religious usages, and above all jealous, even to madness, of the sanctity of the harem.

It was the explanation which, with minor variations, would be generally accepted by all concerned. It was combined in Macdonald's case with genuine grief at Griboyedov's death. In concluding his report, he paid a moving tribute to his qualities:

To the generous, manly, though perhaps somewhat unbending character of the deceased, no one can bear more ample testimony than myself, having long lived with him on terms of personal intimacy, been connected with him in the transaction of business, as well public, as private, and in short, enjoyed numberless opportunities of duly appreciating the many virtues which adorned his mind, and of perceiving that a high sense of honour, formed on all occasions, the rule, and guide of his actions.

The wheels of diplomacy now began to turn. In the absence of Amburgherr, Macdonald's brother, Captain Ronald Macdonald, travelled to Tehran to receive apologies and an explanation from the Shah, and to escort Mal'tzov back to Tabriz. Meanwhile, the news had reached Paskievich in the field. Amburgherr, briefed in Nakhichevan by Abbas Mirza's first minister, reported that neither the Shah nor his ministers were responsible for the catastrophe, which were entirely due to an outburst of fanaticism from the mob. Macdonald wrote to him on the same lines, adding that he was declaring public mourning for two months for all British nationals, and protesting formally to the Persian Foreign Minister. The abject self-abasement of the Shah and Abbas Mirza, who promised to send a resplendent mission of apology to the Tsar, headed by a prince of the blood, made it easier for Paskievich to do what he already wished, that is to make threatening noises but do nothing. 'It is quite impossible,' he told Nesselrode, 'to start another war with Persia.'[5] On 16 March, he received his first official guidance from St Petersburg. The Tsar, he was told, was gratified to learn that the Shah and the heir to the throne had nothing to do with the inhuman and despicable events that had taken place. The occurrence must be attributed to 'the impulsive and excessively zealous efforts of the deceased Griboyedov',[6] and his misunderstanding of the 'crude and vulgar customs' of the Persian rabble. Griboyedov's own team had disowned him.

No-one in Tabriz had dared to break the news to Nina, now six months pregnant, and staying with Macdonald's wife. Macdonald had the difficult task of explaining to her why the stream of letters from her husband had dried up, using the weather and the appalling state of the Persian roads as an excuse. The return of Amburgherr to Tabriz, and the arrival of Mal'tzov from Tehran, made his position easier. Mal'tzov was charged to tell her that her husband was well, but too busy to write, and that he had asked her to return to her mother in Tiflis to await him. Her father wrote separately with the same request. The sixteen-year-old had little option but to accept, however suspicious she might be. Escorted by Amburgherr, she left for Tiflis. Upon arrival at her mother's, she found no letter from her husband. Paskievich's wife, Griboyedov's cousin, called on her to explain away Griboyedov's silence. Bursting into tears, she lost control and blurted out the truth. Nina became hysterical, and on the following day gave birth prematurely to a son, who lived only a few hours. (Muravyov-Karsky, in a different version of the story, says that it was Madame Akhverdova who gave her the news, and was severely blamed for doing so; which version is correct is impossible to know.)

Griboyedov's coffin travelled slowly back to the Russian border. When it passed through Tabriz, it received no special recognition from Abbas Mirza, nor from the British mission. On 2 May, it reached Nakhichevan, and once on Russian soil was treated with appropriate honours. At the Araxes river, a Major-General greeted it with a battalion of the Tiflis infantry regiment drawn up in two ranks. Arms were presented, the Russian equivalent of the Last Post was sounded. Later, the coffin was placed on a hearse, pulled by six horses draped in black, accompanied by black-clad mourners, and a service according to the Armenian rite was held in the church at Nakhichevan.

On 11 June, there took place the famous meeting between the coffin and Pushkin,[7] on his way to join his brother at the Turkish front. His description of the circumstances is so evocative that it is worth quoting in full:

> I began the ascent of Bezobdal, the mountain which separated Georgia from ancient Armenia. A wide road shaded by trees winds around the mountain. On the peak of Bezobdal I passed through a small gorge called, it seems, the Wolf's Gate, and found myself on the natural border of Georgia. New mountains rose before me, a new horizon; below me stretched fertile green wheatfields. I glanced once more at scorched Georgia and began to descend: along the sloping side of the mountain toward the fresh plains of Armenia. With indescribable pleasure I noted that the heat had suddenly decreased: the climate was already different.
>
> My man lagged behind with the pack-horses. I rode alone in the flowering wilderness surrounded by mountains in the distance. Absent-mindedly I rode past the post where I was to change horses. More than six hours went by and I began to be surprised at how long it was taking between stations. Off to one side I saw piles of rocks resembling native saklyas and set off toward them. Indeed, I arrived at an Armenian village. A few women in colourful rags were sitting on the flat roof of an

underground saklya. I made myself understood somehow. One of them went down into the saklya and brought me some cheese and milk. Having rested a few minutes, I set out again and saw opposite me on the high bank of a river the fortress of Gergery. Three streams plunged down the high bank foaming noisily. I crossed the river. Two oxen harnessed to a cart were descending the steep road. Some Georgians were accompanying the cart. 'Where do you come from?' I asked them. 'From Teheran.' – 'What do you have on your cart?' – 'Griboyed.' This was the body of the slain Griboyedov, which they were taking to Tiflis.

On 17 July, after an inspection of the body at the quarantine station of Dzhelal Oglu (Muravyov-Karsky was told later that one hand was missing), the coffin arrived in Tiflis. The doleful procession entered the precincts of the city along the right bank of the river Kura, passing along the tall city walls and the vineyards they enclosed. It was night-time. In the flickering torchlight, one could barely distinguish the white veils of the Georgian women, their weeping mingling with the mournful dirges of the clergy. The whole population, both military and civil, had turned out to do honour to the fallen majesty of the Tsar's representative, who had married one of them. His widow, surrounded by her family, led the mourners. At the first sight of the coffin, she fainted, and did not recover consciousness for some time. The next day, the Military Governor of Tiflis attended the requiem mass in Sion Cathedral sung by the Exarch of Georgia, the Metropolitan John. His mutilated body was finally laid to rest in the monastery of Saint David on the hillside above Tiflis. Before leaving for Tehran, Griboyedov had told Nina that if he died in Persia, it was his wish to be buried there. Later Nina ordered a funeral monument for him, where she was eventually buried beside him. She had the following words engraved on it, still to be seen today: 'Your spirit and your works remain eternally in the memory of Russians; why did my love for thee outlive thee?'[8]

XXV

The Aftermath

The Persian mission to St Petersburg was headed by Abbas Mirza's twenty-three-year-old son Khosraw Mirza, accompanied by the Crown Prince's diplomatic adviser Mirza Saleh (familiar to Griboyedov from Tabriz and Karaziadin) and a numerous suite. He carried with him a personal letter of apology from the Shah to the Tsar, together with a variety of gifts from the Shah's treasury, of which the most important was an enormous diamond, the Nadir Shah, which had been looted from Delhi in 1739. The diamond, which, without being too fanciful, can be described as the price of Griboyedov's blood, can be seen in the Kremlin today.

Khosraw Mirza, young, good-looking and well-spoken, was lionised in St Petersburg. (In Tiflis, he had been made to feel by Paskievich that he had come not as a guest but to ask pardon.) A palace was put at his disposal, and during his two months there he was feted at balls and dinners, as if the reason for his embassy had been a happy one. On 13 August, after a solemn audience at the Winter Palace, at which the Shah's apology, blaming the 'unheard of evil deeds' of the mob, was read out before the Tsar, Nicholas pronounced 'that he consigned the ill-fated affair in Teheran to eternal oblivion'.[1] Better still, after further discussions, Nicholas struck one kuror off the remaining two still owing as war reparations, and postponed the payment of the other for five years. Griboyedov, whose life had been so bedevilled by the 'accursed contribution' might well feel his efforts had been in vain.

It is pleasing to note that on his way through Moscow, without telling anyone of his intention, Khosraw Mirza called on Griboyedov's mother to express his sympathy at the loss of her son; sadly there is no record of the interview. Meanwhile, the Tsar, showing some compunction at the fate of his murdered envoy, had written to Paskievich to ask about the financial situation of Griboyedov's dependants, namely his mother and his wife. Paskievich replied that all Griboyedov's loose cash had been looted in Tehran, and that his mother was in very straitened circumstances due to the money she had spent on her son's education. (We may be sure that Madame Griboyedova had been at pains to make this clear.) Nesselrode later passed on the news of his master's generosity: both Nina and Griboyedov's mother were granted pensions of 5000 roubles each, one sixth of Griboyedov's salary, together with a lump sum of 30,000 roubles. As we know, this did not prevent Griboyedova from accusing Bulgarin of embezzling her son's gratuity after Turkmanchai, an accusation Bulgarin vigorously rejected.

Nina never remarried. She died in 1857 of cholera, having rejected all suitors. She is occasionally glimpsed in the memoirs of visitors to Georgia, and must have known Lermontov (a cousin of Madame Akhverdova's) when he was stationed in Tiflis. She always found solace in the piano, and is recorded as knowing all Griboyedov's compositions by heart. Their delight in music had been one of the closest bonds between them.

Griboyedov's friends mourned him in their different ways. Despite his sometimes irascible nature, few people had a greater gift for friendship. His mother and sister in Moscow saw relatively little of him as an adult. His long periods of absence, either in Persia or the Caucasus, had forced him to select an alternative family, comrades and friends drawn from the camps, regiments and headquarters where he spent most of his working time. In St Petersburg, in the flowering of the arts that followed the war of 1812, a passion for literature, music and the theatre had drawn him to those of like mind and talents. These were the days, as Herzen wrote, 'in which Pushkin reigned supreme; in which the Decembrists...set the tone; in which Griboyedov laughed'.[2]

Following the débacle of 1825, he remained intensely loyal to his friends: Odoyevsky, Bestuzhev, Küchelbecker. In his last letter to Paskievich before leaving Tabriz, Griboyedov had made an impassioned plea for Odoyevsky, though it was not until 1833 that his transfer to the Caucasus came through; he was killed in action six years later. Bestuzhev was more leniently treated; possibly thanks to Griboyedov's efforts, he was transferred to Georgia at the end of 1829, there to begin a second life as a soldier and the author of a string of bestselling novels with Caucasian settings. One of his first actions on arrival in Tiflis was to visit Griboyedov's tomb. 'How much this man did for me,'[3] he wrote. 'He died, and all is turned to ashes.' In 1837, following the death of

Pushkin in a duel, he arranged a requiem for his two fellow writers. 'I wept then as I am weeping now,' he wrote to his brother afterwards,

> with hot tears, for a friend [Pushkin] and a comrade in arms [Griboyedov], and for myself. When the priest chanted, 'for the immortal souls of the two murdered boyars Alexander and Alexander' my sobs tore at my breast. The phrase seemed to me to be not only a remembrance, but also a premonition...Yes, I feel that my death will be just as violent and unexpected, and that it is close at hand.

He died in battle three months later.

Küchelbecker alone was never allowed to leave Siberia. He was sustained in his 20 years of imprisonment and exile by his memories of his friends, his deep Orthodox faith, and his reading of the Bible. 'Farewell!'[4] he wrote in a last, smuggled letter to Griboyedov. 'Until we meet again, in that world you forced me to believe in.' The letter, intercepted by the censor, was written in May 1829; he had not yet heard the news of his friend's death.

Beguichov, Griboyedov's oldest and most faithful friend, lived on until 1857. There was an element of simplicity in his character: it was sometimes suggested that he was the model for the good-natured Platon Mikhailovich, overwhelmed by Moscow and his wife, in *Woe from Wit*. But for Griboyedov, he was the first person who recognised his true value as a writer; he also helped him out in various financial difficulties, regarding his loans, as he said, 'almost as a subsidy to art'.

Beguichov's biographical article about Griboyedov, written just before he died, for *Plyushar's Universal Enyclopedia* of 1858, was the first official memoir of his friend; he had been helped in writing it by a number of Griboyedov's contemporaries, including Zhandr and Vladimir Odoyevsky. He had also talked earlier to Griboyedov's distant cousin and would-be biographer, Dmitri Smirnov. Born in 1819, and therefore only ten at the time of Griboyedov's death, Smirnov had taken it upon himself to interview as many as possible of Griboyedov's surviving friends. These valuable findings began to be published after 1874, and were eventually published in their entirety under the title *Griboyedov in the Memoirs of his Contemporaries* by the Griboyedov scholar S.A. Fomichev in 1980. The picture that emerges is not always flattering. Griboyedov could be coldly ambitious, ungrateful to former benefactors, such as Yermolov and Shakhovskoy, prickly and sarcastic in company. But he remained a hero to those who knew him best, not only for his courage, gifts and patriotism, but at the simplest level: in the words of Beguichov,[5] he was 'a good son, a good brother, a true friend'. Bulgarin, whom Smirnov privately regarded as 'an appalling shit', had staked his claim to Griboyedov early in his essay 'My Unforgettable Friend', published in the *Northern Bee* in 1830. He gained reflected glory from his friendship and thanks to his possession of Griboyedov's manuscript of *Woe from Wit* – Zhandr owned another – was able to quote from the play in his articles, though still with an eye to the censor. Griboyedov's mother, predictably, accused him of breaching copyright.

The first full-length, but still censored, versions of *Woe from Wit* were performed in Moscow and St Petersburg in 1831. From then on it became part of the repertoire, but it was not until after the reforms of the early 1860s that a complete version, collating the various manuscripts, was able to be published or performed. Interpretations varied. There were those who saw the play as an intimate personal drama, centring on the characters of Sophie, Chatsky and Molchalin, others who loaded it with political meaning, taking Chatsky as the spokesman for their reforming views. Others again portrayed his protest as essentially futile and irrelevant. Some debated whether or not it was a comedy. Byelinsky feted it as a tragedy, as opposed to Griboyedov, who had called it a 'comedy'. A famous production by Meyerhold in 1927 portrayed him as an aristocratic idealist, doomed to fail in confrontation with the confident philistinism of Moscow society. An isolated, fragile figure, he spends much of the performance seated at the piano playing Mozart and Beethoven; the false rumour of Chatsky's madness in the party scene is relayed from character to character to the sound of a tranquil nocturne by Field. Dismissed as perverse by many critics, the production's greatest contribution was in bringing out the musical qualities of the play, reflecting Griboyedov's gifts as a a pianist and composer.

For the twentieth-century poet Alexander Blok, Griboyedov was the most original and talented writer in the history of Russian drama. Fascinated by his character, he sees him as a divided personality,[6] 'on the one hand a Petersburg civil servant...an unloveable fellow with a cold expression, a poisonous mocker and sceptic', on the other a subversive, whose hidden rebelliousness and restlessness force him into unceasing experiment aesthetically. In an essay in 1907, coming down from the fence after an extended summary of all the critical literature on Griboyedov, he describes *Woe from Wit* as the 'most magnificent creation of all our literature'. It is a bold claim, and one which will always be open to discussion. But Griboyedov's place in the pantheon of Russian literature is secure. His epitaph remains as relevant as it was on the day his widow had it carved on his tomb: his spirit and his works live eternally in the memory of Russians.

APPENDIX I

Griboyedov's Death and the 'British Conspiracy' Theory

The theory that the British secretly masterminded the massacre of Griboyedov and the Russian mission in Tehran was put forward by a number of Russian literary historians during the Cold War era: these included such well-regarded writers in Russia as S.V. Shostakovich, V.T. Pashuto, I.O. Popova and L.M. Arinshtein. It was alleged that the British were seeking revenge on the Russians, and Griboyedov in particular, for the humiliations inflicted on them in Persia by the Treaty of Turkmanchai; and that the Duke of Wellington, Prime Minister from January 1828, and Lord Ellenborough, President of the Board of Control (in charge of India) were the chief proponents of this anti-Russian policy.

According to their interpretation, British interests in Persia were divided into two groupings: the first was the peace party, led by Sir John Macdonald; the second 'hawkish' grouping consisted of Sir Henry Willock, his brother George Willock and Dr McNeill in Tehran. This second grouping supposedly represented the 'imperialist minded British aristocracy', led by Wellington, Ellenborough and the Governor of Bombay, Sir John Malcolm, who wished to embarrass Russia in its war with Turkey, and undermine its hold on Persia by provoking a further Russo–Persian war. Extensive quotations from Ellenborough's *Political Diary*, nearly all misunderstood and out of context, are used to justify this theory. In the distorted perspectives of these writers, it is only a short step from Ellenborough's expressed distrust of Russia's expansionist policies to the assumption that the 'hawkish' party masterminded the massacre in Tehran, using its agents to incite the fanaticism of the Persian crowd.

Before taking a detailed look at these suggestions, it is worth returning to the broader picture of British policies in the area at the time. The best picture of these is given in Professor Malcolm Yapp's exhaustive and authoritative study, *Strategies of British India: Britain, Iran and Afghanistan, 1798–1850* (Oxford, 1980). In describing the British perception of Persia in their search for a system which would safeguard India from the dangers of an attack from the northwest, he writes:

From 1798 to 1838 Britain experimented with a system of defence in which the central role was played by Iran in alliance with British India. Iran was thought to offer an insurmountable obstacle to any would-be invader of India. Disappointed with the fruits of the Iranian alliance, Britain began in 1830 to investigate alternatives.

He points out that India and its defence had a low priority in British foreign policy at the time; the first place was always held by Europe. British Foreign Secretaries tended to look on India as an embarrassment, whose interests demanded arrangements which hampered negotiations with other foreign powers, notably France and Russia. In the early years of the century, when Britain was at war with France and allied with Russia, Britain was anxious to avoid any appearance of opposition to Russia in Western Asia. Only at the end of the 1820s did fears that Russian ambitions might cause the dismemberment of the Ottoman empire cause a revision of this attitude.

> Britain's new, still uncertain view of Russia as a menace to British interests was then reinforced by a new perception of Russia as a major threat to those European liberties for which Britain had become the chief spokesman. The growth of Russophobia in Britain coincided with the enhanced sense of the value of India. [p.94]

At the time of Griboyedov's death, these views were only beginning to take hold. The previous few years had seen a gradual loss of British interest in Persia. Abbas Mirza had been roundly beaten in the war of 1826–8; the Shah was broke, and financially unwilling to back any policies which might benefit Britain or India; the East India Company, according to Wellington, Prime Minister from January 1828, was almost insolvent. The British mission in Persia had been drastically reduced on the grounds of cost. As Yapp remarks, 'The apparent triumph of the Iranian buffer system was an illusion' (p.95).

Macdonald, as we have seen, had done his best to bring about some kind of stability in the area by acting as a trusted intermediary between the Russians and Persians in their peace negotiations. But he was power-less to prevent the growth of Russian influence, and in any case regarded the Persians as hopelessly unreliable. He constantly complained of their perfidy and foolishness, and even included Abbas Mirza: 'a wretched devil on whom it would be folly to place dependence' (Macdonald to Malcolm, 17 June 1829, EM D 556/1). In her defeated state, it was clear that Persia could never resist Russia successfully, and could only survive by not providing her neighbour with excuses for intervention. Although the Russo–Turkish War of 1828–9 was to heighten British fears of Russian imperialism in Western Asia, there is nothing to suggest that the murder of the Russian envoy and his mission in Tehran would have done anything to strengthen the defences of British India. On the contrary (but for both Russia and Britain's concern to play down the affair) it would have opened a veritable Pandora's box of fresh threats to the British position in the area.

The most convincing refutation of the Russian accusations, which for years were accepted by Soviet historians, even going so far as to make Wellington and Ellenborough directly responsible for engineering the massacre, can be found by examining the correspondence between Wellington and Ellenborough, now in the Wellington archives in Southampton University. It shows Wellington as being closely consulted on almost every policy issue to do with Persia and the defence of India, and taking a hand in redrafting instructions and despatches both to India and Tabriz. He was also in frequent consultation with Sir John Malcolm, the Governor of Bombay, who seems to have had direct access to him.

On 30 March 1828, for instance, Wellington received a direct communication from Malcolm about the progress of the Russo–Persian War: 'Persia is, as anticipated, at the fist of Russia... The throne of Persia will not recover from the blow. We shall soon have that bear you are hugging for our Asiatic neighbour' (WP 921/8). On 30 May, he warned Wellington of the effect which the arrival of Griboyedov's embassy in Tehran might have: 'The evacuation of Persia by the Russians is a significant event... If the Russian ambassador due to arrive in Persia is an able person, Russian ascendancy may be established. This could be counteracted by a British mission' (WPI/934/23). Wellington, however, was unwilling to upgrade Macdonald from his position as representative of the East India Company to that of envoy of the British Crown, and thus equal in status to the Russian envoy.

Ellenborough, who took office at the Board of Control in September 1828, was outspoken in his dislike of Russia. He complained that British Residents in Persia had acted too much in Russia's interests, from 1813 onwards, and saw the Russian conquest of Persia as a real threat to India. 'I would in Persia and everywhere,' he wrote, 'endeavour to create the means of throwing the whole world in arms upon Russia at the first convenient moment' (Ellenborough, *Political Diary*, 1 October 1828, p.132). Wellington was more pragmatic. There was nothing that could be done to stop the Russians, short of declaring war; any attempt by the Persians to come in on the Turkish side against the Russians would only lead to the destruction of the Qajar monarchy. Once peace between Russia and Persia had been concluded, his chief concern was to prevent any recurrence of hostilities. He set out his views at some length in a letter to Ellenborough, on 8 October 1828:

> I have read your proposed despatch to Colonel Macdonald. I think that
> Mr Canning [the Foreign Secretary] did not behave handsomely or wisely

in leaving the Persians to the moderation and mercy of the Emperor Nicholas. We were bound to mediate in their favour, and we ought to have started from the post, not by taking their part, for the Persians were really in the wrong, but by moderating both parties...The contest is now over, however, and we must look to the means of preventing its renewal. It is quite obvious that the King of Persia is not equal to a contest with the power of Russia even upon its Georgian frontier, and when Russia is occupied otherwise in Europe. No combination that can be made in Asia and no improvement in the state and resources of the Persian Government which we think will probably occur, would enable the King of Persia to become a formidable enemy to the Emperor of Russia.

That which we ought to inculcate then is peace and good neighbourhood. A strict and good-humoured performance of treaties and the manifestation of a strong desire to continue in good terms would have a good effect, and such measures are not at all inconsistent with an entire independence of, and freedom from Russian control and even counsel, and great attention to the resources of the country, financial as well as military...

We must observe that the advice which we have under consideration is to be given to a semi-barbarous, but very corrupt, court and people. The ministers, the Prince, the King himself would sell our advice for half a crown, and we must take care that while peace is our real object and policy and the real intention which we have in view, we are not accused as the Persians were two years ago, and the Turks more recently, of exciting war against the Emperor or his Eastern frontier' [WP1/963/23].

The restrained and moderate views expressed by Wellington give not the slightest encouragement to the idea that he was hatching a murderous plan to assassinate the new Russian envoy and his mission; indeed, they make clear that it would have totally contrary to British interests to engage in any such conspiracy.

The Soviet version of events, still widely accepted in Russia, is based on a series of speculations. Some of them can be factually refuted. To start with, there is no evidence that the Willocks or Dr McNeill were in Tehran at the time of the massacre, and there are a number of significant indications to the contrary. De Gamba, the French Consul in Tiflis, who would have received first-hand reports very soon after the massacre, states categorically: 'None of the staff of the English legation were in Tehran during these horrible events' (Archives Diplomatiques du Ministère des Affaires Etrangères, C. Russie, vol. 176, Letter, 9298, 7 March 1829). The First Secretary, Sir Henry Willock, cast in the role of one of the chief plotters, had in fact left the mission two months before the massacre. Having been acting Chargé in Tabriz for 11 years, he had been replaced by Macdonald in 1824; after two years' leave he had returned to Persia as First Secretary, but had been relieved of his post in November 1828. It is scarcely likely that he lingered on in secret in Tehran or that he would have been supported with funds or official approval in mounting such a dangerous and uncertain operation. Griboyedov, in his letter to Macdonald shortly before his death, makes no mention of the presence of either of the Willock brothers; George Willock, a junior officer seconded from the Madras Cavalry Regiment, in any case would not have had the authority to act on his own.

Dr McNeill, having failed in his mission to help Griboyedov to obtain a contribution to the eighth kuror from the Shah, was almost certainly in Tabriz, as the mission's doctor, in attendance on Macdonald, who was already suffering from the lingering illness (probably TB) from which he would die the following year. We find McNeill certifying the translation of a letter from the Shah to Abbas Mirza into English for Macdonald on 19 February 1829, to be used in Macdonald's report on the affair (IOL/S & P/9/90, 69-61). As a close friend and colleague of Macdonald's, it is unthinkable that he would act in direct contradiction to his superior's peacemaking policies by planning an uprising, or that, as an honourable man, he should lend himself to such a course.

Interestingly, we find McNeill's own account of the affair in the memoirs of Prince V.S. Tolstoy, who met him in Tiflis in the summer of 1839; McNeill, then British envoy to Persia, was travelling to Russia via the Georgian military highway, and Tolstoy had been appointed as his escort. In view of earlier suggestions of British involvement, Tolstoy asked McNeill somewhat timidly about Griboyedov's death. He received essentially this reply:

> McNeill highly appreciated Griboyedov's qualities. It is well known that before the beginning of the last war with the Persians, gangs of their marauding brigands irrupted into our borders, and kidnapped many of our German settlers of both sexes. Upon the conclusion of the peace, Persia obliged herself to return all these slaves, a condition they fulfilled unwillingly and in bad conscience. Griboyedov was implacable, insisting to the Persians that they should fulfil this clause. He used agents to seek out the candidates, these agents reported to him. There were three young German women hidden in the very capital of Persia. Griboyedov insisted on a search of the suspected houses, the police failed to find them. The agents denied this, saying that during the searches the girls had been hidden. Griboyedov knew how much the Persians were dissembling and acting hypocritically, and demanded that they should be brought to the embassy. The Teheran police brought three young Persian women as hostages until the Germans should have been delivered. They were installed in a room by the stairs, which communicated with the flat roof. Griboyedov's personal valet, Alexander, who had shared his wet nurse with him, and to whom he was specially attached, at night crept

into the Persian girls' quarters. A great uproar and cries were then heard. Alexander slunk away back to his room. At dawn when the call to prayer was heard from the neighbouring mosques, the Persian girls climbed to the roof and called out to the worshippers that they had been violated and dishonoured, whether or not they imagined it we do not know. From the mosques the rumours multiplied, a hysterical and vengeful mob rushed to the embassy, murdering the defending Cossacks. Finally they entered the envoy's room where they killed him with stones. Later they dragged his mangled remains of his body around crying: 'Make way, make way for the Russian ambassador!'

McNeill added that when the episode became known to the British, the British envoy urgently expedited a note demanding punishment of the evildoers; unless this were to happen it would be impossible to remain in Persia, as a country where no security could be guaranteed.

Tolstoy's memoirs were not published till 1874, 35 years after his meeting with McNeill, but the account has the stamp of authenticity. It is noteworthy that McNeill makes no claim to have been an eye-witness of what happened, and that some of the details vary from the accepted version of the affair. In particular, he makes no mention of the defection of Mirza Yakub as the chief factor in precipitating the riot, and ascribes a hitherto unknown (though not necessarily incredible) role to Griboyedov's scapegrace half-brother. However, he was talking 20 years after the event, and the story may well have acquired variations over that period.

On the Russian side, the main contemporary suggestions that the British might have been involved in Griboyedov's murder come from Paskievich and Muravyov-Karsky. In a letter to Nesselrode, immediately after hearing the news, Paskievich confirmed that the British had not been in Tehran at the time, but added darkly, 'One may suppose that the English were not altogether foreign to participation in the disorders that broke out in Teheran, though perhaps they did not foresee the fatal results' (Popova, p.191). However, after receiving Mal'tzov's report in March, he ceased to express any suspicions of British involvement.

Muravyov-Karsky, who was serving with Paskievich at the time, may have been influenced by his commander's first reactions. Although he adduces no new facts, he gave his own interpretation of the episode in his memoirs. The relevant passage is as follows:

> From the course of this business people conclude that the Shah himself and all the Persian government knew of Allah Yar Khan's purpose and connived at the crime. It has even been supposed that the English, seeing that Griboyedov was beginning to outweigh them in influence, endeavoured secretly to incline the principal Persian officials to undertake this audacious stroke. It is impossible to suppose they wished to

carry matters to such a point, but it is very conceivable that they wanted an incident which would lead to the humiliation of our minister and a diminution of his influence.

There are no further references to the possibility by any contemporary players on the scene, most importantly the chief eye-witnesses, Mal'tzov and the secretary, who would certainly have mentioned the British presence had there been one. A further argument against the conspiracy theory (probably used to Paskievich at the time) came from his adjutant, Count Felkersam. He pointed out that the British usually left an official in Tehran to observe the relations of the Russians with the Shah's court; if Griboyedov's mission was so menacing to English interests, why, he asked, did they not follow their usual practice by placing one of their own people there? (Quoted by S.P. Yefremov, Russky Arkhiv, March 1872). Interestingly, de Gamba in Tiflis, in his letter to the French Foreign Office of 7 March 1829, suggested that 'Turkish intrigues' might have been responsible for the massacre, presumably reasoning that a renewal of Russia's war with Persia might have diverted resources from the war with Turkey. The researches of Professor Michael Rogers (see Bibliography) in the Ottoman archives, however, provide no evidence that this was so.

Before abandoning the subject of the so-called conspiracy, let us suppose for a moment (without the slightest shred of documentation to support it) that Wellington, Ellenborough and the Board of Control did determine as a matter of policy to murder the entire Russian mission through the unpredictable agency of the Tehran mob. A number of highly undesirable consequences would then have had to be faced.

The Russians would very possibly have mounted a punitive expedition against the Persians. Since the Shah would be most reluctant to open his remaining coffers to finance any further war, and Abbas Mirza had no money, artillery or any army left to speak of, the Russians would have met with almost no resistance.

In the event of the Persian defeat, the Qajar monarchy would have been overthrown, thus provoking even greater dangers in the short term: an unknown and insecure new ruler would be even more unlikely than the previous dynasty to provide a stable buffer zone for India.

In dealing with the appallingly weak Qajar dynasty, the British were at least confronting a known risk; the extra uncertainty involved a change of power could only cause further concern in London and Calcutta. Not even Ellenborough in his most Russophobic moments believed that such an option was desirable.

Even supposing that the Russians were too committed to the Turkish war to mount a campaign against Persia, they would certainly have claimed a further huge compensation from the Shah. If the British were indeed responsible for the massacre, they would be expected to foot the bill, an unthinkable risk in view of the near insolvency of the East India Company, and the restraints and economies imposed on them by London.

In the final analysis, the strongest arguments against the conspiracy theory lie in the characters of those supposedly involved. Men such as Wellington and Ellenborough and Lord William Bentinck were born aristocrats (a black mark in Soviet eyes) and became honourable and responsible statesmen. We should not cast them as part of a cheap thriller plot, worthy of the sick history of the twentieth century, smacking more of the imagination of a Beria or his henchmen than of the realities of nineteenth-century politics. Had the British been responsible for Griboyedov's death, their role would certainly have been discovered in the extensive enquiries which followed the massacre, and they would have been covered with contempt and ridicule throughout Europe. We must also assume that Nicholas I and Nesselrode would have extracted any advantages they could in blaming the British for such a flagrant breach of diplomatic protocol. It was not a humiliation which Wellington, with his vast prestige as the leading statesman of Europe, would have risked.

To plot the murder of a foreign envoy and his whole staff in a third country was unprecedented in British foreign policy. However perfidious Albion might be, it is unlikely that she would have gone so far. A suspicious mind, of course, might argue that by now incriminating documents could have been removed and destroyed. Nevertheless, there is no written evidence of any conspiracy, and as this appendix seeks to show, a great deal of corroborative evidence as to why it would have been dangerous, counter-productive and contrary to all the existing aims of the key policy-makers at the time. The plain fact is that the conspiracy never took place.

The most extreme statement impugning the British as responsible for Griboyedov's assassination and that of his mission comes in an article by L.M. Arinshtein and I.S. Chistova in a paper delivered at the Khmelita Proceedings in 1989, and later published in the book summarising those proceedings, S.A. Fomichev (ed.), *A.S. Griboyedov, Materialy k biografii (Sbornik nauchnykh trudov)* (Leningrad, 1989; Smolensk 1998), pp.108–33.

Since these allegations are published in Russian, and only available in a very rare *sbornik* (booklet), I feel I should perhaps tax the reader's patience with a longer statement of their case, treated as received wisdom in Russia, giving more details of the events preceding and following Griboyedov's death: accordingly I will seek to paraphrase some of the main extracts from the article.

The first part of Arinshtein's article recapitulates much material from the most comprehensive account of Griboyedov's death available in Russian to Soviet readers, from *Griboyedov in the Memoirs of his Contemporaries*, S.A. Fomichev and V.E. Vatsuro (eds) (Moscow, 1980), namely the secretary to the *mehmendar* of the mission's 'Narrative of the Proceedings of the Russian Mission, from its Departure from Tabreez for Tehran on 14th Jummade 2D [20 December 1828], until its Destruction on Wednesday the 6th Sha'ban [11 February 1829]', *Blackwood's Edinburgh Magazine*, 171 (September 1830), pp.496–512. It also includes the report of Captain Ronald Macdonald following his visit to Tehran after the events:

'All was well, until about six days before his departure. Mirza Yakub, second Eunuch and Treasurer to the Shah, appeared, and claimed protection that, as born in Erevan, and as such now being a Russian subject, he was entitled to repatriation under the Treaty of Turkmanchai. The Envoy tried to dissuade him, arguing he would not return to Erevan to enjoy the same wealth, advantages and privileges that he had had in Persia. All arguments failed and he was accepted into the Embassy. A crowd of Moslems gathered outside the Embassy on 30 January (11 February 1829 old style). The envoy ordered the gates to be closed and the guard strengthened. After the first shots, the whole mission were bestially murdered by, it is alleged, a huge hundred-thousand-strong mob.'

There are, states Arinshtein, more than 30 versions of the storming of the embassy and these fatal events; of these 30, one can summarise explanations to some seven. Possible interpretations include: the anti-Russian activities were the responsibility of the Persian Government, in particular of the Shah's court; the main guilty party was a leading feudal lord, Allah Yar Khan, at court, who had especial scores to settle both with the Russians and with Griboyedov personally; guilt is really attributable to the spiritual leaders of the mob in Tehran, especially Mujtahid Mirza Mesikh, the chief mulla-imam; the attack of the mob was especially noteworthy because of its spontaneous character; the Persians alleged that the person mainly responsible was Griboyedov himself, through his own actions and attitudes, and contributing to this was the conduct of his entourage, notably the Christian Persians and Armenian servants, whom he employed and failed to control; there may have been 'secret manoeuvres-impulses' from St Petersburg, in particular from Nicholas I and Nesselrode. These are not documented; finally responsibility for 'instigating these acts', it is asserted, may lic with the British mission in Persia.

Arinshtein then examines the suggestions in some detail. Because of the absolute nature of Fath Ali Shah's dictatorship and authority as Shah, he dismisses any possibility of any initiative by Allah Yar Khan, as no subject would have dared to interfere with the Shah's relations with a major foreign power. 'Real power in the cities,' he writes, 'was held by the religious leaders, especially the Muslim ones, who combined moral authority with all legal powers. The mobs were especially prone to fanaticism, but did the Mujtahid act on his own initiative, or was he responding to the will of others?'

Only the Shah, or the British (he suggests) at the time had the power to influence events in this way. Could the Shah have profited from such a provocation? Was it in his interests to encourage it? 'In our view, a well-organised and professionally arranged attack on the Russian Mission could suit expansionist-minded British circles'. The more the background is analysed and studied, the less it appears to have been in the Shah's interests to have another major row with the Russians, having just paid them a huge indemnity.

Arinshtein then turns to certain documents: the letter from Sir John Macdonald of 9 February 1829 to his political masters in the East India Company, in which he gave his initial report based on oral information; the personal 'Firman' letter from the Shah, to him, explaining the tragic events; letters from the head of the Shah's Government, Abdul Vehhab-Mirza, and the Minister of Foreign Affairs, Abul Hassan Khan.

These last two were a reply to Macdonald's own diplomatic protest, delivered as the response of a shocked Victorian gentleman; he was, after all, looking after Griboyedov's wife, at the time heavily pregnant. One is dated 5 March 1829, 1 Ramazan 1229. They were translated by Macdonald's Persian-speaking secretaries John McNeill and J. Campbell. The Persian originals are not available, but three copies were sent off to different interested parties by Macdonald: the Political Secretary of the East India Company; the Chairman of the Board of the East India Company; the GOC of Russian Troops in the Caucasus, General Paskievich (the British reference is PRO FO 249.27 IOL).

The Persians did not explain what had happened until a week after the tragedy, on 6/18 February. This was the verbal explanation from a regretful Crown Prince to Macdonald in Tabriz. The Persians only had diplomatic relations with the Sultan, Britain and Russia, and no longer with France. Missions were normally in Tabriz, except extraordinary ones that might find the Shah in Tehran. Arinshtein refers then to those in Persia who favoured an isolationist foreign policy, though this had long been inappropriate, as Persia had already fallen under British influence; and the British in Persia, he alleges, felt themselves to be the complete rulers and owners of the country. They were systematically subsidising the Shah and his court; they had resident Consuls in all the main towns, and British officers staffed the Persian army; British doctors looked after the court. McNeill was the Shah's personal doctor.

But, Arinshtein argues, there was no unity amongst the British representatives in Persia; there were two 'groupings'. One was led by Macdonald, who was the envoy of the East India Company: though the company was formally subordinate to the King, in practice it was a 'state within a state'. J. Campbell who acted as a diplomatic secretary to Macdonald, was the son of the company's chairman. The company wanted Persia to stay at peace with Russia. Stability in Persia was its guiding policy.

The second grouping was headed by Henry Willock, his brother George and McNeill. They represented the 'expansionist' circles of the British aristocracy, especially from 1828 onwards. It is true that Wellington was irritated by Russian policies, and his views are quoted in notes in the Southampton University database. He was supported in this by Lord Ellenborough, who did not exclude the use of force: 'Our policy in Asia must follow one course only – to limit the power of Russia'. 'In Persia we may have to face up to a widely armed struggle against Russia,' he wrote in his *Political Diary* in 1828. 'If the Russians occupy Khiva we will have to occupy Lahore and Kabul.'

Arinshtein recognises the peace grouping, led by Macdonald, in strong contrast, who wanted peace with Russia; in connection with the Turkmanchai negotiations in February 1828, he advised HMG that 'the Peace enables Persia to continue in being as an independent State, and frees us from having to take on the Russians or the Petersburg Court, which considering the successes of Russian arms we would have been dragged into'. Macdonald knew his subject as a professional. He had seen an all-Russian column invade Azherbaijan, and then scatter Persian troops at Deh Kurgan over the valley of Sultaniye, and open the path to Tehran; a renewed war would throw Persia forever into Russia's arms.

In fact Russia had shown restraint; Paskievich's troops had not marched on Tehran, they soon evacuated Tabriz and the lands of Azherbaijan. Macdonald believed in the negotiating table not the field of battle.

This view, it is alleged, was not convenient to the other grouping of 'hawks', the chief 'hawk' among them being Henry Willock. His reports had deliberately distorted the situation and helped to provoke the Russo–Persian War of 1826–8. Other observers, including Muravyov-Karsky, considered Willock a crude and coarse person. Macdonald thought he was a 'conscienceless intriguer'. Malcolm had told Bentinck that he would not have Willock on his staff in Persia in the 1820s. Arinshtein then suggests that Macdonald and Campbell were on bad terms, but no evidence is given for this assertion. As soon as he took up his appointment, Macdonald, not trusting Willock, despatched him to

England with Lieutenant J. Alexander, where Willock intrigued against Macdonald. Events favoured Willock with the arrival in power of Wellington and Ellenborough. In June 1827, Willock was knighted, and by October 1827 he was on his way back to Persia via St Petersburg, where he muddied the waters with Nesselrode, alleging he was the new Chargé d'Affaires. Griboyedov and Willock had been acquainted since 1819, and knew of the differences between the British. Willock was shortly to be recalled (see later Wellington document references). Macdonald shared valuable information with Griboyedov, especially financial, over the scale of British subsidies, to show what fines the Shah could or could not pay at Russia's demand. Griboyedov had seen Campbell frequently during the Turkmanchai negotiations, and in the summer of 1828 learnt from him of the alleged 'new' instructions coming from Wellington and Ellenborough (no evidence given).

To some extent, suggests Arinshtein, the British wanted the defeat of Russia in the Russo–Turkish War of 1828, and generally to weaken Russian influence in the Middle East; if a second war could be provoked for Russia in the area, Russia's fight against two Muslim powers (however impossible) would be extended by thousands of kilometres. It is suggested, without evidence, that Willock felt the British could get advantage from the Russians being dragged into a war on two fronts; if Macdonald and Griboyedov succeeded in their peaceful policies, this would be impossible, and Willock and McNeill were to seek the bloody dénouement to trigger this possibility.

Arinshtein then turns to Macdonald's report (the first document after the murder) to George Swinton, the Political Secretary of the East India Company, dated 19 February 1829:

> I first heard on the 18th of this month that HRH Prince Abbas Mirza wanted to talk to me on a matter of utmost urgency; I found him in the Palace with the 'Kai-mak-am'. He then described the murder. I have not the slightest grounds to think that the Shah or anyone from his Court could be linked to the catastrophe.
>
> The Shah did send his own unarmed guards to repress the riot, a number of whom were killed. There is no advantage whatsoever to the Shah to be gained from this incident. On the contrary he runs the risk of being completely eliminated. The Crown Prince is totally innocent in the matter, which reinforces his views as to the idiocy of his father who cannot control the population where he lives. The Persians are in no position to be able to undertake a new war – in many provinces there are signs of disorder and disobedience.
>
> I deeply regret I did not accompany Mr Griboyedov to Teheran and am inclined to think that my presence and mediation would have played a positive role to avert what happened, but he only went to Teheran to present his credentials and then planned to return to Tabreez. I felt I

should stay with the Crown Prince about to leave on a foreign mission. As a further deepening of the tragedy, I should mention, my wife and I are caring for his seductive, pretty and heavily pregnant young wife, born a Princess Chavchavadze. More than anyone else, I can bear witness to the bold and noble if somewhat inflexible character of the late departed; a mighty sense of honour dictated his conduct. I shall make a determined protest about this shocking infringement of the sacred ties between nations.

The line taken by Abbas Mirza coincides with that of other sources; it may be read as a *ballon d'essai* by the Crown Prince to dissociate the Shah and his Court from any complicity; Abbas and the Foreign Minister wanted to gauge the degree of fury and indignation of the British. What they did not know at the time was that Macdonald was effectively accepting their version. There were indeed softening and mitigating circumstances 'to calm down' the Tsar's anger, and these are reflected in Macdonald's protest. His political analysis confirms this, by saying there were no advantages whatsoever for the Shah in the situation, though there were very considerable risks for him and his dynasty of being wiped out by Russian reprisals. If Arinshtein is right in accepting that the cornerstone of Macdonald's policy was the preservation of peace with the Qajars in this part of the Middle East, the danger was that Persia would read into Russian military reverses on the Danube an excuse to exploit their defeats and repeat again the mistakes that had led them earlier into a foolish war; Arinshtein continues that Macdonald understood very well who sought to encourage a new war and guessed who had been responsible.

Captain Ronald Macdonald, his brother, was in charge of his bodyguard, and was despatched with his written protest to investigate the grisly murders in Tehran. He left Tabriz on 20 February and stayed there two days, saw the Shah and ministers, and returned by 6 March with his own report and two letters, a personal one from the Shah and one from the Chief Minister and Minister of Foreign Affairs. Fath Ali Shah was not accustomed to writing personal letters. The Shah's letter began by saying that Colonel Macdonald already had a good idea of the events leading to General (sic) Griboyedov's fate.

From the moment of his arrival he was surrounded by the maximum goodwill. Our ministers were told to anticipate his every desire and to fulfil all his requests. Unfortunately, in the context of the return of prisoners, the Envoy listened to evil counsels and 'exceeded the bounds of reasonableness'. None of our Ministers committed before him the slightest hostile act. The cause of the shame and disaster were the inhabitants of the City who could not control themselves. You will understand perfectly what a calamity for us this represents.

In every alarming situation we have always found the intervention of the British, giving friendly advice and support, helpful, as we did in the Turkmanchai negotiations with your Excellency last year. We rely on Your Excellency's helpful and friendly disposition to do all in your power to advise the Crown Prince our Son and to insist with him what should be done in the context of international conduct; we must take necessary steps to contain the evil and remove the stain of shame from our Government.

Arinshtein comments that 'the Shah's letter is a cunning attempt to keep the peace with the Russians'. The Shah had no idea of a preventive war against Russia. Macdonald would not support such a policy, the Shah felt. Guilt as to the parties involved on the 6 Shaban did not concern the Shah overmuch; leave it to the Ministers; what Heaven had pre-ordained could not be stopped. Arinshtein suggests that the Shah knew perfectly well that the alleged policies of the two British groups were at loggerheads with each other.

The second letter was from the Chief Minister. He acknowledged the British protest and confirmed what had happened, repeating that the Government had nothing to do with it. The Chief Minister's letter analyses why the Persian Government could not possibly have chosen a worse moment to hurl defiance again at the Russians; it had paid the bulk of their enormous fine, which, if left in the Shah's coffers, would have been enough to pay for another 50,000 soldiers. Had it been minded to treachery, after the armistice, this would have been a large force to start the war up again. The Persian population thought the fine 10 times too high, but the Russians had not taken Tehran, and had behaved with restraint, and with justice; the Persian army was not exterminated, the population was spared complete confusion. But the Shah had not felt able to behave perfidiously to an invading power that had shown such restraint. He found the fine reasonably fair; acceptance of the clause on repatriation, it was known, would lead to conflicts and trouble; this was the reason for the Crown Prince's proposed St Petersburg good-will mission. For all these reasons, the Government was not involved. Would Macdonald help as best he could to soften the consequences of the tragedy?

It was an extraordinary confession of weakness from a defeated Government that the invading enemy was just, generous in spirit and restrained. Abdul Vehhab-Mirza, the letter's author, belonged to that layer of well-educated and civilised Persians of the profile of Khosraw Mirza, along with the courtier-poet Fazil-Khan, whom Pushkin had described in his *A Journey to Erzerum*. It would seem that the fears expressed by Griboyedov before setting off on his mission to Persia – 'Allah Yar Khan will not forgive Turkmanchai' – were unfounded; his murder was not an act of political revenge by the Persians.

In addition, we have the letter of the Foreign Minister, Abul Hassan Khan. He took great pains again to emphasise that the Government had no interest in provoking the incident, and reminded Macdonald that he had personally warned Griboyedov that the population would react furiously about Mirza Yakub and the two women being apparently held in the embassy. He advised the women to return. They did not agree. As further justification, the mob was mad, he said: Mirza Selliman (a kinsman of Manuchehr Khan) was murdered by the mob. Had the ministers thought he would be killed, he would never have been sent to the Russian embassy. After showing so much honour and attention to the Russian envoy, it was inconceivable that the Government could plan his murder. Had it not wanted him to stay, it could have asked for the envoy to be changed. 'You reproach us for not suppressing the riot. It was so great, we had to close the gates of the Citadel, where the Shah's palace was placed. The riot arose like lightning quicker than one could gather up troops; the mob's intentions were only to seize Mirza Yakub, and free the two women. It was Dadash-Bek on Griboyedov's staff, an Armenian who killed a Muslim, who caused the cup of patience to overflow, and all patience to be lost. The Armenians from the Envoy's suite insulted the religion of Islam in the streets, which infuriated the population. It will be difficult to pin down the guilty murderers, as Teheran receives caravans from all over Persia. To punish the guilty, the Shah would have to kill off the whole population. We will do what we can and continue investigations.'

It is difficult to follow Arinshtein's argument that these letters confirm the impression that the murder was not just the result of a spontaneous uprising but a 'carefully orchestrated and planned provocation, from the side of those seeing advantage in the fanning of hatred between peoples'. It is noteworthy that not one contemporaneous account of the murder by people close to the scene, officially or informally, supports Arinshtein's version, and Macdonald himself would have been a vitally interested party in the subversion of the so-called Willock/McNeill grouping and plan. His reports and letters, and those of the Persians themselves in the three vital letters quoted by Arinshtein, show how the Persians would have had every interest in shifting the blame to another party, i.e. the English. They do not do so, nor even hint at it.

Last but not least is the curious silence from all contemporary Russian sources, including the lone survivor, Mal'tzov. His lengthy report describing the murders and events would surely have mentioned any sinister wicked British involvement, to warn St Petersburg of the duplicity of the British; on the contrary, Mal'tzov admits to limited mistakes of judgement by his own superior and envoy, and lays emphasis on the whole Mirza Yakub scandal and the problem of the women, and stresses too the hideous nature of a fanatical Shiite mob; it would have been tempting for a Russian observer to mention British intrigues in Tehran, and to shift the responsibility entirely from his own envoy, thus making him a patriot and noble victim. As for the suggestion that a separate policy existed, laid down directly to the Willock group in Tehran by Wellington, Ellenborough and the Foreign Office, this 'group' would have needed some accreditation to the Government and Shah, with a staff and finances with which to bribe the mullahs and/or the mob, and would have had to have shown some signs of accountability, by way of reports, to their alleged masters for any expenditure to seduce the mob. Our archival records have been checked for the slightest sign of such policies. They do not exist.

*   *   *

To document Wellington's views, this is a tabulation of his chief policies on Russia and Persia at the time:

Sir Robert Peel to Wellington, 18 August 1828, informing him that Lord Melville's directions concerning the finances of India are correct: 'The East India Company is not very far from insolvency' (WPI/948/3). The conclusion must be drawn that it would not and could not finance riots and murders in Persia.

Letter from Malcolm to Wellington, 3 March 1828, with his plan for administration of Central India, commenting on Russo–Persian War (WP/921/8).

Letter from Malcolm, 30 May 1828, praising Macdonald's work in the Russo–Persian peace, stating that his achievement should be honoured (WP/934/23).

4 August 1828, Malcolm intervenes again on behalf of Macdonald for a reward in 'helping save Persia for the present' (WPI/946/10).

Letter from Malcolm to Wellington, 26 October 1828, on the inadvisability of cutting down too much in Persia, 'whatever can be done with the small means allowed, will be done by Macdonald' (no doc. ref.).

Malcolm to Wellington, 22 October 1828, on the undesirable consequences of recalling Macdonald: 'Willock does not have the qualities of Macdonald, and it would be a disgrace if Willock were allowed to represent British interests' (WPI/961/23).

Letter from Wellington, 16 August 1828, in draft for Robert Peel about Ellenborough being appointed to Board of Control (WPI/950/35).

Letter from Wellington to Ellenborough, 9 October 1828, giving his advice as to keeping the peace in Persia, and achieving stability there: 'we ought to inculcate peace and good neighbourhood'. Wellington also questioned co-operation between Turks and Persians: 'any movement on [the Shah's] part would lead to certain destruction' (WPI/963/23).

Wellington to Ellenborough, 19 November 1828: 'we will call upon the East India Company to put down every expense as well at home as abroad which is not absolutely necessary for the Government and defence of their territorial possessions and for carrying on their trade' (WPI/969/6). This again rules out financing trouble in Persia.

Letter from Ellenborough to Wellington, 6 October 1828, enclosing draft despatches for Macdonald (WPI/959/15).

Ellenborough sends final draft of despatch to Macdonald, 13 October 1828, back to Wellington: 'in conformity with your suggestions and nearly in your own words', i.e. adopting the peace policy (WPI/960/16).

Wellington to Ellenborough, 20 August 1829: 'the Persian despatches are very curious and interesting' (WPI/1042/40).

Minutes of Wellington's meeting with Lieven and Count Matuscewitz on the Eastern question, 4 and 5 September 1829 (WPI/1048/13). Refers to Macdonald as trying to prevent new Russo–Persian War, complains about Paskievich, saying that England was going to war against Russia, referring to the recent outrage; Macdonald persuaded the Shah to give Russia satisfaction. 'Desire of England to keep on good terms with Tsar' (WPI/1048/13).

Draft despatch to Lord Heytesbury, British Ambassador in St Petersburg, 14 October 1829, authorising him to explain to the Tsar that the 'entire independence of the Persian monarchy must ever be object of deep interest to his Majesty, any attempt on part of Russia to extend her conquests in Persia, could be considered by his Majesty as an act unfriendly to HM as an Asiatic power' (no doc. ref.).

Letter from Wellington to Lord Aberdeen, 10–11 October 1829, on how to prevent a death blow to the independence of the Ottoman Porte (WPI/1054/21).

Letter Wellington to Ellenborough, 22 October 1829, agreeing that Henry Willock should be recalled in response to Ellenborough's proposal of 18 October and expressing the need for a guard in Persia (WPI/1054/59).

Ellenborough, *Political Diary*, 12 August 1829, letter from Ellenborough to Wellington, with private letter from Macdonald: 'The Shah is determined not to pay any more money etc'; 'the Russians at Tiflis are violent in their language against England' (WPI/1038/18).

Letter from Ellenborough to Wellington, 22 August 1829, forecasting 'step by step as the Persian monarchy is broken up, the Russians in that quarter will extend their influence and advance their troops, more especially under such a man as Paskievich without quarrelling with us, they have crept up on Kabul' (WPI/1039/22).

Ellenborough, 18 October 1829, proposes recall of Sir Henry Willock, as 'he costs a great deal and does no good', in *Despatches* vol. 6, pp.238–9.

Letter from Ellenborough to Wellington, 18 October 1829: 'Russia will attempt by conquest or influence to secure Persia as a road to the Indies, I have the most intimate connection' (WPI/1051/19). Ellenborough was doing his duty, in re-assessing the right strategy for the defence of India.

Later, Ellenborough, in his *Political Diary*, vol 2, reports the Duke's view that the Russians 'had brought it upon themselves' (the murder of the mission and envoy). On 8 June, he passed conventional judgement on Griboyedov's mistakes committed at Tehran, having evidently read enough about the background of the question by then. These accounts only confirm 'what, we had already heard of the arrogance and violence of the Russians, they deserved their fate'.

APPENDIX II

Table of Russian Ranks (as established by Peter the Great, 24 January 1722)

Military Ranks		Civilian Ranks	Grade
Naval Forces	**Land Forces**		
General-Admiral	Generalissimo Field Marshal	Chancellor or Active Privy Counsellor	I
Admiral	General of Artillery General of Cavalry General of Infantry	Active Privy Counsellor	II
Vice Admiral	Lieutenant General	Privy Counsellor	III
Rear Admiral	Major General	Active State Counsellor	IV
Captain-Commander	Brigadier	State Counsellor	V
First Captain	Colonel	Collegial Counsellor	VI
Second Captain	Lieutenant Colonel	Court Counsellor	VII
Lieutenant-Captain of the Fleet Third Captain of Artillery	Major	Collegial Assessor	VIII
Lieutenant of the Fleet Lieutenant-Captain of Artillery	Captain or Cavalry Captain	Titled Counsellor	IX
Lieutenant of Artillery	Staff Captain or Cavalry Captain	Collegial Secretary	X
		Secretary of the Senate	XI
Midshipman	Lieutenant	Gubernia Secretary	XII
Artillery Constable	Sublieutenant	Registrar of the Senate	XIII
	Ensign Bearer	Collegial Registrar	XIV

Source: Basil Dmytryshyn (ed.), *Imperial Russia: A Source Book 1700–1917*, 2nd cd., Portland State University, Dryden Press, Hinsdale, Illinois, pp.17–18.

APPENDIX III

Anglo–Russian Rivalry in Persia

The circumstances dictating Anglo–Russian rivalry in Persia at the time of Griboyedov's murder are quite incomprehensible without an analysis in depth of an important realignment that took place in London, in the minds of British policy-makers about Russian policies in Persia, and those required for its stability and the defence of India; it is true to say the rules of the game had changed with Russian successes recognised in the Treaty of Turkmanchai; policy-makers such as the Duke of Wellington, Lord Ellenborough at the Board of Control, Lord William Bentinck as Governor General in India, and Sir John Malcolm in Bombay as Governor, primarily responsible for Indian defence strategy, now realised Fath Ali Shah and Abbas Mirza were broken reeds, and the old policy of costly subsidies to keep Persia in place as the buffer-state for India was nullified by Russian victories, and that a new 'forward policy' to contain Russia was required. Such British responses have been treated – almost as a matter of Soviet party policy and, previously, as a patriotic nationalistic judgement – as 'russophobic', and their proponents attacked for hatred of Russia and her agents, notably Griboyedov, Nesselrode and Tsar Nicholas. It is well-documented on the British side, and a shrill though lusty debate; essential background material on this re-alignment in 1827–8 includes many British and Western sources inaccessible to Soviet scholars and researchers, who of course have as a result misjudged British policies: for a list of the key books and articles for an understanding of these issues, see Malcolm E. Yapp, *Strategies of British India, Britain, Iran and Afghanistan, 1798– 1850* (op. cit.). For Yapp's comment about the British realignment, required after Turkmanchai to maintain the defence of India, see p.23; for the view in Britain that Russia had become 'a major threat to those European liberties for which England had become the chief spokesman', see p.95; and for Macdonald's view that Abbas Mirza could not be depended upon, see his letter to the Governor General of Bombay (EM D 556/1.). John McNeill took the same view: 'in every communication with Abbas Mirza on every subject, the Envoy must be prepared for every description of meanness, deceit and treachery' (Mrs Florence [Stewart]

Macalister, *Memoir of the Rt Hon. Sir John MacNeill and of his Second Wife Elizabeth Wilson by their Grand Daughter* [London, 1910], p.74).

The other essential, authoritative and extremely well-researched academic book on the new strategic perceptions in London and in India is by Professor Edward Ingrams, *The Beginnings of the Great Game in Asia 1828–1834* (Oxford, 1979).

Both these books have exhaustive bibliographies. Professor Ingrams, with impeccable scholarship, shows how the Great Game's origins may really be shown to begin with the Treaty of Turkmanchai, removing Persia as a viable buffer-state for the defence of India, and making Afghanistan the next *cordon sanitaire*, thus raising the value to Britain of the Punjab, the Northwest Frontier and the basin of the Indus, ultimately requiring the Sikhs to become reliable and compliant allies in the 'forward policy' which so materially changed the old lines drawn in the 1820s. Modern scholarship, as detailed above, has unveiled most effectively the dominant ideas in the minds of the policy-makers, notably Ellenborough, Wellington and Malcolm, in the case of Wellington as Prime Minister. We even have, in the second volume of Lord Ellenborough's *Political Diary*, Wellington's actual reaction to the outrage in Tehran.

Having recorded the foregoing, it is relevant here to mention the general change in tone of British public opinion, recording the growth of Russian imperialism, described even today in Russian minds crudely as 'russophobia'; most experts on Persia, and travellers there and to Georgia in the late 1820s, were not slow to voice their worries about the growth of Russian territorial ambitions at the expense of the Sultan and the Shah.

S.V. Shostakovich recognises this by quoting one of the most obvious examples, notably the early views of J.B. Fraser in his *Travels and Adventures in the Persian Provinces in 1826*. Later he refers to De Lacy Evans's book, *On the Designs of Russia, on the Practicability of an Invasion of British India* (London, 1829) (in S.V. Shostakovich, *Diplomaticheskaya deyatel'nost' A.S. Griboyedova* [*The Diplomatic Activity of A.S. Griboyedov*] [Moscow, 1960], p.177. 3). He rightly quotes Ellenborough's *Political Diary*, already foreseeing Anglo–Russian blood spilt on the Indus (p.178). Sir John McNeill, in *Progress and Present Position of Russia in the East* (2 vols, London, 1836), was to publish his own concerned pamphlet on the same theme, pp.1810–12. Shostakovich failed to read the second volume of Ellenborough's *Political Diary*.

Amongst contemporary experts raising their voices in alarm, mention must be made of Lieutenant-General Sir William Monteith, in *Kars and Erzerum, with the Campaigns of Prince Paskiewitch in 1828 and 1829*, and an account of the *Conquests of Russia Beyond the Caucasus, from the Time of Peter the Great to the Treaties of Turcoman Chie and Adrianople*

(London, 1856), and Captain R. Mignan, in *A Winter Journey through Russia, the Caucasian Alps, and Georgia, thence into Koordistan* (2 vols, London, 1839), especially Chapter 6, 'Russian Ambition'.

I must also mention the honourable roll-call of early minor players in the game, such as Burnes and Connolly – these are all to be found in Peter Hopkirk's excellent survey of the later moves, in *The Great Game*.

Brief mention should also be made of early Russian explorers sent either by Yermolov or the Tsar on Central Asian reconaissances, men such as Count Muravyov with his *Voyages en Turcomanie et à Khiva faits en 1819–20*, and Baron Georg von Meyendorff, whose *Voyage d'Orenburg à Bokhara fait en 1820* was calculated to excite and alarm the anti-Russian imperialist lobby in Britain.

Amongst other valuable contributions to the debate about the defence of India, attention should be drawn to the Raleigh Lecture on history given by Professor H.W.C. Davis, entitled 'The Great Game in Asia 1800–1844', published in *The Proceedings of the British Academy*, vol. 12 (1926). Davis addresses the necessary changes after Turkmanchai, which had nullified Wellesley's earlier policies of treating Persia as the buffer state for India (pp.230–3).

Notes on the Text

General Notes

1. All dates in the text are in old style (OS), according to the Julian calendar, which in the nineteenth century was 12 days behind the Gregorian calendar used in the West. They follow the chronology established by Piksanov and Shlyapkin in *Complete Collected Works* (see Bibliography).
2. The complex story of Russian influence in Persia after 1828 requires clear ideas of British views on 'the Eastern question', notably the cause of Greek independence at the expense of the Sultan, and secondly the disintegration of the Ottoman empire, and Russian policies affecting this. Some general reading about British foreign policy in the Middle East is germane to these issues; the literature is vast, but a good start for foreigners interested in the background can be made by reading the following works: Bourne, *The Foreign Policy of Victorian England* (see Bibliography), especially helpful about Canning's policies and views (see introduction and later Palmerston on the perceived threat to India, pp.34–5). A major point of British diplomacy before Griboyedov's death was the abrogation of the obnoxious treaty clauses requiring subsidies to Russia; this issue is clearly dealt with in Macalister, *Memoir* (see Bibliography), pp.114–24. Dodwell, *The Cambridge History of the British Empire* (see Bibliography), is most relevant to all these issues. It describes the development of the 'forward policy' after Griboyedov's death. Ward and Gooch, *The Cambridge History of British Foreign Policy* (see Bibliography) covers the ground in respect of Greece and its independence and the Treaty of Adrianople; chapter V, dealing with India between 1833 and 1849, treats adequately the beginnings of the Great Game (pp.199–201).

Chapter I: A Moscow Education

1. Griboyedov family background: P. Nikolayev, G.D. Ovchinnikov and Ye.V Tsymbal, 'The History of the Griboyedov Family' in Fomichev (ed.), *A.S. Griboyedov, Materialy k biografii* (see Bibliography), pp.76–83.
2. Payment of Father's debts: ibid., pp.90–1.
3. Birthday 4 January 1795. For the best summary of the known evidence and arguments for or against the date for Griboyedov's birth, 1790 or 1795: M.V. Stroganov, 'The date of birth of Griboyedov, or halfway through his life' in ibid., pp.10–19.

4. M.V. Fekhner, 'The house of the Griboyedovs in Moscow', *Memorials of Culture* (see Bibliography), pp.124–5.

5. Childhood years in Moscow and Khmelita: Volkov-Muromtsov, *Yunost' ot Vyazma* (see Bibliography); Razgonov, *Penati Vtoraya Zhisn Khmelita* (see Bibliography); Sychev, *Vyazma* (see Bibliography); Fomichev (ed.), *A.S. Griboyedov, Materialy k biografii* (see Bibliography); Gershenzon, *Griboyedov's Moscow* (see Bibliography); Roosevelt, *Life* (see Bibliography), pp.22–5, including excellent plans and photos of Khmelita.

6. On his mother: Piksanov and Shlyapkin (eds), *Complete Collected Works* (see Bibliography), vol. 1, pp.i–iv; on family origins: p.iv; on school and Moscow: pp.i–xvii.

7. Khmelita details: N.A. Tarkhova, 'The Griboyedov Country House, Khmelita' in Fomichev (ed.), *Materialy k biografii* (see Bibliography), pp.48–60.

8. 'In my time': Nicholas Volkov-Muromtsov, private letter to author, 1991.

9. 'This was nothing extraordinary': Volkov-Muromtsov to author, 1991.

10. 'The restorers': Volkov-Muromtsov to author, 1991.

11. 'A heedless, merry sort of fellow': applied to Fyodorovich in Fomichev and Vatsuro (eds), *Griboyedov* (see Bibliography); Lykoshin on his Khmelita childhood shared with Alexander as youths; his uncle was a 'bespechny veselchak', p.32.

12. The full text of *The Character of my Uncle*: Piksanov and Shlyapkin (eds), *Complete Collected Works* (see Bibliography), vol. 2, p.118.

13. '...It will fall to the lot', ibid., vol. 2, p.118.

14. Griboyedov's musical education and association with John Field: S. Bulich, 'Griboyedov: A Musician' in ibid., vol. 2, pp.305–28.

15. Griboyedov's childhood and education in Moscow: Meshcheryakov, *The Life and Activity of Alexander Griboyedov* (see Bibliography), pp.4–45; also includes some evidence on Griboyedov's date of birth. Regrettably, this author also includes some unsustainable Tynianov 'factional material'.

16. 'Our mentor' referring to Griboyedov's governor Petrosilius: Griboyedov, *Woe from Wit*, tr. Waring (see Bibliography), p.56.

17. His examination with Lykoshin by Professor Aviat de Vattoy: Fomichev and Vatsuro (eds), Lykoshin's memoirs, *Griboyedov* (see Bibliography), pp.32–8.

18. 'A certain indeterminate power': ibid., pp.32–8.

19. Griboyedov's admiration for and interest in Voltaire as a leading prophet of the Enlightenment and French Revolution: Nechkina, *A.S. Griboyedov* (see Bibliography), pp.86, 93, 97–9, 101, 107, 344. The 'bronze bust' refers to Houdon's bust of Voltaire in the Hermitage for Catherine the Great: letter 11 July 1824 to P.A. Vyazemsky in Piksanov and Shlyapkin (eds), *Complete Collected Works* (see Bibliography), vol. 3, pp.158–9.

20. Beguichov's recollections of Griboyedov's childhood: Fomichev and Vatsuro (eds), *Griboyedov* (see Bibliography), pp.23–4.

21. 'A little Frenchman from Bordeaux': Griboyedov, *Woe from Wit*, tr. Waring (see Bibliography), p.94.
22. Dmitri Dyranskoy: Fomichev and Vatsuro (eds), *Griboyedov*, (see Bibliography), pp.23–4.
23. For the English Club: Memoir Series No. 10: Vigel', *Zapiski* (see Bibliography); Buyotov, *Moskovsky Anglisky Klub* (see Bibliography); Lopatina, *A.S. Pushkin* (see Bibliography).
24. Bagration and Count Rostov's dinner at the Club: Tolstoy, *War and Peace*, tr. Garnett (see Bibliography), pp.503–4 (also pp.282–88).
25. All references to Marya Ivanovna Rimskaya-Korsakova: Gershenzon, *Griboyedov's Moscow* (see Bibliography).
26. Translation of and reference by Famusov to his Diary: Griboyedov, *Woe from Wit*, tr. Waring (see Bibliography), p.59.
27. Tatiana at the Assembly of the Nobility: Pushkin, *Eugene Onegin*, tr. Johnston (see Bibliography), p.202.
28. Reference to King of Prussia: Griboyedov, *Woe from Wit*, tr. Waring (see Bibliography), p.67.

Chapter II: The War of 1812

1. Recollections of Erström on the French invasion of Moscow and its effect on the university: Roginsky (ed.), *Our Heritage*, pp.640–73.
2. Baron Shtein's view, 'Russia should keep her original customs': Nechkina, *A.S. Griboyedov* (see Bibliography), pp.112–3; Griboyedov's introduction to him by Professor Bühle: p.568.
3. All details relating to Griboyedov's military service and the story of the Saltykov and Irkutsk Hussars merging, S.V. Sverdlin, 'The War Years': Fomichev (ed.), *A.S. Griboyedov, Materialy k biografii* (See Bibliography), pp.61–75. For military details, including description of the regiment's uniform: Nechkina, *A.S. Griboyedov* (see Bibliography), pp.111–25. With thanks to Sophie Lund for her useful translation (see Bibliography).
4. 'Letter from Brest-Litovsk' written to praise General Kologrivov: Piksanov and Shlyapkin (eds), *Complete Collected Works* (see Bibliography), vol. 3, pp.3–9.
5. Article on the importance of the Cavalry Reserves: ibid., vol. 3, pp.10–4.
6. 'Strange destiny of the Slavonic race' and the occupation of Paris in 1814 by the Russian army: Mikhailovsky-Danilevsky, *History* (see Bibliography), pp.340–95.
7. Cruelties practised in Russia under Arakcheyev, 'the blood was never dry on the floors': Herzen, *My Past* (see Bibliography), vol. 1, pp.198–200, 203.
8. Griboyedov's pleasant recollection of his times in the saddle, as expressed by Chatsky to Platon Mikhailovich in the play: Griboyedov, *Woe from Wit*, tr. Waring, p.83.

9.   War memoirs of Beguichov: Fomichev and Vatsuro (eds), *Griboyedov* (see Bibliography), pp.24–5.
10. The church episode and riding to a ball on the first floor on horseback: Zhandr had the stories from Beguichov, ibid., pp.247–8.
11. 'Kamarinskaya' anecdote and escapade, D.A. Smirnov interviewing Zhandr after Griboyedov's death many years later: ibid., pp.247–8.
12. Griboyedov's retirement negotiations due to ill health: S.V. Sverdlin, 'The War Years' in Fomichev (ed.), *A.S. Griboyedov, Materialy k biografii* (see Bibliography), pp.64–6.

Chapter III: Literary Beginnings: St Petersburg

1.   Skalozoop's view that the fire of 1812 improved the appearance of Moscow: Griboyedov, *Woe from Wit*, tr. Waring (see Bibliography), p.67.
2.   Pushkin's views on the position of writers in Russian society: see his letter to A. Bestuzhev of June–August 1825 from his Mikhailovskoye estate in Pushkin, *The Letters* (see Bibliography), pp.199, 221–4; letters to A. Bestuzhev, end of January 1825, describing *Woe from Wit*: pp.200–1.
3.   Griboyedov's letter of 9 November 1816 to Beguichov: Piksanov and Shlyapkin (eds), *Complete Collected Works* (see Bibliography), vol. 3, p.121; also exclamation about cheap porter: p.122. The same letter describes his mild attack of VD and visit to the Shuster Club: p.122.
4.   Griboyedov's early plays under the influence of Prince Shakhovskoy: Bonamour, *A.S. Griboyedov* (see Bibliography), pp.131–69. These pages also describe his joint comedy with P.A. Katenin, *The Student*. Bonamour has painted the best and most comprehensive picture of literary St Petersburg when Griboyedov arrived there after his military experiences: pp.78–123.
5.   Griboyedov's prank disguised as a monk and other anecdotes of Azarevicha alleged to have taken place in Shakhovskoy's garret: Davydov, 'Tale of the Past' in *Zima-Kazan* (see Bibliography), 1871–2 and 1880–2. Kindly made available by the courtesy of Mr Evgeny Tsymbal in Moscow.
6.   For a lively description of Shakhovskoy's influence on Griboyedov, his dominant position in the Russian theatre and trail-blazing role in Russian comedy: Karlinsky, *Russian Drama* (see Bibliography), pp.239–51; chapter on Shakhovskoy: pp.226–48, 269–77.
7.   On Shakhovskoy: Vigel', *Zapiski* (see Bibliography), pp.278–309; for an excellent summary by Karlinsky of *Woe from Wit*'s plot and place in Russian drama: Karlinsky, *Russian Drama* (see Bibliography), pp.330–5; also pp.278–309.
8.   Suggested division of garret into archaists and romantics: Nabokov in Pushkin, *Eugene Onegin*, tr. Nabokov (see Bibliography), vol. 2, p.450. As Nabokov writes, reverting to the issues of the day that enjoyed the

attention of the garret: 'Küchelbecker was not alone in preferring the old Lomonosov-Derzhavin type of ode to the romantic elegy of his time. Sheviryov, a forerunner (in certain tricks of archaic demeanor and mythopoeic imagery) of Tyutchev (whose genius he lacked), had similar predilections. Classifiers distinguish two main groups of poets: the Archaists (Derzhavin, Krylov, Griboyedov, Küchelbecker) and the Romanticists (Zhukovski, Pushkin, Bariatinski, Lermontov). In Tyutchev the two lines merged.'

9.   Shakhovskoy's invitation to Griboyedov and Khmel'nitsky to help him compose his successful comedy *The Married Fiancée*: Fomichev and Vatsuro (eds), *Griboyedov* (see Bibliography), p.25 (Beguichov), p.341 (note only). Griboyedov and Prince Shakhovskoy: V.P. Meshcheryakov, *A.S. Griboyedov* (see Bibliography), pp.22–36. All the texts of Griboyedov's apprenticeship translations of plays from the French theatre are in Piksanov and Shlyapkin (eds), *Complete Collected Works* (see Bibliography), copiously annotated.

10. On Griboyedov's relationship with Katenin and young Pushkin: Meshcheryakov, *A.S. Griboyedov* (see Bibliography), pp.38–63. Proud of his success in September 1815 in having his French play *The Newly Weds (Le Secret du Ménage)* performed in St Petersburg by such well-known actors and actresses as Semyonova, Sosnitsky and Bryansky, Griboyedov took up the cudgels in defence of his clever new friend Pavel Katenin, denouncing an unsigned attack on him by N.I. Grech, the editor of *Son of the Fatherland*, who had already obliged him by publishing in November 1815 his review of Prince Shakhovskoy's comedy *The Lipetsk Spa*, otherwise known as *A Lesson to Coquettes*.

Katenin (1792–1853) was an adherent of the classical school of poetry, a translator of Corneille and author of many tragedies, poems and articles. Like Pushkin, he was a great theatre-goer. Pushkin often visited Katenin's quarters in the barracks of the first battalion of the Preobrazhensky Regiment in Millonaya Ulitza (Million Street). In *Eugene Onegin* Pushkin refers to Millonaya Ulitza, and to the late hours at which he used to leave Katenin's quarters when 'everything was still, only the sentries called to one another, and the distant clatter of some cab resounded suddenly from Million Street.' In his reminiscences, Katenin recalls Pushkin's first visit to his rooms: 'My visitor met me at the door, offered me his stick with its thick end and said, "I came to you as Diogenes to Antisthenes: give me a beating, but teach me." I replied: "To educate an educated man is to spoil him", and taking him by the arm led him to my rooms. A quarter of an hour later the courtesies were over, our conversation became animated, time passed imperceptibly and I invited him to dine with me. Someone else came in and my new friend left late at night.'

Much overrated by his friend Pushkin – who overrated also le grand (Pierre) Corneille, whose bombastic and platitudinous *Cid* (1637) Katenin 'translated' into Russian (1822). In the draft of a poem referring to a theatrical feud (18 lines composed in 1821, published posthumously, 1931), Pushkin had already found the formula (II 16–7):

And for her [Semyonova]...
Youthful Katénin will revive
Aeschylus' majestic genius...

N. Nabokov in Pushkin, *Eugene Onegin*, tr. Nabokov (see Bibliography), p.83.

See also Meshcheryakov, *A.S. Griboyedov* (see Bibliography), who devotes a whole chapter to their relations as far back as their collaboration on the play *The Student*, pp.38–63.

11. Griboyedov's attack on Zagoskin: With thanks to Sophie Lund for a sprightly translation of *The Puppet Theatre* of 1819 (see Bibliography).
12. Griboyedov's relationships with Grech: Fomichev and Vatsuro (eds), *Griboyedov* (see Bibliography), pp.33–4; for an excellent social picture of the city and leading literary personalities, including Grech: Yatsevich, *Pushkinsky Petersburg* (see Bibliography), p.308.
13. For the text of his article defending Katenin's translations against the sentimentalist school: Piksanov and Shlyapkin (eds), *Complete Collected Works* (see Bibliography), vol. 3, p.241; also useful notes: pp.281–3.
14. More details about Shakhovskoy's garret and Pushkin's happy evenings there: Magarshack's readable *Life of Pushkin* (see Bibliography), pp.52; pp.60–65 on the Green Lamp.
15. The literary and social circles of Grech and Osip Senkovsky's salon: Yatsevich, *Pushkinsky Petersburg* (see Bibliography), pp.304–7; for his links with Grech: pp.272–4, 309.
16. The general background to Admiral Shishkov's views: Nabokov in Pushkin, *Eugene Onegin*, tr. Nabokov (see Bibliography), vol. 3, pp.169–73. Griboyedov had no direct relations with the Admiral, but was fully aware of his views and his role as a conservative.
17. On Admiral Shishkov's role: ibid., pp.170–1.
18. For a caustic and witty description of the Arzamas dining society: ibid., pp.171–2; also Vigel', *Zapiski* (see Bibliography), pp.63–65, vol. 2, pp.100–4.

On Zhukovsky: Nabokov in Pushkin, *Eugene Onegin*, tr. Nabokov (see Bibliography); on Karamzin's reforms: vol. 3, pp.143–5: 'In his truly marvelous reform of the Russian literary language, Karamzin neatly weeded out rank Church Slavonic and archaic Germanic constructions (comparable, in their florid, involved, and uncouth character, to bombastic Latinisms of an earlier period in western Europe); he banned inversions, ponderous compounds, and monstrous conjunctions, and introduced a lighter syntax, a Gallic precision of diction, and the simplicity of natural-sounding neologisms exactly suited to the semantic needs, both romantic and realistic, of his tremendously style-conscious time. Not only his close followers,

Zhukovski and Batyushkov, but eclectic Pushkin and reluctant Tyutchev remained eternally in Karamzin's debt. Whilst, no doubt, in the idiom Karamzin promoted, the windows of a gentleman's well-waxed drawing-room open wide onto a Le Nôtre garden with its tame fountains and trim turf, it is also true that, through those same French windows, the healthy air of rural Russia came flowing in from beyond the topiary. But it was Krylov (followed by Griboyedov), not Karamzin, who first made of colloquial, earthy Russian a truly literary language by completely integrating it in the poetic patterns that had come into existence after Karamzin's reform.'

19. A lively 'insider's view' of Freemasonry written by the generally well-informed Vigel': *Zapiski* (see Bibliography), vol. 2, pp.114–8; Nabokov in Pushkin, *Eugene Onegin*, tr. Nabokov (see Bibliography), vol. 2, p.226.

20. The relief afforded to Pierre Bezukhov in *War and Peace* by belonging to the Masons: Tolstoy, *War and Peace*, tr. Garnett (see Bibliography), pp.328–337.

21. The whole story of the rise of secret societies, leading eventually to the Northern Society in St Petersburg and the Southern Society in Tulchin, fusing to collapse in the Decembrist uprising of 1825, and Griboyedov's 'elective affinities' with their members, created by propinquity at the Noble Pension, Moscow University and in St Petersburg by shared institutions such as the Green Lamp, and his Masonic Lodge, 'Les Amis Réunis' to which Pestel' also belonged: Nechkina, *Sledstvennoye* (see Bibliography); Nabokov in Pushkin, *Eugene Onegin*, tr. Nabokov (see Bibliography), vol. 3, pp.345–51.

For thorough English accounts: Ulam, *Russia's Failed Revolutions* (see Bibliography), pp.3–65; Zetlin, *The Decembrists* (see Bibliography); Mazour, *The First Russian Revolution* (see Bibliography); the excellent references in Lynn Barratt, *The Rebel* (see Bibliography).

Finally, a reaffirmation of the party line in 1989, that of Griboyedov's role as a Decembrist, is the principal question to be addressed in Griboyedov's biography: Yu P. Fesenko in Fomichev, *A.S. Griboyedov, Materialy k biografii* (see Bibliography), pp.92–108.

Chapter IV: The Duel

Additional Background Material

Notes from Reyfman, *Ritualized Violence* (see Bibliography). On the Sheremet'yev–Zavadovsky duel: *Sbornik biografii kavalergvardov, 3*: pp.241–3 (this account relies heavily on archival materials that have since been lost; it is reprinted in Fomichev and Vatsuro (eds), *Griboyedov* (see Bibliography), pp.268–71; S.N. Beguichov, 'A.S. Griboyedov' and D.A. Smirnov, 'Rasskazy ob A.S. Griboyedov, zapisanniye so slov ego druzei', both in Fomichev and Vatsuro (eds), *Griboyedov* (see Bibliography), pp.26–37, 212–14 (B.I. John's account, pp.231–43). For

J.A. Zhandr's account: Sosnovsky (P.P. Karatygin), 'Aleksandr Sergeyevich Griboyedov' (see Bibliography), pp.161–3; Przhetslavsky, 'Begliye ocherki' (see Bibliography), pp.384–6; 'Veliky Knyaz' Konstantin Pavlovich v somneniyakh i otritsaniyakh sovremennykh emu poryadkov (Iz perepiski egos N.M. Sinyaginym)'. Sinyaginym's letter of 14 November 1917: *Russkaya Starina*, 102 (see Bibliography); Pylyaev, 'Znamenitiye dueli v Rossii' (see Bibliography), pp.497–502. On the Griboyedov–Yakubovich duel: N.N. Muravyov-Karsky, 'Iz zapisok' in Fomichev and Vatsuro (eds), *Griboyedov* (see Bibliography), pp.41–5.

1. For the unsavoury and greedy exploitation of her serfs in the province of Kostroma by Griboyedov's mother, and Griboyedov's tacit acceptance of this by accepting 'tainted' revenue as income to support himself in St Petersburg: 'Griboyedov and serfdom' in Piksanov, *Griboyedov: Researches* (see Bibliography), pp.83–158. The second part of the article deals with Griboyedov's views as expressed in writings and his play, and starkly refutes Nechkina, on the essence of her case that *Woe from Wit* is a denunciation of serfdom, in line with Decembrist doctrine and later Soviet doctrines about the Revolution. Nechkina ignores all this evidence inconvenient to her.

2. On 9 June 1817, Griboyedov, together with Pushkin and Küchelbecker, was enrolled as a trainee diplomat at the Collegium of Foreign Affairs, Arkhivny Yunost: Nabokov in Pushkin, *Eugene Onegin*, tr. Nabokov (see Bibliography), vol. 3, pp.119–20. The finest authority on this institution, its customs and procedures and training methods, and the policies of its ministers at the time (notably Count Nesselrode, Count Capodistrias, reporting directly to Tsar Alexander I) is Grimsted, *The Foreign Ministers* (see Bibliography).

3. The confusing division of work between Capodistrias and Nesselrode and the difficulty of foreign diplomats in St Petersburg in addressing the correct Minister on any given issue: Grimsted, *The Foreign Ministers* (see Bibliography), pp.250, 275. Nesselrode became sole director of Foreign Policy from summer of 1822: ibid., p.276. For the trainee system at Tsarskoye Selo under Capodistrias: ibid., note p.241, and Griboyedov's languid complaint that he studied only the Trojan War. At the Foreign Ministry: Fomichev, *Griboyedov in Petersburg* (see Bibliography), p.40; for his new friendship with Count Zavadovsky: pp.21–2.

4. Pushkin's description of the blows of fate, namely the consequences for Griboyedov of the death of Sheremet'yev, in the famous duelling *partie carrée* of 1817: Pushkin, *A Journey* (see Bibliography), pp.46–7.

5. To reconstruct events in the *partie carrée* – without question one of the most exciting events in Griboyedov's until then blood-free life up to 1817, but treated as a marginal event by serious literary historians – detailed detective work across a variety of sources is needed to re-establish the chronology of events. Chief witnesses are Zhandr's report to D.A. Smirnov, and Beguichov, for the sake of any future

scriptwriter making a film of this thrilling event, in its way the most famous of duels in Russia, except for the killing of Pushkin by d'Anthés in 1836, and Lermontov by Martynov. One of the few consecutive accounts is in Fomichev, *Griboyedov in Petersburg* (see Bibliography), pp.45–9. See also Gordin, *Dueli* (see Bibliography), pp.66–75, for quite a full account. Nabokov in Pushkin, *Eugene Onegin*, tr. Nabokov (see Bibliography), pp.42–51, has some very useful comments to make on duelling in Russia, including that which killed Pushkin; see also pp.54–6. For Beguichov's description of Count Sheremet'yev: Fomichev and Vatsuro (eds), *Griboyedov* (see Bibliography), pp.26–7.

6.   Pushkin's stanza describing Istomina dancing, in his *Eugene Onegin*, tr. Johnston (see Bibliography), pp.43. Nabokov's general description about Istomina, Nabokov in Pushkin, *Eugene Onegin*, tr. Nabokov, pp.88–90, vol. 2, p.86. For Pushkin's ribald verses, years later about Istomina in another context:

• Orlov s Istominoi v postel
  V ubogoi nagote lezhal:
  Ne otlichisya v zharkom dele
  Nash postoianny general.
  Ne dumav milogo obidet',
  Vzyala Laisa mikroskop
  I govorit: 'Pozvol' uvidet'
  Chem ty menia, moi mily, yob

  [Orlov in bed with Istomina
  In abject nakedness lay:
  He had not distinguished himself in the hot battle,
  Our inconstant general.
  With no thought of offending her lover
  Laisa took a microscope
  And said: 'Permit me to inspect
  What it was, my dear, you fucked me with.]

From Tsyavlovsky (ed.), *Pushkin's Complete Works* (see Bibliography), with a learned note explaining it was first published in a booklet (*sbornik*) by N.P. Ogaryov entitled *Lost Russian Literature in London 1861*. This was from a copy obtained from Bartenev, 'K biografii Griboyedova' (see Bibliography), vol. 1, p.685. Cross, 'Pushkin's bawdy notes from the Literary Underground' (see Bibliography), pp.216–7 for translation.

7.   The attribution to Zavadovsky of qualities of an Englishman not unlike Repetilov in *Woe from Wit*: see Griboyedov, *Woe from Wit*, tr. Waring (see Bibliography), p.93. For more details about Zavadovsky's family and spoilt background: Vigel', *Zapiski* (see Bibliography), p.60; Madariaga, *Russia* (see Bibliography), pp.353–4; Haslip, *Catherine the Great* (see Bibliography), pp.260–1; *Lermontovskaya Encyclopaedia* (see Bibliography), p.172.

8. Zavadovsky's disreputable 'proposals of love' to Istomina: for Istomina's terrified confession to Sheremet'yev that Zavadovsky had enjoyed her favours: Zhandr in Fomichev and Vatsuro (eds), *Griboyedov* (see Bibliography), p.242; for the sleuthing of her by Sheremet'yev, in particular the recollections of V. Sheremet'yev: ibid., p.270. Also interview of Zhandr with D.A. Smirnov on 9 June 1858: pp.239–42. It is the first time Yakubovich says the insult deserves a *partie carrée* and 'bullets only will settle the matter', see pp.240–3, including the duel itself.

9. About the other participants, especially Pushkin's fascination with Yakubovich: Tsyavlovsky (ed.), *Pushkin's Complete Works* (see Bibliography). For his draft short story *The Adventures of a Russian Pelham*, ibid., vol. 1, p.766, Pushkin names Yakubovich directly and describes others of Griboyedov's immediate St Petersburg circle, such as Ilya Dolgorukov, S. Trubetskoy, all members of the 'Circle or Society of the Clever Ones'; Nikita Muravyov, another prominent Decembrist, is in the list: see vol. 1, p.775, and notes, pp.366, 774–5.

10. More about Yakubovich, the duel and his career in Fomichev and Vatsuro (eds), *Griboyedov* (see Bibliography), notes, pp.353–4. These notes refer for the first time to the memoirs of O.A. Przhetslavsky in *Russkaya Starina* of 1883, suggesting that Griboyedov at the duel insisted Sheremet'yev reject the proposal by Zavadovsky for a truce, which would have saved his life; this version was corroborated by Yakubovich for Zhandr's evidence quoting Dr John, also an eye-witness: Gribo in ibid., p.242.

11. Zavadovsky's crying 'à la barrière': ibid., p.242. For Fomichev's details: Fomichev, *Griboyedov in Petersburg* (see Bibliography), pp.41, 44–7.

12. The hidden presence of Kaverin at the duel: Kaverin was a former Göttingen student (1810–1), of whom Pushkin says (c. 1817), in an inscription to his portrait:

> In him there always boils the heat of punch and war;
> a warrior fierce he was in fields of Mars;
> 'mid friends, staunch friend; tormentor of the fair;
> and everywhere hussar!

Kaverin was able to stow away at one meal four bottles of champagne one after the other, and leave the restaurant at a casual stroll. For Pushkin's verses about him: Nabokov in Pushkin, *Eugene Onegin*, tr. Nabokov (see Bibliography), vol. 2, pp.71–2. For Kaverin's comment 'Vot tebe i repka': Zhandr in Fomichev and Vatsuro (eds), *Griboyedov* (see Bibliography), p.242.

13. Evidence that Griboyedov told Sheremet'yev to reject a truce, Fomichev and Vatsuro (eds), *Griboyedov* (see Bibliography), pp.352–3. Views of Muravyov-Karsky quoting from Przhetslavsky explaining the circumstances of the second duel in Tiflis resulting from the impossibility of holding it in 1818, because of Sheremet'yev's death.

14. Details of the ensuing official inquiry, and the possibility that the Tsar personally exempted Griboyedov from any formal punishment, Fomichev and Vatsuro (eds), *Griboyedov* (see Bibliography), p.27.

Chapter V: Into Exile

1. Griboyedov's appalling gloom (*uzhasnaya toska*) and grief after the duel, and his friend's death, Beguichov: Fomichev and Vatsuro (eds), *Griboyedov* (see Bibliography), p.27. In Piksanov and Shlyapkin (eds), *Complete Collected Works* (see Bibliography), vol. 1, p.28, Piksanov's biographical sketch states in a letter to Beguichov that apart from this sorrow, Griboyedov could not dismiss nor forget the sight of the dying Sheremet'yev.

2. Griboyedov paying the price for participating in the duel by involuntary exile, joining Mazarovich's mission to Persia as a junior official: Fomichev and Vatsuro (eds), *Griboyedov* (see Bibliography), pp.343–4. Also his letter to Beguichov describing his impertinent repartee with Minister Nesselrode: Piksanov and Shlyapkin (eds), *Complete Collected Works* (see Bibliography), vol. 3, pp.128–9.

3. Griboyedov's musical accomplishments and passion for the piano: S. Bulich in Piksanov and Shlyapkin (eds), *Complete Collected Works* (see Bibliography), vol. 1, pp.305–28. There are even facsimile reproductions of some of his waltzes.

4. Ksenofont Polevoi's recollections of Griboyedov accompanying the baritone Tosi: Fomichev and Vatsuro (eds), *Griboyedov* (see Bibliography), p.161. For his complaint that Mozart was being murdered in *The Magic Flute*, pp.164–5: 'better play Boieldieu, rather than play Mozart badly; they will understand that,' he added contemptuously about the average audience, see p.165.

5. Oliver Williams's comments: private letter to the author.

6. Bestuzhev's remarks about Griboyedov's dismissive quotation about womankind from Lord Byron: Bestuzhev in Fomichev and Vatsuro (eds), *Griboyedov* (see Bibliography), p.102. Alexander Bestuzhev's nickname was 'Marlinsky' and he should be distinguished from Peter Bestuzhev, who was his brother.

7. Zavalyshin's statement that Griboyedov in his early St Petersburg years lived a very dissolute life, with many adulterous affairs, a claim quite unsubstantiated: Fomichev and Vatsuro (eds), *Griboyedov* (see Bibliography), pp.128–43. Zavalyshin, an ardent Decembrist, is especially interesting about Griboyedov's relationships with other prominent future Decembrists, such as Bestuzhev and A.I. Odoyevsky.

8. Griboyedov's letter of 18 April 1828 to Beguichov about 'Didon', and his income through Ogaryov: Piksanov and Shlyapkin (eds), *Complete Collected Works* (see Bibliography), vol. 3, pp.132–4.

9.   Griboyedov's reference to his Moscow contemporaries as 'the local Hottentots': letter of 5 September to Beguichov in Piksanov and Shlyapkin (eds), *Complete Collected Works* (see Bibliography), vol. 3, p.131. Also for insult levelled against Kokoshkin the actor: ibid., vol. 3, p.133.

10.   Griboyedov's important admission that Moscow was 'my country, my family, my home': letter of 18 September to Beguichov sent from Voronesh in Piksanov and Shlyapkin (eds), *Complete Collected Works* (see Bibliography), vol. 3, p.133; also for the anecdote that his mother was sarcastic about his literary efforts and poetry, and for the admission that Zhandr alone took him at his own valuation. The same letter refers for the first time to his travelling companion, the future Head of Chancery and junior archivist in Mazarovich's ministry, Amburgherr, p.134.

11.   Griboyedov's promise to reform and treat his mother better on return from Persia: letter of 18 September in Piksanov and Shlyapkin (eds), *Complete Collected Works* (see Bibliography), vol. 3, p.133.

12.   Griboyedov's 'Travel Notes', in practice the equivalent of a prose letter to Beguichov dated October 1818 from 'The Caucasus – from Moscow to Tiflis': Piksanov and Shlyapkin (eds), *Complete Collected Works* (see Bibliography), vol. 3, pp.30–4. For the remainder of the journey, Kumbaleyevka, Terek, Vladikavkaz, Kazbek, the Daryal Gorge and Kashaur Pass, pp.31–3, until arrival in Tiflis, p.33. He arrived on 21 October 1818, p.368.

13.   'What an absurd country': letter to Beguichov of 5 September from Moscow; this was a rumour based on a report of a certain Heier in Piksanov and Shlyapkin (eds), *Complete Collected Works* (see Bibliography), vol. 3, p.132.

14.   Obstacles to crossing the main Caucasian passes, slippery trails, ice and snow, see 'Travel Notes to Stepan Beguichov': Piksanov and Shlyapkin (eds), *Complete Collected Works* (see Bibliography), vol. 3, pp.30–4.

15.   The complaint that there were pheasants in the Caucasian countryside but nowhere to eat them: Piksanov and Shlyapkin (eds), *Complete Collected Works* (see Bibliography), p.31.

Reference has already been made to Griboyedov's intention to avoid sentimentalism and romantic clichés in his 'Travel Notes', on p.40 of his letter of 31 January to Beguichov, describing the journey from Tiflis to Sogan Li: Piksanov and Shlyapkin (eds), *Complete Collected Works* (see Bibliography), vol. 3, pp.37–40. An interesting article and analysis of his travel writing has been made by Krasnov, *Travels* (see Bibliography), pp.207–10.

Chapter VI: Arrival in Tiflis

Additional Background Material

The serious student of this period, turbulent and bloody as it is in the history of Georgia and the Caucasus, under its three active and notorious warlords, namely Prince Tsitsiyanov, A.P. Yermolov and Field Marshal Ivan Paskievich will find invaluable evidence as to their failures and successes in the many volumes of the publications by Potto, *Kavkazskaya* (see Bibliography), and Dubrovin, *Istoriya* (see Bibliography); and later in the family archive of Paskievich, made fully available to Shcherbatov for his life of Paskievich, *General-Fel'dmarshal* (see Bibliography).

It is not possible to quote from every page of these books, which in themselves draw on Archives, an essential part of Russian political, diplomatic and military history; I shall only indicate where they are especially relevant to Griboyedov's story as Yermolov's diplomatic advisor, and later history, in that these sources include the still fresh personal reminiscences of participants in the Caucasus and are free of any Soviet class-war and Marxist distortions.

Especial attention is drawn to the very valuable and original contributions made by Potto and Dubrovin. Baddeley himself used these authors enormously, recognising how they extracted their material from the main Georgian source of the *Akti Sobranniye Kavkazsko Arkheograficheskoi Kommissiei* (AKAK).

The early days of the Russian occupation of Georgia after its unification in 1801 are well set out, as are the corrupt dealings of Kovalensky and the desperate final wriggles of the Bagration Dynasty; in Chapter 11, Dubrovin, as befits a general, gives a convincing account of Yermolov's Order of Battle and the full panoply of force, allocated by the Tsars to the 'pacification' of the Caucasus: pp.215–9.

1. The first Russo–Persian War until the 1813 Treaty of Gulistan: Atkin, *Russia and Iran* (see Bibliography), pp.57–73; also Baddeley, *The Russian Conquest* (see Bibliography), p.99, including General Kotlyarevsky's famous victory over the Persians at Aslanduz, p.88.

2. Russo–Georgian history and background since Georgia's absorption into the Russian empire in 1801: Avalov, *Georgia's Unification* (see Bibliography); 'Muslim resistance to the Tsar' in Gammer, *Shamil* (see Bibliography); Allen, *A History of the Georgian People* (see Bibliography); Atkin, *Russia and Iran* (see Bibliography), including a very useful modern Bibliography, pp.191–203; Baddeley, *The Russian Conquest* (see Bibliography); Curtiss, *The Russian Army* (see Bibliography); Russo–Persian diplomatic relations: Shostakovich, *The Diplomatic Activity* (see Bibliography), pp.26–41.

3. Prince Tsitsiyanov: Lang, *The Last Years* (see Bibliography), pp.255–61. Consolidation of Russian power: ibid., pp.267–84.

4. Russian imperial ambitions to control the delta of the river Araxes in the eastern Caucasus as a strategic barrier: Atkin, *Russia and Iran* (see Bibliography), p.44, also p.59; for Tsar Alexander: pp.63–5.

5. Colonial imperialism and the exploits of General Prince Tsitsiyanov, Yermolov's predecessor, and also of General Rtitshchev: see the excellent nineteenth-century works of Potto, *Kavkazskaya* (see Bibliography), and Dubrovin, *Istoriya* (see Bibliography), vol. 6 on Russia's conquest of the Caucasus.

6. Georgia and Tiflis when Griboyedov arrived there in October 1818: Montpereux, *Voyage* (see Bibliography), vol. 2, pp.64–6; also p.226, p.230–46. For another contemporary description of Tiflis, Sir Robert Ker Porter travelled through the towns at the same time on his way to Tehran: Porter, *Travels* (see Bibliography). See also all travellers' accounts listed in Bibliography: Atkin, *Russia and Iran* (see Bibliography), pp.191–203, notably J. Johnson and Capt. Mignan, p.193. Also Tiflis references, Allen, *A History of the Georgian People* (see Bibliography), p.426.

7. The newly arrived Griboyedov settling into the Court of the GOC: memoirs of Muravyov-Karsky in Fomichev and Vatsuro (eds), *Griboyedov* (see Bibliography), pp.41–7; also V.A. Andreyev, pp.157–9. For a useful overview of Georgia and Persia when Griboyedov first arrived there: Yenikolopov, *Griboyedov and the East* (see Bibliography), pp.3–47.

8. General background to General Yermolov's life and career until he became the GOC and Viceroy of the Caucasus: Baddeley, *The Russian Conquest* (see Bibliography), pp.92–9. Baddeley's index entry for Yermolov shows how fully he is placed in the Caucasian context.

9. Yermolov's failed embassy to the Shah in 1817: see Mr and Mrs Freygang (tr.), *Letters* (see Bibliography); Kotzebue (tr.), *Narrative* (see Bibliography); Lyall, *Travels* (see Bibliography). For a Russian nationalist point of view: Shostakovich, *The Diplomatic Activity* (see Bibliography), pp.30–8.

10. Griboyedov's second duel in Tiflis on 23 October 1818, an almost minute-by-minute account from Muravyov-Karsky, who was present: Fomichev and Vatsuro (eds), *Griboyedov* (see Bibliography), p.42.

11. 'I respect your actions': ibid., p.44.

12. 'I could not but derive pleasure', ibid., pp.43–4.

13. Griboyedov suspected that Yakubovich damaged his hand on purpose, out of sheer meanness.

14. 'O sort injuste': ibid., p.46.

15. 'If you are so well informed', ibid., pp.44–5.

Chapter VII: Yermolov and Russian Imperialism

Additional Background Material

The earlier volumes of Potto cover essential parts of Griboyedov's life in Georgia and the Caucasus, in particular vol. 2, no 4 (1888), pp.739–60, which describes Yermolov's almost desperate resistance to giving up his command to Paskievich. He describes the very real danger initially of a Persian victory, and General Paskievich's intervention and mission to Georgia: pp.755–7.

Potto describes in considerable detail Griboyedov's early years under Yermolov, notably vol. 2, no 1 (1887), the foundation of Grozny in 1817, Colonel Velyaminov's role on the river Sundja, the erection of fortress Vnezapnaya ('unexpected'); Yermolov's policies of scorched earth and genocide and no mercy: pp.108–13. The cruel activities of General Grekov in 1825 are set out: pp.138–41; and finally the double murder of Generals Grekov and Lissanievich at Gerzel-Aoul in 1825: p.153.

Vol. 2, no 2 shows very clearly the major disturbances in 1819/20, which Yermolov was seeking to repress at the very time when Griboyedov wrote his misinforming article reporting that the Northern Caucasus was in a state of happy pacification. Potto describes at length the Kazi–Kumikh March of 1820: pp.272–408.

Lieutenant-General Dubrovin's history of the Russian conquest of the Caucasus supplements Potto invaluably, describing Russian military strategies and tactics against the Persians and operations in the intervening khanates between Georgia and the Araxes, an area that tied down great numbers of troops and able officers.

In vol. 3, Dubrovin provides a most useful description of the Sack of Tiflis in 1795: pp.11–5. He also shows openly the incompetence of Catherine's Chief General in Georgia: General Gudovich, pp.13–49.

Yermolov's very frank description of his personal way of life is given in his letter to Kazadayev: p.229; he makes no mention of his two Tartar concubines, by whom he was to have three children. Dubrovin has enlightening pages on Yermolov's abortive 1817 embassy to Persia: pp.238–47, 244–81.

1. 'I shall wash my boots' and 'I desire that the terror of my name', quoting General Tsitsiyanov to the Ruler of Elisou in Daghestan: Baddeley, *The Russian Conquest* (see Bibliography), p.68. For terror of Yermolov's name: p.97; quoting General Potto: p.15.

2. 'On n'est pas plus entraînant', Griboyedov about Yermolov: 'Travel Notes to Stepan Beguichov' in Fomichev and Vatsuro (eds), *Griboyedov* (see Bibliography), vol. 3, p.35.

3. There are useful pages in Nechkina describing Griboyedov's relationship with Yermolov: Nechkina, *A.S. Griboyedov* (see Bibliography), pp.191–211; for his verdict that Yermolov could not be more seductive as the 'Proconsul of Iveria': Griboyedov's letter to Mazarovich of 12 October 1818 in French: ibid., pp.194–5; also pp.195–9.

4. Pushkin's description of Yermolov as having 'the head of a tiger on the torso of Hercules': Pushkin, *A Journey* (see Bibliography), p.13.

5. 'He seems to love me very much': Griboyedov about Yermolov in letter of 29 January to Stepan Beguichov in Piksanov and Shlyapkin (eds), *Complete Collected Works* (see Bibliography), vol. 3, p.35; more about his relationship with Yermolov on pp.36–7.

6. His dismissive remarks to Beguichov about the *Russian Invalid* article, 'they wrote nonsense in the *Russian Veteran* [*Invalid*] and I replied with similar nonsense!': Piksanov and Shlyapkin (eds), *Complete Collected Works* (see Bibliography), vol. 3, p.367.

7. His description of the onward journey to Tehran being like death, letter to 'my Petersburg friends' from Tiflis, 27 January 1819, 'Forget not the wandering Griboyedov 1500 versts away!': Piksanov and Shlyapkin (eds), *Complete Collected Works* (see Bibliography), vol. 3, p.361.

8. Griboyedov's joking repartee with Yermolov when leaving Tiflis, letter to Beguichov, 'Ne nous sacrifiez pas. Excellence, si jamais vous faites la guerre à la Perse': Piksanov and Shlyapkin (eds), *Complete Collected Works* (see Bibliography), vol. 3, p.35.

9. His hope now to forgive Yakubovich, who accompanied the embassy to speed it and say farewell, Piksanov and Shlyapkin (eds), *Complete Collected Works* (see Bibliography), vol. 3, p.37.

Chapter VIII: Journey to Tehran

1. Griboyedov's private reflections to Beguichov in his letter of 31 January 1819, on his new role in involuntary exile, 'the Secretary' to an errant mission: Piksanov and Shlyapkin (eds), *Complete Collected Works* (see Bibliography), vol. 3, pp.37–41.

3. His admiration of the bridge at Dermuchizana: Piksanov and Shlyapkin (eds), *Complete Collected Works* (see Bibliography), vol. 3, p.40.

4. Griboyedov's compliments to the Persian Shahs on their fine architecture: Piksanov and Shlyapkin (eds), *Complete Collected Works* (see Bibliography), vol. 3, p.38; reference to Strabo, p.39; reference to Zhukovsky, p.47.

5. For visit to Erivan and Karamzin and other receptions by its powerful Sardar: 'Travel Notes' for 5–9 February 1819 in Piksanov and Shlyapkin (eds), *Complete Collected Works* (see Bibliography), vol. 3, pp.47–9.

6. For Griboyedov's fury that his mission was not correctly met on arrival at Erivan: Piksanov and Shlyapkin (eds), *Complete Collected Works* (see Bibliography), vol. 3, p.44.

7. The comical English military instructor: ibid., vol. 3, p.46.

8. His analogies exemplified by Olearius: ibid., vol. 3, p.47.

9. Griboyedov's flat declaration, 'No! I am not a traveller!': ibid., vol. 3, p.51.

10. Griboyedov's condemnation of Persian flattery and 'hyperboles', 'Travel Notes' of 10–13 February, ibid., vol. 3, p.52.

11. Arrival in Tabriz, 1819, ibid., vol. 3, p.53.

12. Griboyedov's activity, first visit to Tabriz, lunch with the British and meeting Sir Robert Ker Porter, 'Travel Notes', Piksanov and Shlyapkin (eds), *Complete Collected Works*, vol. 3, p.53.

14. There is an interesting suggestion that the propagandist trumpet-blowing piece describing the successful reception of Mazarovich's mission in Tehran had been written by Mazarovich himself, in the Government-controlled paper in St Petersburg, *Le Conservateur Impartial* (the number in question was of 13 and 20 August 1819). However, the expert about Griboyedov's early diplomatic career, Popova, shows very clearly that the author was Griboyedov, following his earlier precedents of writing fairly treacly and adulatory articles and, in the case of his Tiflis article in 1819, distorting the truth: Ivanov, 'Griboyedov and Yermolov under surveillance' (see Bibliography), pp.215–4. There are also useful notes on this first visit to the Shah.

15. Departure from Tabriz: see 'Travel Notes' in Piksanov and Shlyapkin (eds), *Complete Collected Works* (see Bibliography), vol. 3, pp.54–6.

Chapter IX: Tabriz and the Deserters

1. A general description of Tehran: Porter, *Travels* (see Bibliography), pp.308–12; he also provides a good description of Tabriz: pp.220–9.

2. 'When a great man': ibid., p.311.

3. A far more detailed account of the Nowruz feast, or Shah's New Year reception is given in ibid., pp.32–6, including full description of Fath Ali Shah himself: pp.325–6; the Shah's avarice and passion for riches: p.352.

4. Arrival in Tehran, official reception by the Shah, and the playing of 'God Save the King': Piksanov and Shlyapkin (eds), *Complete Collected Works* (see Bibliography), vol. 3, p.56.

5. Shostakovich's presentation of Griboyedov's patriotic role: Shostakovich, *The Diplomatic Activity* (see Bibliography), pp.24–39, 55; also Griboyedov's vivid phrase that he was in a 'diplomatic monastery': p.38; Abbas Mirza's policies and ambition, and his chief vizier, Mirza Bezurg: pp.43–4.

6. The agreeable picture of Griboyedov relaxing by reading Tom Moore amidst a sea of turtles: Piksanov and Shlyapkin (eds), *Complete Collected Works* (see Bibliography), vol. 3, pp.57–9.

7. Griboyedov's diplomatic notes of complaint to Henry Willock, British Chargé d'Affaires in Persian and Tabriz dated 14–20 August 1820 and 1 September 1820; also Willock's reply of 18–20 August 1820, and Willock's despatch to Lord Castlereagh reporting the incident and describing him on 1 September 1820, as a 'young man of little experience and no prudence': article by Costello, 'Griboyedov in Persia' (see Bibliography).

8. The repatriation of Russian deserters from the Persian Army, as agreed in 1813, had completely eluded Yermolov during his 1817 embassy. Shostakovich, in *The Diplomatic Activity* (see Bibliography), gives the background: pp.35–9, 60–63. This inglorious episode in Griboyedov's

active career as a diplomat is a 'black hole' in his biography for lack of adequate archival material, and the apparent absence of any files establishing the facts as to the number of deserters repatriated: there are confusing numbers quoted by a number of the parties to the episode. The second area of doubt is the eventual fate of all the deserters at Russian hands once safely under Russian military control back in Tiflis in 1822.

9. Yermolov approving Griboyedov's conduct, 'I must judge you as deserving rightful praise': Shostakovich, *The Diplomatic Activity* (see Bibliography), p.63.

10. We have the exact text of his pleading and slightly mendacious arguments put to Abbas at a personal meeting on 30 August 1819 in Tabriz: Piksanov and Shlyapkin (eds), *Complete Collected Works* (see Bibliography), vol. 3, pp.61–3. Griboyedov had to be careful not to offend Abbas Mirza, the Russian battalion's employer, who welcomed their skills as a disciplined experienced fighting force; for the strength of the Russian battalion: Porter, *Travels* (see Bibliography), p.588; also detailed description of Abbas Mirza's 'reformed' army: pp.580–7, 589. Meshcheryakov has an interesting Tynianov-style factional account of the talks between Griboyedov and the men seeking security on the Tabriz Maidan in *A.S. Griboyedov* (see Bibliography), pp.183–274. Yenikolopov, without any supporting evidence, states that repatriates numbered about 250 soldiers: *A.S. Griboyedov v Gruzii* (see Bibliography), p.26. Nechkina also describes the episode, and refers to 80 soldiers, and grimly comments 'their fate was probably far crueller than at first assumed'; she explains how Griboyedov admitted in French to Mazarovich after the event, 'Je suis dupe et trompeur' ('I am deceived and a deceiver'): Nechkina, A.S. *Griboyedov* (see Bibliography), pp.334–5; also note p.591, quoting Popova's book, *Griboyedov-diplomat* (see Bibliography), pp.24–6.

11. Piksanov covers the episode, quoting the few remarks Griboyedov made to Beguichov later: 'I cannot guarantee your security'; 'their number is given as 70', and he is quoted as thinking he 'brought out 110': Piksanov and Shlyapkin (eds), *Complete Collected Works* (see Bibliography), vol. 1, p.61.

12. As will become evident from Griboyedov's simultaneous negotiations through Mazarovich with the military authorities in Tiflis, Griboyedov could not talk the deserters into returning to Russia without promising them full pardons and amnesties from the hideous fate usually applied to Russian deserters, namely flogging to death 'through the ranks', or transportation to Siberia in irons.

13. He met a certain number of the men on the Tabriz Maidan, and gave them assurances that he later qualified as being 'unguaranteeable': Piksanov and Shlyapkin (eds), *Complete Collected Works* (see Bibliography), vol. 3, p.293. For comments on his exchange with Abbas Mirza: vol. 3, p.292; elsewhere in his 'Travel Notes', Griboyedov records

laconically: 'The deserters, negotiations, madness and grief! I will give my head for those unfortunate ones are miserable compatriots': vol. 3, p.61.

14. On arrival in Tiflis, General Velyaminov told him face-to-face, how 'la cohue des barbus agite encore', i.e. for severe punishments and scrapping the deal made with Mazarovich on Griboyedov's behalf: Popova, *Griboyedov v Persii* (see Bibliography), pp.67–8, October 1819.

   To clarify these issues, the author hoped that the Georgian state archives would contain the file. Private research was commissioned in Tiflis. Thanks are due to Tamara Dragadze in London, who made contact with Professor Abzianidze of the Institute of Literature under the Georgian Academy of Sciences, who tried to establish the facts in Tblisi.

   Archives were consulted in Tiflis by Tamila Mgaloblishvili and Liya Kiknadze, to ascertain if possible from Georgian archives the exact number of deserters repatriated by Griboyedov from Tabriz to Tiflis, and the eventual outcome of their cases, whether punishment, flogging or exile to Siberia, or amnesty as promised. The Central States Archives of Georgia (TsGIA) folio 2, op. 1, Affairs 897 of 812 sheets gave no results, by way of explanation. The researchers stated that many of these documents were removed from Tiflis to Russia in 1964, with no reason given. Present whereabouts are unknown. The following documents were checked: Fond (file) 2, 1 Affairs 760 (10 sheets), 897 (812 sheets), 1027 (21 sheets); Fond 4, 2 Affairs 730 (16 sheets); Fond 11, 1 Affairs 2 (70 sheets), 20 (29 sheets), 31 (11 sheets), 3932 (17 sheets); Fond 16, 1 Affairs 4053 (11 sheets), 4477 (19 sheets), 10 Affairs 994 (5 sheets); Fond 1082, 1 Affairs 1061 (45 sheets); Fond 1087, 1 Affairs 1061 (39 sheets), 1069 (11 sheets), 1169 (12 sheets); Fond 1505, 1 Affairs 118 (165 sheets). All these references are regrettably undated. K. Kekelidze, Institute of Manuscripts, of the Georgian Academy of Sciences: Archive of G. Tumanishvili, No. 2417, from the complete Piksanov and Shlyapkin (eds), *Complete Collected Works* (see Bibliography); card index file of the Veidenbaum Archive, G. Leonidze, in the Tiflis Literary Museum. Scrutiny of these archives led the researchers to no new conclusions on these points. There are several books about Griboyedov in Georgian, but all of them are about his poetry. Only one Georgian scholar – Vano S. Shaduri – wrote a PhD thesis about Griboyedov's life in Georgia, published as a book (in Russian) in Tblisi in 1977 (see Bibliography) – in which the author claims that he studied all available Georgian sources, but there is not a word about this episode. The true facts about the deserter issue therefore still elude us.

15. Popova gives the full French text of Griboyedov's complaint to Mazarovich, 'me voici dupe et trompeur': *Griboyedov-diplomat* (see Bibliography), p.24–5.

16. Whilst Soviet biographers and editors of Griboyedov quote enough material to show the unresolved factual problems in this question,

namely the inconsistent numbers, ranging from 70 to 158 soldiers on the Maidan in Tabriz, their fate remains unclear. The only researcher and writer to give us illuminating insights is Popova, in *Griboyedov v Persii* (see Bibliography). The first mention of the deserter question comes in the Introduction, pp.13–4. She bases her sources on papers in the Ministry of Foreign Affairs of 1819, where the exchange of letters between Griboyedov and his superior Mazarovich should by rights be held, but then states that these papers cannot be found. Popova refers to a 'melancholy outcome' of the repatriation for Griboyedov, suggesting that what Griboyedov described to Mazarovich as 'la cohue des barbus' had prevailed on the Chief of Staff, General Velyaminov, to renege on his promise of amnesty to Mazarovich and indirectly Griboyedov, p.15. She suggests that Griboyedov reported fully on his treatment after arrival in Georgia with the soldiers, p.63. This report does not tell us their fate. On p.90, we read how Mazarovich seeking to soothe Griboyedov's outraged conscience at their joint double-cross by the military, states smoothly 'your deserters must expunge their guilt before their country'. There is no explanation how this is to be. There is a reference to a ruling from the Emperor, p.91, in which it is stated that the 40 men who reported for repatriation later became 100. Popova confirms on p.14 that Griboyedov described himself to Mazarovich as 'a fool and a deceiver!' (in Russian, 'ya durak i obman-schchikom'), strong terms to use in such a life-and-death context. The reference is to his letter no. 5 to Mazarovich. On p.60, there is the first reference to a total of 158 unfortunates; by the time they reach Nakhichevan, there were only 155.

In official Russian literature, the figure for deserters who came out of Persia with Griboyedov is 150. There is another figure – 70 – which we find in Piksanov and Shlyapkin (eds), *Complete Collected Works* (see Bibliography), Note 110. Shostakovich quotes 70 in *The Diplomatic Activity* (see Bibliography), p.61, but the origin of this figure we find in Piksanov and Shlyapkin (eds), *Complete Collected Works* (see Bibliography), where on p.26 we read that on 30 August, 70 Russians gathered in front of the mission's office (Griboyedov uses this figure too in his 'Travel Notes'). It took Griboyedov several days to get a travel permit, and on 4 September, when he started his trip, the numbers of Russians swelled to 'around 150', p.28. As to the figure of 80, it is clear from Griboyedov's letter that those (out of 150) were in trouble after his arrival in Tiflis – we know that the group consisted of POWs and deserters, and that only deserters were in trouble. In what kind of trouble, there is no record anywhere. AKAK holds copies of diplomatic despatches from Tabriz only since 1820, a year after this affair, and there were no newspapers or magazines at that time to tell us the story.

Additionally, at the author's request, and through the generous collaboration of the historian and Caucasian expert George A. Putnikov in Moscow, archival research in Moscow was carried out to establish the missing information about the following questions: the numbers finally involved in repatriation to Tiflis by Griboyedov in any files removed from Georgia, or in Moscow in the early nineteenth century, and the sentence and fate inflicted on the deserters. The archives consulted were: Rossiisky Gosudarstvenny Archiv Drevnikh Aktov (RGADA) covering Persian–Russian relations. This work was carried out by K.I.N. Kreipert, G.i.; Rossiisky Gosudarstvenny Istorichesk Archiv, fond Abamelek-Lazarevykh, fond I/F. Paskievich. K.I.N. Kreipert, G.i. did the work; Arkhiv Vneshnei Politiki Rossii (AVPR) Lichny fond (personal file) of A.S. Griboyedov. The research was carried out by two other workers: E.T. Kasumov and I.O. Sviridova. Despite these efforts, no relevant answers were found.

A general conclusion is that perhaps any embarrassing files were removed, possibly by Nechkina. In her book, she hints darkly that she knew some of the answers: Nechkina, *A.S. Griboyedov* (see Bibliography), p.335, where she predicts, if with knowledge, 'their fate in Russia was probably far crueller than that initially promised'; and notes, p.591. She records 80 soldiers being repatriated.

For the aftermath of the deserter episode, and the Foreign Ministry refusing to support Yermolov's request for a decoration: Popova, *Griboyedov v Persii* (see Bibliography), p.15. Nesselrode took a tough line with Yermolov, stating that diplomats should not be engaged in such bloody and messy work.

Chapter X: Diplomatic Diversions

1. From Piksanov and Shlyapkin (eds), *Complete Collected Works* (see Bibliography), p.26, we find out that at the time of Griboyedov's arrival in Tiflis, Yermolov was in Chechnya and called him there. Yermolov thanked Griboyedov and wanted to decorate him, but the St Petersburg Foreign Ministry was irritated, as Russo–Persian relations deteriorated because of the affair. As a result, Griboyedov was very disappointed and depressed, as is apparent in his letters. Piksanov confirms that Yermolov wished to praise and reward with a decoration: p.xl.

2. Yermolov's idea of using Griboyedov as a legal codifier of Georgian laws, notably a Russian translation of Tsar Vakhtang's Legal Code: Yenikolopov, *A.S. Griboyedov v Gruzii* (see Bibliography), p.49.

3. Griboyedov's caustic and ironic letter describing Tabriz social life to N.A. Kakhovsky, letters of May and 25 June 1820: Piksanov and Shlyapkin (eds), *Complete Collected Works* (see Bibliography), vol. 3, pp.139–41.

4. Griboyedov's cynical disrespect and carping criticisms of his amiable superior Mazarovich, notably for his Roman Catholic piety (not unnatural for an Italian), and his criticism of Mazarovich for fawning too

much on Abbas Mirza: Popova, *A.S. Griboyedov v Persii* (see Bibliography), pp.8–33; also Muravyov-Karsky in Fomichev and Vatsuro (eds), *Griboyedov* (see Bibliography), pp.45–6, who disliked Mazarovich on the grounds he was not an ethnic Russian, upholding the dignity of the Tsar, and that instead, with his brother, he was seeking business opportunities in the Persian bazaars, as was Griboyedov with the young Frenchman Ettier.

5.   Griboyedov's complaint about the private chaplain Kaplan, 'a house magician': his letter to Kakhovsky in Piksanov and Shlyapkin (eds), *Complete Collected Works* (see Bibliography), vol. 3, p.140.

Griboyedov's description of social life in Tabriz, the burial of Dr Kastaldi: Shostakovich, *The Diplomatic Activity* (see Bibliography), p.37.

6.   Griboyedov's exploitation of his friendship in Tabriz with Ettier and later Vsevolozhsky to develop the possibility of a Russo–Persian trading company: see the original and successful piece of detective work by Kal'ma, 'The commercial projects of Griboyedov' (see Bibliography).

7.   The pretext for Abbas Mirza's 'attack' on the Turks: Fraser, *Travels and Adventures* (see Bibliography), pp.309ff.

8.   Griboyedov's lucky break in promoting Abbas Mirza's armed demonstration against the Turks of 1822, which earned him the Order of the Lion and the Sun later from the Shah, which he was able to pawn later to raise money when – as usual – he was half-broke: Yenikolopov, *A.S. Griboyedov v Gruzii* (see Bibliography), p.35; also for support of Yermolov for the war, though Nesselrode, to his credit, thought it would destabilise the area and weaken the Ottoman empire, thus irritating the British. In practice, it disrupted Anglo–Persian trade quite seriously, a Russian objective: p.58. For conclusion of war by armistice at Erzerum: p.39. Shostakovich comments on this war: *The Diplomatic Activity* (see Bibliography), pp.67–71. Shostakovich rightly claims that Griboyedov, by this dangerous play, scored off the British and diminished their influence; they thereafter saw him as a dangerous player: p.71.

Dubrovin first mentions Mazarovich's mission, including Griboyedov, on p.541. The differences in policies between Nesselrode in the Foreign Ministry vis-à-vis Persia and Yermolov's bullying bluster are well set out: pp.545–53. The Persian–Turkish War of 1822, in which Griboyedov played a significant role as troublemaker is described: p.554. For the difficult hand Mazarovich had to play with Yermolov pursuing his own foreign policy: pp.562–8.

9.   Yermolov's request to Nesselrode to employ Griboyedov in Tiflis, bringing him back from Tabriz: Yenikolopov, *A.S. Griboyedov v Gruzii* (see Bibliography), p.33. Piksanov deals with this move in Griboyedov's life in Tabriz: *Griboyedov: Researches* (see Bibliography), vol. 1, pp.liii.

10.   Yermolov's compliments about Griboyedov's skills are quoted from Yermolov's letter to Nesselrode of 12 January 1821, referring to his broken arm from a riding accident needing treatment in Tiflis as a

justification: Piksanov and Shlyapkin (eds), *Complete Collected Works* (see Bibliography), vol. 3.

11. In a fascinating postscript in his letter, presumably to Prince Shakhovskoy, in Piksanov and Shlyapkin (eds), *Complete Collected Works* (see Bibliography), vol. 2, pp.144–5, Griboyedov tells his old tutor and literary mentor what his present skills were in languages, and how he wishes to return from a 'gloomy Kingdom'. Nechkina, in her obsessive desire to prove *Woe from Wit* is a Decembrist manifesto, and, as it were, a propaganda and reforming and political document, devotes more space and analysis of the creative history of the play, beginning, Chapter VI, 'Concept of the Comedy': Nechkina, *A.S. Griboyedov* (see Bibliography), pp.169ff. Piksanov, too, devotes the whole of vol. 1 of Piksanov and Shlyapkin (eds), *Complete Collected Works* (see Bibliography) to the play, and in his book of ideologically clean essays about Griboyedov has much to say about the genesis and conception of the play: Piksanov, *Griboyedov: Researches* (see Bibliography). All the average Russian-reading English admirer of Griboyedov needs to know of his masterpiece *Woe from Wit* can be found in Grishunin and Fomichev (eds), *New Collected Works* (see Bibliography), commentary, pp.345–59. This covers all extant manuscripts of the play and the evidence of important eye-witnesses to its composition, notably Wilhelm Küchelbecker in Tiflis; also Fomichev and Vatsuro (eds), *Griboyedov* (see Bibliography), pp.257–63, especially p.259. Each edition of the Khmelita *sbornik* in the latter book includes valuable specialised articles about aspects of the play, especially in 1998. Without question, the two most readable accounts in English of the play and influences affecting its conception are by two distinguished Slavic American scholars, namely Karlinsky, *Russian Drama* (see Bibliography), and Professor William E. Brown, *A History of Russian Literature* (see Bibliography), vol. 2. The invaluable insights of Bonamour must also be mentioned: *A.S. Griboyedov* (see Bibliography).

12. Beguichov's summary of Griboyedov's hard-won experience in Persia: Fomichev and Vatsuro (eds), *Griboyedov* (see Bibliography), p.27.

13. Beguichov's evidence about the creation and early drafts of *Woe from Wit* being started in Persia: ibid., pp.25–8.

14. Bebutov's evidence that Griboyedov recited part of the play to him in 1821: ibid., pp.342–3. Bebutov's meeting was in 1819.

15. Griboyedov's letter, presumed to be to Prince Shakhovskoy, about his dream in which he promised the Prince to write his play, is quoted in full in Piksanov and Shlyapkin (eds), *Complete Collected Works* (see Bibliography), vol. 2, pp.144–5.

Chapter XI: Return to Tiflis

1. Griboyedov's life in 1822–3 in Tiflis, describing his links with Prince Chavchavadze and Dadashvili and the aristocracy of Orbelianis etc: Yenikolopov, *A.S. Griboyedov v Gruzii* (see Bibliography), pp.43–53.

2. Of the liberal sympathisers thronging Yermolov's court in the south, there is ample evidence from Nechkina, who describes Yermolov's pre-disposition to enlightened liberalism, himself condoning the hotheads: Nechkina, *A.S. Griboyedov* (see Bibliography), pp.198–200, 202, 206; also van Halen, *Narrative* (see Bibliography), p.209. Yermolov even jokingly called Fonvisin a 'Carbonarist' for his role in bailing Küchelbecker out from a disagreeable position in Moscow by allowing him to join his staff: Nechkina, *A.S. Griboyedov* (see Bibliography), p.213. For the storm in a teacup between Küchelbecker and Pokhvisnyev, leading to a duel and Griboyedov's ill-judged role in it, evidence of Muravyov-Karsky about the details: Fomichev and Vatsuro (eds), *Griboyedov* (see Bibliography), pp.50–1.

3. Beguichov's evidence about the writing of *Woe from Wit* and the reading of the Slavonic Bible, and his invaluable statements about hearing early readings of every scene almost as soon as it was written: Fomichev and Vatsuro (eds), *Griboyedov* (see Bibliography), p.159, and all extracts pp.257–63.

4. Griboyedov's gloomy confession, after Küchelbecker had to leave Tiflis, that he no longer had an appreciative audience, and had to read to the walls, in his melancholic letter to Küchelbecker of 1 October 1822, continued in January 1823: Fomichev and Vatsuro (eds), *Griboyedov* (see Bibliography), pp.145–6.

5. Griboyedov attending Dr Lyall as an 'unofficial minder' around Kakhetia: Yenikolopov, *A.S. Griboyedov v Gruzii* (see Bibliography), p.51; also Lyall's own memoirs and travel book: Lyall, *Travels* (see Bibliography), pp.20–40.

6. Griboyedov's poem, 'There where the Alazan meanders': Fomichev (ed.), *The Dramatic Works* (see Bibliography), vol. 2, poem p.220, notes, pp.481–2.

7. Griboyedov's letter to Küchelbecker of January 1823, and on death of Amlikh, his servant: Fomichev and Vatsuro (eds), *Griboyedov* (see Bibliography), pp.145–6.

Chapter XII: Theatrical Campaigns, Moscow

1. Beguichov's marriage and Griboyedov's trembling hands, and his curious fantasy: Fomichev and Vatsuro (eds), *Griboyedov* (see Bibliography), p.28.

2. The literary situation in Russia upon Griboyedov's return in 1823: useful summary in Bonamour, *A.S. Griboyedov* (see Bibliography), pp.194–201;

the influence of French classicists and English Romantics: p.201; the rise of Pushkin and position of Zhukovsky: pp.198–201.

3. Prince Vyazemsky's denunciation of Caucasian atrocities and colonialism, in his letter of September 1822 to A.I. Turgenev, a well-known liberal; also Pushkin's letter of 6 February from Kishinyov: Wolff and Bayley (eds), *Pushkin on Literature* (see Bibliography), p.63.

4. Beguichov writing that Griboyedov 'would rise with the sun' to compose his play: Fomichev and Vatsuro (eds), *Griboyedov* (see Bibliography), pp.27–8.

5. Beguichov's praise of Griboyedov's knowledge of the Persian court and its customs: ibid., pp.27, 29.

6. Griboyedov's close relations with Küchelbecker stretch from 1817 to after Küchelbecker's exile as a convict to Siberia. Griboyedov tried to help him financially, and every detail of their relationship and friendship is painstakingly charted by Meshcheryakov in *A.S. Griboyedov* (see Bibliography), pp.186–208. Küchelbecker, being a future notorious Decembrist, is of great interest to Nechkina in *A.S. Griboyedov* (see Bibliography), pp.213–9, for their collaboration and exchanges in Tiflis. There are numerous other references to their friendship later: e.g. p.614.

7. 'Yunost' Vyeschchovo' ('The Youth of the Prophet'), his pageant for the competition for the opening of the Bolshoi Theatre in 1823: Piksanov and Shlyapkin (eds), *Complete Collected Works* (see Bibliography), vol. 1, p.212, note p.297. Griboyedov humiliatingly lost this commission to Dmitriyev. Also Beguichov in Fomichev and Vatsuro (eds), *Griboyedov* (see Bibliography), p.29.

8. Griboyedov's winter in Moscow and his relations with Prince Vyazemsky in composing jointly, to Verstovsky's music, the vaudeville *Who is the Brother? Who is the Sister?*: Meshcheryakov, *A.S. Griboyedov* (see Bibliography), pp.91ff. It was Vyazemsky who nicknamed Griboyedov 'G-persidsky': p.921. There is also the fullest description of the 'war of epigrams' between Dmitriyev and Pisarev, Griboyedov and Vyazemsky. Their collaboration is described by Vyazemsky in his memoirs: Fomichev and Vatsuro (eds), *Griboyedov* (see Bibliography), pp.78–88; also for the war of epigrams and for his comments on *Woe from Wit*, p.87; and notes, pp.257–360.

9. Griboyedov's genial exchanges with the composer Verstovsky: letter of December 1823 in Piksanov and Shlyapkin (eds), *Complete Collected Works* (see Bibliography), vol. 3, p.150.

10. Vyazemsky's recollection of the opening night and Griboyedov's coolness: Fomichev and Vatsuro (eds), *Griboyedov* (see Bibliography), p.85; for nicknaming Griboyedov 'Gribus': p.93.

11. The childish abuse exchanged in the war of epigrams, including Griboyedov's 'snake-like stare': Meshcheryakov, *A.S. Griboyedov* (see Bibliography), pp.91–5.

12. 'There is no call to praise him': ibid., pp.94–5,

13. Beguichov's evidence as to Griboyedov's carelessness about his manuscript: Fomichev and Vatsuro (eds), *Griboyedov* (see Bibliography), pp.28–9.

Chapter XIII: *Woe from Wit*

1. Griboyedov's return to St Petersburg in 1824: Fomichev, *Griboyedov in Petersburg* (see Bibliography), pp.58–63, especially his first visit to the veteran fabulist Krylov, 63–4; Griboyedov duly read to him his revised comedy, p.64; and to Prince Shakhovskoy, p.63.
2. Griboyedov's post-Persian adjustment to all new literary developments since 1819 in Moscow and St Petersburg is described by Bonamour, *A.S. Griboyedov* (see Bibliography), pp.192–214, as are his new friendships with intellectuals like Prince V.F. Odoyevsky in Moscow. Bonamour deals with Nechkina's claims that Griboyedov was, as it were, an honorary Decembrist, and analyses the so-called Decembrist themes from *Woe from Wit*.
3. Griboyedov made advances to the bemedalled war hero General Miloradovich to get his play on stage and past the censors: Piksanov and Shlyapkin (eds), *Complete Collected Works* (see Bibliography), vol. 3, p.66; on the way to St Petersburg he had made some important last-minute changes, as he told Beguichov: letter of 10 June 1824, pp.153–5. The same letter describes the enthusiastic response his readings elicited from St Petersburg's theatrical and literary elite. He told Beguichov how Count Lanskoi might intervene to get the play approved: p.154; and that visiting Miloradovich, he found the Grand Duke Nicholas, the future Tsar. For the very first time, he referred to Bulgarin as a friend amongst such distinguished future Decembrists as Odoyevsky and Mukhanov: p.155.
4. Griboyedov and Alexander 'Marlinsky' Bestuzhev, see especially the chapter describing their late-flowering friendship: Meshcheryakov, *A.S. Griboyedov* (see Bibliography), pp.140–6. The book also tracks the relationship with Prince A.I. Odoyevsky: pp.124–39.
5. Details of Bestuzhev's reconciliation with Griboyedov, and the decision that they could become friends: Fomichev and Vatsuro (eds), *Griboyedov* (see Bibliography), pp.89–90. Vyazemsky was writing much later, in particular in 1828: see 'Letter of Petersburg 1828' in ibid., p.90.
6. Griboyedov's plan to translate Shakespeare's *Romeo and Juliet*, collaborating with Zhandr: Bonamour, *A.S. Griboyedov* (see Bibliography), pp.215–6.
7. His stay in Petersburg and extensive exposure to Decembrists: Nechkina, *A.S. Griboyedov* (see Bibliography), pp.383–93. These pages are useful for his life with Prince A. Odoyevsky. See p.391 in particular for his failed attempt to get von Fock, the censor, to agree to the play's performance.

8. The aborted performance of *Woe from Wit* that never took place at the Imperial Theatrical School: Peter Karatygin, 'My acquaintance with A.S. Griboyedov' in Fomichev and Vatsuro (eds), *Griboyedov* (see Bibliography), p.104–6; he too recounted how Griboyedov was rude to Fyodorov: p.108.

9. Griboyedov's breakthrough to getting the first two acts of *Woe from Wit* published in *The Russian Thalia* thanks to Bulgarin: Meshcheryakov, *A.S. Griboyedov* (see Bibliography), pp.152–9; for the rest of their relationship, see up to p.185.

10. Karatygin's account: Fomichev, *Griboyedov in Petersburg* (see Bibliography), pp.107–8.

11. Mass handwritten copying of the manuscript 'a whole Chancery': Fomichev and Vatsuro (eds), *Griboyedov* (see Bibliography); Zhandr speaking to D.A. Smirnov: p.348. 'The chief MSS handed to Zhandr was corrected by A.S. Griboyedov and remained with me [Zhandr]', hence the reliability of the 'Zhandr' manuscript.

12. Griboyedov's special friendship with Zhandr: Meshcheryakov, *A.S. Griboyedov* (see Bibliography), pp.64–75.

13. Pushkin's receipt of a copied handwritten version of the play brought at the end of January 1823 by his old friend Pushchin (a future Decembrist): Pushkin, *The Letters* (see Bibliography), letter No. 101 to Alexander Bestuzhev, pp.200–1; also letter No. 100 to Prince P.A. Vyazemsky of 28 January 1825, p.199.

14. Griboyedov and Molière: Bonamour, *Alceste and the Influence of the Misanthrope* (see Bibliography), p.256; on influences of Molière: pp.200–1, 286, 294–5, 296–9; on French influences on Griboyedov: pp.290–3.

15. 'More than seven hundred leagues': Griboyedov, *Woe from Wit*, tr. Waring (see Bibliography), p.54.

16. Sophie's dream about 'devils and love, flowers and fear': ibid., p.50.

17. Sophie's rebuke: ibid., p.572.

18. Nechkina, concerned with the play's Decembrist content, claims roundly that the image of Repetilov as a fiery radical prattler dates only to 1823: Nechkina, *A.S. Griboyedov* (see Bibliography), p.373–5. He cannot be interpreted as ridiculing Decembrists.

19. 'Parliament and jury service', Griboyedov, *Woe from Wit*, tr. Waring (see Bibliography), p.99.

20. Chatsky's diatribe about the people he has been with: ibid., p.111.

21. Famusov's denunciation of Chatsky as mad: ibid., p.111.

22. Pushkin's judgements to Bestuzhev: Pushkin, *The Letters* (see Bibliography), p.201. Bonamour, *A.S. Griboyedov* (see Bibliography), pp.365–6, also has a very pertinent comment about listening to the play, in particular the musicality in the play's rhymes. Bonamour notes how operatic much of the play is, with its choruses and important silences: pp.242–3. The most famous production of the play to emphasise its musicality was that by Meyerhold in 1928, using John Field and Beethoven as background music: Braun, *Meyerhold, A Revolution in*

Theatre (see Bibliography), pp.243–8. Meyerhold particularly urged his actors to work on the verse with its peculiarly Griboyedovian lightness; he nevertheless added another dimension of sound. Music was super-imposed; largely to counterbalance Chatsky's intellectuality, he was made to improvise at the piano, as if to express emotion as well. Griboyedov's nature, so intensely musical, expressed his ideas and theories very directly through the speeches of Chatsky; it has not escaped some critics that music was an important message in this theatrical medium, a point adopted by Meyerhold in his production of the play in 1928 and 1935, at the Maly Theatre in Moscow.

Griboyedov was himself a musician and collected folk melodies; indeed, he passed one on to Glinka, for which Pushkin then wrote words, now well known as the 'romance' 'Never sing for me that sad song of Georgia...' ('romance' designates the Russian art song, as the term *Lied* does the German). Shortly before opening night, Meyerhold thus explained his reason for the music; in a newspaper interview, as reported by A.V. Fevralsky (*Pravda*, 12 March 1928), he said: 'The show is saturated with music. The approach to Chatsky's character through music will make it possible to overcome its apparent intellectuality. The emotional charge in Chatsky will be revealed in his musical improvisation, taken from the enormous musical culture of the age (Beethoven, Mozart, Bach). So Meyerhold's Chatsky was made to represent not only 'wit', or intellect, in his critical attack on an indifferent age.' Article by Hoover, *Russian Literature Triquarterly* (see Bibliography).

23. The exchange of letters between Katenin and Griboyedov in January 1825: Piksanov and Shlyapkin (eds), *Complete Collected Works* (see Bibliography), vol. 3, pp.167–9; notes, pp.327–8.

24. Griboyedov's allusion to Molière and his characters being portraits: Piksanov and Shlyapkin (eds), *Complete Collected Works* (see Bibliography), vol. 3, p.168. For Bonamour's comments on Griboyedov and Molière: *A.S. Griboyedov* (see Bibliography), p.196; for further comments on the Katenin exchange: p.230.

25. Herzen's interpretation of Chatsky: Herzen, *My Past* (see Bibliography), vol. 2, pp.200–1.

26. 'A shot that rang out': ibid., vol. 2, pp.261–3.

27. Bonamour, *A.S. Griboyedov* (see Bibliography), analyses Nechkina's Marxist interpretations, namely that Chatsky is a revolutionary and proto-Decembrist, a theme borrowed from Herzen: see pp.263–6; for the play about serfdom issues: pp.323–4; also p.312; summary p.344.

28. The most useful commentaries on the play's richness and felicities of language are to be found in Karlinsky, *Russian Drama* (see Bibliography), pp.226–311; also the subtle and careful presentation by Bonamour, *A.S. Griboyedov* (see Bibliography), pp.223–307. Bonamour pursues his analysis with a further essential chapter on '*Woe from Wit* and society': pp.308–47; also pp.348–78.

29. Griboyedov's reference to the abuse of serfdom, in which a serf owner suddenly 'swapped three of his key serfs for three borzoi hounds': Griboyedov, *Woe from Wit*, tr. Waring (see Bibliography), p.68.

30. Goncharov's essay (in Russian) on the play *A Million Torments*: Konovalov and J. Richards (eds), *Russian Critical Essays* (see Bibliography), pp.113–4.

31. Griboyedov's affirmation that Moscow was 'my country, my family, my home': letter to Beguichov of 18 September 1818 in Piksanov and Shlyapkin (eds), *Complete Collected Works* (see Bibliography), vol. 3, p.133.

32. Byelinsky's essay about the play: Byelinsky, *Sochineniya* (see Bibliography), vol. 1, pp.583–603. Piksanov and Shlyapkin (eds), *Complete Collected Works* (see Bibliography) also give an excellent summary of all Russian critics' views, including Byelinsky, vol. 3, pp.303–51; about Byelinsky himself: pp.315–21. Byelinsky points out that the play is not a comedy, but a tragic satire, p.317, and that Chatsky is a failed Don Quixote figure, and essentially tragic.

33. Griboyedov's arrogant, if not rude reference to 'the whole tribe of literary critics as such swine' *svoloch*: letter to Beguichov of 4 January 1835 in Piksanov and Shlyapkin (eds), *Complete Collected Works* (see Bibliography), vol. 3, p.165; the same letter has his admission about his affair with Teleshova.

Chapter XIV: Love and Politics, St Petersburg

1. For Griboyedov's close attachment to Prince Alexander Odoyevsky, who saved his life in the great flood of 1824, see especially essay about both of them: Meshcheryakov, *A.S. Griboyedov* (see Bibliography), pp.124–39; also Fomichev, *Griboyedov in Petersburg* (see Bibliography), pp.79–86. There are also interesting references in Zavalyshin's memoirs to their close friendship: Fomichev and Vatsuro (eds), *Griboyedov* (see Bibliography), pp.128–31; Zhandr also touches on them: pp.348–9.

2. Griboyedov's touching letter to Beguichov recommending Odoyevsky as 'l'enfant de mon choix': Piksanov and Shlyapkin (eds), *Complete Collected Works* (see Bibliography), vol. 3, pp.348–9.

3. The mysterious reference to Odoyevsky's infatuation with a married woman 'V.N.T.': Meshcheryakov, *A.S. Griboyedov* (see Bibliography), p.127; the woman's identity is still unknown today.

4. Odoyevsky's watchdog role supervising Griboyedov at the theatre: Zhandr in Fomichev and Vatsuro (eds), *Griboyedov* (see Bibliography), p.234.

5. Karatygin's compliments to Griboyedov on his multiple talents: ibid., p.107.

6. The Gribov anecdotes: ibid., pp.109–10.

7. The anecdote whereby Griboyedov took his revenge: ibid., p.109.

8. There are three chief sources for Griboyedov's affair with the ballerina Katherine Teleshova: his confession in a letter to Stepan Beguichov of 4 March 1825, that he was temporarily madly in love with her, and describing how General Miloradovich was his rival for her favours: Piksanov and Shlyapkin (eds), *Complete Collected Works* (see Bibliography), vol. 3, pp.165–6; Zhandr, in his interview with D.A. Smirnov of 28 April 1858, was quite indiscreet: Fomichev and Vatsuro (eds), *Griboyedov* (see Bibliography), pp.216–26; the Russian text of his love poem to Teleshova published in *Son of the Fatherland*, thus telling all St Petersburg he was in love: Piksanov and Shlyapkin (eds), *Complete Collected Works* (see Bibliography), vol. 1, pp.13–5; notes, pp.280–1. Fomichev deals very briefly with this human moment in Griboyedov's life, *Griboyedov in Petersburg* (see Bibliography), pp.89–90.

9. Herzen's dismissal of the war hero Miloradovich: Herzen, *My Past* (see Bibliography), vol. 1, pp.295–6.

10. His ardour cooling: Piksanov and Shlyapkin (eds), *Complete Collected Works* (see Bibliography), vol. 3, p.165.

11. Griboyedov's familiarity with the Northern Society and future Decembrists, such as Kondraty Ryleyev, and his 'Russian breakfasts', and Bestuzhev: Meshcheryakov, *A.S. Griboyedov* (see Bibliography), chapters about future Decembrists and Griboyedov, notably Odoyevsky and Bestuzhev and Küchelbecker. Nechkina gives the subject priority: Nechkina, *A.S. Griboyedov* (see Bibliography), pp.365–79; or his St Petersburg years 1823–5: pp.384–401.

12. 'A hundred second lieutenants', D.A. Smirnov interviewing Zhandr on 3 June 1858: Fomichev and Vatsuro (eds), *Griboyedov* (see Bibliography), p.243; on the same page, Zhandr confirms his weighty opinion that Griboyedov's involvement was 'as full as possible'. Zhandr, from intimate inside knowledge, has much to say about the Decembrists and their organisation: pp.232–4. He gives a very detailed account of Griboyedov's arrest as a suspect Decembrist: pp.207–11.

13. 'You all make a lot of noise': Griboyedov, *Woe from Wit*, tr. Waring (see Bibliography), p.99.

14. 'Liberalism, scepticism and nationalism': Piksanov and Shlyapkin (eds), *Complete Collected Works* (see Bibliography), p.175; for the limits of Griboyedov's opposition: p.173; for his scepticism: p.175.

15. Bestuzhev's remarks to the interrogatory commission: Fomichev and Vatsuro (eds), *Griboyedov* (see Bibliography); the transcript of his trial: pp.272–91; on Bestuzhev particularly: pp.181, 275–6, 283. Bestuzhev had told him about the secret society.

16. Lavrentyeva anecdote of his party upon joining the society: Meshcheryakov, *A.S. Griboyedov* (see Bibliography), pp.322–5.

17. The story (not used by Nechkina, who queried the source's reliability) about Griboyedov's frenzied dish-breaking party upon being received

into the Northern Society: Meshcheryakov, *A.S. Griboyedov* (see Bibliography), pp.322–5.

18. The fullest interpretation of the inspiration and true meaning of the tragedy *Radamist and Zenobia*: Vatsuro, 'Problems of the creativity of A.S. Griboyedov' in Fomichev, *Griboyedov in Petersburg*, pp.162–94. Bonamour sees *Radamist and Zenobia* as one of Griboyedov's most ambitious literary projects and an attack on oriental despotism and indirectly on Persia: Bonamour, *A.S. Griboyedov* (see Bibliography), pp.400–2; also treatments of the draft: Yenikopolov, *A.S. Griboyedov v Gruzii* (see Bibliography), pp.135–6, for full text of the draft: Piksanov and Shlyapkin (eds), *Complete Collected Works* (see Bibliography), vol. 1, pp.256–61; notes, pp.300–1.

19. A predictable analysis by Nechkina that the theme of a slaves' revolt is in line with Decembrist forecasts, in their case that a revolt by aristocrats against tyrants would be bound to fail: Nechkina, *A.S. Griboyedov* (see Bibliography), pp.532–7.

Chapter XV: Crimea and the Northern Caucasus

1. 'I am virtually convinced': Piksanov and Shlyapkin (eds), *Complete Collected Works* (see Bibliography), vol. 3, p.175. He was not against marriage, but was denied the possibility of supporting parents: such dependence was bound to suppress creativity and artistic independence.

2. There is copious analysis of Griboyedov's journey south through Kiev and the Ukraine, as to whether or not he brought important conspiratorial messages from the Northern Society in St Petersburg to the conspirators of the Southern Society at Tulchin. See Nechkina, for whom this is a burning issue: *A.S. Griboyedov* (see Bibliography), pp.450–66. Piksanov also describes his journey: Piksanov and Shlyapkin (eds), *Complete Collected Works* (see Bibliography), vol. 1, pp.lviii–lxii.

3. 'Vladimirs and Iasyaslavi': ibid., vol. 3, p.175.

4. Nechkina examines the evidence of all Decembrists, giving evidence about Griboyedov's possible membership: *A.S. Griboyedov* (see Bibliography), pp.405–11, where the 'on nash' ('he is ours') question is ventilated; the debate continues, pp.412–7. It is necessary to temper Nechkina's conclusions with the well-founded judgements of Piksanov in *Griboyedov: Issledovaniye* (see Bibliography), especially the essay on Griboyedov and serfdom, pp.83–158; Griboyedov and Bestuzhev: pp.161–90. For the interesting suggestion that Griboyedov was only an *affilié*, in other words a 'sleeping supporter' waiting to see which way the conspiracy might develop, succeed or fail, we must turn to Prince P.V. Dolgorukov, quoting the evidence of a certain Batenkov (a former Decembrist) that there was a category of *affiliés*, who did not sign up formally: Meshcheryakov, *A.S. Griboyedov* (see Bibliography), pp.317–8; it is further suggested, p.318, that Griboyedov was the

sleeping liaison of the society to Yermolov. This was all published by Dolgorukov in 1863. Even Nechkina accepts this possibility: p.46; she treats Dolgorukov as 'well-informed'.

5.   When Griboyedov reached the Crimea after Kiev, he resumed his practice of keeping admirable 'Travel Notes'. There are none about Kiev, and all we have of his visit is in his sparse letters at this time to Odoyevsky and Beguichov. None of the Decembrists wrote up his visit later, though they had to answer in detail questions on the content of their talks with Griboyedov: see the 'Proceedings of the Interrogatory Commission', Fomichev and Vatsuro (eds), *Griboyedov* (see Bibliography), p.272; evidence of Muravyov-Apostol: p.278; about Kiev talk: p.282; Griboyedov's own testimony: p.284; the Commission's questions to him: p.286.

6.   Griboyedov's beautiful 'Travel Notes' of the Crimea in Piksanov and Shlyapkin (eds), *Complete Collected Works* (see Bibliography), vol. 3, pp.68–81; also Piksanov's useful topographical notes. Meshcheryakov, *The Life and Activity of Alexander Griboyedov* (see Bibliography), gives a useful timetable: pp.310–3. He also describes Griboyedov's contacts with local Poles, such as Count Olizar, and his meeting at Parthenit with Mickiewicz: pp.72–3. For gypsy music in Crimea: Piksanov and Shlyapkin (eds), *Complete Collected Works* (see Bibliography), vol. 3, p.69.

7.   Balaklava and St George's Monastery: ibid., vol. 3, pp.74–5.

8.   The 'view from the gallery' at Gursuf: ibid., vol. 3, p.72.

9.   His musings about St Vladimir: ibid., vol. 3, p.75. Griboyedov's 'Travel Notes' here are supplemented by two excellent descriptive letters to Beguichov, one from Simferopol in the centre of the Crimea, dated 9 September 1825, vol. 3, pp.177–8, the other from Feodosiya, letter of 12 September 1825, vol. 3, pp.179–81.

10.   Griboyedov's relationship with A.N. Muravyov: Piksanov and Shlyapkin (eds), *Complete Collected Works* (see Bibliography), vol. 1, pp.lx–lxl; also note p.333.

11.   Bonamour summarises usefully the Crimean visit: *A.S. Griboyedov* (see Bibliography), pp.386–7.

12.   'In 1825 my dearest wish': A.N. Muravyov's own memoirs in Fomichev and Vatsuro (eds), *Griboyedov* (see Bibliography), pp.113–4.

13.   'It is time to die': Piksanov and Shlyapkin (eds), *Complete Collected Works* (see Bibliography), vol. 3, p.116, 177–9, 181. The same letter recommends A.I. Odoyevsky to Beguichov: 'Do you recall how I was before leaving for Persia?'

14.   The reference to the Decembrist Orzhritsky in letter of 9 September from Simferopol to Beguichov, in letter to A.A. Bestuzhev from the post station of Ekaterinengrad dated 27 November 1825, N.K. Piksanov and I.A. Shlyapkin (eds), 1917, vol. 3, p.182.

15.   The military situation in the northern Caucasus upon Griboyedov's return there in late 1825: Piksanov and Shlyapkin, *Complete Collected Works* (see Bibliography), p.122–3. Also Potto, *Kavkazskaya* (see

Bibliography), vol. 2, issue 4, p.663–68. For Potto on the situation in 1825, and on the murders of Generals Lissanievich and Grekov: ibid., pp.436–82, 637–9; Dzhambulat's raid: pp.503–32; 'Kabardin Revolt': pp.1025–532; death of Dzhambulat: pp.548–58; for notes on murder of Grekov/Lissanievich: vol. 1, 1887, p.153; also Gammer, *Shamil* (see Bibliography), pp.35–7. Gammer's notes are invaluable for detailed substantiation of details. Baddeley, *The Russian Conquest* (see Bibliography), is also eloquent on Yermolov's genocidal policies in the Northern Caucasus: pp.13, 135–51; General Grekov: pp.147–8; for their joint murder: pp.148–51, 152–4. Shostakovich gives the diplomatic background at the time with Persia: *The Diplomatic Activity* (see Bibliography), pp.71–5, and picks up the story again from 1825 and the end of his leave: see pp.85–7. Also Yenikolopov, *A.S. Griboyedov v Gruzii* (see Bibliography), pp.54–6.

There is a valuable supplement to Potto's account of the situation in the Northern Caucasus in 1825 under the scorched earth policies of Grekov and Lissanievich: pp.527–9; we hear how Yermolov personally ordered Dtchechoyev to be flogged to death, with six strokes each from 1000 men, totalling 6000 strokes: Dubrovin, *Istoriya*, p.529. Grekov reported 'the understanding of the Chechens does not exceed that of cattle': p.529. Gerzel-Aoul murders: pp.532–6. The heroic Imam who slaughtered two Generals with his *kinjal* was Aled Ucharadzhi; these exciting pages are amongst some of the most vivid ever written about the bloody events in the Caucasus under Yermolov.

The gory reduction of Kabarda by Yermolov in 1821–2 with fire and sword carried as far as the fastness of Chegem, gave every opportunity for Caucasian daredevils such as Yakubovich to distinguish themselves, pp.425, 431. In the ranks of the Nijegorodsy's dragoon Regiment: Yakubovich again on p.433.

However much Yermolov put the highlanders to fire and slaughter or massacred their women and children, there was almost always a highlander ready to raise the banner again and lead armed raids against the Russians, such was the case of Dzhambulat in 1824, in Kabarda, pp.503–16.

When Griboyedov returned in 1825 to the Northern Caucasus to find Velyaminov considering how to dominate the mutinous province, we can read the whole complicated war game facing the Generals. Potto describes the situation bluntly: 'The Kabardin Revolt' [bunt], p.533. There is an especial chapter devoted by Potto to the death of 'Dzhambulat Kutchuk', described so vividly by Griboyedov in his letter to Küchelbecker of 27 November: Piksanov and Shlyapkin (eds), *Complete Collected Works* (see Bibliography), vol. 3, pp.183–4. He misspells the youth's name, calling him 'Kutchuk Djankhoto'. Potto describes this cruel and merciless example of Yermolovian imperialism: pp.549–58, and calls this murder a 'tragedy': p.557.

16. The Brigands of the Tchegem: Piksanov and Shlyapkin (eds), *Complete Collected Works* (see Bibliography), vol. 1, pp.15–7, notes, pp.281–3. Also Meshcheryakov, *A.S. Griboyedov* (see Bibliography), about the poem: pp.330–1.

17. Letter to Küchelbecker of 27 November about the hideous massacre of Kuchuk Dzhambot: Piksanov and Shlyapkin (eds), *Complete Collected Works* (see Bibliography), vol. 3, pp.183–5.

18. 'The fight for the mountains': letter to S. Beguichov of 7 December 1825 from Ekaterinengrad in Piksanov and Shlyapkin (eds), *Complete Collected Works* (see Bibliography), vol. 3, pp.185–6. In the same letter he passes judgement on Yermolov, Velyaminov and other generals in distinctly critical terms; despite his reservations, he still wishes to join an armed demonstration against the Chechens.

19. 'I must tell you': letter to Küchelbecker of 27 November 1825 in Piksanov and Shlyapkin (eds), *Complete Collected Works* (see Bibliography), vol. 3, p.183. He wished to describe to him the local garrison life and the success or otherwise of Yermolov's genocidal policies.

20. His dismissal of other generals: letter to Beguichov in Piksanov and Shlyapkin (eds), *Complete Collected Works* (see Bibliography), vol. 3, p.186.

21. Griboyedov's aside that annihilating the unruly highlanders in their mountain fastness is not the problem, it is to find them there: letter to Stepan Beguichov of 7 December 1825 from Ekaterinengrad, Piksanov and Shlyapkin (eds), *Complete Collected Works* (see Bibliography), vol. 3, pp.186–7.

22. The Rebrov warning showing Griboyedov's foreknowledge of events in St Petersburg: Fomichev and Vatsuro (eds), *Griboyedov* (see Bibliography), p.152; also for eye-witness account by N.V. Shimanovsky (one of Yermolov's adjutants): pp.115–21. This gives the dramatic details of the search for his now burnt papers. P.M. Sakhno-Ustimovich was another officer who was a direct eye-witness to the scenes in the Northern Caucasus: pp.122–3. For the pre-arrest details: Nechkina, *A.S. Griboyedov* (see Bibliography), pp.397–9. Also Meshcheryakov, *The Life and Activity of Alexander Griboyedov* (see Bibliography), pp.331–40.

Chapter XVI: The Decembrist Débacle

1. Events in the Senate Square on 15 December 1825: see Mazour, *The First Russian Revolution* (see Bibliography); Barratt, *The Rebel* (see Bibliography); Ulam, *Russia's Failed Revolutions* (see Bibliography).

2. Odoyevsky's exaltation, 'We shall die, oh how gloriously': Meshcheryakov, *The Life and Activity of Alexander Griboyedov* (see Bibliography), pp.124–32; also Barratt, *The Rebel*, p.22.

3. Yermolov instructing the courier to read him the news: Fomichev and Vatsuro (eds), *Griboyedov* (see Bibliography), p.487. For Shimanovsky's

account of those days at Grozny in his memoirs: pp.118–9; it was Feld Jaeger Damish who told the story in particular: p.116.

4. 'Now, stand by for a real stir'. This was said with his fists tightly clenched and a smile: Fomichev and Vatsuro (eds), *Griboyedov* (see Bibliography), pp.116–7.

5. The detailed circumstances of Griboyedov's arrest, presumably as told by him to Zhandr, who later told D.A. Smirnov: Zhandr interview in Fomichev and Vatsuro (eds), *Griboyedov* (see Bibliography), pp.207–9; telling how Yermolov ordered him to burn compromising papers: pp.220–1; Yermolov greatly helping him after arrest: p.244.

6. Shimanovsky's arguments about Moscow with Griboyedov: Fomichev and Vatsuro (eds), *Griboyedov* (see Bibliography), p.130.

7. Yermolov's love of Griboyedov, and extraordinary attentions to him after arrest: D.A. Smirnov interviewing Zhandr in Fomichev and Vatsuro (eds), *Griboyedov* (see Bibliography), p.208; for another witness corroborating this especial treatment, see D. Davydov in Fomichev and Vatsuro (eds), *Griboyedov* (see Bibliography), for 'loving him as a son' and other favours: pp.152–3, V.A. Andreyev reports the same: pp.157–9. Yermolov duly reported to General Dibich, Chief of the Army General Staff that, as ordered, all Griboyedov's papers had been seized: Nechkina, *A.S. Griboyedov* (see Bibliography), p.484; Yermolov's praise for Griboyedov as a useful diplomat is recorded by Veidenbaum, p.602. For a useful account of the arrest: Piksanov and Shlyapkin (eds), *Complete Collected Works* (see Bibliography), vol. 1, pp.lxi–lxv. Also, E. Brimmer's farewells to Griboyedov as he left camp under escort: Fomichev and Vatsuro (eds), *Griboyedov* (see Bibliography), pp.124–5.

8. Griboyedov's admission that quite a few of his papers would have been 'highly dangerous': Zhandr's opinion to D.A. Smirnov in Fomichev and Vatsuro (eds), *Griboyedov* (see Bibliography), pp.221–2. Zhandr uses the phrase 'the papers might have been compromising'.

9. 'Why are you staring at him': D.A. Smirnov interviewing Zhandr in ibid., pp.208–9.

10. The proposed execution of monarchy and large gallows: Mazour, *The First Russian Revolution* (see Bibliography), p.122, on the Decembrist programme based on Pestel's plans: Ulam, *Russia's Failed Revolutions* (see Bibliography), pp.26–7, and for killing Tsar Alexander, p.40.

11. Griboyedov's mother, classifying him disloyally as a 'Carbonari': Nechkina, *A.S. Griboyedov* (see Bibliography), p.502. The source for this was Beguichov: Fomichev and Vatsuro (eds), *Griboyedov* (see Bibliography), p.209.

12. Griboyedov under arrest in the headquarters of the General Staff, St Petersburg: Fomichev, *Griboyedov in Petersburg* (see Bibliography), pp 124–9; also Nechkina, *A.S. Griboyedov* (see Bibliography), pp.404–17, 474–502.

13. Beguichov, speaking about his interrogation and time under arrest: see his interview with Zhandr in Fomichev and Vatsuro (eds),

Griboyedov (see Bibliography), pp.220–2; for Griboyedov's relaxed contacts with Bulgarin: pp.222–3; for help during the interrogation received from Secretary Ivanovsky and Yermolov and Paskievich: Zhandr to Beguichov, p.244; also useful notes, pp.398–9. Zavalyshin, another Decembrist incarcerated in the headquarters of the general staff, also left a memoir: ibid., pp.132–6; he gives the picture of Griboyedov playing the piano at Laredo's tearooms, p.136, and the advice the good Colonel Lyubimov gave him in framing his answers, pp.138–40.

14. The actual text of questions and answers at the commission: Fomichev and Vatsuro (eds), *Griboyedov* (see Bibliography), pp.272–87, including the evidence of other Decembrists relevant to his incrimination. The support Griboyedov received from Bulgarin during his ordeal is fully described by Meshcheryakov in *The Life and Activity of Alexander Griboyedov* (see Bibliography), pp.160–1; Piksanov's biographical sketch describing arrest and later events is still very reliable: Piksanov and Shlyapkin (eds), *Complete Collected Works* (see Bibliography), pp.lxvi–lxviii, lxix.

15. Griboyedov's outright denial to General Levashov that he belonged to the Society: see transcript of the interrogation, Fomichev and Vatsuro (eds), *Griboyedov* (see Bibliography), pp.272–87; also Nechkina, A.S. *Griboyedov* (see Bibliography), pp.493–6.

16. Griboyedov's letter of complaint and personal justification to Tsar Nicholas of 15 February 1826: Piksanov and Shlyapkin (eds), *Complete Collected Works* (see Bibliography), vol. 3, p.189, and later for brief messages to Bulgarin: pp.190–1. For Dibich's reproving minute on his letter to the Tsar: notes, vol. 3, p.137.

17. His remarks to Bulgarin asking for *Childe Harold*: Piksanov and Shlyapkin (eds), *Complete Collected Works* (see Bibliography), vol. 3, p.190; also Meshcheryakov, *A.S. Griboyedov* (see Bibliography), p.161.

18. Griboyedov's comment that he agreed with the conspirators on certain mild reforming propositions, see transcript: Fomichev and Vatsuro (eds), *Griboyedov* (see Bibliography) pp.273–4, 280–1, 283.

19. The Menshikov mission, and the special surveillance the Tsar requested of Yermolov also included Griboyedov by name: Ivanov, 'Griboyedov and Yermolov under surveillance (secret) by Nicholas I' (see Bibliography), pp.241–2.

20. Menshikov's favourable report about Yermolov's troops being loyal: Fomichev, *Griboyedov in Petersburg* (see Bibliography), p.142.

21. The Tsar's decision to release Griboyedov with a certificate of innocence: Nechkina, *A.S. Griboyedov* (see Bibliography), pp.507, 510–2.

Chapter XVII: The Persian Campaign

1. Griboyedov's first audience with Tsar Nicholas, when he was included in a group of 'whitewashed' well-connected possible Decembrists on 2 June 1826: Piksanov and Shlyapkin (eds), *Complete Collected Works* (see Bibliography), vol. 3, p.372; also Nechkina, *A.S. Griboyedov* (see Bibliography), pp.512–3; Meshcheryakov, *The Life and Activity of Alexander Griboyedov* (see Bibliography), pp.373–4.

2. Nicholas's 'pewter eyes': Edward Crankshaw, *The Shadow* (see Bibliography), quoting Herzen, p.41; Herzen especially noted how his eyes were 'without a trace of mercy': pp.40–1, notes, p.395. The future Queen Victoria's letters and de Custine on the same subject: Herzen, *My Past*, (see Bibliography), vol. 1, p.63. For a further readable account of Tsar Nicholas's behaviour during the crisis days of December 1825 and his appearance: Lincoln, *Nicolas I* (see Bibliography), pp.17–67; the future Queen Victoria's comments: p.68; investigating commission: pp.80–5.

3. Griboyedov and Bulgarin: Meshcheryakov, *The Life and Activity of Alexander Griboyedov* (see Bibliography), pp.152–85; also Fomichev and Vatsuro (eds), *Griboyedov* (scc Bibliography), p.421, notes, pp.394–8; Zhandr in his interview with D.A. Smirnov also referred to their relations: p.223. Nechkina lists six lines of references to Bulgarin: Nechkina, *A.S. Griboyedov* (see Bibliography), p.609.

4. Bonamour quotes a useful text on Griboyedov's sombre mood post-release: Bonamour, *A.S. Griboyedov* (see Bibliography), p.391; also Piksanov's biographical sketch: Piksanov and Shlyapkin (eds), *Complete Collected Works* (see Bibliography), vol. 1, p.17; text of the poem 'Liberated' and references to A.I. Odoyevsky: p.18.

5. The new Orthodoxy dictating ideas, and the ideology of Nicholas's reign: Reitblat (ed.), *Vidok Figlyarin* (see Bibliography), p.637. This gives details of Bulgarin's 'Memoir of his friend', from *Son of the Fatherland*, in 1830; for the new Orthodox ideology: Riasanovsky, *Nicholas I* (see Bibliography). The book is especially valuable on the ideas of Pogodin and Shevyrev. For a shorter version of the same issues, see the same author's *A Parting of Ways* (see Bibliography): the beginnings of slavophilism and the almost public worship of Peter the Great and Nicholas I's views of nationalism and nineteenth-century growth are fully described in these two useful studies.

6. Peter Ya. Chaadayev, a contemporary of Griboyedov's in Moscow at the university: Nechkina, *A.S. Griboyedov* (see Bibliography), p.620; Herzen, *My Past* (see Bibliography), rightly makes the connection between the impact of the *Philosophical Letters* on the educated and the reading Russian public, and *Woe from Wit*: vol. 2, pp.261–2. For Ya. Chaadayev's ideas and letters: Tarasov, *Ya. Chaadayev* (see Bibliography). Also in Rouleau (ed.), *Lettres* (see Bibliography).

7. Griboyedov's admission, in his letter of 11 December 1828 to Bulgarin, 'I haven't a single kopek', and notes of 19 March on borrowing 150

roubles from Bulgarin: Piksanov and Shlyapkin (eds), *Complete Collected Works* (see Bibliography), vol. 3, p.192.

8. 'I have stopped being clever': letter to Beguichov recommending him to read Plutarch in Piksanov and Shlyapkin (eds), *Complete Collected Works* (see Bibliography), vol. 3, p.195.

9. Griboyedov's passage across the mountains with D. Davydov: Fomichev and Vatsuro (eds), *Griboyedov* (see Bibliography), pp.144–51; Muravyov-Karsky reports again from Tiflis on their life together there: pp.30, 52–5.

10. The wider background and the causes of the 1826–8 war, somewhat distorted by Russian patriotism and chauvinism: Shostakovich, *The Diplomatic Activity* (see Bibliography), pp.87–93. Shostakovich is frequently inaccurate, accusing the British of fomenting the war: p.87. One of the best modern overviews of the causes of the 1826–8 war is to be found in Atkin, *Russia and Iran* (see Bibliography), pp.66–90, 154, 156–7.

11. The diplomatic background to worsening relations between the new Tsar and Persia, and the detailed account of the failed negotiations between Prince Menshikov, the Tsar's special envoy, and Yermolov: see the reports from the Shah's camp at Sultaniye, as sent back by Henry Willock to the East India Company before John Macdonald's arrival to replace him, in archival references in the Bibliography.

At an early stage in the preparations for war, we find Abbas Mirza playing a peaceful role, writing to Prince Menshikov in July 1826: 'I have directed the Sardar of Erivan not to disturb the peace', IOL/S/P/ enclosure to letter of Willock to the secret committee dated 23 July 1826, p.321, forwarding Abbas Mirza's *ruckum* (decree) to Menshikov. 'I knew the Shah to be peaceable, and the Prince of the same mind', IOL/S/P/P/. Extracts from Willock's journal, 23 July 1826, p.285; 'HRH at heart was determined on peace', p.293.

As well as Willock's journal, we also have McNeill's for evidence of Abbas Mirza's aversion to war, IOL/SP/P, pp.242–3; the Shah asked McNeill, freshly arrived from Tabriz, if Abbas Mirza had collected any troops to make war; the Shah laughed at the negative reply. McNeill replied that the Prince was inclined to peace, p.242. The Shah pointed out that the Prince had dismissed Major Hart (his chief British military instructor and advisor), p.243.

The run-up to the 1826 War, Dubrovin is illuminating on Menshikov's irrelevant mission: pp.594–7. Menshikov's failure to agree policies with Yermolov: p.600. *Casus belli* crystallising around Lake Gokcheh: p.609. Allah Yar Khan's hard-line role as a warmonger: p.609. For Abbas Mirza's order of battle: p.611. Yermolov's desire Persia should open belligerent activities: p.614. Evidence Yermolov's forces were too widely dispersed in garrison and police duties: pp.629–30. In general, it should be said the military evidence marshalled by Dubrovin and Potto about Yermolov's failure to 'pacify' the

Caucasus is a necessary counter-balance to the pro-Yermolov story of Soviet writers such as Shostakovich and Pashuto.

And for Yermolov's naive account of the beginnings of the 1826 war, for which his obstinacy was largely responsible: Yermolov, *Zapiski* (see Bibliography), pp.417–29.

12. The abortive Menshikov mission: Shostakovich, *The Diplomatic Activity* (see Bibliography), pp.92–3.

13. For an excellent account of the preliminaries leading to the 1826 war and the Persian incursions under Abbas Mirza, and Yermolov's curious failure to protect Georgia: Baddeley, *The Russian Conquest* (see Bibliography), pp.152–6.

14. Meshcheryakov, *The Life and Activity of Alexander Griboyedov* (see Bibliography), describes Griboyedov's return to the Caucasus on 9 December 1826: pp.388–90. Griboyedov described very frankly his difficulties in serving two masters, Paskievich and Yermolov: Fomichev and Vatsuro (eds), *Griboyedov* (see Bibliography), vol. 3, p.195; by serving Paskievich, General Davydov later accused him of plain disloyalty to his original patron, Yermolov: pp.152–4; also Popova, *Griboyedov-diplomat* (see Bibliography), pp.65–97.

In 1826, we can trace the events affecting Paskievich's takeover of military and supreme power from Yermolov, in his daily Journal covering August to 1 September 1826. Paskievich was to receive a most useful despatch from Prince Menshikov detailing the Persian Order of Battle sent from Tiflis on 12 September: pp.57–62. The journal continues from September to November 1826, Paskievich noting the numerous supply problems for his soldiers caused by General Madatov. We must assume that Yermolov would not have disapproved of Madatov's covert sabotage in his favour. Madatov traduced Yermolov and blamed Russian officials' acts for the disaffection in the province of Elizavetpol: p.87. After his victory there, essential to check the Persians, he continued to have supply problems with Madatov: p.89.

Vol. 3 includes in full the personal and other letters of General Dibich sent to intervene and facilitate Paskievich's takeover of power: p.212. Dibich reports Yermolov's illegitimate children as a cause of his concern, and the Tsar authorises Paskievich to sack Madatov and Velyaminov and any others he considered 'nuisibles': p.216. On p.242 there is Nesselrode's announcement of the arrival of Obreskov as Griboyedov's immediate diplomatic superior; Paskievich writes triumphantly from the walls of Erivan: pp.256–61. Shcherbatov deals with the armistice talks at Karaziadin with Mirza Saleh's earlier approach: p.254.

15. Griboyedov's impertinent comments about Paskievich compared to Yermolov: D. Davydov in Fomichev and Vatsuro (eds), *Griboyedov* (see Bibliography), pp.153–4, notes, p.382.

16. Paskievich's career and role as a war hero from 1812 and his having been the new Tsar's former commander of the Guards Division: see

the biography of him by Shcherbatov, *General-Fel'dmarshal* (see Bibliography). For evidence, Nicholas called Paskievich 'my father, my commanding officer', a relationship begun in Paris in 1814: Nechkina, *A.S. Griboyedov* (see Bibliography), pp.509–14. The following books are also relevant: Monteith, *Kars and Erzerum* (see Bibliography); Fowler, *Three Years in Persia* (see Bibliography); Fraser, *An Historical and Descriptive Account of Persia* (see Bibliography) are all relevant contemporaries. Also Atkin, *Russia and Iran* (see Bibliography), p.181.

The final major work of history relevant to Griboyedov's diplomatic and paramilitary career is Shcherbatov's *General-Fel'dmarshal* (see Bibliography). This touches on Griboyedov's life at a number of essential points, notably in vols 2 and 3, and has the importance of being based on entirely original and genuine documents – original sources, we may say, and as such bearing the imprint of being quasi-archival, though not held in a State Archive, but made available to Shcherbatov from Paskievich's personal family archives in the nineteenth century.

Vol. 2 opens with Yermolov's final year of power in the Caucasus in 1826, and his residual attitudes towards Persia. Paskievich and Griboyedov would inherit these prejudices, mostly contrary to Russia's true interests.

17. Paskievich about Yermolov, laying blame on him for the desperation that led Persia to war: Baddeley, *The Russian Conquest* (see Bibliography), p.159; Yermolov's departure: pp.160–1.

18. 'With whom was buried all my good fortune': ibid., p.160.

19. 'Factotum': Shostakovich, *The Diplomatic Activity* (see Bibliography), pp.99, 120.

20. 'Do not expect any poetry from me': letter to Bulgarin from Tiflis, 16 April, 1826 in Fomichev and Vatsuro (eds), *Griboyedov* (see Bibliography), pp.198–9.

21. 'What he says becomes holy writ', and for his essential diplomatic role advising Paskievich: Shostakovich, *The Diplomatic Activity* (see Bibliography), pp.96–9, 100–1, 120.

22. Paskievich's successful campaign to repel the Persians, including the capture of Abbas Abad and the intervening khanates, and finally the storming of Erivan and the occupation of Armenia: Baddeley, *The Russian Conquest* (see Bibliography), pp.164–90. For Griboyedov's diplomatic contribution: Popova, *Griboyedov-diplomat* (see Bibliography), pp.76–97, 99–103. Yenikolopov covers the ground too, in *A.S. Griboyedov v Gruzii* (see Bibliography), pp.63–9. Davydov, as a fellow fighter in the campaign, has occasional comments: Fomichev and Vatsuro (eds), *Griboyedov* (see Bibliography), pp.154–6. Shostakovich is also useful: *The Diplomatic Activity* (see Bibliography), pp.115–9, 121–2. Griboyedov fully described the Erivan campaign in his resumed 'Travel Notes': Piksanov and Shlyapkin (eds), *Complete Collected Works* (see Bibliography), vol. 3, pp.82–7. He was present at

all key moments, i.e. the visit to the Monastery of Etchmiadzin, p.86; the taking of Nakhichevan, p.87; the fall of Abbas Abad, p.87; the crossing of the Araxes by 2000 cavalry, p.88.

Vol. 3 of Potto published in 1888 describes especially the Russo–Persian War of 1826–8, pp.361–72. There is a full account of the first round of talks with Mirza Saleh, and then later at Karaziadin. The remaining chapters are explicit and detail the capture of Erivan and the heroic role of General Krasovsky at Ushakan, pp.452–7, 466–77. Throughout this volume there are the most useful city and fortress plans of Erivan, p.503, and Chapter 30 describes the fall of Erivan. Potto continues with the fall of Tabriz: Chapter 31 onwards. He acknowledges how useful British mediation proved to be on p.551, and describes Dr McNeill personally: p.557. He states openly that McNeill had been 'an opponent of the war' on p.557, thus contradicting Shostakovich's distortions. He also delineates clearly the role of Volkhovsky in the negotiations at Deh Kurgan: pp.561–9. For General Sukhtelen's capture of Ardebil and the shrines of Sheikh Seffi ed-Din with its precious manuscripts see pp.574–8, and for Sukhtelen's cunning measures to allay Persian suspicions see pp.576–9. Potto discusses the Treaty of Turkmanchai: pp.578–601. He describes the eagerness of Macdonald and the British mission to receive Russian orders for their essential contribution: pp.592–3. Finally, it should be recorded, Potto devotes a whole chapter to Griboyedov's final mission and death: vol. 3, pp.603–35. This also includes a useful biographical summary.

23. 'All this makes life more cheerful': letter to Akhverdova in Piksanov and Shlyapkin (eds), *Complete Collected Works* (see Bibliography), p.200.

Chapter XVIII: Armistice Negotiations

1. Paskievich's brusque reprimand, 'Come! Come! Let us have no shuffling': Mirza Saleh's previously unpublished report, India Office Library, despatch No. 21 of 20 August 1827, p.621, IOL, P&S/9186, pp.589–96. Mirza Saleh was an exceptionally interesting and favoured man. In the 1810s, Abbas Mirza, with a long-term plan for the future of building trust and confidence between Persia and Britain, had selected two groups of young Persians of promise to visit England to acquire knowledge in a number of areas. In 1815, one such group was formed, and Colonel d'Arcy of the Royal Artillery was asked to arrange studies in England for five of them, including Mirza Saleh Shirazi. Described as a 'secretary', he was expected to learn English and other languages with a view to becoming a government translator on return. Mirza Saleh eventually applied himself to English, French, Latin, natural philosophy and printing; he kept a diary whilst in England, which reveals how Colonel d'Arcy treated his group as servants or prisoners. Sir John Malcolm

fortunately befriended him, and Saleh travelled to Oxford, Bristol and Salisbury. He called England the *vilayet-i-azadi* ('land of freedom'). On his return from Tabriz, he set up a printing press and was to publish Persia's first newspaper in Tehran in 1836.

In 1822, Mirza Saleh returned to London, entrusted with diplomatic tasks of some delicacy by Abbas Mirza. On this occasion, he stayed for ten months, being sent to buy arms and stores. He was also to secure the arrears of Britain's subsidy to Persia, and to get Captain Willock replaced by an ambassador. Canning agreed about the subsidies being overdue, and in 1823 Mirza Saleh returned with Canning's decision: the Indian Government would be appointing a 'new arrangement of the Mission to Persia'. The Indian nominee would be Colonel John Kinneir Macdonald of the 24th Madras Infantry, who would arrive in 1826.

Mirza Saleh had proved himself an able young negotiator on vital issues for the Persians, and he had dealings with the essential decision-makers most influential in Anglo–Persian relations, such as Sir John Malcolm and the Foreign Secretary, Canning. On leaving, he wrote to the Foreign Office, 'Having been myself educated in England and very much attracted by your nation and having always spoken warmly in private of it...'. He returned to Persia via St Petersburg. For the background on Mirza Saleh: Wright, *The English amongst the Persians* (see Bibliography), notably pp.74–5, 77, 80–1, 84–5.

Vol. 3 of Shcherbatov relates directly to Griboyedov's diplomatic activity supporting Paskievich's military successes. Thus in Chapter 1 we have the fall of Tabriz captured by Prince Eristov, the crystallising of peace talks and brief given to Obreskov on p.3 – the place-name of Deh Kurgan first appears on p.26. Instructions to Obreskov: pp.30–7; these pages also cover the courteous offer of mediation of Macdonald and the British mission, rejected as impertinent by the Russians. We find Allah Yar Khan, despite his craven surrender of Tabriz, still plays a role as an intermediary to the Shah; he was released to go to Tehran: p.39. Ch. 2 describes the capture of Ardebil and its precious library as war-loot by General Sukhtelen: pp.57, 62, 67, 69. The work of Obreskov and Griboyedov is cited: p.51; the role of McNeill is also highlighted in bringing the Shah's moneys: pp.51, 54–6. Negotiations between Obreskov and Griboyedov are detailed on p.51; also those with Abul Hassan Khan, the Persian Foreign Minister: pp.56–7, 61. Final round of talks at Turkmanchai: pp.73,75–8, from Paskievich's diary of events, show very clearly the leading role played by Macdonald and McNeill in convincing Abbas Mirza and Abul Hassan Khan (Foreign Minister) as to the best deal that Griboyedov and Paskievich would give them: pp.75–7. Final terms at Turkmanchai, 7 February: pp.78, 82. One-hundred-and-one-gun salute for peace; the problem of resettling 80,000 Armenians: p.91. Role of British guaranteeing some of Abbas Mirza's payments of the indemnity: pp.93–5. Griboyedov's mission to St Petersburg with the Treaty: p 95.

In his Despatch No. 21 of 20 August 1827, pp.597–637, Lieutenant-Colonel John Macdonald enclosed the full translation of the journal kept by Mirza Saleh during his late mission to the Russian headquarters. Macdonald sent this to the Secret Committee of the Court of Directors in London, IOL/S P/9/96. The despatch is endorsed 'Secret and Political 1119/1'; received from Foreign Office 8 October 1827, read 9 October 1827. Macdonald mentions that 'Mirza Saleh was received by Paskievich's first aide de camp (no name given) apart from the ADC. There was Mr Gribaodoff [sic], Hamburger [sic] and Prince Dolgoruki, of whom I had previously known at Tabreez.' Shostakovich was aware of the earlier round of talks with Mirza Saleh, before Griboyedov and not Obreskov went officially to Karaziadin: Shostakovich, *The Diplomatic Activity* (see Bibliography), pp.123–4, also pp.126–7, 128–9.

2. Griboyedov's armistice negotiations at Karaziadin on behalf of Paskievich, and his carefully drafted report for Paskievich to forward to the Tsar and Nesselrode: Shostakovich, *The Diplomatic Activity* (see Bibliography), p.123, also p.126; for full text of report: Piksanov and Shlyapkin (eds), *Complete Collected Works* (see Bibliography), vol. 3, pp.594–60.

3. 'I left the Persian camp': ibid., vol. 3, p.265. References to his talks with the different Persians, including Abbas Mirza, are in the full *compte-rendu* and Report to Paskievich: pp.252–67. Piksanov gives a useful note about this draft document: Piksanov and Shlyapkin, *Complete Collected Works* (see Bibliography), p.364.

Chapter XIX: The Treaty of Turkmanchai

1. Capture of Erivan and the campaign: Baddeley, *The Russian Conquest* (see Bibliography), pp.165–70, 172–4. Also Potto, *Kavkazskaya* (see Bibliography), vol. 3, pp.437, 496–519.

2. 'I suddenly saw old Simonich': letter to Madame Akhverdova of 3 October 1827, written from Erivan immediately after the Te Deum to offer thanks for the victory in Piksanov and Shlyapkin (eds), *Complete Collected Works* (see Bibliography), vol. 3, pp.204–5.

3. Yenikolopov describes the impromptu performance of *Woe from Wit*: Yenikopolov, *A.S. Griboyedov v Gruzii* (see Bibliography), pp.94–5. Also Shostakovich, *The Diplomatic Activity* (see Bibliography), pp.123–9. Bonamour summarises these exciting times in Griboyedov's life: Bonamour, *A.S. Griboyedov* (see Bibliography), pp.393–4.

4. Griboyedov's theory of willpower enabling one to overcome fear as expressed to Polevoi: Fomichev and Vatsuro (eds), *Griboyedov* (see Bibliography), pp.185–6; reference to Prince Suvorov during recent Persian campaign: p.162.

5. 'The matter was decided': Potto, *Kavkazskaya* (see Bibliography), vol. 3, pp.321–544; also Baddeley, *The Russian Conquest* (see Bibliography), pp.172–4.

6. 'Europe is not Katerina Akakiyevna': Fomichev and Vatsuro (eds), *Griboyedov* (see Bibliography), quoting E.V. Brimmer, pp.124–5.

7. The brilliance of the winter season and the numerous receptions given either by the triumphant Russians, or the rather despondent and worried British, is well attested by contemporaries, such as Fowler, *Three Years in Persia* (see Bibliography) and Monteith, *Kars and Erzerum* (see Bibliography).

8. On the peace talks at Deh Kurgan (Dei-Kargan) and finally at Turkmanchai (villages near Tabriz), the most relevant account to follow is that of McNeill, whose crucial contribution was in squeezing out of Fath Ali Shah the minimum number of kurors (as part of the Russian indemnity): Macalister, *Memoir* (see Bibliography). His book describes very comprehensively the days immediately before the war in 1826, pp.72–98, including references to the 'almost universal disaffection' of the subjects of Russia in the provinces ceded to Russia by the Treaty of Gulistan, p.86. Pages 92–101 show very clearly the trouble McNeill had in extracting every kuror from the Shah. The embarrassing mission of Colonel Volkhovsky and the help McNeill gave him is chronicled at pp.102–3. The break-up of the conference at Deh Kurgan is at pp.104–5; the British double-cross of Persia on payment of their annual subsidy is at pp.106–9.

9. The cynical negotiation whereby Macdonald obtained the abrogation of terms in the Treaty of Tehran still unacceptable to the British, Macalister, *Memoir* (see Bibliography), pp.106–120.

10. A useful explanation of Macdonald's help to Abbas Mirza in providing him with a further 200,000 tomans in return for abandoning the third and fourth articles of the Treaty of Tehran is provided in Watson's *A History of Persia* (see Bibliography), pp.242–3.

11. A nationalistic and patriotic account of Turkmanchai and Russia's imperialist gains, and in detail Griboyedov's hardworking contribution: Shostakovich, *The Diplomatic Activity* (see Bibliography), pp.134–157.

12. 'The General has promised': letter of 21 January 1828 to George Swinton at the Political Department, Fort William, pp.107–8, IOL/S/P/9/88/ Letter to the Secret Committee of the East India Company.

13. Talks with Abbas Mirza on the surrender of Ardebil after Paskievich and Griboyedov called off the Armistice at Deh Kurgan in early January 1828: Dubrovin, *Istoriya* (see Bibliography), vol. 3, p.62; for Sukhtelen's capture of Ardebil on 25 January: pp.67–8. Potto also covers the capture of the Province of Urmia and Ardebil by Sukhtelen: Potto, *Kavkazskaya* (see Bibliography), pp.571–2; for the mosque of Sheikh Seffi ed-Din: pp.575–7.

14. 'For the love of Allah': Fomichev, *Griboyedov in Petersburg* (see Bibliography), p.151.

15. 'Where they are all illiterate', Griboyedov's advice to Paskievich of 30 October 1828 from Tabriz by letter: Piksanov and Shlyapkin (eds), *Complete Collected Works* (see Bibliography), vol. 3, p.227.

16. 'The man of the greatest influence at court', McNeill's notes on various courtiers: quoted in Macalister, *Memoir* (see Bibliography), p.75.

17. Macdonald's judgements on the Treaty of Turkmanchai: Lang, 'Griboycdov's last years in Persia' (see Bibliography); Macdonald to the Indian political department and, by the same token, to George Swinton, No. 84 of 14 February 1828, IOL S/P/P 249-26, p.322.

18. Paskievich's tribute to Griboyedov's handling during the negotiations quoted in Paskievich's letter to Nesselrode: Shcherbatov, *General-Fel'dmarshal* (see Bibliography), vol. 3, p.95. Also Shostakovich, *The Diplomatic Activity* (see Bibliography), pp.146–7; these references cover Paskievich's important letter; again at pp.150, 154, 158–9.

Paskievich's warm personal recommendation of Griboyedov to the Tsar as 'a person who was exceptionally reliable to me on political questions; I am obliged to him for the principle we should not sign until receiving a goodly sum of the Indemnity in advance'. 'Subsequent events showed without this, we would never have achieved our stated aims': report of 11 February 1828 from the private family archives of the Paskievichco, p.05.

Paskievich also sent with Griboyedov a letter to the Grand Duke Michael Pavlovich, in it he admitted to a certain exhaustion upon successful conclusion of the campaign: p.96. Excitement in St Petersburg at the first victory of arms of the new reign was very high, as we learn from Benckendorff's letter to Prince Vorontsov in Odessa: p.97. Essential material connected with Griboyedov's murder and Paskievich's response to the party line preached by Nesselrode from St Petersburg, dictated largely by the need not to upset the British, in the light of general Middle Eastern situation and Russia's war with Turkey: p.13.

Chapter XX: A Hero's Return

1. Griboyedov's tactlessness in calling on Yermolov in disgraced semi-exile in Orel: Yermolov was visited by Pushkin in 1827, as we know from Pushkin, *A Journey* (see Bibliography).

2. Yuri Tynianov's 'factional' inventions on the Yermolov–Griboyedov dialogue: *The Death of the Vazir Mukhtar*, translated into English as *Death and Diplomacy* (see Bibliography).

3. Confirmation that Griboyedov's affairs and those of his mother were in a messy and confused state: Beguichov in Fomichev and Vatsuro (eds), *Griboyedov* (see Bibliography), p.30. Griboyedov linked his demand to Paskievich for a purely financial reward chiefly to his need to bail out his mother.

4. Griboyedov's triumphant reception with the Treaty in St Petersburg: Piksanov and Shlyapkin (eds), *Complete Collected Works* (see Bibliography), biographical sketch, vol 3, pp.lxxix–xi. Also Fomichev,

Griboyedov in Petersburg (see Bibliography), p.143. For Tynianov's account of Griboyedov's formal reception by the Foreign Minister and the Tsar at the Winter Palace with the Treaty: Tynianov, *Death and Diplomacy* (see Bibliography), pp.37–43. Evelyn Harden in her PhD thesis, 'Truth and Design' (see Bibliography), describes very fully Griboyedov's last stay in St Petersburg, based on Tynianov's factional account.

5. Griboyedov's pecuniary rewards and knighthood of St Anne (second class): Popova, *Griboyedov-diplomat* (see Bibliography), pp.103–4.

6. 'Without doubt he [Griboyedov] was the chief architect of the Peace': Fomichev and Vatsuro (eds), *Griboyedov* (see Bibliography), p.89. For Griboyedov's protestation that he was suited only to a life of study ('kabinetnaya jisn'): letter to Madame Akhverdova in Piksanov and Shlyapkin (eds), *Complete Collected Works* (see Bibliography), vol. 3, p.205; Piksanov biographical sketch, vol. 1, lxxxll.

7. Griboyedov's fearless and morally courageous request, in his letter of 3 December 1838 from Tabriz to Paskievich, to intervene for Odoyevsky: Piksanov and Shlyapkin (eds), *Complete Collected Works* (see Bibliography), vol. 3, pp.238–42; there is a postscript entitled 'the most important'. As Piksanov notes drily, this request remained without result: p.361. Griboyedov also intervened with Paskievich on behalf of Bestuzhev: notes, pp.367–8. The occasion that made the Tsar blanch was when Nicholas received Griboyedov in audience a second time, to receive the Treaty of Turkmanchai; we have no record of this conversation, but predictably Nechkina makes the case; for 1828 interview: Nechkina, *A.S. Griboyedov* (see Bibliography), p.528.

8. 'He is the cleverest man in Russia', Ksenofont Polevoi in March 1828: Fomichev and Vatsuro (eds), *Griboyedov* (see Bibliography), p.160. His report of his talks with Griboyedov is of overwhelming interest, recording the latter's views on music, Mozart's *Magic Flute*, and Shakespeare: pp.160–67.

9. We hear from Prince Vyazemsky how Griboyedov joined the elite of Russian literature at Princess Laval's to hear Pushkin read his *Boris Godunov* on 17 May: Fomichev and Vatsuro (eds), *Griboyedov* (see Bibliography), p.91; also note, p.362.

10. The abortive plan to visit London: ibid., pp.161–2.

11. Vyazemsky, in his letter to his wife on the Georgian love song: ibid., notes, p.364. Also Piksanov and Shlyapkin (eds), *Complete Collected Works* (see Bibliography), biographical sketch, vol. 1, p.lxxxiv.

12. The reading of *The Georgian Night*: Fomichev and Vatsuro (eds), *Complete Collected Works* (see Bibliography), pp.394–8. Polevoi recalling the reading at Grech's: p.161. For the text of *The Georgian Night*: ibid., vol. 1, pp.266, notes, p.302. Bulgarin records the text, and there is a glancing reference to it by Beguichov, as mentioned by Griboyedov during his last visit to him on the way south in 1828. Piksanov dates its inspiration to 1827, when Griboyedov joined Paskievich on the Erivan campaign: ibid., vol. 1, pp.230–3, 302–3; alternative versions

are on pp.271–2. Nechkina interprets the tragedy as an anti-serfdom declaration, in particular serfdom as practised feudally in Georgia; for the full text of Bulgarin: Nechkina, *A.S. Griboyedov* (see Bibliography), pp.307–8. There are some sharp criticisms of Piksanov's moderate position about Griboyedov denouncing serfdom somewhat tepidly: pp.309–10. All references to Piksanov's position are in notes, p.590. Further comments from Nechkina on this short creative draft: *A.S. Griboyedov* (see Bibliography), pp.531–2. Fomichev reminds us that Griboyedov gave a reading from *The Georgian Night* at Svinin's dinner party: pp.157–60; Yazykov wrote praising it to his brother in Derpt: Fomichev and Vatsuro (eds), *Griboyedov* (see Bibliography), p.159.

13. For the concept of Griboyedov's Russo–Transcaucasian Trading Company, to give Georgia something of an East India Company, there is considerable controversy and a weighty literature: in the context of the project being for or against Decembrist principles in its proposals for the use of indentured serf labour, equivalent, in the view of some, to slave labour in the American colonies: Tynianov, *Death and Diplomacy* (see Bibliography), pp.537–8, who introduces a fictional scene in which Griboyedov tries to sell the project prematurely to the Ministry, in the shape of K.K. Rodofinikin, as a good future investment for him: Nechkina, *A.S. Griboyedov* (see Bibliography). The keenest scholarship about this issue is in an article and analysis by Malshinski, who shows how General Paskievich gave the proposal draft, edited jointly by Griboyedov and a Pole, the Civil Governor of Tiflis, Zavileisky, to Colonel Burtsov. Burtsov was a former Decembrist on Paskievich's staff who recommended against the project on the grounds that it would create an empire within the state and circumscribe Paskievich's authority in an unacceptable way, and furthermore increase serfdom and slave labour. There is also useful evidence from Muravyov-Karsky about the project: Fomichev and Vatsuro (eds), *Griboyedov* (see Bibliography), pp.66–7, also notes, pp.355–6. The two articles by Malshinski and later Markova, 'Noviye materialy' (see Bibliography), tell the Russian-reading scholar almost all he should know about this question, except for the very pertinent comments of Piksanov in his *Griboyedov: Researches*. There are references to Markova's work in Nechkina, *A.S. Griboyedov* (see Bibliography), notes, p.606. Nechkina also summarises the full debate: pp.539–45. Malshinski wrote in 1891 on the issues: p.606, reference no. 704. Yenikolopov also describes the issues in *A.S. Griboyedov v Gruzii* (see Bibliography), pp.125–8. Popova comments: *Griboyedov-diplomat* (see Bibliography), p.135.

14. Griboyedov's self-drafted instructions, and Rodofinikin's amending minutes are neatly shown together by Pashuto, 'Diplomaticheskaya deyatel'nost' A.S. Griboyedova' (see Bibliography). These texts were also published in *Russkaya Starina* (1874).

15. 'The Minister [Nesselrode] first proposed': Beguichov in Fomichev and Vatsuro (eds), *Griboyedov* (see Bibliography), pp.30–1. Yenikolopov

deals with this period of Griboyedov's life: Yenikopolov, *A.S. Griboyedov v Gruzii* (see Bibliography), pp.107–9. For the fullest and best account of Griboyedov's nomination as Resident Minister Plenipotentiary in Persia: Popova, *Griboyedov-diplomat* (see Bibliography), pp.108–13. Griboyedov's draft for his own terms of reference as Resident Minister Plenipotentiary and Resident in Persia, as corrected by his Under-Secretary K.K. Rodofinikin, are given in Piksanov and Shlyapkin (eds), *Complete Collected Works* (see Bibliography), vol. 3, pp.271–8, notes, p.365. The improved version was approved by the Ministry in final form.

16. The choice of Ivan Mal'tzov as First Secretary of the mission on the advice of Sobolevsky was, as Shostakovich tells us, largely dictated by the wealth of his father, who was a leading shareholder of the American–Russian company, which in Griboyedov's mind may have been a model for his Russian–Transcaucasian Trading Company; 'the nomination of Mal'tzov as Secretary may have been fully consistent with the idea of promoting the future Transcaucasian trading empire': Shostakovich, *The Diplomatic Activity* (see Bibliography), p.163. More details are given of Mal'tzov's later career in Fomichev and Vatsuro (eds), *Griboyedov* (see Bibliography), p.412. In old age, Mal'tzov was to become a senior member of the Foreign Ministry.

    There is some interesting marginal information on Ivan Mal'tzov from the gossipy memoirs of a well-known bluestocking, Smirnova-Rosset, later also a contemporary of Lermontov, the Empress's 'lady-in-waiting' or 'Freiling'. She tells of a card party where a certain Serafina Sterich presented Mal'tzov to her, suggesting that she should marry him as he was very rich; 'he looked at me with lovesick silly eyes but otherwise produced no impression. Yegermeister also told me he was mean'. She adds the detail that Griboyedov requested his services from Nesselrode; Nesselrode agreed, saying 'I have retained young Kiselyov for an important Embassy', e.g. Paris; she then castigated Mal'tzov for not dying gallantly like Griboyedov, but hiding himself: Smirnova-Rosset, *Autobiography* (see Bibliography), p.255.

17. Dr Malmberg being seconded from the Erivan military hospital: Fomichev and Vatsuro (eds), *Griboyedov* (see Bibliography), p.390. For the presents: Meshcheryakov, *The Life and Activity of Alexander Griboyedov* (see Bibliography), p.406.

18. The story of Griboyedov relying on Bulgarin for the safe investment of his Turkmanchai prize money: article by Piksanov, 'The altercation between Bulgarin and Griboyedov's mother' (see Bibliography), pp.715–7.

19. His dedication of *Woe from Wit* to Bulgarin before leaving St Petersburg: Fomichev and Vatsuro (eds), *Griboyedov* (see Bibliography), p.31.

20. Zhandr's final lunch party when Griboyedov left St Petersburg: ibid., pp.224–5. Piksanov quoting Zhandr: Piksanov and Shlyapkin (eds), *Complete Collected Works* (see Bibliography), vol. 1, biographical sketch, pp.lxxxiv–v.

21. Griboyedov's final farewell to Stepan Beguichov: Fomichev and Vatsuro (eds), *Griboyedov* (see Bibliography), p.31.
22. 'Nothing but flies, dust and heat': letter to F.V. Bulgarin of 27 June 1828 in Piksanov and Shlyapkin (eds), *Complete Collected Works* (see Bibliography), vol. 3, p.212.

Chapter XXI: Courtship and Marriage

1. 'The further I am from Petersburg': letter of 12 June 1828 from Moscow to Bulgarin in Piksanov and Shlyapkin (eds), *Complete Collected Works* (see Bibliography), vol. 3, p.209. The same letter referred to his 'inordinate gratitude to Nicholas I', being so overwhelming that he could never dare in any respect to be disrespectful to him, or ungrateful: p.209.
2. The grand state which Griboyedov kept as Minister, offering champagne and pineapple, and the services of a good chef and diary: letters of Karl Adelung, the junior secretary attached to the mission in Fomichev and Vatsuro, *Griboyedov* (see Bibliography), pp.170–7.
3. Nina Chavchavadze's suitors before Griboyedov, and in particular Senyavin's obsessive suit, thinking about her every day: V.F. Shubin, 'Nina Chavchavadze in the letters of contemporaries' in Fomichev (ed.), *A.S. Griboyedov, Materialy k biografii* (see Bibliography), pp.162–8, 172–4; his letter to Bulgarin: pp.219–20. He unromantically compared Nina to Bulgarin's German wife Lenotchka, and called Nina 'a second volume, Lyenotchka'.
4. Griboyedov's delight and joy at receiving permission to get married from his future father-in-law, Prince Alexander Chavchavadze: letter to Bulgarin of 24 June 1828 written from a bivouac near Kasanchi on the Turkish frontier in Piksanov and Shlyapkin (eds), *Complete Collected Works* (see Bibliography), vol. 3, p.221. His last comment is 'I shall slave for the Tsar, to feed my children': p.221.
5. For Muravyov's criticisms of the plan for the Transcaucasian Trading Company: Fomichev and Vatsuro (eds), *Griboyedov* (see Bibliography), pp.66–7. Muravyov shows Griboyedov's self-interest in proposing to make himself a director of the company: p.355. Markova's essay about the alleged critical comments by the Decembrist Colonel Burtsov: these were not by Burtsov, but by an establishment General, namely Lt General M.A. Zhukovsky, a Quartermaster-general on Paskievich's staff, thus removing much of Nechkina's dismay at Griboyedov being accused by a Decembrist of promoting serfdom; all this is set out in Nechkina, *A.S Griboyedov* (see Bibliography), p.539.
6. 'Our Sovereign could not make a better choice': Piksanov and Shlyapkin (eds), *Complete Collected Works* (see Bibliography), vol. 3, p.69.
7. Griboyedov's feverish paroxysms just before the wedding and wedding celebrations: Fomichev and Vatsuro (eds), *Griboyedov* (see Bibliography), pp.180–2.

8. 'All Tiflis loves and cherishes the groom and bride': Adelung, 'Letters to his Father' in ibid., pp.177–9.

9. 'Little Mannikin': letter to Bulgarin (nicknamed here 'Pikulo Tchelovekulo'), 12 June 1828 in Piksanov and Shlyapkin (eds), *Complete Collected Works* (see Bibliography), p.209.

10. The description of Ninushka as playful and cheerful: letter to Miklashevich of 17 September from Etchmiadzin in Piksanov and Shlyapkin (eds), *Complete Collected Works* (see Bibliography), vol. 3, pp.226–7.

11. 'Disgusting': Adelung's letters to his father in Fomichev and Vatsuro (eds), *Griboyedov* (see Bibliography), p.164.

12. 'There was no trace of a Georgian in him': ibid., p.185.

13. 'He may well imagine': letter to Amburgherr of August 1828 in Piksanov and Shlyapkin (eds), *Complete Collected Works* (see Bibliography), vol. 3, p.223; he reported again on the Armenian issue to Rodofinikin: letter of 30 October 1828 from Tabriz in vol. 3, p.238–9. Griboyedov hoped McNeill would actively support his financial pressure on the Shah. When he got to Tehran, the Shah had sent McNeill packing.

14. Griboyedov's efforts to extract the eighth kuror from the Shah, for the background and the desperate measures to which Abbas Mirza was reduced, even to unsewing his concubines' silver buttons: Shostakovich, *The Diplomatic Activity* (see Bibliography), pp.200–1.

15. Macdonald's useful role underwriting part of the payment is given credit by Shostakovich, ibid., pp.202–3. More on this issue in Yenikolopov, *A.S. Griboyedov v Gruzii* (see Bibliography), pp.115–6.

16. Whilst living on a shoestring in Tabriz, Griboyedov found himself driven to distraction by the constant invasion of Armenians in his embassy on the move to Georgia, officially being legally repatriated. Yenikolopov, ibid., gives the details, pp.118.

17. 'We are so poorly lodged': Griboyedov's letter of complaint to Count Nesselrode of 9 December 1828 in a special article in *Russkaya Literatura*, no 3 (1985). The author is grateful to Evgeny Tsymbal, who sent an offprint of this publication. Other letters in the same article dated earlier in October detail the tortuous course of obtaining the eighth kuror.

18. Griboyedov's complaint about cholera and the plague raging at the time: letter to Rodofinikin of 30 October 1828 from Tabriz in Piksanov and Shlyapkin (eds), *Complete Collected Works* (see Bibliography), vol. 3, pp.228–9.

19. 'A swine': letter to Amburgherr of 20 September in ibid., p.225. He even wrote 'he is a swine and no more' in a letter to Paskievich himself, dated 3 December from Tabriz: ibid., p.239. His fury was triggered by being denied one month's salary.

20. 'After a fretful and alarming day': letter to Varvara Miklashevich from Tabriz of 3 December 1828 in ibid., p.240.

21. 'Hanging in the Malmaison Gallery': Griboyedov's letter to V. Miklashevich dated 3 December from Tabriz in ibid., p.238. The shepherdess was an idealised version of the Virgin Mary.

22. 'I have been married for two months': letter to K.K. Rodofinikin of 30 September 1828 from Tabriz in ibid., pp.227–8.

23. 'Perfectly poisonous letter': ibid., p.240.

24. Macdonald's letter to the Foreign Office confirming the excellent relations at the time between Britain and Russia: Lang, 'Griboyedov's last years in Persia' (see Bibliography), p.323, quoting Macdonald's Government letter of 18 October 1828.

25. Macdonald, after Griboyedov's murder, and regretting that he had not accompanied him to Tehran (see his despatch to George Swinton of 19 February 1829) sought an audience with Abbas Mirza and his Kaimakam, both of whom wanted to know how to limit the damage after the murders: Arinshtein 'Proceedings at Khmelita' in Fomichev (ed.), *A.S.Griboyedov, Materialy k biografii* (see Bibliography). For Macdonald's regrets: Arinshtein in ibid., pp.119, 198.

Chapter XXII: Tabriz to Tehran

1. For the full text of the 'Mehmendar's Narrative': a Russian translation of it is given in Fomichev and Vatsuro (eds), *Griboyedov* (see Bibliography), pp.303–29. Whatever doubts Soviet nationalist scholars entertain concerning the validity of the text, Fraser, the leading Anglo–Persian expert and scholar of the time, had none, as we know from his letter of 30 June to the editors of the magazine: 'As to its authority it bears the stamp of that in every line, nor do I doubt that it has originated in something of the sort which it purports to be, a native journal or account of the whole proceeding.' Fraser added, on a personal note, 'Poor Grebayadoff [sic], I knew him well, he was an amiable or rather depressive person, but as the Author of the MSS says, too young or at least inexperienced to be put at the head of so important Mission', National Library of Scotland, MSS 4207 F 118–9 Blackwood Archive.

   At this point, some relevant evidence as to its authenticity should be recorded from the Russian side: two of Griboyedov's best informed contemporaries, namely Zhandr, in speaking to D.A. Smirnov, replied to the question of which was the most reliable account of the murder. Zhandr told Smirnov that he had asked General Yermolov in retirement the same question, and Yermolov had advised him that the secretary's account was the fullest and most detailed description of the causes of the catastrophe. Yermolov must have had in mind the French version (which was to be the basis for the English version in *Blackwood's Magazine*). Zhandr about Yermolov: Fomichev and Vatsuro (eds), *Griboyedov* (see Bibliography), pp.223–4. Fomichev, in his suggestion the English version was doctored, conveniently omits the very telling approval of the 'Narrative' by both Zhandr and Yermolov: notes, pp.414–15. For the secretary's laying the blame for unruly and disorderly conduct on the Georgians and Armenians acting as servants, uncontrolled by Griboyedov: 'Mehmendar's Narrative' (see Bibliography), pp.498–9. The full name of the French publication was *Nouvelles Annales des voyages et des sciences geographiques*.

2. Rustem-Bek's reprehensible conduct: 'Mehmendar's Narrative' (see Bibliography), pp.498–9.

3. The humiliating arrest of Allah Yar Khan by Muravyov-Karsky: article in *Russky Arkhiv* (1891) (see Bibliography), pp.188–91.

4. Mirza Nabi Khan episode: 'Mehmendar's Narrative' (see Bibliography), p.498.

5. 'Manifestation of justice': ibid., p.499.

6. The Secretary considered Griboyedov was aware of Rustem-Bek's abuses in accounting and quartermaster issues: ibid., p.499.

7. 'The prisoners have driven me mad': letter to Nina from Kasvin, 3 December in Piksanov and Shlyapkin (eds), *Complete Collected Works* (see Bibliography), vol. 3, p.244.

8. 'Now I really feel I know': ibid., vol. 3, p.245.

9. 'To begin with the cold was unbearable': this letter in French was dated by Evelyn Harden to early February 1829, and found by her in the Portland papers at Nottingham University. Harden, 'Griboyedov and the Willock Affair' (see Bibliography), pp.74–91.

10. Though more official and sober in tone, we have another eye-witness account of the mission, from the official report to Paskievich and Nesselrode, by Mal'tzov. The full text is given in Fomichev and Vatsuro (eds), *Griboyedov* (see Bibliography), p.292. Mal'tzov's account was accepted by the Foreign Ministry: notes, p.412. It is noteworthy that Mal'tzov at no point in his report sees fit to mention, or incriminate the British in any way; there were simply none in Tehran for him to mention. For his confirmation that Griboyedov was very well received: report, p.292. Shostakovich also deals with the mission in Tehran, drawing heavily on the 'Mehmendar's Narrative': Shostakovich, *The Diplomatic Activity* (see Bibliography), pp.210–3. Shostakovich uses Mal'tzov selectively: pp.216–7, 221.

11. The description of the arrival of the envoy's procession, 'Mehmendar's Narrative' (see Bibliography), p.500.

12. 'I perceived that the anxiety to please': the junior secretary to the *mehmendar*, ibid., 1830, p.501.

13. The tangled story of the Shah's presents so foolishly mislaid by careless shipping arrangements by the Russians, ibid.; about Dadash-Bek, p.502.

14. Griboyedov's joy at departure and the thought of being reunited with his bride, ibid., p.503.

Chapter XXIII: Countdown to the Massacre

1. 'Five times more than my digestion can take': Griboyedov's last letter from Tehran to Macdonald, discussed at length in Harden, 'Griboyedov and the Willock Affair', (see Bibliography), p.86.
2. The secretary's tone of alarm about the application of Mirza Yakub for asylum: 'Mehmendar's Narrative' (see Bibliography), p.504. All the details in the Secretary's narrative about Mirza Yakub are corroborated by Mal'tzov in his report: Fomichev and Vatsuro (eds), *Griboyedov* (see Bibliography), pp.293–5; for the Mujtahid's key role in condemning Mirza Yakub to death as an apostate (the fatal *fetva*): Mal'tzov, p.296.
3. 'It is not on Mirza Yakub they have spat': 'Mehmendar's Narrative' (see Bibliography), p.505. Mal'tzov confirms this.
4. 'He could not believe': Mal'tzov in Fomichev and Vatsuro (eds), *Griboyedov* (see Bibliography), p.298.
5. The folly of sending Allah Yar Khan's women to the Russian baths: 'Mehmendar's Narrative' (see Bibliography), p.507.
6. 'To prevent a rupture between two mighty powers': ibid., p.508.
7. 'Showers of stones': ibid., p.508.
8. 'The noise of your guns': ibid., p.509.
9. Griboyedov's vain attempt to address the crowds: ibid., p.509.
10. 'Look! They have killed Alexander': ibid., p.510.
11. 'Fath Ali Shah. J'enfoutre': ibid., p.510. These words were printed in French in the first version of *Nouvelles Annales des voyages et des sciences geographiques*. It is unlikely that the secretary's French would have been of a standard to have heard these words correctly.
12. 'Almighty God!': ibid., p.511. One may speculate he was an Afshari trained by General Comte Claude Gardanne during the period of the Franco–Persian Treaty of Finkenstein.
13. Mal'tzov's fear at being 'in imminent expectation of death': Mal'tzov in Fomichev and Vatsuro (eds), *Griboyedov* (see Bibliography), pp.297–9; Mal'tzov's account of how he escaped: pp.298–9.
14. The mob's insults shouted at the mangled body, mistakenly supposed to be that of Griboyedov, whilst it was being dragged round the city: 'Mehmendar's Narrative', (see Bibliography), p.511.

Chapter XXIV: Diplomatic Repercussions

1. For the aftermath of the riot and murders, there is supplementary Russian research, mainly nineteenth-century, in certain learned articles: A.P. Berzhe, 'Smert' A.S. Griboyedova' (see Bibliography). Another version, introducing some new details is Alaverdiyanets, 'Konchina A.S. Griboyedova po armyanskim istochnikam' (see Bibliography).

   Yefremov in 1872 wrote a lengthy article about the murders, 'O smer-ti Griboyedova v Tegerane' (see Bibliography), casting doubt on the

'Mehmendar's Narrative', though admitting it is a genuine Persian account, and suggesting that Europeans 'doctored' it, notably British from the mission.

A most interesting further explanation is the interview snatched from McNeill whilst travelling through Georgia in 1839 by his escort, a bold young Russian officer: Tolstoy, 'Ser Dzhon Maknil' (see Bibliography). McNeill introduced a new detail, namely that Gribov had tried to seduce one of Allah Yar Khan's ex-wives overnight, to the shock of Muslim susceptibilities, by creeping up to their rooms: p.898.

This account of Tolstoy's bears the stamp of authenticity, though communicated 20 years after the event and 35 years after the McNeill–Tolstoy meeting. It is noteworthy in that McNeill nowhere thinks it politic nor desirable to explain where he was at the time. He does not state that he was not an eye-witness at all. More remarkable is the fact he attributes no part of the Persian fury to the presence of Mirza Yakub, which other accounts consider to be the chief factor infuriating the population, and leading the Mullas to preach a holy war. The chief factor alleged by him to have caused the riot was fury and outrage at the alleged sexual humiliation of the hostage girls, who were Allah Yar Khan's ex-wives. Though McNeill was speaking almost 20 years after the event, we must assume that he remembered enough of the true facts that he had translated so carefully from the Persian justifications at the time. He chose to put a different construction on events, one which was convincing enough, and helpful to Griboyedov's reputation, as the blame could be placed on the lustful, irresponsible young half-brother. At all events, Tolstoy's account offers no support to the Soviet conspiracy theory against the British, as there is no evidence that they were present. Tolstoy, 'Ser Dzhon Maknil' (see Bibliography), pp.884–94.

Otherwise the chief article of value about his death posthumously is Kommissarov, 'Iranian authors' views on A.S. Griboyedov's death' (see Bibliography), pp.190–5. The standard Persian account is from Fassai, *Forsnama-e-Naseri* (see Bibliography), pp.18–90: the Persian author accuses Griboyedov of great arrogance in interpreting the Treaty, and tells us that the mob from Tehran numbered 100,000 people. Persian sources yield no new facts.

McNeill's reaction at the time is quoted in his granddaughter's book: Macalister, *Memoir* (see Bibliography), pp.128–9. For a reliable English account: Costello, 'The Murder of Griboyedov' (see Bibliography). Costello quotes all the official Foreign Office and Government of India reports relevant to the murder, and deals fairly with suggestions from Russian nationalists about British complicity, pp.79–89. Ingram, 'The Defence of British India I: The Invasion Scare of 1798', (see Bibliography) deals fully with the dangers of destabilising the Qajars; Abbas Mirza's expectation of succeeding Fath Ali Shah: Ingram, 'The succession crisis in Persia, 1833–4' from *The Beginnings of the Great*

Game in Asia (see Bibliography); Ingram, 'The Rules of the Game' (see Bibliography).

Lang, in his cogent article 'Griboyedov's last years in Persia' (see Bibliography) deals with the post-murder political situation, including the pressures upon Paskievich to fight the Turks effectively, making punitive reprisals quite impossible, whatever Nesselrode's fears of upsetting the British: pp.317–39, especially pp.332–9.

In 1829, an unexpected English visitor, T.B. Armstrong, arrived in Tehran still to find 'some blood upon the stones of the English Embassy Palace, where six Russian grooms had been massacred': Armstrong, *Journal of Travels* (see Bibliography), p.129. For his conventional – English-style – account of the massacre: pp.69-74.

Another conventional English explanation of the catastrophe is given by Alcock in *Travels* (see Bibliography), pp.69–75.

Thanks are due to Sir Denis Wright, whose wide-ranging scholarship drew attention to these accounts.

Of genuine scholarly relevance to interpreting the issues surrounding Griboyedov's murder and Persian ideas and attitudes, it is well worth turning to the article 'Conspiracy theories on the British' by Ashraf in the *Encyclopaedia Iranica* (see Bibliography), pp.139–347. The article deals specifically with the whole murder question, and a certain Khan Malek is alleged to have described a supposed 'great British plot' to dismantle Persia, of which the murder was to be an essential part, p.139. Ashraf neither accepts nor dismisses this proposition for the fantasy that it is; elsewhere he tells how in Persian conspiracy theories the British are depicted as 'cold-blooded, foxy and cunning and able to cut off the heads of their enemies even with cotton'. There is a fair-minded comment concluding that these ideas contribute to a political malaise that sometimes precludes rational responses to internal crises': p.145.

Another interesting virtually contemporary account of the murder after the event is to be found in Fowler's *Three Years in Persia* (see Bibliography): vol. 2 gives the conventional account of events, very heavily loaded towards the Persian side of the story. Fowler had access to the most confidential letters of the Shah to his son, and also Abbas Mirza's letter to Paskievich attempting damage limitation; Zil-li Sultan, Commander of the Shah's troops, is described as attempting to control the crowds, but no mention is made of the unfortunate fact that his men were not issued with bullets or bayonets, and thus remained impotent at the moment of truth: pp.216-7. The published letters reflect the Persian party line; 'the Persian government has purchased the friendship of the Russian Government with heart and soul'. Fowler estimates the Tehran mob at only 30,000.

From another account published in the *Asiatic Journal*, vol. 27 (see Bibliography), we learn a further detail exemplifying the arrogant carelessness of the Russian mission within their quarters, on the same night that Allah Yar Khan's two ex-wives took refuge in the Embassy. Mirza Yakub was allowed to have a dinner party at which, so the *Journal* alleges, 'he brought in a prostitute', p.626. This detail could be dismissed as irrelevant, Mirza Yakub being a eunuch. But curiously, Charles de Gamba, the French Consul in Tiflis, has the same story as an example of Shiite passions becoming more inflamed: de Gamba's letter in *Archives Diplomatiques du Ministère des Affaires Etrangères* (vols 176, 178C. C.C. Tiflis vol. 1, letter No. 9298 of 24 February and 7 March 1829 and letter of 13 March No. 2661) refers to the prostitute introduced to the Armenian womens' rooms 'to their great indignation...'

A copy of Charles de Gamba's report to Paris was given, in the interests of scholarship, to Sergei Fomichev at the Khmelita Conference Proceedings of January 2000 by the author. It contains the interesting statement that not a single Englishman was in Tehran at the time. To date, Pushkin House has made no scholarly comments on this new piece of evidence.

Before leaving the facts and existing accounts of Griboyedov's death and the conduct of the Russian mission, and Persian responsibilities in this context, one of the fullest, though not most reliable, accounts is in Shostakovich, *The Diplomatic Activity* (see Bibliography), pp.218–50. Shostakovich uses the 'Narrative', Mal'tzov's report and most learned articles since then already quoted in these notes. According to Shostakovich, both the Foreign Minister, Abul Hassan Khan, and the Shah were ready to allow the mob to start a riot 'to teach the Russian Envoy a lesson': pp.228–9. Allah Yar Khan, insulted by the removal of his two wives, could join this cabal: p.229. To the court party, Shostakovich then adds the Shiite clergy, furious at Mirza Yakub's apostasies and reported blasphemies: p.230. Shostakovich alleges the Mujtahid Mirza Mesikh pronounced the fatal *fetva* against Griboyedov personally: p.230. Shostakovich himself calls Mirza Mesikh the chief instigator of the crowd, p.234, and mentions the essential point that the *sarbazi* sent to protect the mission were without ammunition. On p.235, we find Shostakovich using the 'Narrative' as published in *Blackwood's Magazine*. On p.236 Shostakovich begins to suggest that the British were responsible; McNeill's perfectly reasonable remark to his wife, 'I do not doubt that if I had been in Teheran I should have been as safe there as anywhere' is used as evidence that he was a ringleader amongst the crowds. Shostakovich treats Mal'tzov's report as placing full responsibility for the atrocities on the Shah and his wretched Government: p.238. Shostakovich devotes two or three pages to the miraculous survival of Mal'tzov: p.241; using the evidence of another survivor, Ambartsum Bek, published in Fomichev and Vatsuro (eds), *Griboyedov* (see Bibliography), p.198, Ambartsum was a *gholam*, a mounted escort guard and courier. Then Bek adds some vivid details of Griboyedov's last-minute courage in refusing to hide in the chimney or fireplace: p.199. Ibrahim Bek escaped the mob's fury as he was disguised in Persian uniform and lay as dead after suffering 18 wounds: p.240.

A difference of degree of guilt was established early on, in that the fury of the mob could easily be attributed to Mirza Yakub's apostasies; Mal'tzov later wrote in his report that the problems arising out of the conduct of the Armenian women, under Russian protection, were in fact the principal cause of the envoy's assassination. Mal'tzov wrote to Paskievich that it was only after the murders that there was any mention of the women: Shostakovich, *The Diplomatic Activity* (see Bibliography), p.243.

Fath Ali Shah, in his letter to Abbas Mirza apportioned much blame to the servants of the mission inflaming Shiite prejudices with their conduct. Mal'tzov lays very little store by this factor, though the author of the 'Narrative' gives it full weight: Shostakovich, *The Diplomatic Activity* (see Bibliography), p.244.

Shostakovich rejects this line of excuses by the Persians as one facilitating direct guilt being placed on Griboyedov personally for mistakes of tact and lack of control: ibid., p.245. Shostakovich feels himself obliged to link the Persian leaders and fanatical clergy with 'the English residents', by which he means the mission in Tabriz under Macdonald. No evidence is offered in support of this. The issue is further explored on pp.250–3, see refutation notes (Appendix III).

For Paskievich's speculations about the British, see his letter to Nesselrode quoted by Popova, *Griboyedov-diplomat* (see Bibliography), p.191; to be fair, this must be juxtaposed with Paskievich's adjutant's view (Count Felkersam, who pointed out that the British usually had an official on duty to supervise any Russian prosecuting Russia's interests in Tehran. Why, asked Felkersam, did the British not oversee Griboyedov's activities?) This anecdote is quoted by Yefremov, not too well-disposed to the British otherwise, in 'About Griboyedov's death in Teheran' (see Bibliography). Shcherbatov, *General-Fel'dmarshal*, p.76, tells us more of Paskievich's views: 'Il y a donc du louche dans ce qu'il n'y avait pas un seul anglais lors du sejour de Griboyedoff à Teheran, tandis que dans toute autre occasion ou les russes étaient a cette capitale, ils ne les quittaient pas de vue.'

Paskievich to Nesselrode dated 13 April 1829 from Tiflis. Paskievich speculated equally that the British were not completely exempt from involvement in the disturbances: 'perhaps they contemplated quite impartially the new superiority of our mission in Persia. At all events they did not foresee the disastrous consequences of the disturbances.' So much for Paskievich's suspicions of the British, flatly contradicted by his admission that they were not present in Tehran, his despatch to Nesselrode of 8 February 1829, pp.80–1. Nesselrode agreed that the Shah and his court were completely foreign to the issue of implicit responsibility for Griboyedov's assassination, p.59. Further complications were not to be created with the Persian,s embarrassing the prosecution of the war with Turkey, p.60. The Shah's lachrymose *firman* apologising for the murder is in full in French, together with his feeble excuses about Mirza Yakub, p.70. The remaining documents in Shcherbatov show the measures taken by the Russians to receive the mission of Abbas Mirza's son Khosraw Mirza, apologising to the Tsar, as a prince of the blood, for the murders.

For Muravyov's views: Fomichev and Vatsuro (eds), *Griboyedov* (see Bibliography), for a number of post-murder details, namely how Akhverdova broke the news to Nina: p.67. Muravyov even repeats the sexual advances possibly made by Gribov: p.70. His conclusions on pp.72–3 do not incriminate the British seriously. Muravyov is of especial interest, as knowing all the gossip in Tiflis at the time, immediately after the events. Muravyov hazards the opinion that the British certainly would not have wished to push matters to such a gory end, though 'a diminution of our Envoy's influence would not have displeased them': p.73.

For the research of Professor Rogers in the Ottoman archives on my behalf, showing conclusively there was no Ottoman connivance, as suggested by Gammer, *Shamil* (see Bibliography). The combined evidence of Paskievich personally, his adjutant Felkersam and the French Consul in Tiflis, all separately stating that not a single Briton was in Tehran at the time, is overwhelming. All Mal'tzov wrote on the issue was, quite truthfully, that 'the English feared the very considerable influence of our Envoy on the Persian government'. Paskievich, in his final report to Nesselrode, confirms he was far from suspecting the British: Shostakovich, *The Diplomatic Activity* (see Bibliography), pp.252–3.

Potto, *Kavkazskaya* (see Bibliography), vol. 3, pp.602–32, devotes a whole chapter to Griboyedov's last mission and murder. He gives no sources, but it is a readable version, clearly using Mal'tzov's report. Potto uniquely describes the sad reception of the body in Tiflis by his widow, and his eventual burial on Mtatsminda Hill.

For Mal'tzov's final summary of the causes of the riots: his report in Fomichev and Vatsuro (eds), *Griboyedov* (see Bibliography), pp.301–2.

2. Allah Yar Khan's jealousy and hatred of Abbas Mirza: Potto, *Kavkazskaya* (see Bibliography), p.619.

3. Pushkin's epitaph, 'I do not know of anything more enviable than the final years of his stormy life': Pushkin's *A Journey* (see Bibliography); when he meets the coffin bearing his friend's mangled remains at Gergery, between Armenia and Georgia: Fomichev and Vatsuro (eds), *Griboyedov* (see Bibliography), p.265 in Russian; for English translation: Pushkin, *A Journey* (see Bibliography), pp.45–7.

4. 'At a late hour': Macdonald to FO 60/31, quoted by Lang in 'Griboyedov's last years in Persia' (see Bibliography), pp.328–9.

5. 'It is quite impossible to start another war with Persia': Berzhe, 'The Death of Griboyedov' (see Bibliography), quoting letter to Nesselrode of 20 February, pp.188–94.

6. 'The impulsive and excessively zealous efforts', the new party line from St Petersburg: Shostakovich, *The Diplomatic Activity* (see Bibliography), quoting Nesselrode to Paskievich in his letter of 16 March: p 363. Popova, *Griboyedov v Persii* (see Bibliography), for same text; Nesselrode hid behind the Tsar's opinion: p.215.

7. Pushkin's meeting with Griboyedov's coffin near Besobdal: Pushkin, *A Journey* (see Bibliography), pp.45–8. Piksanov, in his biographical sketch in Piksanov and Shlyapkin (eds), *Complete Collected Works* (see Bibliography), vol. 1, describes Griboyedov's death without any incrimination of the British.

8. Nina's eternal valediction to her husband, 'Your spirit and your works remain eternally in the memory of Russians; why did my love for thee outlive thee?': ibid., vol. 3, p.11.

Chapter XXV: The Aftermath

1. 'He consigned the ill-fated affair': Lang, 'Griboyedov's last years in Persia' (see Bibliography).

2. 'In which Pushkin reigned supreme': Herzen, *My Past* (see Bibliography), vol. 1, p.280.

3. 'How much did this man do for me?': Fomichev and Vatsuro (eds), *Griboyedov* (see Bibliography), pp.367–8.

4. Küchelbecker's farewell to Griboyedov: ibid., p.263. Küchelbecker refers to their shared belief in the books of the Old Testament, in his diary entry for 25 May 1845.

5. 'A good son, a good brother, a true friend'. For Beguichov's misleading compliment that Griboyedov was a 'good son' to his irritating mother: Fomichev and Vatsuro (eds), *Griboyedov* (see Bibliography), p.31.

6. 'On the one hand a Petersburg civil servant': Veselovsky, *The Complection of Russian Literature* (see Bibliography), pp.49–57. For Blok's actual comments: Fomichev, *A.S. Griboyedov Tvortchestvo* (see Bibliography), pp.126–7.

Bibliography

Journals, Papers, Theses & Pamphlets

Asiatic Journal, vol. 27 (January–June 1829)

'Biographical Sketch of His Late Royal Highness Abbas-Mirza', *Journal of the Royal Asiatic Society*, no 1 (1834), p.322

Campbell, J., 'The Russo–Persian Frontier, 1810', *Journal of the Royal Central Asian Society*, no 18 (1931), pp.223–32

Costello, D.P., 'Griboyedov in Persia in 1820: two diplomatic notes', *Oxford Slavonic Papers*, SP, no 5 (1954), pp.66–9

Costello, D.P., 'The Murder of Griboyedov', *Oxford Slavonic Papers*, SP, no 8 (1958), pp.66–89

Costello, D.P., 'A Note on the Diplomatic Activity of A.S. Griboyedov by S.V. Shostakovich', *Slavonic and East European Review*, no 40 (December 1962), pp.235–44

Cross, Anthony, 'Pushkin's bawdy notes from the Literary Underground', *Russian Literature Triquarterly*, 'The Golden Age' (Michigan, 1975), pp.216–7

Davis, Prof. H.W.C., 'The Great Game in Asia 1800–1844', *The Proceedings of the British Academy*, no 12 (1926)

Dessaix, Robert, 'On Chatsky as Antihero', *Forum for Modern Language Studies*, no 10 (1974), pp.379–87

Griboyedov, A.S., *Woe from Wit*, rhyming translation by Professor A.G. Waring, *Russian Literature Triquarterly* (Michigan), no 24 (Spring 1990)

'Griboyedov in Persia: December 1818', *Slavonic and East European Review*, no 57 (1979), pp.255–67

Harden, Dr Evelyn Jasiulko, 'Griboyedov and the Willock Affair', *Slavonic and East European Review*, no 30 (1971), pp.74–92

Harden, Dr Evelyn Jasiulko, *Truth and Design in the Historical Novels of Jurij N. Tynjanov, in particular* The Death of the Vazir Mukhtar (PhD thesis, Harvard University, Cambridge, MA, January 1966)

Hoover, Marjorie L., article in *Russian Literature Triquarterly*, no 7 (1974), p.285–93

Ingram, Prof. E., 'The Defence of British India I: The Invasion Scare of 1798', *Journal of Indian History*, no 48 (1970)

Ingram, Prof. E., 'The Rules of the Game', commentary on the defence of British India 1798–1829, *Journal in Commonwealth History* (1974–5), pp.257–79

Jones, Malcolm, 'Andrew Hay and the Griboyedov Affair', *Journal of Russian Studies*, no 42 (1981), pp.16–21

Lang, David M., 'Griboyedov's last years in Persia', *Slavonic and East European Review*, no 7 (December 1948), pp.317–39

'The Late Affray at Teheran', *The Asiatic Journal*, 28 (November 1829)

'The Massacre of the Russian Legation', *The Asiatic Journal and Monthly Register for British India and Dependencies*, Periodical Publications (London) 1–25: pp.xxvii, 783–4

McNeill, Sir John, 'India, Great Britain and Russia', pamphlet (London, 1838)

McNeill, Sir John, 'Russia, Persia and England', *Quarterly Review*, no 128 (London, 1839)

Proffer, Carl R. and Ellendea (eds), *Russian Literature Triquarterly* (Michigan), no 24 (Spring 1990)

Secretary to the Mehmendar of the mission, 'Narrative of the Proceedings of the Russian Mission, from its Departure from Tabreez for Tehran on 14th Jummade 2D [20 December 1828], until its Destruction on Wednesday the 6th of Sha'ban [11 February 1829]' ['Mehmendar's Narrative'], *Blackwood's Edinburgh Magazine*, no 171 (September 1830), pp.496–512

English Language Books

Alcock, Thomas, *Travels in Russia, Persia, Turkey and Greece in 1828–9* (E. Clarke & Son, London, 1831)

Alexander, J.E., *Travels from India to England* (London, 1827)

Algar, Hamid, *Middle Eastern Studies* (1970), vol. 6, pp.276–96

Algar, Hamid, *Religion and State in Iran 1785–1906. The Role of the Ulama in the Qajar Period* (Berkeley, Los Angeles, London, 1969)

Allen, W.E.D., *A History of the Georgian People: From the Beginning down to the Russian Conquest in the Nineteenth Century* (Routledge & Kegan Paul, London, 1932)

Allen, W.E.D., and P. Muratoff, *Caucasian Battlefields* (Cambridge, 1953)

Anderson, M.S., *Britain's Discovery of Russia, 1552–1815* (New York, 1958)

Armstrong, T.B., *Journal of Travels in the Seat of War, during the Last Two Campaigns of Russia and Turkey* (A. Seguin, London, 1829)

Ashraf, Ahmad, 'Conspiracy Theories on the British', *Encyclopaedia Iranica*, vol. 6, pp.138–147

Atkin, Muriel, *Russia and Iran 1780–1882* (University of Minnesota Press, Minneapolis, 1980)

Avery, P.W., 'An Enquiry into the Outbreak of the Second Russo–Persian War, 1826–1828', *Iran and Islam*, ed. C.E. Bosworth (Edinburgh, 1971), pp.17–45; also contribution by Vladimir Minorsky

Baddeley, J.F., *The Russian Conquest of the Caucasus* (New York, 1969, facsimile reprint of Russian Campaigns in 1908 London edition)

Barratt, Lynn, *The Rebel on the Bridge* (Elek Books, London, 1975)

Bettes, J.H., ed., *Russian Studies*, series ed. Neil Cornwell (Bristol, 1995)

Blanch, Lesley, *The Sabres of Paradise* (London, 1960)

Boulger, D.C., *Lord William Bentinck* (Oxford, 1892)

Bourne, Kenneth, *The Foreign Policy of Victorian England 1830–1902* (Oxford, 1970)

Braun, Edward, *Meyerhold, A Revolution in Theatre* (London, 1979), especially Chapter 8

Browne, E.G., *Modern Times, 1500–1924*, (Cambridge, 1930), vol. 4, *A Literary History of Persia*, no 5

Brown, Prof. William E., 'Alexander Griboyedov before 1823. Alexander Griboyedov and Woe from Wit', in his book *A History of Russian Literature of the Romantic Period* (4 vols, Michigan, 1986), vol. 2

Buckingham, James Silk, *Travels in Assyria, Media and Persia* (London, 1829), vols 1 & 2

The Cambridge History of the British Empire (Cambridge, 1923), H. Dodwell (ed.), vol. 4

Chaadayev, Peter Ya., *The Major Works of Peter Ya. Chaadayev*, tr. and with commentary by Raymond T. McNally (London, 1969)

Chesney, Colonel, R.A., *The Russo–Turkish Campaigns of 1828 and 1829, with a view of the Present State of Affairs in the East* (3rd edn, Smith, Elder & Co., London, 1854)

Crankshaw, Edward, *The Shadow of the Winter Palace* (London, 1976)

Curtiss, John Shelton, *The Russian Army under Nicholas I, 1825–1855* (Duke University Press, Durham, NC, 1965)

Curzon, Hon. G.N., *Persia and the Persian Question* (2 vols, London, 1915)

Davis, H.W.C., *The Great Game in Asia* (1926)

Dmytryshyn, Basil, ed., *Imperial Russia: A Source Book 1700–1917* (2nd edition, Illinois, 1974), pp.17–8

Ellenborough, *Lord Edward Law, A Political Diary 1828–1830*, ed. Lord Colchester (2 vols, London, 1881)

Fowler, George, *Three Years in Persia; with Travelling Adventures in Koordistan* (2 vols, Henry Colburn, London, 1841)

Fraser, J.B., *An Historical and Descriptive Account of Persia, including a description of Afghanistan and Beloochistan* (Edinburgh, 1834)

Fraser, J.B., *Narrative of a Journey into Khorasan, in the Years 1821 and 1822* (London, 1825)

Fraser, J.B., *Travels in Koordistan, Mesopotamia, & c* (vol. 1, London, 1840)

Fraser, J.B., *A Winter's Journey from Constantinople to Teheran* (vol. 1, London, 1838)

Fraser, J.B., *Travels and Adventures in the Persian Provinces on the southern banks of the Caspian Sea* (London, 1826)

Freygang, Mr W. & Mrs F.K. (tr. from German), *Letters from the Caucasus and Georgia* (London, 1823)

Gammer, Moshe, *Shamil and the Conquest of Chechnia and Daghestan* (Frank Cass, London, 1994)

Goncharov, I.A., 'A Million Torments' (in Russian), *Russian Critical Essays of the 19th Century*, S. Konovalov and D. J. Richards (eds), (Oxford, 1972), pp.111–17

Bibliography

Griboyedov, A.S., *Gore ot Uma [Woe from Wit]*, ed. with introduction, bibliography and vocabulary by Richard Pearce; notes by D.P. Costello, Russian Series (Bristol, 1995)

Griboyedov, A.S., *The Misfortune of Being Clever*, tr. S. Pring (Nutt, London, 1914)

Griboyedov, A.S., *Woe from Wit*, in *Four Russian Plays*, tr. Joshua Cooper (London, 1972), also his introduction

Griboyedov, A.S., *The Puppet Theatre*, tr. Sophie Lund, private translation for author, unpublished (original published in Russian, 1819)

Grimsted, Patricia Kennedy, *The Foreign Ministers of Alexander I: Political attitudes and the conduct of Russian diplomacy 1801–1825* (Berkeley, 1989)

Harden, Dr E.J., *The Murder of Griboyedov: New Materials* (Birmingham, 1979), no 6

Haslip, J., *Catherine the Great* (London, 1977)

Herzen, A, *My Past and Thoughts: Memoirs of Alexander Herzen*, tr. Constance Garnett (6 vols, London, 1924)

Imlah, A.H., *Lord Ellenborough* (Massachusetts, 1939)

Ingram, Prof. E., *The Beginnings of the Great Game in Asia 1828–1834* (Oxford, 1979)

Johnson, Prof. John, *Sketches from India to England in the year 1817* (London, 1818)

Jones Brydges Bart, Sir Harford, *An Account of the Transactions of His Majesty's Mission to the Court of Persia in the Years 1807–11* (2 vols, James Bohn, London, 1834)

Karlinsky, Prof. Simon, *Russian Drama from its Beginnings to the Age of Pushkin* (Berkeley, Los Angeles, 1985)

Kazemzadeh, F., *Russia and Britain in Persia, 1864–1914* (New Haven, 1968)

Keep, John, *Soldiers of the Tsar: Army and Society in Russia 1462–1874* (Oxford, 1985)

Kiernan, V.G., *'The Duel in European History', Honour and the Reign of Aristocracy* (Oxford, 1988)

Kinneir, J. McDonald, *A Geographical Memoir of the Persian Empire* (London, 1813)

Kotzebue, M. Von (tr.), *Narrative of a Journey into Persia in the Suite of the Imperial Russian Embassy in 1817 of General A.P. Yermolov* (London, 1819)

Lang, D.M., *The Last Years of the Georgian Monarchy, 1658–1832* (New York, 1957)

Lincoln, W. Bruce, *Nicholas I, Emperor and Autocrat of all the Russians* (London, 1978)

Lyall, Dr R., *Travels in Russia, the Crimea, the Caucasus and Georgia* (2 vols, 1st edn, Cadell, London, 1825; reprinted New York 1970)

Macalister, Mrs Florence (Stewart), *Memoir of the Rt Hon. Sir John MacNeill and of his Second Wife Elizabeth Wilson by their Grand Daughter* (London, 1910)

Madariaga, Isabel de, *Russia in the Age of Catherine the Great* (London, 1981)

Magarshack, D., *Life of Pushkin* (London, 1967)

Malcolm, Sir John, *History of Persia From The Most Early Period* (2 vols, London, 1815)

Malcolm, Sir John, *Sketches of Persia* (London, 1845)

Mazour, Anatole G., *The First Russian Revolution, 1825, The Decembrist Movement, Its Origins, Development, and Significance* (reissue, Stanford University Press, California, 1961)

McNeill, Sir John, *Memoir*, see Macalister, Mrs Florence (Stewart)

McNeill, Sir John, *Progress and Present Position of Russia in the East* (2 vols, London, 1836)

Mignan, Capt. R., *A Winter Journey through Russia, the Caucasian Alps, and Georgia, thence into Koordistan* (2 vols, London, 1839)

Mikhailovsky-Danilevsky, A., *History of the Campaign in France in the year 1814* (Smith Elder, London, 1839)

Minorsky, Vladimir, see Avery, Peter, Iran and Islam

Mirsky, Prince D.S., *A History of Russian Literature*, ed. and abridged by Francis J. Whitfield (London, 1964)

Monteith, Lt-Gen. Sir William, *Kars and Erzerum, with the Campaigns of Prince Paskiewitch in 1828 and 1829; and an account of the Conquests of Russia Beyond the Caucasus, from the time of Peter the Great to the Treaties of Turcoman Chie and Adrianople* (London, Longman, Brown, Green, 1856)

Morier, J.J., *Journey through Persia, Armenia and Asia Minor to Constantinople* (London, 1818)

Noyes, G.R., 'Wit Works Woe', tr. Sir B. Pares, *Masterpiece of the Russian Drama* (New York, 1933), pp.85–155

Philips, Sir Cyril Henry, *The East India Company, 1784–1834* (Manchester, 1961)

Porter, Sir Robert Ker, *Travels in Georgia, Persia, Armenia, Ancient Babylonia, etc. during the Years 1817, 1818, 1819 and 1820* (2 vols, London, 1821)

Proffer, Carl R., and Ronald Meyer (eds), *Nineteenth-century Russian Literature in English. A Bibliography of Criticism and Translations* (Michigan, 1990)

Pushkin, A.S., *Eugene Onegin*, tr. Sir Charles Johnston (Harmondsworth, 1979)

Pushkin, Alexander, *Eugene Onegin*, tr. and with a commentary by Vladimir Nabokov (4 vols, 1st edn, Routledge & Kegan Paul, London, 1964; Princetown University Press, 1975)

Pushkin, A.S., *A Journey to Erzerum*, tr. Birgitta Ingemanson (Ann Arbor, Ardis, Michigan, 1974)

Pushkin, A.S., *The Letters of A. Pushkin*, T. Shaw, (ed.) (Wisconsin, 1967)

Rawlinson, Major-General Sir Henry C., *England and Russia in the East* (London, 1875)

Reyfman, Irina, *Ritualized Violence Russian Style* (Stanford University Press, California, 1999)

Bibliography

Riasanovsky, Nicholas V., *Nicholas I and Official Nationality in Russia, 1825–1855* (Berkeley and Los Angeles, 1959)

Riasanovsky, Nicholas V., *A Parting of Ways* (Oxford, 1976)

Roosevelt, Prof. Priscilla, *Life on the Russian Country Estate* (New Haven, 1995), pp.22–5, including excellent plans and photos of Khmelita

Rosselli, John, *Lord William Bentinck, The Making of a Liberal Imperialist, 1774–1839* (India, 1974)

Sheil, Lady, *Glimpses of Life and Manners in Persia* (London, 1856)

Stuart, Charles, *Journal of Residence in Northern Persia and the adjacent provinces of Turkey* (London, 1854)

Swietochowski, *Tadeusz, Russia and Azerbaijan, A Borderland in Transition* (2 vols, New York, 1934)

Sykes, P.A., *History of Persia* (2 vols, 3rd edn, London, 1930)

Tancoigne, J.M., *A Narrative of a Journey into Persia* (London, 1820)

Temperley, H.W.V., *The Foreign Policy of Canning 1822–7* (1925)

Tolstoy, L., *War and Peace*, tr. Constance Garnett (New York, n.d.)

Tynianov, Yuri, *Death and Diplomacy in Persia*, tr. Alec Brown (London, 1938)

Ulam, Adam B., *Russia's Failed Revolutions from the Decembrists to the Dissidents* (Weidenfeld & Nicolson, London, 1981)

Van Halen, Don Juan, *Narrative of Don Juan Van Halen's Imprisonment in the Dungeons of the Inquisition at Madrid, and His Escape in 1817 and 1818; to which are added, His Journey to Russia, His Campaign with the Army of the Caucasus, and His Return to Spain in 1821*, edited from the original Spanish manuscript by the anonymous author of Don Esteban and Sandoval (2 vols, Henry Colburn, London, 1827), vol. 1

Veselovsky, Alexei G., *The Complexion of Russian Literature*, ed. Andrew Field (Penguin, New York, 1971), pp.49–54

Wagner, Dr Moritz, *Travels in Persia: Georgia and Koordistan; with Sketches of the Cossacks and the Caucasus* (3 vols, Hurst & Blackett, London, 1856), vol. 2

Ward, A.W., & G.P. Gooch (eds), *The Cambridge History of British Foreign Policy (1783–1919)*, (Cambridge, 1923), vol. 11 (1815–1866)

Watson, R.G., *A History of Persia from the Beginning of the Nineteenth Century to the Year 1858* (Smith Elder, Cornhill, London, 1866)

Weaver, J.R.H., and Austin Lane Poole (eds), *Henry William Carless Davis, 1874–1928, A Memoir and a Selection of his Historical Papers*, Raleigh Lecture (London, 1933)

Wilbraham, Captain Richard, *Travels in the Trans-Caucasian Provinces of Russia and along the Southern Shore of the Lakes of Van and Urumiah, in the Autumn and Winter of 1839* (John Murray, London, 1839)

Wolff, Tanya, and Bayley, John (eds) *Pushkin on Literature* (1st edn, London, 1971; Stanford, 1986)

Wright, Sir Denis, *The English Amongst the Persians, during the Qajar Period 1787–1921* (London, 1977)

Wright, Sir Denis, *The Persians Amongst the English* (London, 1985)

Yapp, Prof. M.E., *Strategies of British India, Britain, Iran and Afghanistan, 1798–1850* (Oxford, 1980)
Zetlin, M., *The Decembrists* (New York, 1958)

French secondary sources

Bonamour, Jean, *A.S. Griboyedov et la vie littéraire de son temps* (Paris, 1965)
Bonamour, Jean, *Alceste and the Influence of the Misanthrope* (1965)
Drouville, Gaspar, *Voyage en Perse faite en 1812 et 1813* (Paris, 1825)
Hofman, Professor M., *Histoire de la littérature russe, depuis les origines jusqu'à nos jours* (Paris, 1934)
Montpereux, N. Dubois de, *Voyage autour de Caucase, chez les Tcherkesses et les Abkases* (6 vols, Paris, 1856)
Nesselrode, Count K.V., *Lettres et papiers du Chancelier Comte de Nesselrode 1760–1856* (2 vols, Paris, 1908–1912)
Rouleau, Alain (ed.), *Lettres philosophiques* (Paris, 1970)

Russian language titles

Akti Sobranniye Kavkazskoi Arkheografícheskoi Kommissiei (AKAK), (12 vols, Tiflis, 1866–1904)
Alaverdiyanets, M.I., 'Konchina A.S. Griboyedova po armyanskim istochnikam', *Russkaya Starina*, no 10 (1910), pp.43–65, ed. G. Shermazan
Andreyev, V.A., 'Yermolov i Paskievich', *Kavkazsky Sbornik*, no 1 (1876), pp.197–213
Andronikov, I., *Lermontov v Gruzii v 1838 godu* (Tblisi, 1958)
Arsenishvili, E., and I. Yenikolopov, *Griboyedov v Gruzii* (Tiflis, 1929)
Avalov, Z., *Prisoyedineniye Gruzii k Rossii [Georgia's unification into Russia]* (2nd edn, St Petersburg, 1906; New York, 1981)
Bartenev, P. 'K biografii Griboyedova', *Russky Arkhiv*, no 2 (1881), pp.177–90
Bartolomei, F.F., 'Posol'stvo Knyazya Menshikova v Persiyu v 1826 godu'. Dnevnik General-Leitenanta F.F. Bartolomeya', *Russkaya Starina*, no 4 (1904), pp.65–92
Bebutov, D., 'Zapiski', *Kavkazsky Sbornik* (Tiflis), no 23 (1902)
Berzhe, A.P., 'A.S. Griboyedov. Deyatel'nost' kak diplomat 1827–29', *Russkaya Starina*, no 10 (1874), pp.516–34
Berzhe, A.P., 'A.S. Griboyedov v Persii i na Kavkaze 1818–28', *Russkaya Starina*, no 10 (1872), pp.276–300
Berzhe, A.P., 'Aleksei Petrovich Yermolov v ego pis'makh k Kn. M.S. Vorontosovu, 1816–1852', *Russkaya Starina*, no 12 (1876), pp.523–50
Berzhe, A.P., 'Smert' A.S. Griboyedova: Podrobnosti tragicheskoi ego konchiny (1829 g.)', *Russkaya Starina*, no 8 (1872), pp.163–207

Bibliography

Buyotov, Aleksei, *Moskovsky Anglisky Klub, stranitsi Istorii* (Moscow, Isdaniye Moskovskogo Angliiskogo Kluba, 1999)

Byelinsky, V.F., *Sochineniya, 1834–1840*, Ivanov-Razumov (ed.) (3 vols, St Petersburg, 1911)

Davydov, A. (ed.), *A.S. Griboyedov. Ego zhizn' i gibel' v memuarakh sovremennikov* (Leningrad, 1929)

Davydov, V.N., '"Rasskaz o proshlom". Razmyshleniya Griboyedova i Chatsky. Rasskaz Arzarevichevoi ob igrakh Griboyedova na cherdaka u Shakhovskogo', ['Tales of the Past, Recollections about Griboyedov and Chatsky'] (Moscow-Leningrad, 1931), pp.198–389, article from *Zima-Kazan* (1871-2), p.199

Dubrovin, Lt. Gen. N.F., *Istoriya voiny i vladychestva russkikh na Kavkaze* (6 vols, St Petersburg, 1871-74), vol. 6 (1888)

Eidel'man, N. Ya., *'Byt' mozhet za khrebtom Kavkaza'; Russian literature and social thought in the first half of the nineteenth century in its Caucasian context*, ed. M.S. Lazarev (Moscow, 1990)

Fekhner, M.V., 'The House of the Griboyedov's in Moscow', *Memorials of Culture, Research and Restoration* (Moscow, 1959)

Fomichev, S.A. (ed.), *The Dramatic Works, Poems and Travel Notes of A.S. Griboyedov* (2 vols at time of publication, St Petersburg, 1999)

Fomichev, S.A., *Griboyedov in Petersburg*, ed. S.A. Remizov (Pushkin House, Leningrad, 1982)

Fomichev, S.A., *A.S. Griboyedov Tvortchestvo, Biografiya, Traditsii* (Leningrad, 1977)

Fomichev, S.A., *Problemi Tvortchestva A.S. Griboyedov, Trast Imakom* (Smolensk, 1994), esp. on Radamist and Zenobia, pp.162–193

Fomichev, S.A., and S. Krasnov, *The Life and Creativity of A.S. Griboyedov* (Moscow, 1994)

Fomichev, S.A. (ed.), *A.S. Griboyedov, Materialy k biografii (Sbornik nauchnykh trudov)* (Leningrad, 1989; Smolensk State University, 1998, covers subsequent years), includes article by L.M. Arinshtein and I.S. Chistova, and others

Fomichev, S.A., and V.E. Vatsuro (eds), *Griboyedov in the Memoirs of his Contemporaries* (Moscow, 1980)

Gershenzon, M., *Griboyedovskaya Moskva [Griboyedov's Moscow]* (2nd edn, Berlin-Moscow, 1922)

Gershenzon, M., *O.P. Chaadeyev zhisn' u myshleniye* (St Petersburg, 1908)

Gertsen (Herzen), A.I., *Sobraniye sochinenii* (30 vols, Moscow, 1954–64), esp. vols 1, 8–9

Glinka, V., and A.V. Pomarnatsky, *Voyennaya Gallereya Zimnego Dvortsa* (Leningrad, 1974)

Goncharov, I.A., *Sobraniye sochinenii* (8 vols, Moscow, 1955)

Goncharov, I.A., 'A Million Torments' (in Russian), *Russian Critical Essays of the 19th century*, ed. S. Konovalov and D.J. Richards (Oxford, 1972), pp.111–17

Gordin, Ya. A., *Dueli i Duelyanti* (Pushkin Fond, St Petersburg 1997)

'A.S. Griboyedov', *Literaturnoye Nasledstvo* (Moscow) pp.19–21 (1946) pp.143–176 (see also Kal'ma below)

'A.S. Griboyedov: Two Letters to A.I. Rykhlevsky', ed. I.O. Popova; 'letter to P.A. Vyazemsky', ed. V. Nechayeva; 'Letter to P.A. Karatygin', ed. M. Baronovskaya, *Literaturnoye Nasledstvo* (Moscow) pp.47–48 (1948), pp.225–8, 228–40, 367

'A.S. Griboyedov: 'Works in Verse', *Sochineniya v Stikhakh*, ed. V.P. Meshcheryakov (Leningrad, 1987)

Grishunin, L. (ed.), *A.S. Griboyedov, Sochineniya* (Moscow, 1989)

Grishunin, L., and S.A. Fomichev (eds), *New Collected Works of A.S. Griboyedov* (St Petersburg, 1983)

Herzen, A.I., see Gertsen

Ivanov, O., 'Griboyedov abd Yermolov under surveillance (secret) by Nicholas I', *Literaturnoye Nasledstvo*, nos 47–8, special issue (1946)

Kal'ma, N., 'Kommercheskiye zamysli Griboyedova' ('The Commercial Projects of Griboyedov'), *Literaturnoye Nasledstvo*, nos 19–21 (1935), pp.143–76

Kamensky, D.N., *Slovar' dostopamyatnykh lyudei Russkogo zemli* (Moscow, 1836), parts 4–5

Karatygin, P.A., 'Aleksandr Sergeyevich Griboyedov. Iz moyikh zapisok', *Russkaya Starina*, no 3 (1872), pp.423–30

Karatygin, P.A., *Zapiski*, ed. B.B. Kazansky (Leningrad, 1929)

Kommissarov, D.S., 'Iranian authors' views on A.S. Griboyedov's death', *Voprosi Istorii*, no 8 (1975)

Krasnov, P.S., 'The Travels of Griboyedov', *A.S. Griboyedov, Tvorchestvo, Biografii i traditsii* (Leningrad, 1977)

Krasnov, P.S., and A. Tarkova, *A.S. Griboyedov, Zhizn' i tvorchestvo* (Moscow, 1994)

Lermontovskaya Encyclopaedia (Pushkin House, Leningrad, 1981)

Lopatina, M.N., *A.S. Pushkin i yevo sovremmeniki v Moskovskom Angliiskom klube* (Moscow, 1999)

Malshinski, A., 'An unedited note of A.S. Griboyedov's', *Russki Vyostnik*, no 9 (1891), p.15

Markova, O.P., 'Noviye materialy o proyekte Rossiskoi Zakavkazskoi Kompanii A.S. Griboyedova i P.O. Zaveleyskogo', *Istorichesky Arkhiv*, no 6 (1951), pp.324–390

Meshcheryakov, V.P., *A.S. Griboyedova, Literaturnoye okruzheniye u vospriyatiye ikh–nachalo xx* (*A.S. Griboyedov, his literary circle and background: 19th–early 20th centuries*), ed. C.C. Priima (Leningrad, 1983)

Meshcheryakov, Viktor P., *Zhizn' i deyaniya Aleksandra Griboyedova* (*The Life and Activity of Alexander Griboyedov*) (Moscow, 1989)

Minorsky, V., 'An original Letter of Fath Ali Shah's', *Russkaya Mysl* (Berlin) (1924), pp.32–45

Minorsky, V., 'Tsena krovi Griboyedova. Neizdanny dokument', *Russkaya Mysl* (Prague-Berlin), nos 3–4 (1923), pp.332–45

Miyansarov, M.M., *Bibliographia Caucasica et Transcaucasia* (St Petersburg, 1874–76)

Bibliography

Myasoyedova, Natasha, *Griboyedova i Pushkin* (Moscow, 1997)

Nashe Nasledstvo [Our Heritage], ed. V. Roginsky, no 5 (Moscow, 1991)

Nazarova, L.N., A.M. Gordin and V.N. Orlov, *A.S. Griboyedov v portretakh, illyustratsiyakh, dokumentakh* (Leningrad, 1955)

Nechkina, M.V., *A.S. Griboyedov i dekabristy (A.S. Griboyedov and the Decembrists)* (Moscow, 1947; 2nd edn 1951)

Nechkina, M.V., *Sledstvennoye dyelo A.S. Griboyedov* ('Mysl', Moscow, 1982)

Nikitenko, A.V., *Zapiski i dnevnik 1826–1877* (2 vols, St Petersburg, 1893)

Orlov, V.L., *Griboyedov, kratkii ocherk jiznii tvortchestva* (Moscow, 1952)

Pashuto, V.T., 'Diplomaticheskaya deyatel'nost' A.S. Griboyedova', *Istoricheskiye Zapiski*, no 24 (1947), pp.111–59

Piksanov, N.K., 'Stolknoveniye Bulgarina s mater'yu Griboyedova [The altercation between Bulgarin and Griboyedov's mother]', *Russkaya Starina*, no 12 (1905), pp.706–18

Piksanov, N.K., *A.S. Griboyedov. Biografichesky ocherk* (St Petersburg, 1911)

Piksanov, N.K., *Griboyedov i Mol'yer* (Moscow, 1922)

Piksanov, N.K., *Griboyedov: Issledovaniya I Kharakteristiki [Griboyedov: Researches and Characteristics]* (The Writer's Publishers, Leningrad, 1934)

Piksanov, N.K., *Griboyedov I staroye barstvo (po neizdannym materialam)*, extracts from the Memoirs of V.I. Lykoshin (Moscow, 1928)

Piksanov, N.K. (ed.), *Griboyedov v vospominaniyakh sovremennikov* (Leningrad, 1929)

Piksanov, N.K. & I.A. Shlyapkin (eds), *Polnoye sobraniye sochinenii A.S. Griboyedova (Complete Collected Works of A.S. Griboyedov)* (3 vols, St Petersburg, 1911–17)

Pokrovsky, V.I., (ed.), *Alexander Sergeyevich Griboyedov: his Life and Works, a collection of historical and literary essays* (Moscow, 1911; Norwich, 1985 (in Russian).

Popova, I.O., *A.S. Griboyedov v Persii v 1818–1823 (po novym dokumentam)* (Moscow, 1964)

Popova, I.O., *Griboyedov-diplomat* (Moscow, 1964),

Potto, General A.V., *Kavkazskaya voyna v otdel'nykh ocherkakh, epizodakh, legendakh i biografiyakh* (3 vols, St Petersburg, 1887–8)

Przhetslavsky, O.A., 'Begliye ocherki', *Russkaya Starina*, vol. 10, no 3 (1883)

Pylyaev, 'Znamenitiye dueli v Rossii', *Samechatelnye chudaki i originaly* (1898, Moscow, 1900)

Razgonov, S.N., *Penati Vtoraya Zhisn Klimelita, v Almanakh Parnyatniki Otcchestra* (Moscow, 1996)

Reitblat, A.I. (ed.), *Vidok Figlyarin* (Moscow, 1998)

Rozanov, V., *Literaturniye ocherki* (St Petersburg, 1889)

Russkaya Starina, no 2 (1900)

Russky Arkhiv, vol. 10 (1891)

'Samson Yakovlev [sic] Makinstsev i russkie begletsy v Persii', *Russkaya Starina*, no 15 (1876)

Shaduri, V., *Griboyedov i gruzinskaya kul'tura* (Tblisi, 1946)

Shaduri, V., 'Tam, gde vyiotsya Alazan', Rojdeniya A.S. Griboyedov' (Tblisi, 1977)

Shavrigin, S.M., *Tvortchestvo Knyazya A.A. Shakhovskogo v istorii literaturnovo protsessa 1800–1840* (St Petersburg, 1996), esp. pp.52–3, 94–113

Shcherbatov, Prince A.S., *General-Fel'dmarshal Knyaz' Paskievich, ego zhizn'i deyatel'nost'. Po neizdannym istochnikam* (7 vols, St Petersburg, 1888–1904)

Shostakovich, S.V., *Diplomaticheskaya deyatel'nost' A.S. Griboyedova* (*The Diplomatic Activity of A.S. Griboyedov*) (Socio–Economic Literature, Moscow, 1960)

Sidorova, I.S., 'A.S. Griboyedov: The Letters of M.M. Bakunina', *Russky Arkhiv*, 11–111

Skabichevsky, A.M., *A.S. Griboyedov, ego zhizn' i literaturnaya deyatel'nost* (St Petersburg, 1893)

Smirnova-Rosset, A.O., *Avtobiografiya [Autobiography]* (Moscow, 1931)

Sosnovsky, T.A. (P.P. Karatygin), 'Aleksandr Sergeyevich Griboyedov', *Russkaya Starina*, vol.10, no 2 (1874)

Sychev, Father A.M. Danil, *Vyazma Ocherki Istorii*, ed. R.V. Okin (Moscow, 1997)

Takho-Godi, A. (ed.), 'Pis'ma k Generala A.P. Yermolov, A.A. Zakrevskomu', *Sbornik Russkogo Istoricheskogo Obshchestva* no 73 (1890), pp.188–459

Tarasov, Boris, *The Life of Remarkable People: Ya. Chaadayev* (2nd edn, Moscow, 1990), vol. 1

Tolstoy, Count V.S., 'Ser Dzhon Maknil [Sir John McNeill] (Iz sluzhebnykh vospominanii) ', *Russky Arkhiv*, no 14 (1874), pp.884–98

Tsyavlovsky, M.A. (ed.), *Pushkin's Complete Works* (6 vols, Moscow, 1938)

Tynianov, Y., *Smert' Vazir-I Mukhtara* (*The Death of the Vazir Mukhtar*) (Moscow, 1948)

Van Khalen, J., 'Zapiski', *Istorichesky Vestnik*, no 5 (1884), pp.402–19; no 6, pp.651-78

Vigel', F.F., *Zapiski* (*Notes*), ed. S.Y.A. Shtraikh (2 vols, 1st edn, Moscow, 1928; reissued with introduction by Professor Allen McConnell, ed. Marc Raeff, Oriental Research Partners, 1974).

Volkov-Muromtsov, N.V., *Yunost' ot Vyazma do Feodosii, 1902–1920* (Paris, 1983)

Vvedensky, A.R.V. (ed.), *Polnoye sobraniye sochinenii A.S. Griboyedova* (St Petersburg, 1892)

Ya. Chaadayev, P., *The Life of Remarkable People* (Moscow, 1990)

Yatsevich, A., *Pushkinsky Petersburg [Pushkin's Petersburg]* (Petropol', St Petersburg, 1993)

Yefremov, P.A. (ed.), 'Aleksandr Sergeyevich Pushkin. Ocherk ego zhizni i perepiska s bratom, druz'yami i znakomymi', *Russkaya Starina*, no 27 (1880), pp.129–48

Yefremov, P.A., 'O smerti Griboyedova (po persidskim istochnikam)', *Russky Vestnik*, no 3 (1890), pp.350–5

Yefremov, P.A., 'O smerti Griboyedova v Tegerane' ('On the death of Griboyedov in Tehran'), *Russky Arkhiv*, nos 7–8 (March 1872), pp.1492–1538

Yenikolopov, I.K., *A.S. Griboyedov v Gruzii i Persii* (Tiflis, 1929)

Yenikolopov, I.K., I.O. Popova and M. Zaverin, *Griboyedov v Gruzii* (Tblisi, 1951)

Yenikolopov, I.K., *Griboyedov i Vostok [Griboyedov and the East]*, (Ayastan Erivan, 1974).

'Yermolov po ego pis'mam k N.P. Voyekovu i N.M. Shimanovskomu', *Russky Arkhiv*, no 9 (1905), pp.38–89

Yermolov, A.P., *Pis'ma* (Makhach-Kala, 1926)

Yermolov, A.P., *Zapiski 1798–1826*, ed. V.A. Fyedorova (Moscow, 1991)

Yuzefovich, M.V., 'Vospominaniya M.V. Juzefovicha o Pushkine', *Russky Arkhiv*, no 3 (1880), pp.431–46

Zakhrov, L.I., *A.S. Griboyedov, Sochineniya (Collected Works)* (St Petersburg, 1995)

Zavalyshin, D.I., 'Vospominaniya o Griboyedove', *Drevnyaya i Novaya Rossiya*, no 4 (1879), pp.311–21

Zilbershtein, I., *The Decembrist Artist Nicholas Bestuzhev* (Moscow, 1977)

Persian titles

Abdullayev, F., *Iz istorii russko-iranskikh otnoshenii i anglisskoy politik i v Irane v nachale*, vol. 21, no 5 (Tashkent, 1971), p.117

Bamdad, M. *Tarikh-i rijal-i Iran* (Tehran, 1347/1968), vols 1, 2 and 3, Tehran 1347/1968. See introduction to Rauzat al-Safa, vol. 1, Tehran, 1339/1950, E.G. Browne, *A Literary History of Persia*, vol. 4 (Cambridge, 1930); Jan Rypka, History of Iranian Literature (Dordrecht, 1968)

Eqbal Ashtiyani Morza Yragi-Khan Ashire Kabir, Abbas, 'Tch. Baiburdi, about the Death of Griboyedov, Tehran 1861', from the *Persian Press* 15 October 1958, *Ettelaat* newspaper, interview with alleged 150-year-old Kanbar Alish

Fassai, Hasan, E., *Farsnama-e-Naseri*, tr. Herbert Busse (New York/London, 1972), pp.180–191

Jahangin Qaem-Magam, Sarkhang, 'Nokati dar Barayeh Katle Griboyedov', *Madjaleyiye Barra sikhane Taariki*, 5–6, Asef Esfaid XI, 1969

Mirkhvand/Muhammad to Sayyid Borhan al Din, *Rauzat al-Safa-yi Nasiri*, compiled by Riza Quli Hidayat about 1858 (6 vols, c. 1858), vol VIII, 'The History of the Safavids', with an account of the Ulema and notables of the time; vol. 4, 'The History of the Zands', with an account of the Ulema and their successors, the reign of Aqa Muhammad Khan Qajar and that of Fath Ali Shah as well as the Russo–Persian Wars and the coronation of Muhammed Mirza; vol. 10, 'The Reign of Muhammad Shah Qajar, Until the Year 1274/1857'

Navvabilyak, Hussein, *Fasli-az-i-Tarikh Iran, Moujebate-i Qatl-e Griboedov* (Madjaleiye Yaghma, 22nd year, no 12, esfahid 1348, 11–111–1970)

Pakravan, Emineh, *Life of Abbas Mirza* (2 vols, in French, Editions de l'Institut Franco–Iranian, Tehran, 1964)

Sipehr, Mirza Muhammed Taqi, *Lisan-al-Molk, Nasih-al-Tawarikh* (Tehran), vol. I (1344/1965), pp.3–4, 75–8

Teimuri Bakieye-Katle, Ibrahim, *Griboyedov, dar zamane Fath Ali Shah Nash va Zarate omure kharedjeozshakrivar*, 1345, VIII, IX (1970)

India Office Library archival material

Causes of the war of 1826–8, India Office Library Series (IOL/S/P9/86), giving Macdonald and Willock versions, detailing Menshikov's mistakes and incompetence and Yermolov's intransigence, and pressures on the Shah from the 'war party', i.e. the clergy, Abbas Mirza and Allah Yar Khan.

Early March 1826, Willock reports negotiations at Tiflis, between Beylerbey from Tabriz, with General Velyaminov in Yermolov's absence.

Further IOL (IOL/S/P9/90) papers, 'Run-up to 1826 War' in 1826; mainly Willock and later Macdonald, reporting to the court of directors of the East India Company, dated September 1826, and to George Canning. Refers to Yermolov's 'haughty language and unbending demeanour', and misrepresentation 'of General Yermoloff': see enclosure letter of 19 September 1826, pp.683–731. Signed by John Macdonald, envoy.

Letter of 23 December 1826, describing a possible deal over Talish for Gokcheh; peace could have been achieved and negotiations brought to a 'happy and early termination': pp.779–83. Shah wishes to know if English will pay subsidy, Macdonald passes buck to Ambassador at Porte: p.793. On 23 December 1826, memo of 'Conference' with Abbas Mirza: pp.805–25. Willock translation of decree from Abbas Mirza to Prince Menshikov, forwarded by Willock to the court of directors, 23 July 1826, p.337, from Camp at Sultaniye.

Willock's journal, 23 July 1826, covering negotiations at Sultaniye sent as enclosure to letter of the same date, refers to talk with Amburgherr, and expulsion of Russian troops from Balikloo and Gokcheh: pp.351–63.

There is ample evidence in the despatches, letters and reports of Willock, before being relieved by Macdonald at Sultaniye, as to their efforts to mediate a peaceful solution; they both reported quite clearly that the Shah desired peace, fearing the drain on his coffers of a war, and not confident that Abbas Mirza's 'new' army would be capable of beating such a formidable old gunner as Yermolov; the 'war party' essentially consisted of the Imams, convinced that the Russians in the captured khanates were persecuting their Shiite flocks; on the secular side, Allah Yar Khan was a convinced *revanchiste* warmonger, hoping to embarrass Abbas Mirza with his apparently patriotic stance. At an early stage in the countdown to war, Abbas Mirza was to be found playing a peaceful role, writing to Prince Menshikov in July 1826, 'I have directed the

Sardar of Erivan not to disturb the peace': IOL/S P enclosure to letter of Willock to the Secret Committee, dated 23 July 1826, p.321; forwarding Abbas Mirza's decree to Menshikov. 'I knew the Shah to be peaceable, and the Prince of the same mind': IOL/S P/P/. Extracts from Willock's Journal, 23 July 1826, p.285. 'HRH at heart was determined on peace': p.293.

We also have McNeill's Journal, as well-informed as Willock, for evidence of Abbas Mirza's aversion to war, IOL/S P/P pp 242–3; the Shah asked McNeill, freshly arrived from Tabriz, if Abbas Mirza had collected any troops to make war; the Shah laughed at the negative reply. McNeill replied 'the Prince was inclined for peace': p.242. The Shah pointed out that the Prince had sent away Major Hart (his chief English military instructor and advisor): p.243. Translation of *firman* from Shah to Macdonald, 22 August 1826.

Turkmanchai Peace Talks

Macdonald's despatch no 21 of 20 August 1827 giving Mirza Saleh's journal, during his late mission to the Russian headquarters, a dummy run for Griboyedov's Karaziadin armistice and truce negotiations, the first preview of the terms of Turkmanchai: IOL/P and S/9/86, pp.638–663, endorsed 'Sec and Pol' 111/9/1, received from the Foreign Office, 8 October 1828; pp.587–637 for Mirza Saleh's journal.

For India Office Library correspondence covering the Deh Kurgan negotiations, in which Macdonald and McNeill intervened very effectively between the Russians (Paskievich, Griboyedov and Obreskov) and the Shah and Abbas Mirza before the final deal was struck in 1828, leading to the Treaty of Turkmanchai. This series is referenced 10L/S and P/9/98.

Covering letter from Macdonald to McNeill in Tehran, from Deh Kurgan, 8 January 1828; also Macdonald's reports to Swinton at Fort William, despatch no 79 of 10 January, on the problem of getting the Shah to pay the first instalment of the indemnity; also covers letters to Persians such as Mu'tamad al-Dawla (Abu'l-Vahhab), and McNeill's reply and reports from Tehran; includes the formal decree from Abbas Mirza to Macdonald, 21 January 1828.

Despatch no 81 to Swinton, 21 January 1828, describing break-off of negotiations ordered by Paskievich, at Griboyedov's insistence, a 'hard line' being required: pp.107–9.

Letter in French, 21 January 1828, to Macdonald from Paskicvich (perhaps and probably drafted by Griboyedov), thanking the British for their services at Turkmanchai, and giving text in French of all articles proposed for the Treaty.

Further letters, in French, of thanks from Paskievich, dated 11 March 1828, thanking Macdonald again for 'l'influence salutaire de vos bons conseils'.

Ottoman archival material

Letter from Professor J.M. Rogers FSA FBA, Khalili Professor of Islamic Art, Department of Art and Archaeology, SOAS, London, to author, 5–8 November 1997:

I've been through the principal catalogue of Foreign Ministry documents in the Istanbul archives, *Cevdet Tasnifi Hâriciye,* and the relevant catalogues of the *Hatt-i Hümâyûn,* orders signed by or issued in the name of the Sultan, in this case Mahmud II.

The former contains 9325 documents and covers the periods 1616–1896: the only problem is that, for some incalculable reason, it's not arranged in chronological order, so one has to go through the whole thing. There are only a very few documents from the period 1820–35.

There are mentions of Persian ambassadors, principally those travelling to Paris and to London through Turkey, but there was no permanent Persian embassy in Istanbul and Persian missions to Istanbul were sporadic. Though the documents in this collection do not mention it, Tayyibî Efendi was sent to Persia in 1829 with the mission of promoting an anti-Russian alliance. It is frustrating that although some of his predecessors on such missions wrote up their Relations (cf. Faik Rsit Unat, *Osmanli sefirleri ve sefaratnameleri* (Ankara, 1968; 1992) Tayyibî Efendi is not known to have done so…even the exact dates of Tayyibî Efendi's and Sharif Shirvani's respective arrivals. However, since the date given is 1829 and ambassadors would not have travelled before the spring, Griboyedov would have been dead and done with well before their arrival. So that exonerates Tayyibî Efendi at least.

That the Ottomans relied for most of their information on reports from the governors of Erzerum of Cildir or military officials in Erivan suggests that they did not maintain a post in Tblisi. There are no reports from Tblisi at all.

Much of the material is what you or I would describe as Consular…

Mahmud II was only concerned with Persia, as far as I can see, when internal disorders (provoked by Russian interferences as much as anything) threatened the Eastern Provinces of Turkey.

The volumes of *Hatt-i Hümâyûn* for the reign of Mahmud II are even less illuminating about Persia. They are mostly concerned with administrative matters within the Ottoman empire. Although Russian moves in the East were obviously of concern to Istanbul there's nothing on the war, or Paskievich (whose name appears nowhere in any of the documents I've looked at) or the Treaty of Turkmanchai, or Griboyedov, Mahmud's officials evidently didn't know about what was going on; but equally they didn't care.

I have also looked at some of the six volumes of the military (Askerî) series of the Cevdet papers, but they are no use at all.

Yours

J.M. Rogers

Cevdet Tasnifi. Hâriciye. Documents most relevant to Persian–Russian–Turkish relations

These are mostly reports to the capital, which is not to say that they are true, or even correct.

752 M 1237/ Unrest in Eastern Turkey and Iraq caused by Abbas Mirza's movements.

1342 Ra 1224/ Russian attacks on the eastern provinces are feared: the governors in question have been put on alert and overtures have been made to Abbas Mirza.

2017 17 Za 1226/ Letter from Abbas Mirza, delivered by an emissary, reporting the killing of the Ottoman governor of Baghdad.

4784 S 1236/ Damage in the eastern Ottoman provinces by tribes recognising Persian authority.

4801 5 Z 1243/ Persian announcement that Russian troops have occupied the province of Khoi, and the measures to be taken by the Ottoman governors of Van and other provinces.

5258 N 1236/ Advice from the governor of Erzerum that measures should be taken, with Russian agreement, against hostile activities on the part of Persia.

5574 22 Ca 1242/ Letter from Abbas Mirza, brought by an emissary, asking for Ottoman aid in the war against Russia. Since, however, the Porte and Russia are not at war the letter is (merely) acknowledged.

5849 17 M 1243/ Because of Abbas Mirza's depredations, the population of Azherbaijan is turning towards Russia.

6716 22 B 1246/ Disraeli's visit to Palestine.

7144 M 1229/ As many as 55 British soldiers and 200 of the Shah's troops are reported to have set off from Tblisi in the direction of Hüdallah, and have occupied Russian fortresses along the Terek with a view to putting an end to the war between Russia and the Kizilbas. Although the persons making the report went 'to Russia' to check, they were not able to verify it.

7997 4 B 1239/ A Persian ambassador, Muhibb Ali Khan, is returning to Iran, but possibly in transit from a European mission.

8029 23 S 1235/ (cf. 8326 7 R 1239/) Ottoman peace treaty with Persia.

The Hatt-i Hümâyûn series

14301 1222/ Haci Ibrahim Efendi is sent (as a special envoy) to congratulate Fath Ali Shah on his accession.

17354F 1241/ Report from the Ottoman commander in Erivan and the governor of Erzerum that the rulers of Daghestan and Shirvan have sought refuge in Persia from Russian repression, and have been well received and provided with troops. With these troops they have secured a victory over the Russians at Kemerî.

19446 1233/ Ten Janissary regiments are to be levied for the forthcoming Persian campaign. Later, of course, there were no Janissaries.

Index

Index